The Mind, the Body and the World

Psychology after Cognitivism?

edited by
Brendan Wallace, Alastair Ross
John Davies & Tony Anderson

ia

imprint-academic.com

Copyright © Brendan Wallace and the contributors, 2007
The moral rights of the authors have been asserted.
No part of this publication may be reproduced in any form
without permission, except for the quotation of brief passages
in criticism and discussion.

Published in the UK by
Imprint Academic, PO Box 200, Exeter EX5 5YX, UK

Published in the USA by
Imprint Academic, Philosophy Documentation Center
PO Box 7147, Charlottesville, VA 22906-7147, USA

ISBN-13: 978 184540 0736

A CIP catalogue record for this book is available from the
British Library and US Library of Congress

Contents

Introduction, *Brendan Wallace* ... 1

Section One: Theory

1. The Embodied Mind & the Illusion of Disembodied Thoughts, *Mark Johnson* ... 33
2. Mental Life, *Xabier E. Barandiaran* ... 49
3. The Radical Constructivist Dynamics of Cognition, *Alexander Riegler* ... 91
4. Unifying Experience: Imagination and Self-Consciousness, *Susan A. J. Stuart* ... 116
5. The Human Stain, *Pamela Lyon and Fred Keijzer* ... 132
6. How Will We Know When We Have Become Are Post-Cognitivists? *Alan Costall* ... 166

Section Two: Language

7. Symbols Without Rules, *Steve Croker* ... 185
8. Distributional Accounts of Language, *Gary Jones* ... 208
9. Variation, Competition and Selection in the Self-Organisation of Compositionality, *Paul Vogt* ... 233
10. On Human Temporality, *Yanna Popova* ... 257
11. Is Language the Ultimate Artefact? *Michael Wheeler* ... 269

Section Three: Practice

12. Grounding Visual Object Representation In Action, *Rob Ellis* ... 309
13. Ecological Cognition: A New Dynamic for Human-Computer Interaction, *Jonathan Bishop* ... 327
14. The Elusiveness of Cognition, *Erik Hollnagel* ... 346

Conclusion: The Future of an Illusion, *Brendan Wallace and Alastair Ross* ... 356

Index ... 362

Editors & Contributors

Tony Anderson, Psychology Dept., University of Strathclyde.

Xabier Barandiaran, IAS-Research Group, Dept. of Logic and Philosophy of Science, University of the Basque Country. *xabier@barandiaran.net*

Jonathan Bishop, Glamorgan Blended Learning, University of Glamorgan. *jonathan@jonathanbishop.com*

Alan Costall, Psychology Dept., University of Portsmouth. *alan.costall@port.ac.uk*

Steve Croker, Centre for Psychological Research in Human Behaviour, School of Social Sciences, University of Derby. *s.croker@derby.ac.uk*

John Davies, Centre for Applied Social Psychology, University of Strathclyde.

Rob Ellis, School of Psychology, University of Plymouth. *rellis@plymouth.ac.uk*

Erik Hollnagel, Dept. of Computer and Information Science, Linköping University. *eriho@ida.liu.se*

Mark Johnson, Philosophy Dept., University of Oregon. *markj@uoregon.edu*

Gary Jones, Psychology Dept., Nottingham Trent University. *gary.jones@ntu.ac.uk*

Fred Keijzer, Section of Theoretical Philosophy, University of Groningen. *f.a.keijzer@rug.nl*

Pamela Lyon, University of Adelaide. *pamela.lyon@adelaide.edu.au*

Yanna Popova, Department of Cognitive Science, Case Western Reserve University. *yanna.popova@case.edu*

Alexander Riegler, Center Leo Apostel for Interdisciplinary Research, Free University of Brussels. *ariegler@vub.ac.be*

Alastair Ross, Centre for Applied Social Psychology, University of Strathclyde.

Susan Stuart, Philosophy Dept., University of Glasgow. *S.Stuart@philosophy.arts.gla.ac.uk*

Paul Vogt, Department of Communication and Information Sciences, Tilburg University. *p.a.vogt@uvt.nl*

Brendan Wallace, University of Glasgow. *bjw5y@clinmed.gla.ac.uk*

Mike Wheeler, Philosophy Dept., University of Stirling. *m.w.wheeler@stir.ac.uk*

Brendan Wallace

Introduction

Given that this is a book on 'cognitivism', what it is (was?), how it originated, and whether or not it is now desirable to look for ways to go beyond it, it would perhaps be expected to begin with the 'standard story' of psychology: in which modern psychology 'started' with introspective psychology in the late nineteenth century, moved onto behaviourism in the 1920s, and, finally, embraced the 'information processing' or 'cognitivist' view of human cognition in the 1960s. However, there are (at least) two main problems with this 'standard' approach. First, as Alan Costall points out in his chapter of this book, this view of psychology is something of an oversimplification, and it should perhaps be viewed as a way of justifying the 'cognitivist revolution' (by implying that after two 'false starts', psychologists finally 'got it right') rather than a genuinely historical account of the progress of twentieth century psychology.[1]

But the second problem cuts more deeply, and is, perhaps, more interesting. As Hubert and Stuart Dreyfus have demonstrated, the roots of cognitivism lie deep in the history of Western thought, and we will have to go back much further than merely the 19th century if we wish to illuminate the real roots of cognitivism. Moreover: if we are ever to go 'beyond' or 'past' cognitivism, it will not be enough to merely return to behaviourism, or change our terminology without changing our core assumptions. If we are to develop a genuinely *post*-cognitivist psychology, our investigation into 'the roots of cognitivism' should begin at the *very* beginning.

---

[1] Which isn't to say it's false as such, merely that it greatly overstates, for example, the popularity of behaviourism before the 'cognitivist' or 'information processing' viewpoint became popular.

Plato

As the philosopher Hubert Dreyfus has pointed out, one of the most important and fateful decisions in the history of Western philosophy and (therefore) psychology took place at

> the beginning of Western culture when the first philosopher, Socrates, stalked around Athens looking for experts in order to draw out and test their rules. In one of his earliest dialogues, The Euthyphro, Plato tells us of such an encounter between Socrates and Euthyphro, a religious prophet and so an expert on pious behavior. Socrates asks Euthyphro to tell him how to recognize piety: 'I want to know what is characteristic of piety … to use as a standard whereby to judge your actions and those of other men.' But instead of revealing his piety-recognizing heuristic, Euthyphro does just what every expert does when cornered by Socrates. He gives him examples from his field of expertise, in this case mythical situations in the past in which men and gods have done things which everyone considers pious. Socrates gets annoyed and demands that Euthyphro, then, tell him his rules for recognizing these cases as examples of piety, but although Euthyphro claims he knows how to tell pious acts from impious ones, he cannot state the rules which generate his judgments. Socrates ran into the same problem with craftsmen, poets and even statesmen. They also could not articulate the principles underlying their expertise. Socrates therefore concluded that none of these experts knew anything and he didn't know anything either. That might well have been the end of Western philosophy, but Plato admired Socrates and saw his problem. So he developed an account of what caused the difficulty. Experts, at least in areas involving non-empirical knowledge such as morality and mathematics, had, in another life, Plato said, learned the principles involved, but they had forgotten them. The role of the philosopher was to help such moral and mathematical experts recollect the principles on which they acted. Knowledge engineers would now say that the rules experts — even experts in empirical domains — use have been put in a part of their mental computers where they work automatically. … On this Platonic view, the rules are there functioning in the expert's mind whether he is conscious of them or not. (Dreyfus and Dreyfus, 2004)

This initial move, which seems so innocent and (indeed) inevitable, is in fact such a crucial one that it's well worth pausing here and looking at what's really being implied. The basic problem Socrates was dealing with was: what does it mean to say that someone is an expert, or, to put it even more bluntly, what does it mean to say that someone is good at something? Now it should be noted that Socrates was dissatisfied with the answers he got because he was looking at the problem in a specific way. Why Socrates expected the answer to the 'expertise' question in the form of rules is lost in the mists of time, (although he probably picked up this idea from earlier philosophers whose teachings are now lost to us). However, regardless as to how he arrived at the idea, the key point is that Socrates seemed to believe that expertise that was context specific and (to use the language of Roger Schank [1982]) *case based*, was necessarily trivial: after all, this could simply be gained by empirical practice: i.e. doing something a lot. *Real* expertise could only be in the form of rules, and since at least some human beings were unquestionably expert at some things, the obvious leap was to then deduce that *all* human cognition *must* therefore be in the form of rules 'whether one is conscious of these rules or not'.

As the reference to 'other philosophers' above should make clear, Socrates and Plato were not alone in their psychological and philosophical speculations. Indeed, Athens was probably more of a cosmopolitan place than we tend to think, and the influence of Eastern (Persian, but also, perhaps, Indian) and Egyptian metaphysical and mystical ideas was probably more influential on Greek thought than is generally realised. Two influences in particular have left their trace, the mystical speculations of the Pythagoreans and Eastern dualism (Lomperis, 1984).

The Pythagoreans stand at the origin of Western mathematics. However, what is relevant here is the extent to which they believed that numbers (i.e. not the things counted but the numbers themselves) were real, metaphysical (spiritual) entities, and that each number had a mystical significance. Therefore everything in the Cosmos could be related back to mathematics, and, of course, being spiritual (not material) it followed that mathematics was the real world, and the alleged 'real' world of matter was only an illusion. (In this and his other mystical views [such as his belief in dualism] Pythagoras seems to have been influenced by the mystical cult of Orphism [Lomperis, 1984].)

Of course, attribution is complex at this late date, but it seems likely that Plato was influenced by this view, and also by the Pythagorean view of the soul (which was dualistic). Therefore Plato was led to posit the idea that human beings consist of two elements: matter and (and immortal) soul. It was by combining these two views that Plato developed his theory of the Forms: timeless elemental metaphysical phenomena which we 'perceive' with our souls, and of which real, 'material' phenomena are mere copies. So for example, the tables we eat and work off are merely pale shadows of the 'real' Platonic Table which exists in metaphysical 'space'.[2] And so on (Lomperis, 1984).

This essential point that must be grasped here, before this essay becomes merely a commentary on Platonic metaphysics, is that Plato was setting out his pre-requisites for an explanation of what we would call 'cognition'. The three most important points of his explanation are as follows:

A: Rules. Plato/Socrates argued that expertise (and, implicitly, therefore, all cognition) is and must be codifiable in the form of rules, and that these rules must be 'stored' in the brain which is the seat of the soul.

B: Dualism. There is immortal metaphysical 'mind' stuff and the 'mere' world of matter. In other words, thinking is a purely disembodied, spiritual phenomenon.

C: Mathematics. Mathematics ('quantitative' analysis) is one of the best ways to access this world of metaphysical truth.

Now it must be stressed that these speculations derive directly from metaphysical (and, in the case of Pythagoras, openly religious) ideas that made sense in the socio-cultural environment of Athens c. 500 BC. Given this almost inconceivable remote period of time, and the fact that its cultural assumptions seem deeply alien to us now, it is more than a little strange that even nowadays much 'scientific' psychology still upholds this essentially Platonic metaphysics (as we will demonstrate).[3]

The Scientific Revolution

Christianity was created in an atmosphere saturated in the neo-Platonic assumptions of thinkers such as Plotinus, and as a result, for the next 1000 years, the Western tradition was, broadly speaking, Platonic. However, by the year 1000 most of the works of Plato had been lost (except in the Byzantine, and, to a lesser extent, Muslim worlds), and Aristotle became far more influential, until by the fourteenth century Aristotle was normally referred to simply as *the*

---

[2] We will remember from the Dreyfus quote earlier that Plato tied this idea in with the concept of 'cognition is rule following'.

[3] This is complicated by the fact that much psychology which seems to be monist, is in fact dualist, when its core assumptions are looked at.

philosopher. (Aristotle preferred to posit logic, not mathematics, as the basic 'language' of nature [Lakoff and Johnson, 1999].)

This altered immediately before the fall of Constantinople in 1453 AD, when Giovanni Aurispa brought many Platonic works which had been held in the Byzantine library to the West: this was the first time many of these works had been made available in Europe for 1500 years.

It is in this context, the rediscovery of Platonism, that we should look at the 'scientific revolution' and, more specifically, the effects this would have on the development of psychology.

Again, here, historians of science have had to clear aside many of the myths that still surround the so called 'scientific revolution'. This work does not imply that the innovations of Galileo and, later on, Newton were not considerable: they were. But what Galileo and (even more so) Newton introduced was more than merely new theories and discoveries. They also introduced a new way of looking at science, and, therefore, the world. For what Galileo in particular represented was a radical shift in Western philosophy away from Aristotle (who, to reiterate, based his philosophy on logic) back to Plato (who based his mystical speculations on mathematics). As Shea writes, quoting Galileo (Galileo's original in italics):

> (According to Galileo) the human mind is restricted in many respects, *but it can attain certainty in the pure mathematical sciences [...] of which the divine intellect indeed knows infinitely more propositions, since it knows them all.* ... Galileo owed this view partly to the Platonism which had been popular in Italy ... since the 15th century. As E.A. Burtt has stressed, the *mathematical structure which makes science possible is ultimately grounded in a religious interpretation of the world.* (Shea, 1972, pp. 124-5; 2nd emphasis added.)

We might add that (Western) religions also presuppose a metaphysics. Galileo's metaphysical assumptions and his scientific practice are therefore entwined.

Descartes

It was Descartes who attempted to take Galileo's innovations and develop their implications for 'pure' philosophy (Galileo had a philosophy of science, of course, but as a practicing scientist he was less interested in abstract speculation as such). There is no room here to go into all of Descartes's philosophy (the origin of the now notorious Cartesian dualism) but the following points are relevant to the current discussion:

A: The subject-object division. For Descartes (after 'all' doubt has been explored) the only thing we 'really know' is the knowing subject ("Cogito ergo sum"). Therefore, there is a sharp distinction between the knowing subject and the 'external' 'object' (i.e. the 'objective' world).

B: Representationalism: therefore, the internal subjective brain/mind must 'represent' the 'external' world.

C: Reality is mathematical.

Point 'C' would seem to be an outlier. However, it was taken up and emphasized even more by Newton, who developed the idea that the 'mathematical' language that lay behind and underneath reality functioned in the form of *predicting the future* (via deterministic laws, the classic example being the Law of Universal Gravitation [Cohen 1985]).[4]

Now: it must be emphasized at this point that neither Galileo, nor Newton, nor Descartes were in any sense atheists or materialists, and that all three of them (and all their contemporaries) would have found the concept of materialism incomprehensible. All of them were openly working within a Christian metaphysical system that had, as one of its key components, Platonism. Nor can one argue that one can sharply differentiate between their 'secular' and their 'religious' (i.e. metaphysical) claims and statements. We now know, for example, that Newton's concept of gravity (i.e as an abstract Universal Law) was taken directly from the occult Masonic texts he studied and is directly related to his (heretical) view of Christianity [Hall 2000]. What that must be stressed here is that Cartesian ideas have *metaphysical foundations*.

Cognitivism

This must be kept in mind as we now leap forward 200 years to the mid twentieth century when the seeds of what were to become the 'cognitivist' revolution were sown. The key point that must be borne in mind is that many (perhaps most) of the philosophical antecedents of 'cognitivism' can (implicitly) trace their intellectual roots back to Descartes, and that behind Descartes lies the Platonic view of cognition as being rule following. However, the intellectual scene of the 1940s and 1950s was very different from that of the 18th century.

---

[4] The 'mystical' implications of 'predicting the future' are of course not coincidental: Newton believed that these deterministic laws were created by a transcendent God.

Even though (within the Anglo-American tradition) the assumptions of Cartesianism remained almost unchallenged (as we shall see), the metaphysic that lay behind them had become extremely unfashionable. For the 'revolutionaries' therefore, of the new 'cognitivist psychology' the problem was, therefore, how to 'strip' Cartesianism of its 'metaphysical assumptions' (without throwing the 'baby out with the bathwater' by simply ditching the whole theory).

There is one other thing that is of importance here. Ever since Newton and his (let us not forget metaphysical, indeed, mystical) assumption that reality functions via determinist laws, it had become a commonplace amongst psychologists that psychology was a 'lesser science' (than physics, say) because psychologists had not 'discovered' the deterministic laws of human cognition in the same way that physicists had (it seemed) discovered the deterministic laws the predicted the movements of (e.g.) planets and stars (Newman, 1969). In other words, they suffered from what has been termed 'physics envy' in that they wished to model psychology on physics (and not, say, on biology, which would seem like a far more natural model) [Nichols, 2005].

According to Newton, reality was 'rule bound'. Therefore human behaviour (it seemed) would have to be 'rule bound' as well. But if we remember from the Dreyfus quote earlier, Socrates had also posited the idea that there were 'rules' inside the heads of experts (and, implicitly, inside everyone's heads). The question was; would anyone make the link between Newton's 'laws' and Socrates' 'rules', and say, essentially, these were the same thing? I.e. that because the world was 'rule bound' that, therefore, there had to be rules (algorithms, laws) inside our heads, and that it was the following of these rules that constituted 'cognition'? As we will see, some did.

But they were helped in this leap by a new 'discovery': information. It was Claude Shannon's 'discovery' and 'codification' of the 'laws' of information that gave psychologists in the 1940s a way to secularise Cartesianism (as it were) and therefore (they thought), create a truly scientific psychology.

Information

The foundations of the cognitive revolution were laid in the 1940s with the work of Claude Shannon on information, and Alan Turing on Artificial Intelligence. Whereas the work of Turing (obscure though it was then) might seem to have an obvious link with psychology, the relation between psychology and an attempt to build a mathematical theory of communication is not nearly so obvious. So why did psychology build a gigantic infrastructure (it is not too much of an exaggeration to say that most, if not all, of the 'information processing' view of human cognition derives from Shannon) on such an obscure and technical subject?

This does not become much clearer when one reads Shannon's original paper (1948). As he says himself, it follows on from work by Harry Nyquist and R. Hartley, both of whom also did work on early telephony and telegraph systems. The problem that faced all these scholars (Shannon was working for Bell labs [the 'phone company] when he wrote his seminal paper 'A Mathematical Theory of Communication') was simple: how was one to calculate what 'bandwidth' would be necessary in terms of laying cables (etc.) for a phone system? In other words, Shannon wished to 'quantify' the amount of 'information' that would be transmitted over the phone line at any given time so one would know how many cables to lay.

Now, the key point here is that Shannon was attempting to solve a technical, pragmatic problem. He was not in any sense attempting to lay out a 'metaphysical' account of what information 'really meant'. Nor was he in any sense attempting to sketch out a theory of human communication. On the contrary: as he stated himself: 'The fundamental problem of communication is that of reproducing at one point either exactly or approximately a message selected at another point. Frequently the messages have meaning; that is they refer to or are correlated according to some system with certain physical or conceptual entities. *These semantic aspects of communication are irrelevant to the engineering problem.*' (emphasis added). Thus: an anthropocentric (human centred) or philosophical investigation of 'meaning' or 'communication' was judged irrelevant by Shannon, and in terms of his own concerns, he was right (Shannon, 1948, p. 379).

So, what was Shannon's definition of 'information'? To quote from the original paper:

> The fundamental problem of communication is that of reproducing at one point either exactly or approximately a message selected at another point. ... The significant aspect is that the actual message is one *selected from a set* of possible messages. The system must be designed to operate for each possible selection, not just the one which will actually be chosen since this is unknown at the time of design. If the number of messages in the set is finite then this number or any monotonic function of this number can be regarded as a measure of the information pro-

duced when one message is chosen from the set, all choices being equally likely (Shannon, 1948, p. 379).[5]

In other words, Shannon's theory assumes that all messages are equally likely (i.e. that they are random) and that all messages have no meaning (or to put it another way, that they are all as meaningful or meaningless as each other). It also presupposes that the amount of possible messages are finite.

Shannon's definition of information is only valid when all these assumptions are met.

So for example, say I have a communication channel, and I have the option of two 'bits' of information I could send, in any combination, '0' and '1'. Of all the possible messages I could choose to send, I have a choice of sending either '0', '1', '01', '10', '00' or '11'. There are only these six possibilities. Shannon's work was an attempt to quantify the amount of bandwidth a telephone or telegraph operator would need to 'handle' this amount of information, when used by a set amount of communicators.

It cannot be stressed enough that Shannon was dealing here with an engineering problem. To quote again: 'Teletype and telegraphy are two simple examples of a discrete channel for transmitting information. ... The question we now consider is how one can measure the capacity of such a channel to transmit information' (Shannon, 1948, p. 381).[6] In other words, how could one work out how much 'information capacity' (i.e. channel capacity) a telegraphy system would need to deal with, for example, the 'information needs' of New York.

---

[5] The measure of 'entropy' was simply a measure of the amount of choice, as Shannon pointed out. For example, if there were, instead, of two possible 'bits' of information ('0' and '1'), three four or five then the amount of entropy or choice would go 'up'. Shannon unfortunately also used the word 'uncertainty' as a synonym for entropy, but this technical use of the word uncertainty has, of course, nothing to do with the word 'uncertainty' in 'ordinary language' which has to do with *meaning*. (When you say you are uncertain of whether your wife is having an affair with the milkman, you are not talking about the degree of entropy in your communication system).

[6] As a matter of fact, Shannon's theory is homuncular. It presupposes that a human being will decide upon the 'number of states possible', what is a 'bit' how many there are (etc.), that a human being will decide to send the message and so forth: and of course in this context Shannon was completely right to assume this. But again, Shannon's theory presupposes conscious human beings to 'get things going': it cannot explain (and to repeat, was not intended to) the existence of these conscious beings, let alone how they might have become conscious in the first place.

Therefore the question is: what does the whole theory of 'information' and 'communication' based on Shannon's theories tell us about human interaction, communication and the way that human beings interpret sentences (or anything) meaningfully? The answer is simple: *it tells us absolutely nothing, and nor was it intended to.* (To quote Raymond Tallis: 'the engineer's use of the word information *cannot apply outside its legitimate provenance*: that of devices designed by human beings designed by human beings to help them communicate with other human beings' (Tallis, 2004, p. 58 [italics added]). The point that Tallis is making is that Shannon's theory *presupposes* 'cognition' (i.e. human beings who cognize): it was not created as an attempt to *explain* cognition).

There are two questions that arise here. The first question is: how did Shannon's theories become used in psychology? The answer is simple: via the psychology of perception. To quote Tallis again:

> From the early 1950s sensory perception (began to be) interpreted as the acquisition of information and sensory pathways (began to be seen as) channels transmitting information from the outside world to the centre ... from this it was a short step to see perception as an (act of) information processing and to regard the function of the nervous system as that of transmitting information from one place to another (Tallis, 2004, p. 57).

And from then on, of course, it became easy to see the 'purpose' of all our cognitive apparatus as being to 'process information'. And so, by the 1960s it was being argued that the brain itself (now conceptualised as a sort of digital computer, see below) was in fact simply a complex information processing device, and by the early 1980s this had become the orthodoxy. To repeat: insofar as these theories are based on Shannon's theories they are simply invalid (it is not true that there is a random chance of all 'states' of information being communicated to you, and it is also not true that all the possible differing communication states that you might receive (in a day, say) can be quantified), and if they are not so based, then why use the word 'information'? It was obvious that using this word would lead to confusion (as people would assume that the scientific (i.e. Shannon's) definition of the word was being referred to, which it wasn't). Indeed, it is not at all clear why more colloquial terms could not be used instead, with little loss of precision (to say that human beings 'process information' sounds interesting and 'scientific', whereas to say that human beings act and think and talk tells us little, but it is not at all clear what one has clarified by using the former phrase and not the latter).

But the much more interesting question is: why did this happen? Why were psychologists (and philosophers) so keen to see the brain as an information processor? The answer comes when one remembers the Cartesian dualism (which, to repeat, is the most obvious way to conceptualise psychology if one decides to model it on Newtonian physics) which is still surprisingly common in psychology.[7] For when one looks at how the phrase information processing was actually used (as opposed to what it originally meant) one sees that the information processing view of cognition is a dualist (that is to say, Cartesian) theory... but it doesn't look like one. Or, to be even more precise that *it seems to be* 'essentially' Monist, but a version of Monism that preserves what was felt to be 'obviously' true about Cartesianism. As Descombes puts it:

> The analogy (i.e. of the brain) with the computer is at the heart of the new mentalist philosophy because it seems to offer a solution to this problem (i.e. the problem of combining materialism with Cartesianism). It presents us with a machine that can be described in two ways: *as if it were* a Cartesian composite made up of a thinking system and a material system but that we know *to be nothing but* a material system. Such a model combines all the advantages of the mentalist doctrine (the mind is dissociated from the world) and the naturalist doctrine (the human person is made up of only one substance and not two) [Descombes, 2001, p. 110; Words inside brackets added; emphasis as original].

Or at least, that's the theory.

To see why this theory might not actually work in practice, we have to look at the way 'information processing' is generally used in psychology (note: the article we are discussing here was selected more or less at random and deals with 'information processing' in the macaque monkey. But the same arguments hold for human 'information processing' as well).

---

[7] Although of course some would deny this ... but what is being argued here is that cognitivism/information processing is inherently a dualist (i.e. Cartesian) theory, and merely stating 'I am not a Cartesian' will not necessarily undo this. As Button et al put it: 'Very few ... cognitive theorists would *characterise themselves* as straightforward 'Cartesian dualists' these days ... but such materialisms as abound are as arid as the ontologies they embrace, and *all* are latter-day variants of the same 17th century world picture which gave us the mind-body dualism against which they pit themselves' (Button et al, 1995: 50). (emphasis added). Of course some psychologists and philosophers are still *explicitly* dualist: See Tibbetts (1990).

The paper begins with a perfectly factual and accurate description of primate vision, thus:

> Each visual center (retina, lateral geniculate nucleus, and primary visual cortex) is a convoluted and/or curved sheet of tissue; they are shown here as flattened, two-dimensional representations that preserves the relative area of each structure. Light from the three-dimensional world is focused by the cornea and lens to form a two-dimensional image on each retina. This image is convened to electrical signals by a dense array of photoreceptors along the back surface of the retina.

So, light comes 'into' the optic system, and focused on the retina, where it is turned into electrical signals. So far so good.

However in the next paragraph we discover that *as well* as this:

> After *processing* within several intermediate layers of the retina, *information* converges onto a population of one million retinal ganglion cells, which comprise several anatomically and physiologically distinct classes of output cell (emphasis added: Essen and Anderson, 1995).

Now, further reading (we are not experts in macaque monkey visual perception!) quickly reveals that this is a highly partisan description of what actually happens, which is that an electrical charge (in the form of Electrical Potential Differences, i.e. voltage) is passed to the ganglion cells via other cells. Again, the 'processing(s)' in the retina are in fact chemical reactions that take place in the presence or absence of light.

So macaque monkey vision is perfectly describable in terms of chemical and electrical reactions. However according to this paper, as well as the physical and observable behaviour that is going on, there is, apparently, *something else* going on: *as well* as engaging in electrochemical relations the visual system is also, apparently 'processing information'. To which one might add? Where? And how? It seems awfully unparsimonious of natural selection (a process that normally tends to select survival strategies that are as simple as possible) that everything in terms of 'cognition' is essentially done twice: one 'at the level' of neurons, linguistic and physical behaviour, and then again at the level of 'information processing'.[8]

But if this was the case it would imply that dualism was, essentially, correct. The brain, according to this view, has two 'aspects':

---

[8] Again, this might seem to be simply one example from one paper, but in fact this problem (how is energy 'turned into' information) is in fact endemic in cognitive science: See Tallis (2004), pp. 58–62.

the material (the actual arrangements of neurons etc.) and the non-material (the mysterious world of 'information'). The world of 'information' is 'mind stuff' and the world of matter is the 'material world'. The Cartesian orthodoxy can therefore be upheld, but within a framework that, as Descombes pointed out, *seems* to be materialist.

So what's the problem? To see why this 'secularised 'version of Cartesian won't work we must again look back at Shannon's original paper. Shannon, to repeat, was not scientist, he was an engineer. In other words, he was not attempting to 'discover' some 'truth' he was attempting to state a useful way of looking at things, to solve a practical problem. The idea that the brain is an information processing device is not in any sense a 'discovery' like the discovery that Saturn has moons or the rediscovery of the Coelocanth. It was instead the elaboration of a certain way of looking at facts that were already known. To make this even clearer, as John Searle has tirelessly pointed out to see the brain as an information processor or a 'digital computer' is not a discovery but a claim, a claim that a certain way of looking at things is useful. It is not and could not possibly be 'true' (Searle, 1980).

Again, information *as that phrase is used in ordinary language* is 'observer relative.' And this is particularly true of the way we use the words 'information' and 'communication' in 'ordinary language' because this use has to do with *meaning*, which is not in any sense 'objective' (which means in this sense 'not relative to an observer'). Chinese symbols are not meaningful to me (they carry no 'information') but they are perfectly meaningful to billions of Chinese people. A piece of information (a 'clue') in an Agatha Christie story is usually meaningless to the main characters bur profoundly meaningful to the detective. And so on.

The solution to the problem of 'everything happening twice' in the paper quoted (perhaps unfairly!) above is simple. Electro-chemical reactions are being *interpreted* as 'information processing' by human beings (in this case the authors of the paper) who *choose to do so*. Now, again, so far as it goes, fair enough. Why shouldn't scientists choose to interpret phenomena as 'information processing' if they want? The problem in this specific example lies, again, with the word information. When you open your eyes in the morning you do not in any sense receive information *(in Shannon's sense).*[9] The world you see in

---

[9] Because, to repeat, Shannon's use of the word would only be relevant if the amount of information available to us in this situation was finite. But this is not the case (Toft, 1996).

front of you is meaningful: it is (presumably) *your* bed, your wall, *your* alarm clock you see. In other words, you recognise what you see, or, to put it another way, it is meaningful to you. But it cannot be stressed enough that, not only is Shannon's definition of information different from that which we use in 'ordinary language' it is actually the opposite. People, of course, discuss and think about and act on *meaningful* information (as in the example above) and Shannon's 'information' can tell us nothing at all about this: indeed, it was defined such that it *could* never tell us anything about this. As Searle puts it: 'The brain, as far as its intrinsic operations are concerned, *does no information processing*. It is a specific biological organ and its specific neurobiological processes cause specific forms of intentionality. In the brain, intrinsically, there are neurobiological processes and sometimes they cause consciousness. But that is the end of the story.' (Searle, 1980: Searle's discussion of why information is, and must be, 'observer relative' is also of great importance here).

To Process

You can justify the view that the brain processes information in two ways. You can see that Shannon's definition gives us objectivity and precision and really puts information on a sound quantitative, mathematical basis. The claim that the brain processes information (in, to repeat, Shannon's sense) therefore becomes a highly tempting prospect. But, as Searle states above, this claim cannot be true. The brain only 'processes' *meaningful* information, but the word 'information' in the first clause of this sentence has nothing to do with Shannon's definition of the word. So we cannot have the objectivity and certainty that his definition offered. But if we abandon this definition we are left with an (implicitly) dualist theory that doesn't even have a sound scientific definition of 'information' on which we can build a coherent theory.

But this leaves the second word in the phrase information processing still unexplained. What does it mean to '*process*' information (or anything)? Again this word seems nice and neutral, but in fact it has a highly specific definition (which is rarely given in psychology textbooks). From the shorter OED:

> Process (verb) to perform a series of operations to change or preserve. 2 Computing: operate on (data) by means of a program. 3 deal with, using an established procedure.

This 'double meaning' (i.e. between definition one and definition two) of the word 'process' enables psychologists to use 'process' as if it was a relatively neutral word while at the same time *alluding* to meaning '2'. In other words, to say that human beings 'process information' is not in any sense a neutral term, but instead predisposes us to seeing cognition as computation, and, therefore, to 'smuggle in' the claim that human beings 'process information' in the same way that *digital computers* process information (i.e. via deterministic algorithms). And in this way the claim that the brain is a digital computer can be assumed without being argued for. But why did psychologists come to believe that the brain was a digital computer?

Turing

The view that the brain is a digital computer can be traced back to the seminal work of Alan Turing in the 1940s. As, again, John Searle has pointed out, it's not clear that one could prove that the brain is a digital computer without a clear description of how the brain works (since we already know how computers work, we could then look for points of similarity between them. But of course at the moment there is no such brain description). But there is a more interesting question that lies behind the one posted above: why was Turing (and those who followed him) so *keen* to see the brain as a digital computer?

The key point to grasp in answering this question is that, as Turing points out:

> The idea behind digital computers may be explained by saying that these machines are intended to carry out any operations which could be done by a human computer. *The human computer is supposed to be following fixed rules* ...[10] (emphasis added)

This assumption that the digital computer follows determinist rules (i.e. a program) and that, therefore, the human brain does the same, is enormously important. Where does it come from? Turing himself attempted to demonstrate that it was true by arguing that

---

[10] Turing was also very keen to stress that the human brain must be not just a computer but a *digital* computer. This again follows from various cultural assumptions that descend, one might argue, from Pythagoras. The idea that that 'quantitative', (i.e. discrete) numbers are somehow inherently more trustable and closer to 'truth' than analogue (qualitative) phenomena is deeply rooted in this tradition: cf. the preference for quantitative over qualitative data in much current psychology. This has of course been challenged in the modern ideas of 'fuzzy logic' (Kosko, 1993).

the contrary idea (the idea that human cognition is NOT rule bound) made no sense. He wrote:

> I shall try to reproduce the argument, but I fear I shall hardly do it justice. It (i.e. the argument he was arguing against, that human cognition is not rule bound [B.W.]) seems to run something like this. 'If each man had a definite set of rules of conduct by which he regulated his life he would be no better than a machine. But there are no such rules, so men cannot be machines.' The undistributed middle is glaring. I do not think the argument is ever put quite like this, but I believe this is the argument used nevertheless. There may however be a certain confusion between 'rules of conduct' and 'laws of behaviour' to cloud the issue. By 'rules of conduct' I mean precepts such as 'Stop if you see red lights,' on which one can act, and of which one can be conscious. By 'laws of behaviour' I mean laws of nature as applied to a man's body such as 'if you pinch him he will squeak.' If we substitute 'laws of behaviour which regulate his life' for 'laws of conduct by which he regulates his life' in the argument quoted the undistributed middle is no longer insuperable. For we believe that it is not only true that being regulated by laws of behaviour implies being some sort of machine (though not necessarily a discrete-state machine), but that conversely being such a machine implies being regulated by such laws. However, we cannot so easily convince ourselves of the absence of complete laws of behaviour as of complete rules of conduct. The only way we know of for finding such laws is scientific observation, *and we certainly know of no circumstances under which we could say, 'We have searched enough. There are no such laws'*. (emphasis added)

Turing continued:

> We can demonstrate more forcibly that any such statement would be unjustified. For suppose we could be sure of finding such laws if they existed. Then given a discrete-state machine[11] it should certainly be possible to discover by observation sufficient about it to predict its future behaviour, and this within a reasonable time, say a thousand years. But this does not seem to be the case. I have set up on the Manchester computer a small programme using only 1,000 units of storage, whereby the machine supplied with one sixteen-figure number replies with another within two seconds. I would defy anyone to learn from these replies sufficient about the programme to be able to predict any replies to untried values (Turing, 1950).

Therefore according to Turing reality is deterministic (i.e. all material objects (including the human brain) follow deterministic laws,

---

[11] Note: this is Turing's phrase for a digital computer.

just as Newton claimed) and therefore cognition must also be the product of deterministic rules. QED. Now, we have seen that the idea of there being deterministic 'laws of nature' etc. is not a 'given': it is an idea that arose in a very specific time and place. But we now see the link between Newton's laws of nature and Socrates laws of thought. Because (according to Turing) it is a 'fact' that reality is 'programmed' via deterministic laws of nature, therefore (and here is the 'leap') the laws of behaviour (posited by Socrates, as we saw) *must be* a specific kind or variant of these rules. So, according to Turing, cognition is rule bound because *everything* is rule bound. Therefore cognition *must be* the result of deterministic laws, and then Turing makes the final leap: since algorithms are also deterministic laws, then all the 'actions' of the human brain must be replicable by a digital computer.[12]

The Metaphor Objection

Of course at this stage, the objection is usually raised that to view the brain as being as an information processor is 'merely a metaphor'. But this argument refutes itself. The whole use of the word 'information' presupposes that there are phenomena that just are 'objectively' information (to objectively define the word 'information' was the whole point of Shannon's paper). To use the word in any other way is to ignore Shannon's work and to use the word in a 'subjective' way. But to admit that 'information' is observer relative ('subjective') renders the word *useless in this context.* Shannon's information theory presupposes that 'information' is NOT observer relative: the whole purpose of his paper was to define an 'objective' definition of information. Therefore, by the same logic, the claim that the brain processes 'are' (Shannon's kind of) information can't be a subjective call: it must be an objective fact (i.e. not a metaphor). If you admit this description is subjective (and that you are merely *choosing to see* the brain as an information processor), you undermine (and indeed con-

---

[12] Turing is cagey as to what extent he believes that the brain really is a digital computer: indeed, the whole purpose of the Turing Test is, in a sense, to render this point moot. However, he does attempt to prove that because the brain is algorithmic, everything it does can also be carried out by an algorithmic digital computer, so any 'differences' become merely trivialities. The mechanism may or may not be the same, but everything that the brain does can (according to Turing) be simulated on a Turing machine.

tradict) Shannon's theory, *as applied to human cognition*.[13] (Cf Mark Johnson's chapter in this book for a further discussion of this 'quest for certainty').

In any case, many philosophers and computer scientists *literally do believe* that the brain is a digital computer. For example the whole project of 'Good Old Fashioned Artificial Intelligence' presupposed that the brain was a digital computer, and philosophers such as Jerry Fodor have also championed this idea (Fodor, 1975).[14]

Chomsky

The third major 'leg of support' for the 'triad' that is 'cognitivism' or 'the information processing view of human cognition' is the linguistic theorizing of Noam Chomsky. What is of importance here is the extent to which Chomsky is a Cartesian dualist and the fact that Chomsky does (or at least did) view cognition as being rule bound.

There is no space here to deal adequately with Chomsky's theories, nor with the (now) vast amount of empirical data that has qualified or criticised Chomsky's work (cf for example Moore and Carling, 1982 and Lakoff and Johnson, 1999). What will be discussed here is the more interesting question of why Chomsky's theories were seized upon, and why they became so popular in the 1960s, 1970s and 1980s.

There are two main reasons why Chomsky's theories became popular and they are not antithetical: Chomsky's theories are Platonic, and they are Cartesian.

To take the Platonism aspect first. Linguists who support Chomsky's hypotheses about how we learn language sometimes note that Chomsky speaks approvingly of Plato at various points (for example Chomsky, 1966)[15] but they tend to gloss over this, as an

---

[13] However, claiming that your, alleged, 'strong' claim that the brain is a digital computer is 'really' merely a personal preference ('I choose to see the brain as a digital computer because I find it a useful metaphor') is a nice way of making this 'theory' unfalsifiable, in Karl Popper's sense.

[14] A final way out is of course Turing's who ignored the question of whether (metaphorically or not) the brain 'is' a digital computer and merely claimed that all human cognition could, in theory, be *simulated* on a digital computer. This has the benefit of being merely an empirical claim. The problem is that so far there are huge areas of human cognition that have not (at the time of writing) proven to be capable of simulation on a computer, digital or otherwise (Dreyfus, 1978).

[15] In terms of linguistics, Chomsky seems to have been influenced not so much by Plato himself as by the 17th century English Platonists. See Chomsky (1966), pp. 107–108.

Introduction

idiosyncrasy, or a desire to place himself in the 'mainstream' of Western thought. This is misleading. Chomsky takes over not one but two major assumptions from Plato: one overtly and one covertly. The overt assumption is what Chomsky describes as 'Plato's Problem' which is described in Plato's dialogue the *Meno* [Chomsky, 1986]. Without going into this in great depth, this shows (according to Socrates (or at least, Socrates as seen by Plato), and Chomsky) that 'we' must be born knowing certain things (in this case, geometrical proofs): it therefore gives strong evidence for Chomsky's 'nativist' point of view. This is obvious and uncontroversial. What is less obvious is that Chomsky takes over Socrates' main assumption of expertise which we looked at at the beginning of this chapter: that expertise (and, therefore, implicitly, cognition) is rule based. Indeed, Chomsky titled one of his books *Rules and Representations* and the idea that cognition just is the action of rules (i.e. algorithms) acting on representations is the essence of what we would now term 'cognitivism'.[16]

What is also important is that Chomsky sees himself as standing directly in the tradition of Descartes and Galileo and Newton (McGilvray, 2002). Now (and we will return to this point in the Conclusion) it's important to see that if one accepts the assumptions of the role of science of these thinkers then Chomsky's view of things really is the only way to make progress. If one really does take the Galilean/Newtonian/Cartesian/Platonic view that the task of science is to look 'through' the (empirical, material) data (in a Pythagorean manner) to see the timeless (Platonic) 'laws of nature' that lies behind them, then, as Chomsky never tires of saying, his approach is the only one possible (in fact, he has gone so far as to say that if mathematical idealisation (and its corollary, the concept that grammar must be considered as an autonomous area of research, isolated from psychological and sociological issues) turns out not to be possible in linguistics, then language must be a 'chaos' of no interest and scientific linguistics is a contradiction in terms (Chomsky, 1979, pp. 152–153]) . In terms of his own practice Chomsky has consistently attempted to look 'through' the apparent muddle of language to 'see' the quasi-mathematical 'rules' which are programmed ('behind', as it were, our behaviour) in the human brain. (The word 'programmed' seems appropriate: as Chomsky writes the role of the

---

[16] To be fair, Chomsky seems to have abandoned this emphasis on rules in his most recent formulation: the 'minimalist programme'. However, of course he has still retained his basic Cartesian assumptions.

linguist as he sees it is: 'to discover a *computational system* that will account for (linguistic) phenomena' (Chomsky, 1988, p. 65 [italics added]).

The other key aspect (in terms of our current discussion) of Chomsky's thought is the extent to which it is Cartesian. Chomsky even called one of his books *Cartesian Linguistics*. And again, this is not some metaphorical point: as Chomsky himself has never failed to stress, his links with Descartes are deep and profound. The key point is not just the now notorious Cartesian dualism, but the emphasis that Descartes put (following from Plato and Pythagoras) on mathematics (or perhaps mathematical logic) as being 'the' language of 'real' science. For example, Geoffrey Sampson argues that the key work in Chomsky's oeuvre is not the better known *Cartesian Linguistics* or *Syntactic Structures*, but, instead, *The Logical Structure of Linguistic Theory* which attempted to use mathematical logic to model the rules which, according to Chomsky, are 'programmed' into the human brain from birth (Sampson, 2002). And of course, Chomsky also assumes the Cartesian concept of 'subject' and 'object': that is, the idea that there are certain phenomena which are 'mental' 'internal' and (to put this into the language of information theory for a second) 'informational' and other phenomena which are 'out there' and material.[17]

Cognitivism

By this point, hopefully, we have shown that there are three (or perhaps four) major strands to contemporary 'cognitive science': 'cognitivism' (i.e. the belief that thought is and must be the following of rules 'stored' in the brain), 'information processing' (the idea that the brain 'processes information' via algorithms (i.e. rules)), artificial intelligence (the faith that the brain is a digital computer, processing information via algorithms) and, perhaps, Chomskyan linguistics (which views the 'language acquiring device' as a 'computational system' using rules). All these models or metaphors have different emphases and when one gets down to the details, are often subtly different. Nevertheless, all four share a common set of presupposi-

---

[17] The problem with the 'subject' 'object' distinction is that it makes no sense: if there are 'subjects' who decide to study themselves (i.e. us) then obviously we too are 'objects' and so everything is objective. Or perhaps everything is subjective. In any case, this is another example of an analogue phenomena on which human beings impose a digital classification (Cf 'fuzzy logic' again: Kosko, 1993).

tions and that these presuppositions descend from Platonic/Cartesian assumptions and beliefs about the nature of thought.[18]

(Note: this applies not just to psychology but also to much of philosophy. Hilary Putnam writes: 'the dominant view in Anglo-American philosophy of mind today appears to be what we may call "Cartesianism cum materialism", that is to say, a combination of Descartes' own conception of the mental as a kind of inner theatre, with materialism' [Putnam, 1999].)

The purpose of this book is very simple: it is to go at least part of the way to demonstrating that these Cartesian and neo-Cartesian assumptions are not the best ones for 21st century psychology.

So: why do we think that these assumptions are problematic? We have discussed this issue at length elsewhere, and there is no need here to go again over the large amount of experimental (and other) data which challenges the information processing paradigm (Wallace and Ross, 2006). However, briefly, it is enough to say that part of the problem with the reigning 'cognitivist' or 'information processing' orthodoxy is its over-arching nature: cognitivism is not simply the theory itself: it is also 'buoyed up' by a large number of ancillary hypotheses some of which have been clearly stated, and some of have not. For example: cognitivists tend to presuppose a methodological reductionism (in line with the views of science prevalent in the 17th century when the Cartesian orthodoxy was being created) which manifests itself, in an emphasis (and over-emphasis) on the study of *individuals* as opposed to humans as *social beings*. Not only this: cognitivists tend to take their reductionism still further and emphasise (and over emphasise) the workings of the 'brain' *as opposed to* the workings of the body: as though the concept of a 'disembodied' brain without a body was a meaningful or coherent idea.[19] This follows from the reductionist programme: the problems of society can (allegedly) be 'reduced to' the problems of the individual, the actions of the 'individual' can be reduced electro-chemical

---

[18] To repeat again: while it is of course true that some researchers in the AI and cognitivist tradition claim to be anti-dualist, even monist, we are arguing here that this contradicts (rather than enriches or complements) the fundamentally dualist assumptions of the Cartesian framework they tend to use. The fundamental problem is that it is not at all clear that it makes any sense to put Cartesian assumptions into a 'materialist' framework. Cf Alan Costall's chapter in this book for a further discussion of this issue.

[19] Yet again, this might seem to be simply a quirk of cognitivism, but actually to consider cognition as the algorithmic manipulation of digital symbols preconditions one to disregard embodied states: digital computers, of course, do not need bodies (or a society) to 'process information'.

actions in the brain, which can (theoretically) be 'reduced to' the actions of the individual atoms in the brain: in other words, psychology can be (and must be) ultimately reducible to physics, if it is to become a 'proper' science. [20]

Roger Schank

However, perhaps the first major crack in the cognitivist orthodoxy was the work carried out by Roger Schank in the 1970s. Here we must be careful of definitions: Schank was still in the information processing mainstream in that he considered cognition to be fundamentally computational (in the broadest sense of the word 'computation'[21]). However his work is very important in that it calls into question the very key assumption of Socratic cognitivism: that expertise *must be* rule bound (of course, coming from a very different tradition, Hubert Dreyfus made much the same point at about the same time [Dreyfus, 1978]). If we will recall, it was Socrates' 'empirical work' (if one wants to use that term) in asking fishermen, potters, etc. how they did what they did that set up the cognitivist 'research programme'. Socrates assumed that their actions must have been rule bound (whether they were aware of it or not) but Schank questioned this by positing instead that experts might work in a world of cases: not rules. In other words, whereas for Socratic cognitivists to perform an action (go for a walk, say) is to follow an internal algorithmic series of process rules (presumably in the form of a computer program: so, the rules would state 1: lift left leg, 2: put foot forward, 3: place foot on ground and so on) for Schank it is to draw on a library of cases, a library that has been built up, essentially, via empirical experience. In other words, I know how to go to a restaurant because I have been to a restaurant before and I can draw on this experience to perform my current action. In situations where I do not have a precise case (or set of cases) to draw on, I can draw on analogous situa-

---

[20] To make this clear: we are not claiming that ALL cognitivists are reductionists of this stripe. Nevertheless it is a fairly common view, and the key assumptions of cognitivism facilitate its acceptance.

[21] To be clear, the main thrust of this introduction (and this book) is to argue against the idea that the brain is what Turing termed a 'discrete state machine': i.e. a digital computer operating via deterministic algorithms (or algorithm like rules) on 'internal' symbols. We take this to be the basic claim of 'classic' cognitivism. Other approaches (i.e. connectionism etc.) are not open to these specific objections, although of course they may be open to others.

tions. For example, I may never have been to a restaurant before, but I may well have been to a shop before, or a library, or whatever.

In other words: 'In order to understand the actions that are going on in a given situation, a person *must* have been in that situation before' (Shank and Abelson, 1977, p. 67 [italics added]).

So: is there empirical evidence to back up Schank's theories? The short answer is 'yes'. For example, Klein and Calderwood (1988), in a study of firefighters, found numerous examples of using previous experience in the form of specific instances to guide current or future actions. For example, in one case the fire commander remembered that hot tar running off a roof had ignited a secondary fire in an earlier incident and used this learned information to prevent a recurrence by putting water on the hot tar. In another case, the commander recalled administrative problems in an earlier forest fire in which there were two teams working at the same time, so he set up a second camp for the second team, therefore preventing this problem.

However, this simplifies the situation because it makes it sound as if these men always referred back to one specific case. In actuality, after decades of experience, in real-world situations they made reference back to *many* previous cases; their experience consisted of these cases. In any event, as Klein and Calderwood stated:

> We have concluded that processes involved in retrieving and comparing prior cases are far more important in naturalistic decision making than are the application of abstract *principles, rules* or conscious deliberation between alternatives (Klein and Calderwood, 1988, p. 210 [italics added]).

Therefore, the expertise of these men consists of simply having done something a lot. What this would seem to demonstrate is that Socrates' initial presupposition does not necessarily hold: it is not *necessarily* the case that expertise must be codified (even unconsciously) in the form or rules, let alone computer program like algorithms.

Reductionism

As the biologist Steven Rose has pointed out, reductionism is neither true nor false: it is simply a tool which is either pragmatically useful … or not (Rose, 2005). The assumption (rather prevalent in the field of psychology) that all human behaviour *must be* therefore 'reducible' to 'brain states' is just that: an assumption, although again, it is an assumption that fits in well with the 'brain is a digital computer' metaphor. This pragmatic assumption has been challenged in recent years on various fronts, not least in the tradition of ecological psychology (i.e. psychology in the tradition of J.J. Gibson) who created the aphorism 'It's not what's inside the brain that's important it's what the brain is inside of' to re-emphasise the importance of situation and context on cognition. But perhaps earlier work by Roger Barker on Environmental Psychology has been insufficiently appreciated. It's not just the empirical work he carried out (in the Kansas town of Oskaloosa: 'Midwest' in his published work) that is important but his reflections on methodology (which we will return to in the Conclusion). Barker carried out various detailed observational studies of the inhabitants of Oskaloosa from which he derived his idea of a 'behaviour setting', which is an emergent property of the standing pattern of behaviour of the social actor and the milieu (i.e. the environment). The milieu and the pattern of behaviour are stated to be synomorphic: i.e. it is meaningless to talk about a milieu without a social actor 'behaving' in it, and equally meaningless to talk about a pattern of behaviour without a milieu. (For example, what 'is' a 'dentist's waiting room'? It is simply a room, without its social use (i.e. without people waiting to see the dentist in it). In our socially structured world, phenomena acquire meaningful definitions from their social use by human beings). These theories derived from Barker's observations that individual's behaviours in specific settings more closely resembled *other* individual's behaviours in the *same* setting than they did the *same* individual's behaviour in *other* settings. For example: there are ways of behaviour that are appropriate in a Church, in a shop, in a cinema, and it is only possible to make accurate predictions as to how people will behave when one knows the setting/mileu being discussed. (This has been informally summed up thus: 'when people are in [a] "post office," they behave post office, and when they are in [a] "basketball game," they behave basketball game' [Scott, 2005, p. 321].)

Situated Cognition

This leads straight on, of course, to one of the key contemporary challenges to cognitivism/information processing: situated cognition, the hypothesis that cognition is always radically *situated*. This view challenges the idea that there are timeless, non-context specific laws of cognition, and therefore renders pointless the attempt to 'place' these rules (or algorithms as they are normally conceptualised) in the human brain (this is the essence of the Cartesian 'subject-object' distinction). Now Barker's empirical work make clear that the milieu (or situation) in which human beings act and talk and think will probably not be depopulated but will instead tend to be a *social* milieu. In other words: cognition is not just situated but socially situated. Some psychologists have gone on to argue that human cognition is therefore fundamentally and radically social, and that, the idea that the basic research unit of psychology should be the individual (let alone the brain) is questionable. (There is no room here to discuss the arguments of Vygotsky, Luria, Wittgenstein, and the whole social psychological tradition in general which show the empirical evidence for this idea, but there are literally volumes of data which show the social roots of cognition [see for example Vygotsky, 2006].)

Embodiment

As well as the idea that thought is situated there has also arisen, in the last few years, the idea that thought is *embodied*. That is, another fundamental Cartesian division (between 'mind stuff' and the world of material objects) is misleading. Instead, the basic facts of our embodied natures (i.e. the fact that human beings tend to have two arms and two legs, that we are bipedal, that we live on dry land and not underwater, that we can only exist within specific temperature and environmental ranges) have a profound and non-trivial impact on our language (via the medium of the metaphors we use) and, therefore, our thought. This view of cognition has been most strongly propounded in the 'cognitive linguistics' of George Lakoff and Mark Johnson, although there have been other philosophers (mainly in the phenomenological/hermeneutic tradition) who put forward similar views.

Other Challenges

But situated cognition and embodied cognition have not been the only challenges to the 'information processing/cognitivist' orthodoxy. Apart from those previously discussed, there have been other traditions that evolved separately from cognitivism: for example, J.J. Gibson's 'ecological psychology'. There has also been work carried out in the field of artificial life (cf. Brooks, 1990), philosophical work that has developed out of 'cybernetics' (van Gelder, 1995), work in neuropsychology and developmental psychology (e.g. Freeman, 1999 and Karmiloff-Smith, 1992), as well as many others. What these approaches share (apart from an implicit or explicit rejection of the 'brain is a digital computer' metaphor) is a questioning, or even rejection of the Platonic/Cartesian assumptions that have dominated psychology for the last 40 years. In our opinion this is a development to be welcomed.

The purpose of this book

What then is the purpose of this book? The reason for this book's existence is quite simple: whereas there are numerous books that discuss whether or not the 'information processing' viewpoint is or is not the best one for 21st century psychology, and numerous books which discuss various specific alternatives to the information processing/cognitivist view, this (so far as we are aware) is the first one to look at as many of the alternatives as possible to see whether or not a new paradigm for psychology is emerging. It is the underlying thesis of this book that the cognitivist hypothesis has taken us as far down the road of understanding the human mind as it is going to, and that it is now showing its severe limitations as a framework for research. The time has come to look at the possibility of a *post*-cognitivist framework for psychology.

But what might such a 'post-cognitivist' approach consist of? Again, we are not, in this book, trying to suggest that one specific paradigm (e.g. 'connectionism', or 'dynamicism') should replace cognitivism: so we are not looking for the differences between the various alternatives posited. Instead we are looking for the *similarities* between them to enable us to bring together people from various fields (linguistics, artificial life, ecological psychology and so forth) to see to what extent we are seeing the emergence of a genuinely 'post-cognitivist' approach across these various fields. In our opinion we are indeed seeing such a 'paradigm shift'. What these various approaches have in common is that they (implicitly or explicitly) reject the Cartesian orthodoxy that underlay the cognitivist/information processing approach. So it might well be argued that a post-*cognitivist* psychology will also have to be a post-*Cartesian* psychology.

In many ways, therefore, we see this as in some ways the 'successor volume' to Stills and Costall's classic work 'Cognitive psychology in Question'. That work, published in 1987, was the first sign that psychology was going to enter a prolonged period of crisis, which is what happened in the 1990s, with the information processing hypothesis encountering increasing difficulties, and no obvious successor emerging. We view this new book as exploratory, and an attempt to surmount this crisis: to begin to map out what a post-cognitivist, post-information processing psychology might look like.

Towards Post-Cognitivism

The other question this book deals with is perhaps even more difficult. How might psychologists (and linguists, and, for that matter, philosophers) 'do' post-cognitivism? Will the 'normal' practices of psychology take place with merely the 'theoretical 'backdrop' being changed, or will post-cognitivism require the development of new approaches and new methodologies? We will not attempt to answer that question in this introductory chapter, as these are the key questions this book is attempting to answer. *All* the chapters are relevant here.

However, in terms of clarifying these questions we have chosen to structure the book by dividing it into three parts: in order to progress from the 'abstract' questions (Is cognitivism dead? If so, why did it die? Can we go beyond it?) to the 'practical ones' (what will be the practices and procedures that will help to make up 'post-cognitivism?).

In Section One, therefore, ('Theories of Post-Cognitivism') we attempt to sketch mainly theoretical approaches to 'post-cognitivism', and attempt to map out a general philosophical approach to post-cognitivism. In the second: 'Language', we look at attempts within linguistics to go beyond Chomskyan Rationalism (this may seem to be an 'outlier' but since Chomsky and Chomskyan approaches in general have been so widely influential in psychology, it would seem wise to have a specific section dealing with language, and attempts to develop a post-Chomskyan linguistics). And in the final section: 'Practice' we look at specific research projects that attempt to put the lessons of post-cognitivism to work in the real world.

Ultimately post-cognitivism will only thrive as a research paradigm if its practical value and usefulness can be demonstrated not just in the lab or in Universities, but in the real world. Therefore, the book moves from 'theory' to 'practice' in the way we hope the whole 'post-cognitivist' movement (if it can be so described) will eventually move towards becoming an established (or perhaps even *the* established) practice in twenty-first century psychology.

Bibliography

Brooks, R. (1990), 'Elephants don't play chess', *Robots and Autonomous Systems*, 6, pp. 3–15.

Button, G., Coulter, J., Lee, J. and Sharrock, W (1995), *Computers, Mind and Conduct* (London: Polity Press).

Chomsky, N. (1966), *Cartesian Linguistics* (New York: Harper and Row).
Chomsky, N. (1979), *Language and Responsibility* (London: Pantheon).
Chomsky, N. (1988), *Language and Problems of Knowledge* (London: MIT Press).
Cohen I. (1985), *Revolution in Science* (London: Harvard University Press).
Descombes, V. (2001), *The Mind's Provisions: a Critique of Cognitivism* (Princeton and Oxford: Princeton University Press).
Dreyfus, H. (1978), *What Computers Can't Do: The Limits of Artificial Intelligence*, (London: HarperCollins).
Dreyfus, H. and Dreyfus S. (2002), 'From Socrates to expert systems', *Philosophy*, 24, p. 1.
Dreyfus, H., and Dreyfus, S. (2004), 'From Socrates to Expert Systems: The Limits and Dangers of Calculative Rationality' (Unpublished Note: Available online at
http://socrates.berkeley.edu/~hdreyfus/html/paper_socrates.html).
Essen, D. and Anderson, C. (1995), 'Information processing strategies and pathways in the primate visual system.' in *An Introduction to Neural and Electronic Networks*, Mora, eds Zornetzer *et al.* (Atlanta: Morgan Kaufmann).
Fodor, Jerry. (1975), *The Language of Thought* (New York: Thomas Crowell).
Freeman, W. (1999), *How Brains Make Up Their Minds* (London: Weidenfeld & Nicolson).
Hall, A. (2000), *Isaac Newton* (Cambridge: CUP).
Hintzman, D. L. (1992), '25 years of learning and memory: Was the cognitive revolution a mistake?' In D. E. Meyer, & S. Kornblum (Eds.), *Attention and Performance XIV: A silver jubilee.* (Hillsdale, N J: Edbaum)
Hodges, A (1999) *Turing.* (London: Phoenix).
Karmiloff-Smith, A. (1992), *Beyond Modularity* (Cambridge, MA: MIT Press).
Sampson, G. (2002), *Empirical Linguistics* (London: Continuum).
Klein, G., and Calderwood, R. (1988), 'How do people use analogies?' In Kolodner J. (Ed.) *Case-based Reasoning: Proceedings of a Workshop on Case-Based Reasoning,* May 10–13 Clearwater Beach Florida (San Mateo: Morgan Kaufman Publishers)
Kosko, B. (1993), *Fuzzy Thinking: The New Science of Fuzzy Logic* (London: Flamingo).
Lakoff, G. and Johnson, M. (1999), *Philosophy in the Flesh* (New York: Basic Books).
Lomperis, T. (1984), *Hindu Influence on Greek Philosophy* (Calcutta: Minerva).
Longrigg, J. (1993), *Greek Rational Medicine: Philosophy and Medicine from Alcmæon to the Alexandrians* (London: Routledge).
McGilvray, J. (2005), *The Chomsky Companion* (Cambridge: CUP).
Moore, T. and Carling, C. (1982), *Language Understanding* (New York: St. Martin's Press).
Newman, E. (1969), 'Newton, physics, and the psychology of the 19th Century', *The American Journal of Psychology,* 82, 3, pp. 400–406.
Nichols, D (1993), 'Outgrowing physics envy: reconceptualising social research', *Behavioural Science,* 15, 1.
Nunn, J. (1997), *Ancient Egyptian Medicine* (London: British Museum Press).

Putnam, H. (1999), *The Threefold Cord* (New York: Columbia University Press).
Rose, S. (2005), *Lifelines* (London: Vintage).
Schank, R (1982), *Dynamic Memory: A Theory of Learning in Computers and People* (New York: Cambridge University Press).
Schank, R. and Abelson, R. (1977), *Scripts, Plans Goals and Understanding* (New Jersey: Lawrence Erlbaum Associates).
Scott, M. (2005), 'A powerful theory and a paradox: ecological psychologists after Barker', *Environment and Behavior*, 37, pp. 295-329
Searle, J. (1990), 'Is the brain a digital computer?', *Proceedings of the American Philosophical Association*, 64, pp. 2137.
Shannon, C. (1948), 'A Mathematical Theory of Communication', *Bell System Technical Journal*, 27, pp. 379-423, 623-656.
Shea, M. (1972), *Galileo's Intellectual Revolution* (London: Macmillan).
Tallis, R. (2004), *Why the Mind is not a Computer* (Exeter: Imprint Academic).
Tibbetts, P. (1996), 'Residual dualism in computational theories of mind', *Dialectica*, 50, 1, pp. 37-52.
Toft, B (1996), 'Limits to the mathematical modelling of disasters', in C. Hood and D. Jones (eds) *Accident and Design* (London: UCL Press).
Turing, A.M. (1950)' 'Computing machinery and intelligence', *Mind*, 59, pp. 433-460.
Van Gelder, T. (1995), 'What might cognition be, if not computation?', *The Journal of Philosophy*, 91, 7, pp. 345-381.
Young, R. (1990), *Mind, Brain and Adaptation in the Nineteenth Century* (London: OUP).
Vygotsky, L. (2006), *Mind in Society* (Harvard: Harvard University Press).
Wallace, B. and Ross, A. (2006), *Beyond Human Error* (Florida: CRC Press).

Section One

THEORY

Mark Johnson

The Embodied Mind & the Illusion of Disembodied Thoughts

In *The Quest for Certainty* (1929/1984) John Dewey analyzed and criticized our human tendency to seek absolutes in response to the contingency and precariousness of human existence. Dewey argued that human mind, thought, and knowledge emerge from our bodily perceptions and actions within various environments, and, consequently, he rejected the notions of a transcendent ego and 'pure', disembodied reason. Knowledge is always situated, partial, and shaped by values. This pragmatist understanding of embodied mind did not win the day, because pragmatism was subsequently displaced and marginalized by the upsurge of Logical Empiricism and analytic philosophy of mind and language, both of which reverted back to traditional ideals of foundational knowledge and disembodied thought. It appears that the quest for certainty will never die, rooted as it is in our pervasive human desire for security against uncertainty, change, and error.

Recent empirical research in the cognitive sciences tends to regard mind and body as aspects of one ongoing process of organism-environment interaction. Our capacity for thinking emerges from our capacities for sensory experience and motor actions. This research supports Dewey's conception of embodied mind, thought, and language. I want to articulate this view of embodied cognition and then to use my account to suggest why the belief in disembodied concepts and reason persists so stubbornly, despite the growing body of empirical evidence suggesting that all human conceptualization and reasoning are grounded in the body and its interactions with its environment. I will suggest that, once we understand the bodily and experiential grounding of our concepts and learn how imaginative operations extend this bodily-based meaning to structure abstract concepts, we can explain why it is tempting to succumb to the illusion of disembodied mind and thought.

James and Dewey on Embodied Meaning and Thought

One of the founding assumptions of American Pragmatism, as articulated by key figures like William James and John Dewey, is that human mind is not an independent metaphysical entity, but rather a complex bodily, social, and cultural process. Emphasizing a non-dualistic, process-oriented evolutionary conception of human cognition, Dewey proclaimed boldly that,

> To see the organism *in* nature, the nervous system in the organism, the brain in the nervous system, the cortex in the brain is the answer to the problems which haunt philosophy. (Dewey, 1925/1981, p. 224)

James (1890) and Dewey (1925/1981) approached the study of mind—of thought, feeling, consciousness, language, reason, will, and knowledge—looking for 'naturalistic' explanations of various mental phenomena. What this meant to them was that there is no transcendent ego or pure (non-empirical) understanding or reason. Whatever capacities we attribute to mind must arise as emergent functions that are part of an organism's flexible adaptation to changes in its environment. These functional unities result from increasing complexity in (so-called 'lower level') perceptual and motoric bodily processes. Hence, what we call 'mind' and 'body' are not two distinct metaphysical entities; rather, they are dimensions or aspects of a loosely unified flow of experiences.

Dewey recognized the revolutionary nature of this naturalistic orientation. It meant, among other things, that at no point in the explanation of any mental phenomena are you permitted to appeal to any non-natural or transcendent disembodied entity, state, or capacity. There must be continuity between our sensory-motor acts and our highest logical, scientific, and philosophical musings:

> ... there is no breach of continuity between operations of inquiry and biological operations and physical operations. 'Continuity' ... means that rational operations *grow out of* organic activities, without being identical with that from which they emerge. (Dewey, 1938/1991, p. 26)

James and Dewey drew extensively on the biology, evolutionary theory, physiology, and brain science of their day. Were they alive today, they would surely be conversing with the best philosophically-minded cognitive neuroscientists (people like Antonio Damasio, 1994, 1999, 2003; Gerald Edelman, 1992, 2000; and Joseph LeDoux, 2002) about how to construct empirically-responsible explanations of mind that do justice to our lived experience, with all its complexity, ambiguity, emotion, and eros. Their problem would be the problem we face today, namely, to explain how our most glorious accomplishments of abstract thought can be grounded in our embodiment.

Embodied Cognition

I believe that the explanation emerging within the cognitive sciences as to how abstract thought can be grounded in capacities for perception and bodily movement is precisely the same sort of answer given by James and Dewey a century ago. The basic idea is this: structures and processes of bodily perception, feeling, and action provide the basis for 'higher' cognitive functions, such as abstract conceptualization, logical inference, and planning. Based on contemporary lesion studies and neuro-imaging techniques, Antonio Damasio hypothesizes

> that the body, as represented in the brain, may constitute the indispensable frame of reference for the neural processes that we experience as the mind; that our very organism rather than some absolute external reality is used as the ground reference for the constructions we make of the world around us and for the construction of the ever-present sense of subjectivity that is part and parcel of our experiences; that our most refined thoughts and best actions, our greatest joys and deepest sorrows, use the body as a yardstick. (Damasio, 1994, xvii).

Abstract conceptualization and reasoning are tied to the structure and logic of our sensory-motor experience, and these structures are appropriated for our abstract thoughts and inferences. Meaning and reason are embodied.

I propose to illustrate and argue for the plausibility of this claim by examining one set of examples of embodied meaning. My argument will take the following form:

1. Our perceptual and motor experience is structured by hundreds of recurring patterns known as image schemas.
2. Image schemas give rise to 'spatial' or 'corporeal' logics, with different image schemas generating different inferential implications.
3. Our experience and understanding of image schemas and their various logical entailments can be appropriated as a basis for reasoning about abstract entities or events. One of the chief mechanisms for this extension is conceptual metaphor, by which we map structure and knowledge concerning a bodily domain of experience onto our understanding of a specific abstract domain. We thus naturally and normally define our most important abstract concepts via multiple conceptual metaphors.
4. When we mistakenly presume to literalize (to treat as literal and absolute) such metaphors, we fall under the illusion that there are disembodied literal concepts that are radically independent of the ways we experience meaning via our bodies. This false ideal of pure abstract concepts is the source of much mischief in human existence, especially in the form of a search for certain and absolute knowledge.

Image Schemas

From the day we are born, and even earlier, we begin to experience the meaning of our nascent world through patterns of sensory-motor experience. For example, consider the multitude of times each day that you move your body from one place to another, usually to achieve some purpose. In each case, there is an initial phase when your body is stationary at a starting location. Then you begin to move along some trajectory, over a continuously-developing path, finally arriving at some terminal location. This terminus itself may then become the starting point for another movement. Experienced movement of this sort has the basic structure of Source-Path-Goal. Likewise, as you observe the motion of objects across your visual field, they move into your view at some location (source), traverse a series of contiguous points (path), and either stop or pass out of your visual horizon at some other location (goal).

Recent work on the so-called 'mirror neuron system' (Gallese & Goldman, 1998; Rizzolatti & Craighero, 2004) shows that when we observe someone grasping and manipulating an object, our own motor and pre-motor cortices are weakly activated, as if *we* were performing that same action. If such phenomena are generalizable, then this would suggest the possibility that when you observe another person moving from source to goal along a path, areas in your own motor and pre-motor cortices would be weakly activated, *as if you* were performing the same motion you are observing. In other words, part of grasping the meaning of another's motion involves your sense of performing the same motion yourself. However, this is activated mostly beneath the level of conscious awareness on your part and typically without sufficient activation to induce actual bodily movements on your part. This is a very deep sense in which meaning is embodied.

Furthermore, there is a distinct 'logic' to our bodily understanding of the SOURCE-PATH-GOAL image schema (Johnson, 1987; Lakoff, 1987; Lakoff & Johnson, 1999). The internal structure of this image schema permits and constrains inferences that we make about certain kinds of motions. For example, if I am travelling along a path from point A to point Z, at a certain time (say T4) I will be half-way from A to Z. If I then continue along the path farther, at some later time (say T6) I will be closer to my destination Z that I was at T4. Or, if two people start out from location A at time T1, and if person P is moving faster than person Q, then at some later time (T6), person P will be *farther along* the path than person Q. This logic of our corporeal, spatial experience may seem simple, but it is *not* trivial. In fact, it is spatial logic like this that allows us to reason about spatial motion and, as we will see, to reason about various abstract domains of experience.

The key point here is that image schemas, such as SOURCE-PATH-GOAL, CONTAINMENT, BALANCE, FORCED MOTION, ITERATION, and CENTER-PERIPHERY have sufficient internal structure to support inferences. Image schemas structure our thinking and our various forms of symbolic expression (Gibbs & Colston, 1995). The SOURCE-PATH-GOAL schema, for instance, has more than just a source, a path, and a goal. Our experiences of perceived and enacted motion involve additional elements, such as the speed of the moving object, obstacles that might block its path of motion, aids to motion, projected trajectories, actual trajectories, and the rhythm of the motion (speeding up, slowing down, surging, hopping, jerking, etc.). We learn these aspects of motion through our bodily experience, prior to language and often beneath the level of conscious awareness, but it is all part of our ability to grasp the meaning of our experience.

Abstract Conceptualization

It may seem like no great insight that our understanding of our perceptual experience and our acts of object manipulation and bodily movement are grounded in structures of our bodily activity. But what about abstract conceptualization and reasoning, those last great respites of alleged disembodied thinking? How are *they* tied to embodiment, especially since they are *abstract*? The hypothesis that is emerging from recent empirical studies in cognitive neuroscience and certain orientations within cognitive science is that even our most abstract thought is shaped by structures of bodily understanding and reasoning. Our acts of perceiving, making, and doing become the basis for our acts of thinking and knowing. This is an example of Dewey's *continuity thesis*, mentioned earlier, which states that 'rational operations *grow out of* organic activities,' without breach of continuity from the 'lower' (perception and motion) to the 'higher' (rational inference about abstract topics).

According to a large body of empirical research coming out of the field known as Cognitive Linguistics, one of the chief mechanisms for this movement from concrete to abstract thinking is conceptual metaphor. A conceptual metaphor appropriates entities and structures in a sensory-motor domain (the source domain) to structure our understanding of an abstract domain (the target domain). As an example of this process, consider what Grady (1997) calls 'primary metaphor', by which sensory-motor inferences are recruited to perform reasoning about abstract entities. Primary metaphors are based on correlations between the source and target domains that give rise, via neural co-activation, to what may be described as a mapping of sensory-motor structure onto a target domain (usually as subjective judgment or abstract thought).

To see how this might work, let us return to the logic of the SOURCE-PATH-GOAL schema. Numerous times each day you enact the SOURCE-PATH-GOAL schema as part of the realization of some purposive activity. Let's say you want to get a drink of water from the kitchen faucet. Initially you are located at point A (say, the living room) and your initial mental state is a desire for a drink of water. Getting up and beginning to move toward the kitchen is the means for the partial realization of your goal of getting a drink. The more you move along a path toward the kitchen, the closer you come to satisfying your purpose. When you reach your destination at the kitchen sink, you satisfy your purpose of quenching your thirst, or at least you are now in a location (destination) where your purpose will soon be satisfied. Notice that in performing this action there is a point-by-point correlation between motion along a path from a starting point to a destination and the corresponding set of stages in the realization of your purpose, as specified by the following source-to-target mapping:

The PURPOSES ARE DESTINATIONS Metaphor

Source Domain		Target Domain
(Motion through space)		(Achieving a Purpose)
Starting Location A	⇒	Having a Purpose
Terminal Location B	⇒	Satisfying a Purpose
Motion from A to B	⇒	Progression Toward Satisfying Your Purpose

This conceptual mapping, from source domain to target domain, is based on the co-activation of neural assemblies in different cortical and sub-cortical areas of the brain: (1) areas responsible for spatial cognition and locomotion, and (2) areas responsible for reasoning about purposive action. This co-activation, which occurs perhaps hundreds of times each day, is the basis for the primary metaphor PURPOSES ARE DESTINATIONS, by which we understand the achievement of a purpose as, metaphorically, motion through space from one location-state to a final destination (a different state). This metaphoric mapping is the basis for body-based expressions that we use to conceive of the achievement of abstract goals, such as,

> Paul is just *getting going* on his research project. We have a *long way to go* until we finish this report. Mary *stopped short* of her goal of balancing the budget. I can't *see what's around the corner* in our attempt to win the campaign.

Notice that, already with this very basic primary metaphor, we are doing abstract reasoning about purposive action using the spatial logic of the SOURCE-PATH-GOAL schema. The conceptual metaphoric mapping permits us to utilize this spatial logic and to apply it to abstract reasoning about our pursuit of abstract goals. In other words, our bodily logic is the means for rational thought.

The operation of conceptual metaphor and other types of imaginative structure has been a robust and highly significant finding within recent work in various parts of the cognitive sciences, and it is also quite compatible with John Dewey's account of embodied meaning and experience. Dewey appears to have glimpsed this bodily grounding of metaphor in cross-domain correlations:

> Every thought and meaning has its substratum in some organic act of absorption or elimination of seeking, or turning away from, of destroying or caring for, of signaling or responding. It roots in some definite act of biological behavior; our physical names for mental acts like seeing, grasping, searching, affirming, acquiescing, spurning, comprehending, affection, emotion are not just 'metaphors.' (Dewey, 1925/1981, p. 221)

When Dewey says that these are 'not just "metaphors"', he means that they are not mere metaphors in the traditional sense, according to which metaphors are nothing but alternative forms of expression for what are essentially literal concepts. However, they are *conceptual metaphors* with specific source-to-target mapping structures. We appropriate spatial and corporeal logics for abstract reasoning. This makes good sense for creatures like us whose minds are not separate from our bodies and who do not possess a so-called 'innate' language module. We are able to perform inferences about abstract subject matters, precisely because all meaning *is* embodied. We do not need to fall back on alleged non-empirical, disembodied cognitive mechanisms, in order to explain the relevant syntactic and semantic dimensions of natural languages and the conceptual inferences we make.

The principal challenge to any theory of embodied meaning and reasoning is to extend the analysis beyond the bodily grounding of perceptual and spatial concepts to explain our abstract conceptualization and reasoning in all areas of theory and practice. There is a large and growing literature of detailed analyses of central concepts in fields as diverse as the physical sciences (Magnani & Nersessian, 2002), mathematics (Lakoff & Nunez, 2000), ethics (Johnson, 1993; Fesmire, 2003), law (Winter, 2001; Bjerre, 2005), politics (Lakoff, 1996), and psychology (Gibbs, 1994; Fernandez-Duque & Johnson, 1999; 2002), and many other fields.

As an example of this kind of analysis, consider our moral and political conception of *rights*. In English, we speak of 'a right *to*' something, as in, 'The Supreme Court ruled that adult homosexuals have a right to private consensual sexual relations' or 'Felix has a right to practice his religion.' The apparently abstract notion of a political right is understood in our culture via either of two basic conceptual metaphors, one of which conceives of rights as metaphorical paths of motion, while the other conceives them as abstract entities that can be possessed, transferred, and lost. According to the first conceptual metaphor (RIGHTS ARE UNOBSTRUCTED PATHS OF MOTION), a right is understood metaphorically as a 'right-of-way' to some destination, that is, some purpose. This metaphor is based on the Location version of the EVENT STRUCTURE metaphor, which consists of the following mapping:

The LOCATION EVENT-STRUCTURE Metaphor

Source Domain		Target Domain
[Spatial Motion]		[Events]
A location	⇒	A State
Change of location	⇒	Change of State
Forces	⇒	Causes
Forced movement	⇒	Causation
Destinations	⇒	Purposes
Paths	⇒	Means
Impediments to motion	⇒	Difficulties
Absence of impediments	⇒	Freedom of action

This complex conceptual metaphor for conceptualizing events, causes, and change is thoroughly embodied. It makes use of the SOURCE-PATH-GOAL schema and involves multiple primary metaphors, such as PURPOSES ARE DESTINATIONS (discussed earlier), CAUSES ARE FORCES, and STATES ARE LOCATIONS. According to this systematic mapping, we metaphorically understand the activity of pursuing some end or purpose as motion along a path to a desired destination (e.g., 'I have a *long way to go* before I get my Ph.D'). Any difficulty that keeps us from attaining our purpose is understood as something that gets in our way and blocks our motion along the path (e.g., 'My illness *got in the way* of my getting promoted'). Based on the logic of the LOCATION EVENT STRUCTURE metaphor, then, one of our key notions of having a legal right is understood as possessing the freedom to move to your desired destination (goal or purpose) without being hindered, blocked, or diverted from your path. If you have a legal right, then other people in society thereby have an obligation *not* to constrain you or to block your metaphorical path of motion. In this way, rights entail correlative duties of non-obstruction (or, sometimes, even of aid and assistance) by other people.

Our second major conception of legal rights comes from another fundamental metaphorical frame known as the Object version of the

EVENT STRUCTURE metaphor, which is based on the following cross-domain mapping:

The OBJECT EVENT-STRUCTURE Metaphor

Source Domain		Target Domain
[Transfer of Objects]		[Events and Causes]
Objects	⇒	Attributes
Possessing an object	⇒	Having an attribute
Movement of object (acquisition or loss)	⇒	Change of attribute
Transfer of possession	⇒	Causation
Desired object	⇒	Purpose

According to the OBJECT EVENT STRUCTURE metaphor, being in a certain state is coming into possession of an object (e.g., '*I've got* a big cold'). Causing someone to be in a state is transferring some object to them (e.g., 'She *gave* me her cold'). Change of state is the result of acquisition or loss of some object (e.g., 'The chicken soup *took* my flu *away*'). Within this framing of action and causation, having a *right to* something means that you may metaphorically take possession of that object (as in, 'She has a *right* to privacy'). Having a right is thus having an IOU—a letter of credit—entitling you to future possession of some object (i.e., some desired state or attribute). And, insofar as I have a right to possess that metaphorical object, other people have an obligation to honor my IOU upon demand, that is, not to stand in the way or hinder me from getting that abstract object (Johnson, 1993).

The point I want to make with these two analyses is that even our basic concepts for abstract entities like *rights* are grounded, via image schemas and primary metaphors, in our bodily sensory-motor experience. They do not emanate from some allegedly 'pure' reason; rather, they emerge from our shared bodily experience. Winter (2001) has shown how large parts of legal reasoning are based, not on literal concepts, but on conceptual metaphors. His analysis reveals how these metaphorical concepts emerge in the shared experience of a culture and are revised and extended via ordinary imaginative processes of metaphor and metonymy. Our legal concepts tend to be relatively stable, but they are subject to modifications resulting from changing historical, social, economic, philosophic, and moral developments. To think of legal (and ethical) concepts as given for all time and fixed in their meanings is to overlook their metaphorical basis. Indeed, it is the metaphors that make the legal concepts understandable and applicable to changing real-life situations.

Why Do We Think We Have Disembodied Thoughts?

So, the question is, if meaning really *is* embodied, then how are we led to the illusion of disembodied concepts and thought? The chief answer is simply that we are very seldom aware of the metaphors that structure our most important concepts, and so we erroneously regard them as literal and absolute. Conceptual metaphors operate, for the most part, beneath the level of conscious awareness. When we hear the words 'Hannibal Lector has a *right to* legal counsel,' the cross-domain mapping in the OBJECT EVENT STRUCTURE metaphor is activated. We are not self-reflectively aware that we are understanding a right metaphorically as an entitlement to the possession of an abstract entity (legal counsel). There is nothing unusual about the non-conscious operation of metaphorical thought. Indeed, most of our thinking goes on beneath the conscious level (Lakoff & Johnson, 1999).

Because our conceptual metaphors are mostly non-conscious, we are often seduced by the mistaken ideal of situation-neutral, universal truths. We easily forget, if we ever knew, that our thought is *not* disembodied, but always tied back to dimensions of our bodily experience. Our unreflective literalism leads us to believe in pure abstraction and disembodied thought. In *The Absent Body* (1990), Drew Leder shows how the bodily capacities and structures that make perception possible actually recede and hide in our perceptual acts, generating the illusion of disembodied thought. Because our perceptual and motor activities are always directed toward some object, state, or situation (either present or to be realized), those acts focus our awareness on the content of our experience, rather than on the bodily means of having those experiences. Leder describes two basic forms of bodily disappearance:

> One I will call *focal disappearance*. This refers to the self-effacement of bodily organs when they form the focal origin of a perceptual or actional field. An example is the invisibility of the eye within the visual field it generates. ... In contrast, I have recently been discussing what I will now term *background disappearance*. Bodily regions can disappear because they are *not* the focal origin or our sensorimotor engagements but are back-grounded in the

corporeal gestalt: that is, they are for the moment relegated to a supportive role, involved in irrelevant movement, or simply out of play. (Leder, 1990, p. 26).

Likewise, the bodily basis of meaning tends to recede into non-conscious processes of meaning-making, leaving us only with a consciousness of the final products and contents of our thinking. It is this receding that generates the illusion of disembodied thought.

In spite of the embodied nature of meaning, it is quite striking how persistently we cling to our belief in disembodied thought. Perhaps the greatest repository of such views is the Platonist conception of mathematics (and logic) as grounded on disembodied universal concepts that give rise to eternal mathematical (or logical) truths. There is a representative example of this illusion in common mathematical notions of infinity. Lakoff and Nunez (2001) have done a beautiful job of showing that our various concepts of infinity are actually defined by body-based conceptual metaphors, rather than being universal non-empirical concepts. In what they call 'The Basic Metaphor of Infinity,' we understand an iterative process that goes on and on (without end) metaphorically as a completed iterative process. This allows us to produce the concept of 'actual infinity' according to the following mapping:

THE BASIC METAPHOR OF INFINITY

Source Domain		Target Domain
[Completed Iterative Processes]		*[Iterative Processes That Go On and On]*
The beginning state	$\Rightarrow$	The beginning state
State resulting from the initial stage of the process	$\Rightarrow$	State resulting from the initial stage of the process
The process: From a given intermediate State, produce the next state	$\Rightarrow$	The process: From a given intermediate state, produce the next state
The intermediate result after that iteration of the process	$\Rightarrow$	The intermediate result after that iteration of the process
The final resultant state	$\Rightarrow$	'The final resultant state' (actual infinity)
Entailment *E*: The final resultant state is unique and follows every nonfinal state	$\Rightarrow$	Entailment *E*: The final resultant state is unique and follows every nonfinal state

The BASIC METAPHOR OF INFINITY is what makes it possible for us to conceive of a never-ending iterative process (potential infinity) as if it were, in its 'last step' a completed iterative process (actual infinity). We are using this metaphor whenever we think of infinity as an actual number—as a unique final resultant state 'at infinity'— as is done in many types of mathematics. Notice two crucial things: First, the metaphor is based on the embodied source-domain experience of iterative processes, such as taking one step after another. Second, via the metaphorical extension, we are allowed to think of a non-ending process as if there were, in fact, some unique, final resultant state—a kind of absolute number.

Much of our thinking about absolutes works in exactly this way, via metaphors that operate beneath the level of consciousness. In *Philosophy in the Flesh* (1999) George Lakoff and I analyzed the notion of *Being* that first emerged in the pre-Socratic thinking of Thales and Anaximander and that was later developed in Plato and Aristotle, forming the basis for an entire western philosophical tradition for which the ultimate question was, 'What is the nature of Being?' But the very concept of *Being* is the result of a metaphor similar to the BASIC METAPHOR FOR INFINITY, in which we metaphorically conceptualize an iterative process of categorization as if there were some ultimate category of all categories, namely, the category of Being. Here is how the metaphor works. If we believe that every entity is a particular *kind* of thing, then we are on our way to a hierarchy of categories. All we have to do is think of each category, in turn, as an abstract entity that must then itself fall under some 'higher' category. If we continue this hierarchical process of progressive category subsumption, we would go on and on without end. The only way to stop this process is to metaphorically conceive a 'final resultant state' of the process, namely, The Category of Being. Being is what is supposedly possessed by all things that exist.

Numerous philosophies and theologies are based on the quest for the nature of Being as such (or Being-itself, pure Actuality, or pure Act-of-Existing). But 'Being' is the product of a metaphorical mapping, the image schema of Iteration, and the folk theory that every entity is part of a *kind* and that kinds are abstract entities. 'Being' is a metaphorical concept that we use to unify our understanding of our experience, but it is not some ultimate reality that we need to discover and explain.

Moreover, as Dewey showed so thoroughly in books like *The Quest for Certainty* (1929/1984), *Experience and Nature* (1925/1981), and *Logic: Theory of Inquiry* (1938/1991), our human anxiety about change, contingency, and death impels us to search for absolute foundations and certain, unshakeable truths. In morality and politics this takes the form of a belief in absolute moral rules which are alleged to dictate how we should live our lives and how we should treat others. But, in *Human Nature and Conduct* (1922/1988), Dewey argued that we should understand moral principles, not as strict moral rules, but rather as summaries of moral ideals and of collective moral wisdom about certain types of situations. So viewed, these principles are not absolute laws, but reminders of what considerations a group of people has found to be important in certain kinds of morally problematic situations. Such ideals give us moral principles for reflecting on our actions, but they do not underwrite strict moral rules that would dictate universally how we should act or what we should think. Even though well-tested principles will have presumptive weight in our ethical deliberations, each principle or ideal is itself subject to scrutiny (and possible revision) in light of new conditions that may arise. Our highest moral ideals are defined by sets of conceptual metaphors (Johnson, 1993) that are grounded in our shared bodily experience.

From an evolutionary and neural point of view, the very idea of disembodied concepts makes little sense (Edelman, 1992; Edelman & Tononi, 2000). What does make sense is that parts of the sensory-motor areas of the brain should be appropriated to perform inferences about abstract concepts. There is no need to create a second, duplicate independent reasoning system for abstract concepts, when the inferential capacities of the sensory and motor systems can do the job. Regier (1996) has formulated structured connectionist models based on known neural architectures and that can use image schemas and metaphors to make inferences about abstract concepts.

Absolutist metaphorical thinking is so deeply engrained in human cognition that most people are hardly ever likely to change their foundationalist habits of thought. Nevertheless, empirically informed and philosophically self-critical people can (1) be aware that there is no disembodied thought, (2) understand that embodied structures of meaning plus imaginative structures such as metaphor make abstract thinking possible, and (3) learn to live without absolutes like Being, First Cause, Truth, Rights, and Justice. John Dewey, for one, spent much of his long philosophical career trying to help us acknowledge the embodiment of mind and overcome our absolutist pretensions. The result was a view of situated inquiry that could give us the most reliable knowledge available, while curbing our lust for ultimate truths and eternal foundations. Dewey gave us a view of a humble, human, and efficacious form of understanding and knowing — one suited for the embodied creatures that we are.

References

Bjerre, C. (2005), 'Mental Capacity as Metaphor', *International Journal for the Semiotics of Law*, 18, pp. 101–140.

Damasio, Antonio (1994), *Descartes' Error: Emotion, Reason, and the Human Brain* (New York: G. P. Putnam's Sons).

Damasio, Antonio (1999), *The Feeling of What Happens: Body and Emotion in the Making of Consciousness* (New York: Harcourt, Brace & Co.).

Damasio, Antonio (2003), *Looking for Spinoza: Joy, Sorrow, and the Feeling Brain* (New York: Basic Books).

Dewey, John (1925/1981), *Experience and Nature. The Later Works of John Dewey, Vol. 1*. Ed. by Jo Ann Boydston (Carbondale: Southern Illinois University Press).

Dewey, John (1922/1988), *Human Nature and Conduct*. Ed. by Jo Ann Boydston (Carbondale: Southern Illinois University Press).

Dewey, John (1938/1991), *Logic: The Theory of Inquiry. The Later Works of John Dewey, Vol. 12*. Ed. by Jo Ann Boydston (Carbondale: Southern Illinois University Press).

Dewey, John. (1929/1984), *The Quest for Certainity. The Later Works of John Dewey, Vol. 4*, ed. by Jo Ann Boydston (Carbondale: Southern Illinois University Press).

Edelman, G. (1992), *Bright Air, Brilliant Fire: On the Matter of Mind* (New York: Basic Books).

Edelman, G. and Tononi, G. (2000), *A Universe of Consciousness: How Matter Becomes Imagination* (New York: Basic Books).

Fesmire, S. (2003), *John Dewey and Moral Imagination: Pragmatism in Ethics* (Bloomington: Indiana University Press).

Fernandez-Duque, D. Johnson, M. (1999), 'Attention Metaphors: How Metaphors Guide the Cognitive Psychology of Attention', *Cognitive Science*, 23 (1), pp. 83–116.

Fernandez-Duque, D. and Johnson, M. (2002), 'Cause and Effect Theories of Attention: The Role of Conceptual Metaphor', *Review of General Psychology*, 6 (2), pp. 153–165.

Gallese, V. and Goldman, A. (1998), 'Mirror neurons and the simulation theory of mind-reading', *Trends in Cognitive Science*, 12, pp. 493–501.

Gibbs, R. W. Jr. and Colston, H. (1995), 'The psychological reality of image schemas and their transformations', *Cognitive Linguistics* (6-4), pp. 347–378.

Gibbs, R. (1994), *The Poetics of Mind: Figurative Thought, Language, and Understanding* (Cambridge: Cambridge University Press).

Grady, J. (1997), *Foundations of Meaning: Primary Metaphors and Primary Scenes*. Ph.D. Dissertation, Department of Linguistics, University of California, Berkeley.

James, William (1890), *The Principles of Psychology* (New York: Dover).

Johnson, Mark (1987), *The Body in the Mind: The Bodily Basis of Meaning, Imagination, and Reason* (Chicago: University of Chicago Press).
Johnson, Mark (1993), *Moral Imagination: Implications of Cognitive Science for Ethics* (Chicago: University of Chicago Press).
Lakoff, George (1987), *Women, Fire, and Dangerous Things: What Our Categories Reveal About the Mind* (Chicago: University of Chicago Press).
Lakoff, George (1996), *Moral Politics: What Conservatives Know that Liberal Don't* (Chicago: University of Chicago Press).
Lakoff, George and Johnson, Mark (1999), *Philosophy in the Flesh: The Embodied Mind and its Challenge to Western Thought* (New York: Basic Books).
Lakoff, George and Nunez, Rafael (2000), *Where Mathematics Comes From: How the Embodied Mind Brings Mathematics into Being* (New York: Basic Books).
Leder, Drew (1990), *The Absent Body* (Chicago: University of Chicago Press).
LeDoux, J. (2002), *The Synaptic Self: How Our Brains Become Who We Are* (New York: Viking Penguin).
Magnani, L. & Nersessian, N., eds. (2002), *Model-based Reasoning: Science, Technology, Values* (New York: Kluwer Academic/Plenum Publishers).
Regier,T. (1996), *The Human Semantic Potential: Spatial Language and Constrained Connectionism* (Cambridge, Mass.: MIT Press).
Rizzolatti, G. and L. Craighero (2004), 'The Mirror-Neuron System', *Annual Review of Neuroscience*, 27, pp. 169–192.
Winter, Steven (2001), *A Clearing in the Forest: Law, Life, and Mind* (Chicago: University of Chicago Press).

Xabier E. Barandiaran

Mental Life

Conceptual Models and Synthetic Methodologies for a Post-Cognitivist Psychology

*To my grandfather,
whose intellectual dedication and lived subtlety
I will admire forever*

'The question as to the nature of life, I believe, has been finally resolved, and is no longer a philosophical question. I hope something like this will happen to the so-called mind-body problem in the twenty-first century.'

John Searle

'Now what makes the cell living? The soft organization of its inner events and occurrences. Thus, if we are looking for the fundamental laws, for the principle of life, we have to establish the connections of this soft organization'

Tibor Gánti

New Foundations for Psychology?

Psychology is one of the most elusive fields of knowledge for current scientific research. This is not a surprising fact given that the brain (which is at least partly responsible for psychological phenomena) is, as Isaac Asimov synthetically described it, 'the most complex three pounds of matter in the universe', with more possible combinations of neural states in the brain than there are atoms in the universe. In addition, brain activity is not determined in isolation (providing at least a workable experimental control condition). Nor is brain activity fully specified by anything like a computer program or a set of genetic instructions ready for us to understand as a Darwinian textbook. On the contrary, a full range of bodily and environmental interactions shape neural activity, including the interactions with other (social) embrained bodies, historically shaped through multiple cultural and biographical contingencies, organized through externalized technologies and languages.

However, despite these difficulties, the question of what the mind is and how it should be studied cannot be left aside with a 'sorry, not yet accessible to science' sticker on it. The answer (however unsatisfactory our understanding may be at present) is clearly relevant to too many current different scientific (and non-scientific) fields to be ignored or 'put off' forever: from public institutions, business operations and everyday life activity to folk-psychology and psychiatric institutions, from education to neurobiological experiments, from inter-personal relationships to psycho-therapies. Of course, attempts to create 'definitive' scientific and rigorous foundations for psychology have been many. And each of these attempts has equally enabled and limited our understanding of the mind (some of those attempts have included phenomenology, phrenology, behaviourism, gestalt psychology, psychoanalysis, computational functionalism, folk-psychology, eliminativist neuroscience and, of course, cognitivism itself).

Post-Cognitivism

The fact that we ask ourselves here about something like a *post*-cognitivist psychology presupposes two basic ideas: (i) that something like a 'cognitivist paradigm' has dominated mainstream psychological studies for a while, providing a fruitful foundational framework and (ii) that we can 'go beyond this' to make room for something like a post-cognitivist foundation for psychology. Both premises require that we make explicit what cognitivism is in the first place. Following Wheeler's analysis of the Cartesian inheritance in cognitive science (Wheeler 2005), cognitivism states that the foundation and demarcation of mental/psychological phenomena is given by: (i) a subject-object dichotomy (ii) in which the cognizer (the subject) manipulates inner representational states (of an immaterial nature: conscious-phenomenological, computational, or otherwise) (iii) according to the rules of reason (logical, linguistic, etc.) (iv) where representational content is acquired by inferential procedures and (v) used to process (deduce, transform) a plan in order to execute actions in the world. As such, cognitivism has established itself as a form of *computational modernity* with its faith in a universal context-independent reason, its representational realism and its functionalist disembodiment. And considered purely as a research program (i.e. putting aside the question of whether its tenets are 'true' or not) it must be admitted that cognitivism has had considerable success in the fields of Linguistics, Artificial Intelligence (especially within the subfields of expert systems and symbol manipulation based reasoning) and Philosophy of the Mind, among others.

We must be clear in stating here that the prefix in *post*-cognitivism does not imply a refusal of a cognitive subject, her reason, her reality or her linguistically structured behaviour. On the contrary, the 'post' might be understood as the opportunity to test the limits of cognitivist foundations in order to formulate questions beyond those limits and eventually to explore possible answers: what kind of processes make possible the appearance of the subject-object dichotomy that every cognitivist study presupposes? What is the origin of the imperative force of reason as a normative structure of mental processes? What are the physical and biological conditions that make its existence possible? What would happen if action is considered as the very condition for the production of perceived situations, and not as the planned response to an objective state of affairs? These kinds of questions demarcate the landscape where post-cognitivism might be able to flourish. In this sense it is perhaps the right time to review and push forward some of the methodological and conceptual innovations that are available to us and might permit us to speak of a paradigmatic discontinuity that could properly be called 'post-cognitivist'. I shall attempt to tackle these proposed methodological innovations by sketching some of the new insights that computer simulation models of neurodynamic embodied agents have permitted. On the conceptual side, and drawing some analogies from the emergent field of 'synthetic protocell biology', I shall elaborate a conceptual model of Mental Life, merging together and pushing forward some of the conceptual achievements that nowadays populate the post-cognitivist landscape under the labels of dynamicism, embodiment and situatedness.

Conceptual Modelling
A MUNdane Declaration of Principles

Before we attempt to define an alternative methodological and conceptual foundation to that of cognitivism it is worth stating a set of epistemological principles that accurately define what this foundation should look like. This meta-theoretical exercise is unavoidable in any attempt to approach foundational issues in psychology. A great deal of both theoretical and methodological debates in psychology do not directly deal with the content of psychological phenomena but with the definition of the very framework in which such questions should be made and answered. Explicitly stating a set of epistemological constraints should make clear how to evaluate the present approach and how it relates to scientific practice. I shall call these the MUN constraints, standing as an acronym for Minimalism, Universality and Naturalism. But first, let me write some preliminary words on models since these constraints are to be applied to the process of model building and interpretation.

Current philosophy of science has focused on models as the most important units of the scientific production and organization of knowledge (Cartwright, 1983; Giere, 1988; Morrison, 2000). Godfrey-Smith has recently summarized this model-based philosophy of science in the following way:

> A model-builder's usual goal is to construct and describe various hypothetical structures. These structures are used to help us understand some actual target system or systems. Generally, the understanding is supposed to be achieved via a resemblance relationship between the hypothetical and the real system. But both the degree and kind of resemblance that is sought are adjustable. ... [T]he ability to describe and develop model systems in some detail, while remaining cautious or flexible about the particular respects in which the model might resemble the target system, is an essential tool. Modelling is especially useful when our knowledge of the target system is poor, and its workings are complex. (Godfrey-Smith, 2005, p. 3)

We can see a promising avenue to settle some theoretical disputes on the foundations of psychology if we adopt a conceptual and simulation modelling paradigm. What this suggestion involves is that foundational concepts themselves should be conceptualised as models. Thus concepts should be constructed as characterizing a class of hypothetical systems or structures that, through a 'resemblance relationship' with a class of target systems, should help us to understand some of their essential features. In particular, our goal is to model Mental Life as a form of organization: i.e. as a class of hypothetical systems in which a set of component processes relate to each other in a specific (interdependent) manner giving rise to a set of characteristic features.

Linguistically expressed conceptual models can be transformed and implemented into more tractable formal or simulation models which would lead, we hope, to empirically testable research procedures. But a conceptual structure, mathematical construct or computer simulation on its own is not a model of anything, unless accompanied by an auxiliary framework made of the assumptions, generalizations and interpretative relationships that permits to relate the hypothetical structure to the target objects and evaluate its adequacy and epistemic scope. In this sense the MUN constraints shall make explicit not only how the conceptual model is to be built but also how its auxiliary framework should be set up in order to transfer the model to the more empirically testable domain of scientific discourse. Let me start with Naturalism, then move to Universality and finally tackle the Minimalist constraint.

Naturalism

Naturalism is a widely spread philosophical position stating that *ad hoc* substances are not to be introduced in a model in order to explain the target phenomena. Thus, for instance, consciousness or information as theoretical primitives (Chalmers 1995), representations or logical structures, should be avoided as foundationally privileged departure points. However, what constitutes an *ad hoc* substance or property is a difficult matter. The way out of this dilemma is to think of naturalism as a scientifically embodied philosophical practice both at its sensory and motor surfaces (so to speak): i.e. it should be grounded on available scientific knowledge and be able to feed-back to scientific practice (through its capacity to generate new hypotheses, to provide principles to reorganize knowledge, clarify concepts, uncover fallacies, etc.). In addition, it should be asked: which type of scientific field must one be embedded in? In this sense we shall expand our naturalist constraint to encompass an additional requirement: a bottom-up approach. By bottom-up we mean that concepts and components of our conceptual model should be built from the most simple and elementary (in relation to a given level of organization of empirical research) to the most complex and higher order ones. In particular we will defend a *biological grounding* by which components of our model should be derived or closely related to more fundamental *biological processes*.[1] Thus, if we were to model meaning, for instance, it would be inappropriate to attribute seman-

---

[1] The bottom-up approach does not forbid to use top-down methods, in fact a top-down bottom-up circulation will be of significant importance. What the

tic properties to component neural ensembles if meaning is defined strictly in higher level terms (for instance as linguistic performance or in reference to the use of dictionaries, with no reference to its biological and neural grounding). Higher level descriptions should be accompanied and grounded on bottom-up explanations of how those phenomena can be sustained and emerge from lower level organizational principles. A bottom-up approach includes a final naturalist constraint: that observer dependent properties (relational properties that are accessible to the external observer's privileged position such as correlations between internal and environmental states, the designer's intentions, etc.) should not be attributed to the model itself, if no specific procedure is established to reconstruct them in a bottom-up observer-independent manner. This way we shall avoid the risk of projecting observer-dependent properties to the model and from the model to the explanation of the target system.[2]

Thus our first MUN constraint mandates that we build our model from a naturalist perspective, which entails a bottom-up biological grounding of the concepts and components belonging to our model of Mental Life.

Universalism

Our second constraint is Universalism. Currently available biological systems amenable to experimentation and study are the result of a set of historical (evolutionary) contingencies. But knowledge has universalist aspirations. As Artificial Life founder Chris Langton (1989) claimed: it is not life-as-we-know-it but rather life-as-it-could-be that is of interest to the field. We could equally define our object of study as the-mind-as-it-could-be rather than the-mind-as-we-know-it. This forces us to define universalizable patterns of life and mind rather than focusing on particular anatomical details of present mind-supporting brains and bodies. For instance if emotions are to be part of our final model it would be inappropriate to

bottom-up approach emphasizes is that the role of top-down methodologies should be limited to a form of heuristics and guidance of the bottom-up grounding.
[2] This form of projection of observer-dependent properties is a common mistake that appears on many human made and interpreted devices such as computer programs or robots. William Clancey (1989) has strongly argued on the danger of confusing three different frames of reference in robotic modelling: the robot designer's ontological preconceptions, the dynamics of a robot's interaction with its environment and an observer's descriptive theories of patterns in the robot's behaviour.

say that emotions are defined by the signals coming from a particular neural pathway, as if human brain anatomy was to determine what emotions there are to be in the Universe. It might be the case that some psychological processes be unambiguously identified or correlated with certain brain areas, but this is not to say that what that process is be equivalent with certain anatomical components or sets of components that happen to be the locus of such emotions in planet-earth vertebrates.

Minimalism

Minimalism is our third and final epistemological constraint. Minimalism might be seen as a direct consequence of our first naturalist bottom-up constraint but it is worth making it explicit as a specific requirement in itself. It states that our model must contain all *but no more than* those features necessary and sufficient to define the class of systems that it targets. So, rather than taking higher level epistemic properties or 'language like' sophisticated mental phenomena as a departure point, minimalism states that we should proceed making use of the simplest and more amenable components in order to build a model. This being said, and this is an important point, the upper boundary for complexity increase must remain open. So, for instance, Neils Bohr, inspired by Rutherford, proposed the planetary model of the atom taking as a departure point 'a simple system consisting of a positively charged nucleus of very small dimensions and an electron describing closed orbits around it' (Bohr, 1913, p. 3). Bohr's model, although focused on a simple system (the Hydrogen atom) to start with, was built with the rest of atomic forms in mind, so that components (electron orbits, nuclear forces and their relationships) could be aggregated to form more complex models once the minimal one was satisfactorily constructed and tested. Equally, we should tend towards generalizable and expandable models, where a minimalist core stands as a foundational first step that permits us to organize and discuss conceptual and empirical relationships. In the absence of a complete model, some properties might be studied on partial property-specific models. In this sense, formalization and computer simulation permit a common language to recombine and integrate achievements and components from different local or particular modelling experiments.[3]

But, unlike Bohr's case, we face a situation where there is no generally accepted and empirically available minimal target object to model. We are lacking the Hydrogen atom of the mind. What constitutes a genuine example of minimal cognition (not to speak of minimal mindfulness) remains an open issue which deserves much more attention than it currently receives.[4] In such a situation, minimalism is a methodological remedy for the study of complex systems. So let us imagine that there was nothing like a one electron + one single proton atom left in the universe: there were only complex macromolecules to experiment with. In such a case we could proceed by creating something like an artificial atomic-physics by constructing complex simulation models of non-existing atoms, out of which an artificial chemistry could be constructed which, finally, could be compared with experimentally available target macromolecules. The Hydrogen atom of the life and mind must be reconstructed from what we take to be coherent with our present knowledge of biological and neuro-psychological phenomena.

By generating such minimalist (but non-directly empirically correlated) models we pay a considerable price in terms of the abstraction and idealization it necessarily involves. But on the other hand we gain an insight into the nature of complex systems that we could not otherwise have. Elsewhere (Barandiaran & Moreno, 2006a) I have termed these models conceptual simulation models because they do not directly target any specific empirical object but remain, nevertheless, epistemologically useful by providing the means for theoretical investigation, conceptual clarification and illustration, proofs of concept, knowledge reorganization and a set of other epistemic functions. This specific use of conceptual simulation models has been called 'opaque thought experiment'. This phrase is useful in that it highlights the extent to which this concept alludes to the heuristic and conceptual role played by thought experiments in other branches of science, whilst stressing that these models are ana-

---

[3] Such is the case of some robotic systems that integrate partial neural models of functionally distinct anatomical parts (Brooks, 1997; Almássy et al., 1998; Taylor & Taylor, 2000, to mention but a few).

[4] There are a number of recent exceptions like Randall Beer's target article and its commentaries (Beer, 2003) on minimally cognitive robotic agents or van Duijn and colleagues' exploration into the principles of minimal cognition (Duijn et al., 2006). Together with Alvaro Moreno I have also addressed this question elsewhere (Barandiaran & Moreno, 2006b).

lytically opaque due to the complexity of the simulation (Di Paolo *et al.*, 2000; Bedau, 1998)[5]. These models make computers virtual laboratories (Emmeche 1994) where complex interactions among emergent dynamic structures can be extensively and intensively studied; improving our theoretical understanding of those natural phenomena which are more complex than those the unaided human mind or mathematical analysis alone are capable of exploring. In addition computer simulation models permit us to establish systematic experimental set-ups for those natural objects whose control conditions are difficult to fix. The embodied and situated brain/mind is one of these objects and artificial life robotic simulations (and realizations) are some of the most successful tools to model it at the conceptual level. These models remain far from the intricate complexities of natural brains-bodies and their subtle ecological environments, but stand, nevertheless, close to a comprehensive conceptual understanding of the integrated and emergent patterns that might constitute the essence of 'psyche'. I will return to this topic throughout the rest of this chapter.

Life: Lessons from Synthetic Protocell Biology

If we are to develop a model of Mental Life it seems important to spend some time exploring the concept of life first (as it is understood and modelled in some current approaches). But the concept of life is not the only link with biology that we can benefit from. Since biology has suffered from most of the same conceptual and methodological problems of psychology, it should be equally expected that psychology could benefit from those conceptual and methodological remedies that biology is using today. Both the fortunes and the misfortunes of biological sciences will contain important lessons to apply into psychology. In addition, biology has a much more detailed (and minimalist) understanding of living systems than the best available picture of brain activity or any other scientifically grounded psychological research field. As a result, concepts and models developed in biology, with its fine grained molecular experimentalism and its computer modelling implementations, have acquired a high level of conceptual, methodological and empirical sophistication and accuracy. Importing some of this conceptual and modelling apparatus back to the realm of psychology looks like a promising research avenue to explore.

[5]   Going even further Daniel Dennett (1994) has claimed that Artificial Life might be understood as a form of philosophy itself.

As Bechtel recently argued (2006), mechanistic explanations in biology have long underappreciated the importance of organization itself; i.e. how components get together in particular reactive arrangements creating the phenomenon under investigation. Far from the linear decomposition and isolated analysis of a component's properties which mainstream molecular biology has focused on, biological explanations will ultimately require models that include positive and negative feed-back loops, self-organized processes, coupled cycles and network properties that put on centre-stage the critical role of organization in living phenomena: 'Only by keeping a keen eye on the organization at play in living systems is it possible to understand the mechanisms that figure in living organisms' (Bechtel 2006).

Systems Biology (Ideker et al., 2001; Kitano, 2002; O'Malley & Dupré, 2005) is the label under which current attempts to integrate data from molecular biology into organizational models (from developmental genetic regulatory networks to metabolic coupled cycles) are carried out. Of particular interest to us is the set of models of minimal organization of life that Systems Biology has started to develop, taking the cell as the basic unit and expression of life (what Solé and colleagues (2006) have labelled Synthetic Protocell Biology). Some of the early formulations of minimal models of life trace their origins back to Maturana and Varela's autopoietic theory of life (1973), Tibor Ganti's chemoton model (1971; 2003), Stuart Kauffman's autocatalytic network theory (1971), and Robert Rosen's M-R systems (1958). The original formulation of these models was done in a conceptual or linguistic form, accompanied by diagrammatic illustrations and formalized descriptions. But since the early 70's, computer simulation models were used to illustrate the emergent order of the proposed organization, (c.f. for example Varela, Maturana and Uribe's pioneering work [1974]). Also, Kauffman explored autocatalytic systems and other self-organizing biological processes making use of computers (1986) while Tibor Ganti's model's first computer simulation dates from 1975 (Békés, 1975, followed by Csendes, 1984).

Despite being often marginalized by mainstream biology these dynamic and organizational models of life have been further developed by a number of authors within the fields of artificial life, artificial chemistry, theoretical biology, complexity sciences, origins and synthesis of life, etc. As an example of some of the most recent approaches, we shall focus on Mavelli and Ruiz-Mirazo's (2007) simulation model of a minimal self-reproducing cellular system that captures and integrates most of the essential features of the models mentioned above. Figure 1 graphically illustrates their model. At the nucleus of it we have an autocatalytic cycle: this is a network of chemical reactions that reproduces the components of the network itself through a cyclic loop of metabolites (A components). The first core idea is that of *self-organization* at the chemical level: a huge amount of microscopic elements adopt a global, macroscopic ordered pattern in the presence of a specific flow of matter and energy (represented by the continuous inflow of X precursors into the system with the outflow of W waste products, and the set of constraints on the equations that govern the reaction dynamics, expressed as kinetic constants K_n). Given the presence of precursor X the stochastic collision of A1 molecules produces A2 molecules that in turn produces A3 molecules leading to A4 which, closing the loop, generate A1 molecules. The resulting pattern generates a form of identity in which, out of an undifferentiated chemical pool, a self-reinforcing order appears. The internal dynamic cohesion that constitutes this identity is not only a consequence of the material features of their components but also, and most importantly, of the achievement and maintenance of some type of circular dynamic causality. In other words, the very macroscopic pattern itself contributes to the maintenance of the dynamical cohesion at the microscopic level: the chemical cycle continuously regenerates its component processes. Thus, it is not only the local interactions that matter but the global patterns they generate: molecular properties are significant only in the context of massive stochastic collisions where the effect of a particular molecule will depend on the reaction rates of other components whose concentrations are continuously maintained in far-from-equilibrium stability conditions by the network of reactions cycles that constitutes the system.

This form of circular physico-chemical organization is a kind of dissipative structure (Nicolis & Prigogine, 1977), a 'far from thermodynamic' equilibrium system that Schrödinger took to be at the core of living phenomena (Schrödinger, 1946). As such, the system, in order to maintain its constitutive order, needs a continuous flow of matter and energy. And, if it is to be robust against variations of this flow while maintaining its unity, a membrane is necessarily required both to retain or encapsulate the core metabolic organization and to 'negotiate' its perturbations and needs (Ruiz-Mirazo & Moreno, 2004). This requirement is represented in the model by L molecules.

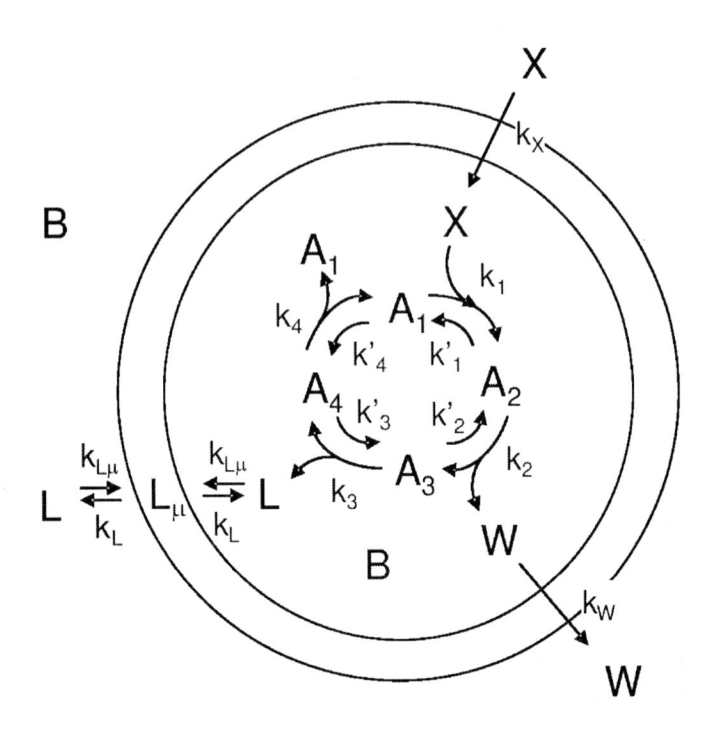

Figure 1: Graphical representation (by Mavelli & Ruiz-Mirazo 2007, with permission) of the simulation model of minimal procell metabolism (what we here take as the basic organization or essence of life).

A core autocatalytic network regenerates the components of the network (A components) and produces a membrane (L components) capable to manage the flow of matter through it (expressed through the precursor X and the waste product W). The value of the kinetic constants (K_n) together with the net flow of matter through the system keep it in far-from-equilibrium thermodynamic conditions: the coupled reactions are continuously sustaining the levels of concentration necessary to keep the system going.

The network produces L molecules that ensemble each other to produce Lμ molecules forming together a membrane that encapsulates the reaction-network. But the membrane is not just an envelope for the autocatalytic network, it selectively controls the diffusion of reactants between internal and external aqueous solutions. This is of fundamental importance since changes in the core autocatalytic network can modulate membrane properties to control the flow of matter and energy between the system and the environment. In turn, this leads to a qualitative difference in organization with regard to that of a single autocatalytic network (like Kauffman's—1986). This (minimal) proto-cell is capable of controlling its boundary conditions for self-maintenance: i.e., it can regulate the input of matter and energy that ensures the ongoing regeneration of components while avoiding osmotic crisis and other organizational threads.[6]

From the simulation model just described and its interpretation as the basic organization of cells, a set of characteristic features or principles of minimal living systems can be extracted:

Emergent Self: Given a set of initial conditions (the presence of X precursor molecules above a certain threshold) a set of macroscopic correlations appear (an interdependent set of concentrations of A types of molecules) as a result of recurrent local interactions (stochastic collisions). In turn the occurrence of these local interactions recursively depends on the macroscopic correlation: the higher the concentration of A1 molecules the higher the probability of a collision between A1 molecules to produce A2 molecules; and the higher the number of collisions of A1 molecules the higher will become its concentration (due to the circular set of reactions A1-A2-A3-A4-A1) until this positive feed-back loop reaches a steady state. The resulting macroscopic order is said to be *emergent* precisely because of the recursive micro-macro/local-global relationship and *self-sustaining* because of the circular causal loop that is established. Due to the chemical substrate of such an organization a physical boundary is required to retain the created emergent order. By producing a membrane as part of the reaction cycle the macroscopic order can be said to distinguish itself from its environment. Although generally expressed in much more sophisticated forms, all living systems ulti-

---

[6] Such a kind of organization has been called *autonomy* (Varela, 1979) or, more concretely specified in the chemical and thermodynamic domain, *basic autonomy* (Ruiz-Mirazo & Moreno, 2004); naming the capacity of the system to create an identity, a self (*autos*) and to define its own rules or norms (*nomos*). It can be said that the system defines or created it norms in the sense that the global order is not determined by local properties in isolation but by the circular dynamics that govern *and* constitute the system as a unity; a unity that depends for its continuing existence on those higher level patterns of activity. A full sense of autonomy would require that the system performs some work, channeling the energy generated through its core metabolic cycle to produce an action on its environment that contributes to its self-maintenance through some control of its thermodynamic and physical boundary conditions (Kauffman, 2003; Ruiz-Mirazo & Moreno, 2004).

mately follow this logic of self-maintenance that determines their integrity as units of life. Now, such an organization cannot exist except as a 'far from thermodynamic' equilibrium system which brings us to the second characteristic feature.

Situated openness: The system (the emergent self understood as a circular macroscopic correlation) can only exist insofar as it is *situated* on a material and energetic environment in order to persist. But what this environment is (in relation to the system) is co-determined by its organization, i.e. by its form of self-maintenance. For instance, the way in which molecule X in the environment becomes relevant for living organization is not something determined exclusively on the basis of its objective molecular properties but in relation to the way in which X becomes a precursor of the nested set of reactions. In this sense, out of an in principle undifferentiated physical surrounding, living organization selectively creates for itself an environment that becomes both a potential source of destructive perturbations and a necessary source of boundary conditions for self-maintenance. The system is thus constitutively *open*.

Normative functionality: As a consequence of the above features certain internal and interactive processes become normative. Independently of how the components of the system are interacting at a given time or the system, as a whole, is functioning, there is something that it 'ought to do' and a set of component interactions that 'ought to happen' in a certain way. First, because of the circular interdependent organization, some internal processes must happen in a particular way for its continuing existence[7]: if collisions between certain molecules do not produce the corresponding molecule at a certain rate so that the reaction chain gets closed, the system collapses. Second, due to its 'far from thermodynamic' equilibrium condition some actions must be carried out by the system in order to ensure its own existence (for instance to avoid an osmotic crisis). I shall call normative the stability dependencies that are created between the macroscopic variables of the system. Thus, a sense of good or bad, appropriate or inappropriate, adaptive or maladaptive, *emerges from the very organization of the system*, and is not externally defined by a designer or observer that projects a desired functionality on it.

---

[7] To use Christensen and Bickhard's terminology (2002) the rest of the component processes of the system *dynamically presupposes* a concrete way of functioning (from all the 'physically' possible ones) for a given component, their stability and consequently their normative functioning, depends on it.

Agency: The emergence of a self-maintained and self-distinguished form of dissipative order, open to its environment will crucially depend (under internal and environmental variation) on its capacity to differentially negotiate the flow with the environment (or even to actively seek for the appropriate sources of matter and energy). Agency appears precisely when the system is capable of adaptively regulating its environmental conditions for self-maintenance.[8] The term adaptive regulation involves here a causal asymmetry on the determination of the system-environment relationship. A minimal example of agency is provided by the membrane's active ion-pumping that avoids an osmotic crisis: the system directs energy against the concentration gradient to control its boundary condition for self-maintenance.

What increasingly sophisticated and accurate simulations models add to the conceptual description of life is the possibility of systematically exploring the emergent patterns and behaviours that such organizations are capable of achieving; thus providing a more precise and insightful understanding of its complexity. Within Mavelli and Ruiz-Mirazo's simulation, out of local stochastic reaction rules, the above characteristic features can be observed and measured along with cell division (driven by autocatalytic growth), buffering and other homeostatic properties, critical thresholds for self-organization and certain system behaviours (oscillations, instabilities, etc.). Computer implementations of mathematical models make possible an automatized intensive and extensive exploration of the full range of organizational configurations. Conceptually, these models are of great importance since they permit to discuss in precise terms what set of components, processes, configurations, etc. are crucial to achieve increasingly more complex biological patterns of organization. These kind of simulation models have become an unavoidable tool to discuss and develop different theories of the origins of life and the necessary conditions for its appearance and synthesis. Ultimately, computer simulation models permit detailed hypotheses to be tested in the 'real' laboratory (Solé *et al.*, 2006).

This conception of life, modelled as a circular, emergent, self-sustaining and 'far from thermodynamic equilibrium' chemical organized system, satisfies the MUN constraints stated above. It is a

---

[8] This feature of agency cannot yet be derived or interpreted within Mavelli and Ruiz-Mirazo's simulation model but it is part of the conceptual model that one of the authors has developed previously (Ruiz-Mirazo & Moreno, 2004).

naturalist model since it is grounded on the material and thermodynamic properties of the components and relationships that make up the system. No reference to vitalist forces is required to specify the essence of life. The model is *universal* for it can generalize the basic organization of life without reference to arbitrary or local contingent properties of life-as-we-know-it, while remaining coherent with its objective/material conditions of possibility. In addition, although the model focuses on a minimal cellular level, all its fundamental properties can be generalized to more complex living forms. Finally, it is a *minimal* model because it integrates only those component processes that are crucial to specify the most fundamental features of life.[9]

The question to be asked next is: can we expect something like this minimal model of *life* to give rise to a minimal model of *mind*?

Simulating Neurodynamic Agents: An Experimental Framework for Theoretical Post-Cognitivist Psychology

Evolutionary robotics (Cliff *et al.*, 1993, Harvey *et al.*, 1997, Nolfi & Floreano, 2000; Harvey, *et al.*, 2005) together with computational

---

[9] I shall note that the above characterization of living organization fails to satisfy the requirement that the upper limit for complexity growth remain open within a minimalist model. The reason is that the complexity that the described chemical organization can achieve remains severely bounded if we don't integrate further, qualitatively distinct, components and processes (Ruiz-Mirazo *et al.*, 2004). We are referring here to the genetic machinery. In fact, Tibor Ganti's original chemoton model already included such components (although in a very preliminary way): energetically stable, non-reactive and recombinable macromolecules. What such 'template' molecules permit is the decoupling of a control regulatory subsystem within the whole organization. In the absence of such kind of components the adaptive capacities of the system are very limited. The introduction of informational talk is used in systems endowed with such components due to their recombinable capacity, energetically stable structure and the fact that they are 'functionally interpreted' by the metabolic organization to produce specific molecules capable to create local constraints. In fact such molecules and processes would be crutial to achieve an open-ended increase of complexity ultimately leading to evolution as we know it and a proper account of life with all its evolutionary potential (Ruiz-Mirazo *et al.* 2004). For some of the authors supporting the picture of life presented here dynamical and self-organization models of biological processes (even autonomy) are not sufficient to account for life; informational or semiotic processes are required for such characterization. However they all agree on that autonomy is the most fundamental requisite and form of organization. Without it the very concepts of information, function or evolution could not be naturalized. For the purpose of this chapter I will take the form of organization described in this section (without recombinable molecular templates) to be an adequate model for the essence of life.

neuroethology (Beer, 1990; Cliff, 1991), evolutionary autonomous agents (Rupin, 2002) and what Randall Beer has called the 'minimally cognitive behaviour program' (Beer ,1996; 2003) are modelling paradigms that permit us to design embodied and situated dynamical agents capable of solving 'minimally' cognitive tasks. The most standard variant of evolutionary robotics works as follows. A robotic body, an environment and a control architecture are simulated as dynamical systems in a computer. It is important to note that the dynamic controllers that are usually implemented in the robotic agent (Continuous Time Recurrent Neural Networks—CTRNN hereafter) are chosen so that, through variations of their parametric values and number of nodes, the controller can potentially approximate any possible dynamical system (Funahashi & Nakamura, 1993). Some parameters of the robotic architecture (especially those of the control system but, additionally, some body parameters too, especially those related to the sensors and motors) are left unspecified. Next, artificial evolution is used to optimize these parameter values. Those configurations that lead the robot (dynamically coupled to its environment) to perform a desired cognitive or behavioural task are selected. The best evolved agent is then tested through intensive experimentation and analysis to provide a dynamical causal explanation of how the task is successfully performed. What this kind of simulation permits (unlike other experimental approaches) is to integrate, in the same explanatory framework, detailed environmental, bodily and neural factors and their complex dynamic interplay. Neural patterns of activity and their stability or synchrony with environmental, body and sensor variability can be precisely determined and their coupled dynamic organization made visible.

Using this artificial experimental framework, models of shape recognition (Cliff *et al.*, 1993), learning (Tuci *et al.*, 2002), communication (Quinn, 2001) and other cognitive phenomena can be built where no theoretical assumptions are previously introduced into the model. This is because the agent is designed in abstract dynamical terms, with no pre-specified anatomical/structural components and predefined functions, and artificial evolution 'blindly' generates behaviourally efficient agents. Selection operates at the level of the brain-body-environment continuum, thus no *a priori* task decomposition or functional presuppositions need to be made in relation to how the agent 'should' solve the task. This leaves room for self-organizing dynamics to emerge in the simulation, and for different and previously 'difficult to imagine' dynamic modes of behavioural organization to appear. What we get is a kind of emergent dynamic functionalist approach in which a potentially universal dynamic controller is constrained to achieve an online embodied functionality out of a previously non-specified sensorimotor architecture.

The main problem with these models is that they involve no reference to real existing biological cognitive agents: i.e. they have no direct empirical target to correlate with. This makes them paradigmatic examples of the conceptual models as described earlier. It is precisely in this sense that evolutionary robotics might help to elucidate the conceptual foundations of psychology and cognitive science. In fact, evolutionary robotic models have already been used to raise some interesting foundational questions (Harvey, 2000; Di Paolo et al., 2003; Beer, 2003; Wheeler, 1996; 2005; Clark, 1997, Chemero, 2000).

Some of the theoretical achievements (that most evolutionary robotists would be willing to accept as post-cognitivist) include precise (even formalized) accounts of the critical role played by a number of key principles in cognitive systems. *Situatedness* defines the environment of an agent as dependent on its controllable relative motion. As a result an agent can exploit environmental cues and sensorimotor correlations to solve cognitive problems that would otherwise require a high cognitive load (or even an exponential growth of context-independent inferences). Early in evolutionary robotics (Cliff et al. 1993) situatedness was made an explicit and tractable feature of intelligent behaviour in terms of exploring the emergent dynamics of shape recognition where cognitive behaviour was the result of distributed system-environment dynamic loops. Sensorimotor *embodiment* is another feature that these models have helped to precisely define. Embodiment is shown as a function of bodily properties in relation to the situated sensorimotor coupling of the agent with its environment, where architectural and mechanical constraints have been shown to be necessary (and sometimes sufficient) to achieve a number of cognitive behaviours that were previously thought to require explicit and sophisticated symbolic procedures. On the one hand motor embodiment defines a limited and biased interface with the world where constrained degrees of freedom (joint angles, elasticity, shape, etc.) facilitate some characteristic interactions (grasping, walking, etc.). On the other hand embodied sensors are not continuous full-range measuring devices but, on the contrary, are limited and specialized within specific ranges, transformations and filtering of sensory perturbations (the coclea, the retina, etc. are sophisticated embodiments of sensory surfaces that exploit physical features to transform environmental perturbations into pre-organized signals). In addition, sensory and motor surfaces that evolved together appear coupled through recurrent sensorimotor and somatosensory interactions increasing the effect of embodiment. *Dynamicism* is another aspect of adaptive behaviour that evolutionary robotic experiments have shown to be irreducible to representational-computationalist concepts. Dynamical concepts and tools have been proved to be the best framework to account for the complex adaptive behaviour that natural and artificial embodied and situated agents can display (Beer, 2003).

Problems with the Situated Robotics Approach

However despite the progress that the situated robotics approach has made, evolutionary roboticist Ezequiel Di Paolo (2003) recently raised concerns about the limits of the current situated, embodied and dynamicist robotic paradigm (although his criticisms are even more valid for traditional AI). His main argument can be summarized as the observation that 'a robot failing in its performance does not show any signs of preoccupation'. Something is missing in current approaches to model minds with robots: a dynamical, embodied and situated sensorimotor loop is not enough to account for mental properties (in particular for intentionality). Unlike human made devices, animals do have concerns about the performance of their actions. Following previous work by Hans Jonas (1966), Maturana and Varela (1980), von Uexküll (1940; 1982) and others, Di Paolo explores the hypothesis that metabolic living organization is the genuine source of value and intentionality that animals benefit from. Due to the circular and 'far from equilibrium' condition of their metabolic body, in their constant precarious existence, organisms are capable of intrinsically evaluating and 'suffering' the consequences of their behavioural performance. Their motivation for action is inscribed on the metabolic constitution of their flesh. It is the intrinsic normative functionality of their interactions as living systems that makes them genuine agents, while robotic machines are externally designed to perform a task that is intrinsically irrelevant to their continuing existence as mechanical systems. This leads to a difficult situation for roboticists, since if survival of metabolic organization is the source of all value and intentionality, there would be no choice other than to create self-producing chemical systems in order to achieve the goal of creating and synthetically exploring genuine intelligent phenomena. The alternative seems to abandon robotics altogether. A way out of this dilemma, Di Paolo argues, might be to create, within the domain of behavioural dynamics, self-sustaining patterns that could be considered to have equivalent properties to those argued here to be the basis of genuine intentionality in living organisms.

Di Paolo built a robotic simulation model to test this concept.[10] Based on previous experiments of visual inversion in humans (Kohler 1962) and the additional neuroscientific evidence that synaptic plasticity is homeostatically regulated (Turrigiano, 1999), Ezequiel Di Paolo (2000b) devised a robotic simulation model where robotic agents (controlled by dynamic recurrent neural networks with homeostatic Hebbian plasticity) were capable of readapting to sensory inversion (without the agents being selected for that task during evolution). After artificially evolving the agents to perform phototaxis (with the additional requirement to maintain internal synaptic stability), Di Paolo's agents were tested for visual inversion. At the beginning of the trial agents performed phototactic behaviour (the agent was able to navigate a 2 dimensional space approaching light). Later on in the trial, right and left light sensors were inverted, subsequently disrupting phototactic behaviour. Agents were not evolved to adapt to sensory inversion ... how then, could phototactic behaviour be recovered? The experiment demonstrated that, by evolving the agents for phototaxis while selecting for internal synaptic stability, both synaptic stability and behavioural stability became evolutionarily coupled. Thus, 'normal' phototactic behaviour was sustained by a stabilized set of synaptic parameters in the agent's control architecture. When the agents' sensors were inverted behavioural coherence was lost and their internal synaptic dynamics entered an unstable region. The instability of synaptic parameters, in turn, produced behavioural instabilities (the agents

---

[10] The experiment was originally inspired by a well documented psychological phenomena that could not be properly explained by available cognitivist approaches. During the 60s Kohler (1962) systematically studied re-adaptation to visual inversion. After a period of two weeks of severe difficulties to coordinate behavior, experimental subjects wearing inverted goggles started to behave coherently, they reported that the whole perceptive up-down regularities started to emerge again in their perceptual experience of the world re-inverting the visual effect of the goggles. After goggles where removed subjects reported that their visual field appeared upside-down and only recovered 'normal' vision after a new process of re-adaptation occurred.

performed 'random' movements). As a result, the synaptic parameter space was explored until phototactic behaviour was recovered again which, in turn, stabilized the values of synaptic parameters.

This mechanism provides a model for neurodynamic behavioural self-maintenance where neurodynamic structures emerge that recursively depend on the behaviour they sustain and inversely behavioural stability and coherency depends on the stability of neurodynamic structures. A stabilized set of synaptic parameters produces phototactic behavior but, if phototactic behavior is disrupted synaptic stability is lost; and, inversely, if synaptic stability is lost coherent behavior disappears until both coupled dynamics are stabilized again. This elementary mode of neurodynamic self-maintenance Di Paolo called 'habits'. And habits might provide an interesting insight into value and intentional phenomena, non reducible to biological adaptive constraints: 'Habits, as self-sustaining dynamic structures, underlay the generation of behaviour and so it is them that are challenged when behaviour is perturbed. An interesting hypothesis is that often when adaptation occurs in the animal world this is not because organismic survival is challenged directly but because the circular process generating a habit is.' The way out of the roboticist dilemma can now be envisioned, the metabolic living organization need not be modelled in order to grasp intentionality: 'The interaction and commerce between these structures of behaviour, and not this or that particular performance, would become the object of robotic design, and the conservation of an organised meshwork of habits, the basis on which to ground artificial intentionality' (Di Paolo 2003).

Mental Life

Di Paolo's conceptual simulation experiments uncover two fundamental issues: (i) that life-like self-sustaining emergent patterns can be found within the behavioural domain and, I shall now argue in more detail, (ii) that metabolically driven agency might be insufficient, even unnecessary, for mindfulness; a specific form of life might be required to achieve psychological properties: Mental Life.

There are many opportunities for sustainability based on fast and flexible motility but the unicellular form of organization is severely limited to occupy such a mode of existence.[11] This had to wait until the appearance of specialised cells, within multicellular systems,

---

[11] The kind of internal organization that is found at the cellular scale does not permit to increase the sensorimotor complexity for two reasons: (i) as more

capable of channelling electro-chemical action potentials connecting sensory and motor surfaces in a fast, integrated and selective manner: the Nervous System (NS hereafter). [12] What we get with the appearance of the NS is that on top of the basic metabolic organization a new dynamical system emerges (controlling the sensorimotor coupling with the environment) whose dynamics are locally decoupled from the underlying metabolic processes.

Thus, unlike plants and unicellular systems, organisms endowed with neural tissues can control their behaviour independently of the continuous processes of metabolism, cell replication and growth. Within multicellular life cycles a new dynamic domain appears (that of electrochemical action potentials) free from having to satisfy more immediate metabolic functions. As a result, behavioural interactions can be quickly and efficiently achieved.[13] But this freedom (that permits a form of decoupling between interactive and constructive living processes) is accompanied by a set of global constraints that ensure the functional integration of the NS within the organism. In particular, if we take a quick overview of the set of constraints that operate to create functional order in neural and behavioural dynamics, we can abstract three general types:

Type 1: Architectural constraints: composed of genetic and developmental constraints specifying some innate conditions of the architecture and 'parameters' of the NS (number and types of neurons, type of connectivity, neuromodulator pathways,

---

complex forms of sensorimotor interaction start to form the more likely it is that catastrophic interferences between the core metabolic network and sensorimotor mediation occur (they both share the same biochemical medium) and (ii) higher complexity requires higher size and a costly trade-off emerges between increase in size and the capacity of the unicellular organism to efficiently connect sensory and motor surfaces while moving as unity in space. As we know, this problem had to wait quite a long evolutionary time to be solved.

[12] A more universalist formulation of this innovation requires to abstract the kind of organizational difference that the NS introduces on living organization. Some of my colleagues and latter on myself (Moreno & Lasa, 2004; Barandiaran, 2004; Etxeberria & Moreno, 2005; Barandiaran & Moreno,2006a,c) have termed this transition *hierarchical decoupling* or *informational decoupling* (Moreno *et al.*, 1997) of the sensorimotor control from metabolism (the underlying chemical self-constructing and self-repair machinery).

[13] In addition, the evolution of the NS is accompanied by a set of changes in bodyplan that enables the channelling of metabolically recruited chemical energy into mechanical work through a musculoesqueletal system. What we get as a result of this hierarchical decoupling of sensorimotor interactions (embedded on a living body) is *adaptive behaviour*.

etc.) and the organism's embodiment (body mechanical properties and sensory modalities).

Type 2: Biological adaptive signals: internal signals from other body organs generally causally correlated with metabolic and sexual needs (pain, pleasure, etc.) with a high modulatory capacity over neural activity.

Type 3: Self-generated constraints: those that the very activity of the NS generates through environmental interactions.

Type 1 and type 2 constraints subordinate the activity of the NS to satisfy biologically adaptive needs and from the point of view of neural sensorimotor dynamics these constraints appear as given, as 'externally' fixed.[14] In such a case, behaviour, so to speak, is the 'slave' of metabolism — as well as other, larger time-scale (philogenetic) self-maintaining needs (sexual mating, kin care, etc.). In some animals neural activity is mostly prespecified by type 1 and type 2 constraints. In fact, C-elegans has been shown to have highly stereotyped behaviours and highly homogeneous neural circuits among different individuals of the same species (to the extent that the number and function of neurons is identical among them — White *et al.*, 1986; Hobert, 2005). If evolution (acting on self-organized developmental processes) fixes a set of constraints that almost fully specifies the behaviour of a C-elegans there is not much of a difference between it and a Braitemberg vehicle. Whether the sensorimotor system is materially constructed by 'the rest' of the organism and functionally integrated in its metabolic self-maintenance (as in C-elegans) or externally built and functionally decoupled from its underlaying structure (as in a Braitemberg vehicle) is completely extraneous to the dynamic causal organization of behaviour.

Take the example of a mutated C-elegans with disrupted sensors producing anti-adaptive behaviour (as there are many and, in fact, these are commonly currently used for comparative studies) and its interactions with the environment (from the point of view of its neurodynamic phenomenology) will be as 'significant' or 'insignificant' as those of a non-mutant (and metabolically sustainable) one.[15]

---

[14] Natural selection operating on internal and interactive self-organizing processes, the inner (non agency-dependent) structure of the organism, the agents organic and material constituency etc., can be viewed as good candidates for this fixation.

[15] Paraphrasing Hans Jonas describing the lack of genuine intentionality of machines, the mutant C-elegans 'may just as well be said, instead of being

But, as the size and connectivity of neural ensembles increases in encephalized animals, adaptive signals and architectural constraints are not enough to instruct the dynamics of the NS so as to produce adaptive behaviour (even if local and interactive self-organizing patterns are evolutionarily exploited). Adaptive signals can be correlated with metabolic needs and can evaluate the effect of behavioral interactions on body dynamics but cannot specify how to achieve adaptive behavioral success. In relation to the architectural constraints, as the size of the NS increases the number of innate constraints play a smaller role on the specification of neural architectures, leaving it open to the recursive activity of the network and its history of interactions with the environment.[16] A space of freedom is thus created when neurodynamic mediation of adaptive behavior overcomes the regulatory capacity of adaptive signals and architectural constraints. Thus the NS needs to generate its own regulatory constraints in continuous interaction with the environment and adaptive body signals, triggering a process of dynamic self-determination that transcends metabolic values. At this point a new form of life appears, embedded on biological life but capable of generating its own normativity and value, its own distinctive identity and world, its own mode of agency: that resulting from the preservation of an internal coherency of experience, the coherency of the developmental organization of neurodynamic patterns. Mental Life appears.

---

distressed, to abandon itself with relish to its wild oscillations, and instead of suffering the frustration of failure, to enjoy the unchecked fulfilment of its impulses. 'Just as well' amounts of course to 'neither" (Jonas 2001: 112). Surely, the C-elegans' metabolism will suffer the effects of its sensorimotor failure and might even get stressed (forcing its metabolic dynamics to compensate the effects of behavioural failure). But this 'metabolic stress' might equally be blind to its causal correlation with a particular behaviour; suffering its maladaptive condition as externally given. If natural selection fixes the correlation between specific behavioural performances and their functional contribution to metabolic self-maintenance then failure on behavioural performance does not necessarily imply that metabolic closure be affected other than externally and inaccessibly to its capacity to detect and compensate that failure as properly behavioural, intentional, failure.

[16] The reason is that a bottleneck exist on how much of the brains circuitry can be genetically specified. As Elman et al. (1996) have noted in human beings only global architectural and chronotopic constraints participate on the development of the NS. *Chronotopic constraints* affect the timing of certain developmental processes and *global architectural constraints* specify global neural pathways, kinds of connectivity between neurons, etc. But none of these constraints can specify the dynamic structures that produce behaviour in adult brains.

Modelling Mental Life

Recalling Di Paolo's notion of habits as dynamic structures, we are now ready to outline a conceptual model of Mental Life in five conceptually distinguishable steps that synthesize its form of organization:

1. Neurodynamic structures are created that sustain different sensorimotor couplings with the environment (the formation of these structures might originally be due to the fixation of self-organized patterns by body adaptive signals and supported by early architectural constraints).

2. Interactive stability dependencies are created between at least some neurodynamic structures and the behaviours they sustain.

3. Internal stability dependencies are created between neurodynamic structures.

4. A nested web of neurodynamic structures appears when dynamic structures become progressively more independent from biological adaptive signals and innate architectural constraints and more dependent on: (a) higher order stability dependencies between them, and (b) the interactions that they altogether sustain with the environment.

5. The adaptive regulation of behaviour to preserve the web of neurodynamic structures becomes the main organizational principle of brain activity and behaviour.

Mental Life appears when the adaptive conservation of the internal organization of neural dynamics becomes the main principle of sensorimotor regulation. From a set of initial conditions of huge developmental plasticity, triggered by biological adaptive signals and channelled by architectural constraints, the NS generates more and more internal constraints and interdependencies between behaviourally emergent self-organized patterns, until the preservation of the internal coherency of these nested structures takes over the regulation of embodied brain dynamics.

This way a 'form of life' appears in the realm of sensorimotor dynamics. The minimal model of cellular organization sketched above represented the essential causal structure of life as a circular network of self-sustaining chemical reactions. It was shown how this network distinguished itself from its environment through a selective membrane that actively regulates the thermodynamic and material flow required for its continuing existence. We can now envision an analogous process in the domain of neurodynamic organization: a web of interdependent dynamic structures is progressively created through a continuous sensorimotor flow, regulated by the behavioural activity of the system. Emergent patterns of brain activity are analogous to chemical reactions, the sensorimotor flow analogous to thermodynamic and material flow, the selective action of the membrane analogous to the behavioural control of the sensory flow and the behavioural and neurodynamic tendency towards the preservation of an internal (experiential) coherence might be equivalent to the metabolic self-sustaining organization of life.

Five Characteristic Features of Mental Life

It is now time to revisit the 4 model features of living organization discussed previously (including an additional one not present in metabolic life: its living and lived embodiment). Both isomorphisms and dissonances between mental and biological life as well as their mutual relationships will help in terms of further elaborating and evaluating the model whilst helping to make it compatible with post-cognitivist research trends.

A. Emergent self

Like minimal cellular chemical dynamics, brain dynamics also involves an irreducible emergent organization where the role of neurons and neural ensembles is contextually defined within a circular causal structure, and where micro and macro levels of correlation mutually constraint each other. Brain activity cannot be appropriately studied by locally decomposing units and putting them back together through simple computational relationships. Rather than a point to point information transfer between functionally specific modules, large scale brain activity responds to the transient correlation of distributed neural ensembles, as a result of multiple feedback loops between different brain regions. Thus, despite the anatomical and functional modularity that might be found among certain brain regions, mental properties such as meaning and intentionality (Freeman, 1997; 2000) or conscious awareness (Edelman & Tononi, 2000) have been argued to be the result of emergent and circular dynamics. There is an increasing number of experiments and simulation models supporting this approach (i.e. of conceptualizing brain activity from a dynamical and holistic perspective): chaotic approaches to large scale brain activity (Freeman, 2000; Tsuda, 2001); the dynamic core hypothesis (Varela, 1995;

Varela *et al.*, 2001); timing nets (Cariani, 2001); adaptive resonance theory (Carpenter & Grossberg, 2003); analysis in terms of transient correlations (Friston, 2000), to mention but a few. Not surprisingly, some analytic and modelling techniques that are used in synthetic protocell biology are also found in neurodynamic research: dynamic and stochastic models, network analysis, chaos, complexity measurements, criticality, power law distributions, etc.

Finally, a crucial feature of our model of biological life was that of self-maintenance. Similarly the activity of the NS can be seen as continuously regenerating itself, through multiple reverberating circuits, self-generated or spontaneous activity, etc. (Cariani, 1999). A significant aspect of this self-maintenance, as we have seen before, is that it is closed through sensorimotor interactions. Which leads us to the second feature of our model:

B. Situated openness

The necessity of all living systems to maintain an open thermodynamic and material flow with their environments in order to sustain their dissipative organization might be seen as somehow isomorphic with the necessity for psychological identity to be situated in a sensorimotor world extracting, through it, a set of coherent correlations that are necessary to maintain its organization (Di Paolo's model of habits provides a minimalist instance of self-maintaining situated openness that certainly inspires this analogy). We are continuously dealing with our biological, emotional, social and cognitive world out of which our psychological identity (our personality) is created and maintained. Consequently, the activity of the NS should *not* be seen as stimulus driven but as continuously engaged with the world in terms of the maintenance and regulation of its dissipative organization; an organization that can only be complete through the environment. This feature of mental life puts action in the centre. Action does not appear as a final step of a representational planning process. On the contrary, the inter-active flow that sustains neurodynamic organization is constitutive of Mental Life. As a result, what-the-system-is is intertwined with what-the-system-does: neurodynamic organization is cause *and* effect of the interactions it sustains. Thus, it is not only that cognitive processes are situated and context-dependent (which is one of the most basic assumptions of the post-cognitivist approach—Wheeler, 2005; Clark, 1997) but, going even further, that Mental Life exploits this situatedness to generate and regulate its internal organization (and not just the structure of behaviour). It follows that isolation from the environment will destroy Mental Life (as a prolonged disruption of the thermodynamic and material flow will destroy a living system). This is, in fact, the case if we are to look at some studies regarding the psychological effects of sensory deprivation and solitary confinement (Haney, 2003), showing how severe personality disorders follow from long periods of isolation.

C. Normativity

The evidence for a specifically mental normativity, distinct from an evolutionary or metabolic one, shows up on the fact that failure of behavioural performance does not necessarily imply failure for biological adaptation. Conversely, success in cognitive performance does not necessarily involve biological success. In mental terms, a neural process or a behavioural interaction becomes functional if it contributes to the self-maintenance of neurodynamic organization. Genuine mindful normativity appears when the adaptive values are lost as initial conditions of the development of the NS and progressively replaced by the web of internal and interactive stability dependencies. As a consequence the model of Mental Life encompasses a wider range of normative dimensions than the purely evolutionary adaptive or the epistemic and referential.

Our model of mental life entails a significant shift from cognitivist assumptions in relation to the normative (truth) status of mental states: a move from a *representational* approach where normativity is defined by the correlation between internal states and external states of affairs to a view where normativity is defined in terms of an *interactively* maintained internal consistency and coherency of experience. This view does not rule out the notion of semantics or even that of adequacy: it just does not reduce it to a causal correlation between internal states and 'states of affairs' in the environment (Dretske, 1988) or to an evolutionary selective history that ensures a correspondence relationship (Millikan, 1984); making semantics, in both cases, external to the internal causal organization of the system (Bickhard, 2000). Within the model of Mental Life just sketched, intentional semantics might be best viewed as affordances or canalizations of possibilities for action which might, or might not, turn out to be relevant to whatever the consequent engagement with the world permits (or requires). The relationships between different dynamic structures within neural organization will be accordingly regulated to preserve an internal coherency regarding future interactive expectations and sensorimotor correlations.

D. Agency

The situated openness of life introduces a problem of demarcation between system and environment. At the level of minimal metabolic life the problem is solved by the encapsulation of the core chemical organization within a self-generated membrane, while the selective action of the membrane on the system-environment diffusion processes demarcates a control asymmetry giving rise to agency. Models of cognitive processes that put the emphasis on extended, distributed and situated dynamics have to face the problem of how to define the identity of the subject as distinct from the environmentally distributed features that are functionally integrated in the production of behaviour. If cognitive behaviour is the result of a non-trivial causal spread, as Wheeler has called it (2005), ... can we really speak of agency? In order to answer this question we need to take into account how the situatedness and agency of metabolic life is different to that of Mental Life.

Metabolism needs to be situated in a material and thermodynamic flow and it needs to regulate the inflow and the outflow. But this flow does not constitute a cycle: i.e. the material and thermodynamic outflow (heat and waste products) does not recursively feed-back into the inflow generating a closed loop. For instance, the effect of a molecule or a change of temperature in a cellular system is directly specified by the relational properties of the molecule (as a physico-chemical entity) and the metabolic organization of the cell. The very appearance of motility (providing the domain in which Mental Life should latter appear) produces a completely different mode of situatedness and, consequently, of agency. As a result, the way in which objects and processes in the world become significant or functional for Mental Life becomes different from its metabolic counterpart. Mental Life's mode of situatedness is circular, transformations in motor surfaces have a direct effect on sensory surfaces and neurodynamic activity is continuously engaged on that circularity. For Mental Life environmental objects and processes have no direct effects except through the way in which they are engaged within the sensorimotor cycle. There are two complementary aspects in which mental agency shows up: (i) the causal asymmetry provided by a circular and self-sustaining organization of internal dynamics that controls its sensorimotor flow and (ii) the selective engagement with the environment that becomes 'cut up' into a world of interactions continuously shaped by the goals and intentions of the subject.

E. Embodiment

Mental Life has an additional characteristic feature not present at the metabolic level: its living and lived embodiment. While metabolism is embodied on non-living components (molecules), Mental Life (as-we-know-it) is embedded on a living body. This includes not only the mechanical musculoskeletal system and sensory organs (as researchers in embodied cognition have repeatedly shown) but also, and more fundamentally, an organismic living body with its metabolic regulatory needs. In fact, as Moreno and Lasa (2003) have pointed out, the appearance of mind is strongly linked to a set of bodyplan transitions where encephalized brains require and enable a neurally regulated bodyplan (i.e. not only the brain is embodied but the body is also embrained). As a consequence, part of the nervous system is not dedicated to deal with the external world but with an internal metabolic environment that is in charge of regulating. As Damasio (1994; 1999) has repeatedly argued, the feedback relationships between body-regulation dynamics and the sensorimotor dynamics constitute the emotional world that becomes constitutive of mental process. The body-regulatory neural activity drives much of the early developmental process of Mental Life since it constitutes a sophisticated form of body signalling. This is a necessary requirement for those neural systems not fully determined by innate architectural constraints since behavioural adaptivity must be continuously adjusted and evaluated on the basis of the effect (on body homeostasis) of the interactions that the NS maintains. Latter in the developmental process the modulatory capacity of the NS of the interior, as Edelman has called it (1989), is recruited by the sensorimotor nervous system to regulate its increasingly complex organization. Thus, the embrained living body takes part in both the formation and the maintenance of Mental Life.

Mental Life from the Point of View of MUN

It is now time to see if the conceptual model of Mental Life sketched here satisfies the MUN constraints stated at the beginning of this chapter; making it explicit how, and to what extent, it might be integrated into scientific research.

The model is **Minimalist** in that it contains all (but no more than) the necessary and sufficient conditions to specify the domain of the mental as a specific domain in itself with its own level of normativity and agency. The mind is not just any sophisticated form of biological adaptation, behaviour, complicated dynamical systems, developmental processes or any situated and embodied neural activity. The hypothesis presented here is that the mind is defined by a *specific form* of organization: Mental Life. For some, the model might be too demanding in that simple forms of sensorimotor behaviour that are often taken to be minimal cases of cognition or mindfulness (such as chemotactic behaviour in bacteria) will be left out as non-mental. For others (especially for those that take human intelligence as the paradigmatic reference) the model might be considered too minimal and below the level of complexity that is necessary to characterize genuine psychological phenomena. But what the conceptual model of Mental Life described in this chapter implies is that there exists a gradient towards the mental, defined by increasingly interdependent number of behaviourally generated neurodynamic structures and, particularly, by the progressive appearance of a regulatory principle of conservation of the resulting organization. Thus, rather than a lower level boundary this model of Mental Life works as a 'limit concept' that specifies a gradient of neurodynamic autonomy (that might never be complete). As such the model itself does not permit us to establish a clear cut point or dividing line which marks the barrier at which Mental Life precisely starts (either in evolution or in ontogenetic development). However if the model is fully and adequately naturalized it should be possible to make measurements and comparisons between different systems regarding their degree of mindfulness; and it might turn out that natural systems are non-homogeneously distributed on the mindfulness axis and that there exists a non-linear transition from the mentally inanimate to mentally alive forms of behaviour (probably due to some complex evolutionary feedback between brain, body an social environment).

The abstract formulation of this hypothetical organization also satisfies the constraint of **Universalism**. No reference to specific anatomical or functional structures is required to define psychological phenomena and, on the other hand, it is in relation to this essential organization that learning, emotions, intentions, etc. can be defined. Not only the organization but the domain in which it appears was also formulated in universalist terms. What the NS is was not defined by any live-on-earth particularity of neural cell types but by abstract properties which functioned as components capable of creating relatively unconstrained sensorimotor dynamics. The satisfaction of a universalist formulation should be able to identify mental-life-as-it-could-be and becomes, thus, of fundamental importance in solving the problem of the possibility of artificial minds. In this sense it is evident that standard robots, isolated or subject to input-output deprivation, are equally stable regardless of the environment they are placed in: what they are is independent from what they do. Current robots do not suffer from the threat of mental death nor do they benefit from Mental Life. But the question is whether it is *in principle* possible for robots to have minds. Unlike the cognitivist hypothesis about the nature of cognition, in which computer implementations of symbolic computations are supposed to be actual instances of cognition, computer simulation models of Mental Life are not realizations. A numerical simulation of the states of the variables of a dynamical system cannot be ontologically equivalent to a real dynamical system (Pattee, 1995). But this still leaves open the question of whether Mental Life can be realized by artificial systems. A more precise universalist formulation of the model, together with a clear definition of the term 'artificial', should be able to provide a definitive answer. In this sense it is crucial to elucidate the nature of the stability dependencies between dynamic structures and the sense in which the sensorimotor organization might be required to be dissipative or far from equilibrium. A strong interpretation of these terms would require that dynamical changes in the system be irreversible which, in turn, will imply that the model would not be realizable as a mechanical system. Thus the most genuine 'artificial' realization of Mental Life we can nowadays try to achieve might require robotic embodiments of cultured cells (living components that are truly 'far from equilibrium', dissipative structures capable of supporting 'far from equilibrium' neurodynamic structures).

But another crucial aspect is the role played by the embrained living body on the formation and regulation of neurodynamic organization in mental-life-as-we-know-it. Does the model of Mental Life necessarily imply that it be embodied on a living system? If Mental Life is about a *specific form* of neurodynamic situated organization and not something directly defined by metabolism, would an artificial internal environment (that feeds-back to the sensorimotor system in the same manner as the living body does) suffice to create genuine Mental Life in a robotically embodied set of cultured neurons?

I do not mean to provide a definitive answer to these questions here but am instead trying to show how the proposed conceptual model permits us to approach these issues and to highlight the relevant themes that need to be further developed. In this sense what is required to answer these questions is to achieve an accurate simulation model of minimal Mental Life that could be tested and complemented with empirically grounded theories of large scale and situated brain dynamics. We are here entering the requirements of the **Naturalist** constraint. As it stands now the model does not break any naturalist constraint: no *ad hoc* substances needed to be included, nor observer dependent properties taken to be causally relevant components of the model, and the five characteristic features of mind were grounded or inferred from the model and its application to known psychological phenomena and neuroscientific studies. Elsewhere (Barandiaran & Moreno, 2006c) I have, together with Alvaro Moreno, traced in more detail the bottom-up transitions that lead from the origin of life to the domain of adaptive behaviour; providing a proper biological grounding of what was here taken as a bottom-line theoretically primitive causal domain for Mental Life: that of embodied and situated neural dynamics. And here stands, one of the epistemological strengths of the model: it takes as theoretically primitive (i.e., as the basis on which the rest of the theoretical foundations are to be built) a mathematically formalizable domain that is, in addition, directly measurable (although not without difficulties) in terms of physical sensory properties, mechanical behaviour and neural activity (electrical and biochemical). In this sense the model integrates some of the tools and theoretical achievements that are most prominently post-cognitivist: for example the dynamical system approach (Beer, 1995; van Gelder & Port, 1995). In addition, the model entails that the mind cannot be defined merely as a causal domain (be it dynamical or computational, disembodied or situated) but as a specific form of organization within that domain and that the different mental properties or features need be formulated in relation to that form of organization (a further development of this topic might be found at Barandiaran & Moreno, 2006b). The question is whether the proposed form of organization can be properly naturalized in the sense of being formalized and introduced into empirical research. If we wish to 'go down that road' the way to proceed requires us to find mathematical formulations for the components and relationships of the model in terms of dynamical system theory. This task that should not, in principle, entail any major difficulties: the notion of dynamic structure can be understood as a local attractor (possibly requiring a more sophisticated formulation such as that of a chaotic attractor, neuronal transient, etc.), stability dependencies might be formulated as a global interdependences between the structure of different local attractors, while transitions between dynamic structures and their mutual transformations might be studied through the concept of chaotic itinerancy (Tsuda, 2001).

Finally the notion of adaptive regulation of the web of dynamic structures (or attractor landscape) implies the major theoretical and mathematical challenge. The difficulty resides in that there is a form of self-reference involved: it is the web itself that regulates its stability dependencies (not an external source of control that can measure and operate separately upon the dynamics of the network) so that an explicit distinction between control parameter, controlled variables and controller subsystem might not be possible. Ashby's notion of ultrastability has been proposed to approach such form of organization (Di Paolo 2003) while there are also other, more radical formulations, that deny the possibility of a dynamical formalization of the kind of closure involved in mental and other forms of life (Rosen, 1991; Kampis, 1991).

In any case, it is clear that simulation models might be able to implement maximal approximations of the conceptual model of Mental Life presented here. A conceptual modelling approach that remains minimalist but universally generalizable and close to what can be implemented in computer simulations is necessary if we are to understand, in its complexity, the kind of interactive and neural organization that supports our mental lives. I have sketched here a conceptual model of Mental Life that meets these demands. However, the construction of this model needs to be tested and continually checked against the latest data from neuroscience (especially from large-scale models of brain activity), while simulation models of embodied neurodynamic agents might be able to integrate the results of this process and actually display the complex and emergent properties that we take to be essential to mind.

Conclusion: There Is Life Beyond Cognitivism

Something analogous to a model of the formation of a circular emergent organization at the origins of life could be in place underlying the elusive foundations of psychological phenomena. The idea that an analogous form of organization might be generating living and mental phenomena has a long standing tradition. What current models of synthetic protocell biology permit is to understand the fundamental and minimal organization of life (its essence) in a much more detailed way than what was previously available (assembling through computer simulation models the huge amount of data that molecular biology has produced during the last decades). The accuracy that present models of minimal life have gained might also help in the task of building analogue conceptual (simulation) models in the realm of neural embodied dynamics. I have outlined how current modelling paradigms in cognitive science (in particular the field of evolutionary robotics) would permit us to construct minimal simulation models of embodied and situated neurodynamic agents. Unlike previous attempts to define the mind in terms of systemic and holistic properties, the binding that nowadays is being carried out between simulation techniques and large scale brain dynamic studies permits us to develop a much more detailed and scientifically fruitful theoretical foundation for psychology than that which was available before. I have proposed here a conceptual model of Mental Life as an organized system consisting of sensorimotor (neuro)dynamic structures which are nested through internal stability dependencies and dependent on the behavioural interactions they sustain, where the preservation of such stability dependencies becomes the main organizational principle. From this model a set of characteristic features were inferred: (i) the formation of an emergent self, (ii) the openness of mental life as a constitutively situated process, (iii) the normative character that certain internal and interactive processes acquire as they are functionally integrated in the regenerative and self-maintaining character of neurodynamic organization, (iv) how mental life provides the means for the constitution of an agent that creates its own world throughout its selective coupling with the environment and (vi) the living and lived embodiment in which the mind-as-we-know-it is embedded on, providing a sort of internal environment that becomes constitutive of the process that bring forth and sustains Mental Life.

We keep trying to make sense of our lives. And science provides extremely accurate and powerful models and metaphors which enable us to do so. As cognitive agents we cannot escape the urge to conceptualize, model, and inhabit our situated and precarious existence. Theoretical foundations for psychology permeate our lives in multiple dimensions: through the institutional policies that they justify, the therapies they design, the technologies that accompany them, the metaphors they inspire. Cognitivism has long dominated our understanding of the mind, conceptualizing it as a computational and representational machine. But however difficult it might turn out to avoid linguistic, propositional and representational descriptions of some of the scenes of our everyday mental lives, reducing them to computational processes of that sort will amount to reduce living phenomenology to a differential reproduction of a set of genetic permutations bearing representational relationships with phenotypic states of affairs. But there is life beyond cognitivism. Other metaphors, models and technologies can populate our cognitive ecosystems. The conceptual model I sketched here, synthesizing existing trends, condenses some of the new opportunities that are opened when models of biological organization together with simulation techniques and dynamicist neuroscience make it possible to reconceptualize the foundations of psychology.

The systemic and integrative (holistic) view of the activity of the NS is not new but the conceptual model of Mental Life proposed here, as a central notion for a post-cognitivist psychology, might be able to integrate some current post-cognitivist trends in psychology and cognitive science (dynamicism, embodiment, situatedness). In particular, the model captures a number of phenomena that remain alien to traditional cognitivist computationalism but that constitute, nevertheless, core phenomenological aspects of our mental lives. In contrast with cognitivism, the basic, fundamental organization of Mental Life is not that of a syntactical representation of the objective world whose correlation is measured by an external observer or natural selector. This is not to say that, as in biological life (where molecular templates permit us to build increasingly complex molecular constraints for self-organized biochemical and biophysical processes) recombinable or compositional structures might not become powerful 'technologies' in the domain of the mental. Symbolic and computational structures might be emergent from the fundamental form of organization that constitutes life. Higher level regularities (such as those found in linguistic structures) might be seen as internally structuring (constraining and enabling) brain dynamics or scaffolding the situated and distributed dynamic environment that the brain is embedded on (like instrumental technologies, cognitively structured environments or socially constrained protocols and institutions). But mental concerns, meanings, intentions, values, habits, pauses, trauma, desires can never be understood without taking into account how the underlying brain-body-environment dynamics *make them be there*, as patterns of the sub-symbolic neurodynamic organization that constitutes our mental lives; continuously engaged in a world that is both the result and the condition of possibility of its permanent re-creation.

Acknowledgements

Funding for this work was provided by grants: 9/UPV 00003.230-13707/2001 from the University of the Basque Country and BMC2000-0764 and HUM2005-02449/FISO from the Ministry of Science and Technology. In addition the author has the support of the doctoral fellowship BFI03371-AE from the Basque Government.

This is an open-access work distributed under the terms of the Creative Commons Attribution License, which permits unrestricted use, distribution, and reproduction in any medium, provided the original author and source are credited.

I would like to express my intellectual debt with the San Sebastian group of Philosophy of Biology (IAS-research). All the ideas presented here are, one way or another, a continuation of the work that has inspired me within that group for several years now. Thanks then to Arantza, Jon, Kepa and specially to Alvaro Moreno for creating such an inspiring intellectual environment. Although the present formulation is mine, most of the ideas presented here have been developed in continuous discussion and joint intellectual work with Alvaro. I have also benefit from Kepa's careful revision of the section on cellular living organization.

Finally I would like to thank Laura for her continuous support and love, as well as multiple revisions and discussion on early and final drafts of this work.

References

Almássy, N., Edelman, G.M. & Sporns, O. (1998), 'Behavioral constraints in the development of neuronal properties: A cortical model embedded in a real-world device', *Cerebral Cortex*, 8, pp. 346–361.

Barandiaran, X. (2004), 'Behavioral Adaptive Autonomy. A milestone in the Alife route to AI?', *Proceedings of the 9th International Conference on Artificial Life* (Boston, Massachussets: MIT Press), pp. 514–521.

Barandiaran, X. & Moreno, A. (2006a), 'A Life models as epistemic artefacts', *Proc. of the 10th Inter. Conf. on Artificial Life* (MIT Press), pp. 513–519.

Barandiaran, X. & Moreno, A. (2006b), 'On what makes certain dynamical systems cognitive', *Adaptive Behavior*, 14(2), pp. 171–185.

Barandiaran, X. & Moreno, A. (2006c), 'Adaptivity: from metabolism to behaviour'. Submitted.

Bechtel, W. (2006), 'Biological mechanisms: Organized to maintain autonomy', In F. Boogerd et al., (Eds.) *Systems Biology; Philosophical Foundations* (New York: Elsevier, in press).

Bedau, M. A. (1998), 'Philosophical content and method of artificial life', In Bynum, T.W. and Moor, J.H. editors. *The Digital Phoenix: How Computers Are Changing Philosophy* (Oxford: Basil Blackwell), pp. 135–152.

Beer, R. (1990), *Intelligence as Adaptive Behaviour: An Experiment in Computational Neuroethology* (Academic Press).

Beer, R. D. (1996), 'Toward the evolution of dynamical neural networks for minimally cognitive behaviour', In Maes, P., Mataric, M., Meyer, J. A., Pollack, J., and Wilson, S., editors, *From Animals to Animats 4: Proceedings of the Fourth International Conference on Simulation of Adaptive Behaviour* (Harvard, MA: MIT Press), pp. 421–429.

Beer, R.D. (1995), 'A dynamical systems perspective on agent-environment interaction', *Artificial Intelligence*, 72, pp. 73–215.

Beer, R.D. (2003), 'The dynamics of active categorical perception in an evolved model agent', *Adaptive Behavior,* 11(4), pp. 209–243.

Békés, F. (1975), 'Simulation of kinetics of proliferating chemical systems', *Biosystems*, 7, pp. 189–195.

Bickhard, M. H. (2000), 'Information and Representation in Autonomous Agents', *Journal of Cognitive Systems Research*, 1(2), pp. 65–75.

Bohr, N. (1913), 'On the Constitution of Atoms and Molecules (Parts 1, 2 and 3)', *Philosophical Magazine*, 26, pp. 1–25, .476–502, 857–875.

Brooks, R.A. (1997), 'From Earwigs to Humans', *Robotics and Autonomous Systems*, 20(2–4), pp. 291–304.

Cariani, P. (2001), 'Neural timing nets', *Neural networks*, 14(6-7), pp. 737–753.

Carpenter, G.A. & Grossberg, S. (2003), 'Adaptive resonance theory', In M.A. Arbib (Ed.), *The Handbook of Brain Theory and Neural Networks, Second Edition* (Cambridge, MA: MIT Press), pp. 87–90.

Cartwright, N. (1983), *How the Laws of Physics Lie* (Oxford: Oxford University Press).

Chalmers, D. (1995), 'Facing up the problem of consciousness', *Journal of Consciousness Studies*, 2(3), pp. 200–219.

Chemero, A. (2000), 'Anti-representationalism and the Dynamical Stance', *Philosophy of Science*, 67, pp. 625–647.

Christensen, W.D. & Bickhard, M.H. (2002), 'The Process Dynamics of Normative Function', *Monist*, 85 (1), pp. 3–28.

Clancey, W. (1989), 'The frame of reference problem in cognitive modelling', *Proceedings of the 11th Annual Conference of the Cognitive Science Society* (Ann Arbor: Lawrence Erlbaum Associates), pp. 107–114.

Clark, A. (1997), *Being There* (Cambridge, MA: MIT Press).

Cliff, D. T. (1991), 'Computational Neuroethology: A Provisional Manifesto', In Meyer, J. A. and Wilson, S. W., editors, *From Animals to Animats: Proceedings of the First International Conference on Simulation of Adaptive Behavior* (SAB'91) (Cambridge, MA: MIT Press).

Cliff, D., Harvey, I. and Husbands, P. (1993), 'Explorations in evolutionary robotics', *Adaptive Behavior*, 2(1), pp. 71–104.

Csendes, T. (1984), 'A simulation study on the chemoton', *Kybernetes*, 13 (2), p. 79.

Damasio, A.R. (1994), *Descartes' Error. Emotion, Reason and the Human Brain* (New York: G.P. Putnam's Sons).

Damasio, A.R. (1999), *The Feeling of What Happens: Body, Emotion and the Making of Consciousness* (London: Heinemann).

Dennett, D.C. (1994), 'Artificial Life as Philosophy', *Artificial Life*, 1, pp. 291–292.

Di Paolo, E. (2000a), 'Behavioral coordination, structural congruence and entrainment in a simulation of acoustically coupled agents', *Adaptive Behavior*, 8(1), pp. 25–46.

Di Paolo, E. (2000b), 'Homeostatic adaptation to inversion of the visual field and other sensorimotor disruptions', In Meyer, J.-A., Berthoz, A., Floreano, D., Roitblat, H., and Wilson, S., editors, *From Animals to Animats 6: Proceedings of the Sixth International Conference on Simulation of Adaptive Behavior* (Harvard, MA: MIT Press), pp. 440–449.

Di Paolo, E. (2003), 'Organismically inspired robotics', In Murase, K. and Asakura, T., (Eds.), *Dynamical Systems Approach to Embodiment and Sociality* (Adelaide, Australia: Advanced Knowledge International), pp. 19–42.

Di Paolo, E., Noble, J. & Bullock, S. (2000), 'Simulation models as opaque thought experiments'. In Bedau *et al.* (eds.), *Proc. Artificial Life VII* (Cambridge MA: MIT Press), pp. 497–506.

Dretske, F. (1988), *Explaining Behavior* (Cambridge, MA: MIT Press).

Duijn, M., Keijzer, F. & Franken, D. (2006), 'Principles of Minimal Cognition: Casting Cognition as Sensorimotor Coordination', *Adaptive Behavior*, 14(2), pp. 157–170.

Edelman, G.M. (1987), *Neural Darwinism: The Theory of Group Neuronal Selection* (New York: Basic Books).

Edelman, G.M. (1992), *Brilliant Air, Brilliant Fire: On the Matter of Mind* (New York: Basic Books).

Edelman, G.M. & Tononi, G. (2000), *Consciousness: How Matter Becomes Imagination* (London: Penguin Books).

Edelman, J. (1989), *The Remembered Present* (New York:Basic Books).

Elman, J.L., Bates, E., Johnson, M.H., Karmiloff-Smith, A., Parisi, D. & Plunkett, K. (1996), *Rethinking Innateness: A Connectionist Perspective on Development* (Cambridge, MA: MIT Press).

Emmeche, C. (1994), *The Garden in the Machine* (Princeton University Press).

Freeman, W.J. (1997), 'Nonlinear neurodynamics of intentionality', *Journal of Mind and Behavior*, 18(2-3), pp. 291–304.

Freeman, W.J. (2000), *How Brains Make Up Their Minds* (New York: Columbia University Press).

Friston, K.J. (2000), 'The labile brain (I, II & III)', *Phil. Trans. R. Soc. Lond. B*, 355, pp. 215–265.

Funahashi, K. and Nakamura, Y. (1993), 'Approximation of dynamical systems by continuous time recurrent neural networks', *Neural Networks*, 6, pp. 1–64.

Gánti, T. (1971), *The Principle of Life*. 1st edition. (In Hungarian; Budapest: Gondolat).

Gánti, T. (2003), *The Principle of Life* (Oxford University Press).

Giere, R. N. (1988), *Explaining Science: A cognitive approach* (University of Chicago Press).

Godfrey-Smith, P. (2005), 'Folk Psychology as a Model', *Philosophers' Imprint,* 5(6). <www.philosophersimprint.org/005006/>.

Haney, C. (2003), 'Mental Health Issues in Long-Term Solitary and 'Supermax' Confinement', *Crime & Delinquency,* Vol. 49 No. 1, January 2003, pp. 124–156.

Harvey, I. (2000), 'Robotics: Philosophy of Mind using a Screwdriver', In Gomi, T. (Ed.) *Evolutionary Robotics: From Intelligent Robots to Artificial Life, Vol. III* (Ontario, Canada: AAI Books), pp. 207–230.

Harvey, I., Di Paolo, E., Wood, R., Quinn, M, & Tuci, E.A. (2005), 'Evolutionary Robotics: A new scientific tool for studying cognition', *Artificial Life,* 11(1-2), pp. 79–98.

Harvey, I., Husbands, P., Cliff, D., Thompson, A., and Jakobi, N. (1997), 'Evolutionary Robotics: the Sussex Approach', *Robotics and Autonomous Systems,* 20, pp. 205–224.

Hobert, O. (2005), Specification of the nervous system of C-elegans. The C. elegans Research Community (Ed.) *WormBook,* doi/10.1895/wormbook.1.12.1, http://www.wormbook.org.

Husbands, P., Harvey, I., Cliff, D., and Miller, G. (1997), 'Artificial Evolution: A New Path for Artificial Intelligence?', *Brain and Cognition,* 34, pp. 130–159.

Husbands, P., Smith, T., Jakobi, N., and O'Shea, M. (1998), 'Better living through chemistry: Evolving GasNets for robot control', *Connection Science,* 10(3-4), pp. 185–210.

Ideker, T., Galitski, T. & Hood, L. (2001), 'A new approach to decoding life: Systems Biology', *Annu. Rev. Genomics Hum. Genet.,* 2, pp. 343–372.

Jonas, H. (1966), *The Phenomenon of Life: Towards a Philosophical Biology* (Evanston, IL: Northwestern University Press).

Kampis, G. (1991), *Self-modifying Systems in Biology and Cognitive Science* (Pergamon Press).

Kauffman, S.A. (1971), 'Cellular homeostasis, epigenesis and replication in randomly aggregated macromolecular systems', *Journal of Cybernetics,* 17, pp. 1–96.

Kauffman, S.A. (1993), *The Origins of Order: Self-organisation and selection in evolution* (Oxford University Press).

Kauffman, S.A. (2003), 'Molecular autonomous agents', *Phil. Trans. R. Soc. Lond. A,* 361, pp. 1089–1099.

Keller, E.F. (2005), 'The Century Beyond the Gene', *J. Bioscience,* 30(1), pp. 3–10.

Kitano, H. (2002), 'Systems Biology: a brief overview', *Science,* 295, pp. 1662–1664.

Kohler, I. (1962), 'Experiments with goggles', *Scientific American,* 206 (5), pp. 62–72.

Langton, C.G. (1989), 'Artificial Life', *Artificial Life* , Chris Langton, (ed.) SFI Studies in the Sciences of Complexity, Proc. Vol. VI (Redwood City, CA: Addison-Wesley).

Maturana, H. & Varela, F. (1980), *Autopoiesis and Cognition: The Realization of the Living* (Dordrecht: Reidel).

Maturana, H.R. and Varela, F.J. (1972), *De Máquinas y Seres Vivos: Una teoría sobre la organización biológica* (Santiago de Chile: Editorial Universitaria).

Mavelli, F. & Ruiz-Mirazo, K. (2007), 'Stochastic simulations of minimal self-reproducing cellular systems', *Philosophical Transactions of the Royal Society of London B*, in press.

Millikan, R.G. (1984), *Language, Thought and Other Biological Categories* (Cambridge, MA: MIT Press).

Moreno, A. & Etxeberria, A. (2005), 'Agency in natural and artificial systems', *Artificial Life*, 11(1), pp. 161–176.

Moreno, A. & Lasa, A. (2003), 'From Basic Adaptivity to Early Mind', *Evolution and Cognition*, 9 (1), pp.12–30.

Moreno, A., Umerez, J. & Ibañez, J. (1997), 'Cognition and Life: The Autonomy of Cognition', *Brain and Cognition*, 34(1), pp. 107–129.

Morrison, M. (2000), *Unifying Scientific Theories* (Cambridge: Cambridge University Press).

Nicolis, G. & Prigogine, Y. (1977), *Self-organization in Non-equilibrium Systems* (New York: Wiley).

Nolfi, S. and Floreano, D. (2000), *Evolutionary Robotics: The Biology, Intelligence and Technology of Self-Organizing Machines* (Cambridge, MA: MIT Press).

O'Malley, M.A. & Dupré, J. (2005), 'Fundamental issues in Systems Biology', *BioEssays*, 27, pp. 1270–1276.

Pattee H.H. (1995), 'Artificial Life Needs a Real Epistemology', In Moran F., et al. (Eds.) *Advances in Artificial Life* (Berlin: Springer), pp. 23–38.

Port, R. & van Gelder, T. (1995), *Mind As Motion: Explorations in the dynamics of cognition* (Cambridge, MA: MIT Press).

Quinn, M. (2001), 'Evolving communication without dedicated communication channels', In Kelemen, J. and Sosik, P., editors, *Proceedings of ECAL01* (Springer Verlag), pp. 357–366.

Rosen, R. (1958), 'A relational theory of biological systems', *Bulletin of Mathematical Biophysics*, 20, pp. 245–341.

Rosen, R. (1991), *Life Itself: A Comprehensive Enquiry into the Nature, Origin and Fabrication of Life* (New York: Columbia University Press).

Ruiz-Mirazo, K. & Moreno, A. (2004), 'Basic Autonomy as a Fundamental Step in the Synthesis of Life', *Artificial Life*, 10, pp. 235–259.

Ruiz-Mirazo, K., Peretó, J. & Moreno, A. (2004), 'A universal definition of life: Autonomy and open-ended evolution', *Origins of Life and Evolution of the Biosphere*, 34, pp. 323–346.

Rupin, E. (2002), 'Evolutionary Autonomous Agents: A neuroscience perspective', *Nature Reviews Neuroscience*, 3 (February), pp. 132–141.

Schrödinger, E. (1946), *What is Life?*

Solé, R.V., Munteanu, A., Rodriguez-Caso, C. & Macía, J. (2007), 'Synthetic protocell biology', *Philosophical Transactions of the Royal Society of London B*, in press.

Steels, L. (1991), 'Towards a Theory of Emergent Functionality', In Meyer, J. and Wilson, R., editors, *Simulation of Adaptive Behaviour* (Cambridge, MA: MIT Press), pp. 451–461.

Stewart, J. (1996), 'Cognition=Life. Implication for higher-level cognition', *Behavioral Processes*, 35, pp. 311–326.

Taylor, N.R. & Taylor, J.G. (2000), 'Hard-Wired Models of Working Memory and Temporal Sequence Storage and Generation', *Neural Networks*, 13, pp. 201–224.
Tsuda, I. (2001), 'Toward an interpretation of dynamic neural activity in terms of chaotic dynamical systems', *Behavioral and Brain Sciences*, 24(5), pp. 793–847.
Tuci, E., Harvey, I., and Quinn, M. (2002), 'Evolving integrated controllers for autonomous learning robots using dynamic neural networks', In *Proceedings of The Seventh International Conference on the Simulation of Adaptive Behaviour (SAB'02)*.
Turrigiano, G.G. (1999), 'Homeostatic plasticity in neuronal networks: the more things change, the more they stay the same', *Trends in Neuroscience*, 22, pp. 221–228.
van Duijn, M., Keijzer, F., & Franken, D. (2006), 'Principles of Minimal Cognition: Casting Cognition as Sensorimotor Coordination', *Adaptive Behavior*, 14(2), pp. 157–170.
Varela, F. (1979), *Principles of Biological Autonomy* (New York: Elsevier).
Varela, F. (1992), 'Autopoiesis and a Biology of intentionality', In McMullin, B. & Murphy, N. (eds.) *Autopoiesis & Perception*. pp. 1—14. Proceedings of a Workshop held in Dublin City University, August 25th and 26th 1992. School of Electronic Engineering Technical Report, Dublin, 1994.
Varela, F. (1995), 'Resonant Cell Assemblies: A new approach to cognitive functions and neuronal synchrony', *Biological Research*, 28, pp. 81–95.
Varela, F., Lachaux, J.P., Rodriguez E. & Martinerie, J. (2001), 'The brainweb: phase synchronization and large-scale inetgration', *Nature Reviews Neuroscience*, 3, pp. 229–239.
Varela, F., Maturana, H., & Uribe, R. (1974), 'Autopoiesis: the organization of living systems, its characterization and a model', *Biosystems*, 5, pp. 187–196.
Varela, F., Thompson, E, & Rosch, E. (1991), *The Embodied Mind: Cognitive Science and Human Experience* (Cambridge MA: MIT Press).
von Uexküll, J. (1940), *Bedeutungslehre* (Bios 10. Johann Ambrosius Barth, Leipzig), [translated by Thure von Uexküll, 1982: The theory of meaning. *Semiotica* 42(1), pp. 25–82].
Wheeler, M. (1996), 'From Robots to Rothko: the bringing forth of world', In Boden, M. (Ed.) *The Philosophy of Artificial Life* (Oxford University Press), pp. 209–236.
Wheeler, M. (2005), *Reconstructing the Cognitive World* (Cambridge, MA: MIT Press).
White, J.G., Southgate, E., Thomson, J.N. & Brenner, S. (1986), 'The structure of the nervous system of the nematode Caenorhabditis elegans', *Phil. Trans. Roy. Soc. London Ser. B*, 314, pp. 1–340.

Alexander Riegler

The Radical Constructivist Dynamics of Cognition

Introduction

The early days of psychology in the 19th century belonged to the 'introspection' movement. However, because introspection is a first-person approach, it doesn't lend itself to objective communicability, one of the pillars of science. With the rise of positivist philosophy (e.g., Carnap, 1932), which demands science stick solely to observable entities, B. F. Skinner and John Watson introduced the behaviorist approach, which rejected any metaphysical speculation about non-observable descriptions such as cognitive processes. The task of psychology was to 'predict, given the stimulus, what reaction will take place; or, given the reaction, state what the situation or stimulus is that has caused the reaction' (Watson, 1930, p.11). After decades of dominating psychology in the US, doubts were cast on behaviorism in terms of whether it is powerful enough to account for more sophisticated phenomena such as language. In his 1959 paper, Chomsky overthrew behaviorist psychology by showing that one has to assume the internalization of linguistic rules, otherwise people would not be able to generate novel and yet grammatically correct sentences that they have never heard before. However, speaking about internal processes was out of bounds for behaviorists as they claimed that 'cognitive constructs give […] a misleading account of what [to] find inside' (Skinner, 1977, p. 10).

As a result, a new paradigm, cognitivism, appeared at about the same time as the discipline of artificial intelligence (AI).[1] Both emphasize internal computations that link sensory input with action output. As Steven Pinker (1997) pointed out, 'cognitive psychology is engineering in reverse [...] one figures out what a machine was designed to do.' Uneasiness with the idea that we are mere machines rather than the unique pinnacle of creation, and especially recollecting holistic philosophies such as phenomenology and early psychological streams such as gestalt-psychology as well as improved computational power that allows for sophisticated dynamical interactions among a huge number of entities, let the post-cognitive movement appear on the horizon, seeking to abandon the information-processing approach of cognitivism. It includes approaches such as embodiment and dynamical systems theory. Starting from philosophical insights such as Heidegger's 'Being in the world' (Dreyfus, 1991) and Merleau-Ponty's (1962) 'Phenomenology of Perception', embodiment (e.g., Riegler, 2002) emphasizes the importance of placing the cognitive being in an environment, something AI failed to do when studying chess playing in isolation. Based on the post-war cybernetic movement and equipped with sophisticated formal and especially computational tools, the dynamical approach to cognition (e.g., van Gelder, 1998) emphasizes the difference between classical digital computation of representational entities and dynamical processes among quantitative variables.

In this chapter I introduce (radical) constructivism as a possible paradigm for a post-cognitive psychology. It, too, borrows from (second order) cybernetics and pushes in the same direction as phenomenology without abandoning the crucial ideas of cognitivists such as Ulric Neisser. To this end, I first point out why mainstream cognitivism is insufficient to explain human cognition by focusing on key notions such as 'information' and 'knowledge'. Then I present the main characteristics of the constructivist approach and present five key challenges for post-cognitive approaches. Finally, I outline a structural-dynamic model based on radical constructivism that provides answers to these challenges.

---

[1] It can be argued whether this change constitutes a 'revolution' in the sense of Thomas Kuhn (1962) who characterized science as a sequence of normality and revolution (O'Donohue, Ferguson & Naugle, 2003).

Cognitivism

> Darwin came along and said we were fancy chimpanzees. Now along come the cognitive scientists saying that we are fancy calculators (Dietrich, 2000).

After Chomsky (1959) had defeated behaviorism, the newly emerging cognitivist paradigm was in search for a new methodological approach, and chose to adopt the information-processing (IP) concept promoted by Broadbent (1958) (which describes cognitive behavior as a sensing-thinking-acting chain). In his 1967 book, Neisser coined the term 'cognitive psychology' and installed the information-processing approach as the dominant paradigm. According to Neisser, cognition is 'stimulus information and its vicissitudes', i.e., 'all processes by which the sensory input is transformed, reduced, elaborated, stored, recovered, and used' (Neisser, 1967, p. 4).[2]

Evidently, the information-processing paradigm resembles what Karl Popper (1979) calls the *bucket theory of mind*. This is the idea that 'there is nothing in our mind which has not entered through our senses.' Cognition is metaphorically considered as a bucket that is incrementally filled with knowledge through our sensory organs. In other words, the information-processing approach describes individuals as 'dynamic information processing machines' (Neisser 1967) that 'compute' perceptual *input* in order to create *output*. Importantly, Heinz von Foerster points out, 'cognitive processes do not compute wristwatches or galaxies, but compute at best *descriptions* of such entities.' And descriptions are computations, too. So he proposes to 'interpret cognitive processes as never ending recursive processes of computation' (Foerster, 1973/2003, p. 217). This poses two questions: (1) How are we to define 'computation'? and (2) What and how much do we actually 'compute'?

As to the first question, computation should not be understood as the mechanical extension of what human professionals used to do in the early 20th century and what our desktop computers are supposed to do, i.e. crunching numbers. Rather, following Foerster's (1973/2003, p. 216) suggestion, computing (from Latin *com-putare*) 'literally means to reflect, to contemplate (*putare*) things in concert (*com-*), without any explicit reference to numerical quantities'.

---

[2] However, as we will see later, Neisser also contributed to the constructivist approach. He emphasized that 'seeing, hearing, and remembering are all acts of construction' and refers to 'continuously creative processes by which the world of experience is constructed' (Neisser, 1967).

The second question, however, cannot be easily answered by referring to etymology. For natural cognitive systems which are engulfed by a huge amount of stimuli every second, computing this amount of sensual input is intractable (NP-complete in the sense of Cook, 1971), i.e. the time required to compute all representations grows exponentially with the number of entities. Not even the navigational skills of bees could be accounted for in terms of information processing. In artificial intelligence research this problem became evident as researchers tried to extrapolate from simplified so-called microworld scenarios to real-world situations. Microworlds (e.g., Shrdlu, Winograd, 1972) were the attempt to find optimal cognitive strategies that could handle simple toy worlds, and to linearly augment their capabilities to deal with more complex environments later on. Since the assumption was that the world and the entities it is populated with can be described in terms of propositions, the representational system of artificial intelligence programs was designed as a network of propositions reflecting the current state of the microworld. However, as soon as the number of objects in a microworld increases and transcends a certain threshold the computational effort necessary to compute them went beyond all borders. Philosophically this was called the *frame-problem* (Dennett, 1984), the problem of how to represent empirical observations, as in any real-world environment the number of possible propositions and their mutual relationships are practically infinite. As Daniel Dennett argues, it makes no sense to focus on processing relevant information either, because making the distinction between relevant and irrelevant input requires an additional cognitive faculty. Therefore, the IP paradigm gets stuck in a bottleneck: which are the essential features that need to be selected among the wealth of information provided by the 'outside' in order to decrease the enormous degree of complexity and ensure survival?

Furthermore, if cognition is the manipulation of propositional knowledge, why then is it so difficult to explicitly describe common sense and human experts' knowledge? In their critique of expert systems, Dreyfus & Dreyfus (1986) argued that only rudimentary levels of expert behavior can be captured by explicit rules and facts. This level of 'competence' is restricted to applying textbook cases and cannot cope with unique and novel situations for which implicit knowledge is required.

Five Challenges

The issues raised so far make it evident that defining cognition as information processing and symbolic computation is a convenient yet insufficient way to explain *human* cognition. It is a convenient theory because it can be readily implemented on a computer, in fact on 'any device that can support and manipulate discrete functional elements — the symbols' (Varela, Thompson & Rosch, 1991, p. 42). Furthermore, it is convenient because it lends itself to functional decomposition, the 'divide-and-conquer' method of society and technical sciences that made modern civilization (based on the division of labor) possible in the first place. Scientifically it enabled the Wrights to invent the airplane (Bradshaw, 1993) as they approached a small number of functional problems in isolation from each other (the 'function space') rather than the much larger 'design space' as their competitors did. However, dividing and scientifically conquering alleged modules of cognition such as memory, attention, perception, action, problem solving and mental imagery does not work. As Foerster (1970b/2003, p. 172) points out,

> [B]y separating these functions from the totality of cognitive processes one has abandoned the original problem and now searches for mechanisms that implement entirely different functions that may or may not have any semblance with some processes that are [...] subservient to the maintenance of the integrity of the organism as a functioning unit.

Such a holistic definition presses for an understanding of mechanisms responsible for the generation of behavior rather than for the specification and implementation of isolated cognitive functions. The situated cognition and embodiment approach defends the idea that cognition is intimately connected with the functioning of the body (Lakoff, 1987). William Clancey (1992) claims that 'perception and action arise together, dialectically forming each other' (p. 5). Furthermore, the concept of representation becomes doubtful as 'we can walk through a *room without referring to an internal map of where things are located*, by directly coordinating our behaviors through space and time in ways we have composed and sequenced them before' (p. 7, italics in the original). This means that sensory, cognitive, and motor functions can no longer be considered independent and sequentially working parts of the cognitive apparatus. And the latter can no longer be described as a computational device, the 'task' of which is to acquire *propositional knowledge* about the mind-independent *reality* by *processing information* that is picked up from that reality.

Based on these considerations we can formulate the following five challenging questions.

Q1. Do people process information?

People are known for the mistakes they make when trying to process information in a logical way (Dörner, 1996). There are at least three reasons for this:

(1) The short-term memory can hold only a rather limited amount of 'informational units', or 'chunks' (Miller, 1956), which favors simple causal explanations.

(2) The bias of human long-term memory for creating conceptual patchworks of associatively linked qualitative statements. For example, Frank Keil (2003) argues that we are prone to the 'illusion of explanatory depth' as his empirical findings reveal that people greatly overestimate their knowledge of facts and procedures.

(3) 'Mental inertia', which is the result of a conservatively working mind that is set to the previously successful strategy (Duncker, 1935/1945; 'if it ain't broken, don't fix it', Riegler, 1998).

The fact that, despite these severe restrictions of human cognition, science has reached such heights, gives rise to the assumption that human scientists, like human chess players (Chase & Simon, 1973), do not use brute 'computational' force in order to cope with the flood of sensory information from the 'outside reality.' History of science suggests that a crucial part of scientific discoveries is to find the relevant details. The classical example is the astronomer Johannes Kepler who had first to process a huge bulk of information collected by his predecessor Tycho Brahe and himself over many years before he worked out which geometrical figure would represent the orbits of the planets (Kozhamthadam, 1994). It took him thirteen years to come up with the answer even though the (from our perspective, simple) solution had been 'there' from the beginning, in the data. However, any simple computational discovery system (e.g., Bacon as described in Langley *et al.*, 1987) can reproduce the astronomer's findings in little more than an instant.

While information processing is slow, there is a huge variety of behaviors people are able to *produce* (Figure 1). For example, in his critique of behaviorism, Chomsky already pointed to the fact that

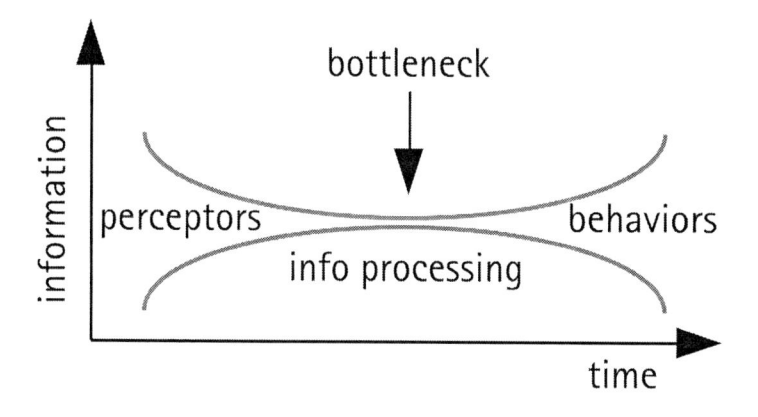

![Figure 1 diagram: information vs time showing perceptors and behaviors curves with info processing bottleneck]

Figure 1. The bottleneck of information processing

people can generate an infinite number of grammatically correct sentences. The conclusion is that humans are miserable processors of information.

Q2. Does cognition need representation and reality?

Terry Winograd and Fernando Flores (1986, p. 73) point out that the common rationalistic view

> accepts the existence of an objective reality, made up of things bearing properties and entering into relations. A cognitive being 'gathers information' about those things and builds up a 'mental model' which will be in some respects correct (a faithful representation of reality) and in other respects incorrect. Knowledge is a storehouse of representations, which can be called upon for use in reasoning and which can be translated into language. Thinking is a process of manipulating representations.

If cognition is supposed to work on descriptions of the outside reality and these descriptions are distilled from sensory information how can we be sure that this picture is accurate? For the correspondence theory of representation (cf. Wittgenstein, 1922, 'In order to tell whether a picture is true or false we must compare it with reality') the subjective picture of the world is accurate if it corresponds to the physical state of the world. However, neurophysiological experiments point in a different direction. In the 1960's Humberto Maturana and colleagues (Maturana, Uribe and Frenk, 1968) investigated whether the spectral composition of colors correlates with the activities in the retina. The results were chastening. It turned out that the activity of the retina can only be connected to the names of colors, which are considered to be rough indicators of how colors are subjectively experienced. Their conclusions were that the objective of their research had turned from establishing empirical support for the correspondence between reality and subject to comparing 'the activity of the nervous system with the activity of the nervous system' (quoted in Pörksen, 2004, p. 61). In other words, cognition does not seem to compare pictures with 'reality'.

Ernst von Glasersfeld (1981, p. 89) summarizes the 'skeptical dilemma' (Figure 2) as follows.

> [I]t is impossible to compare our image of reality with a reality outside [...] because in order to check whether our representation is a 'true' picture of reality we should have to have access not only to our representation but also to that outside reality *before* we get to know it. [italics in the original]

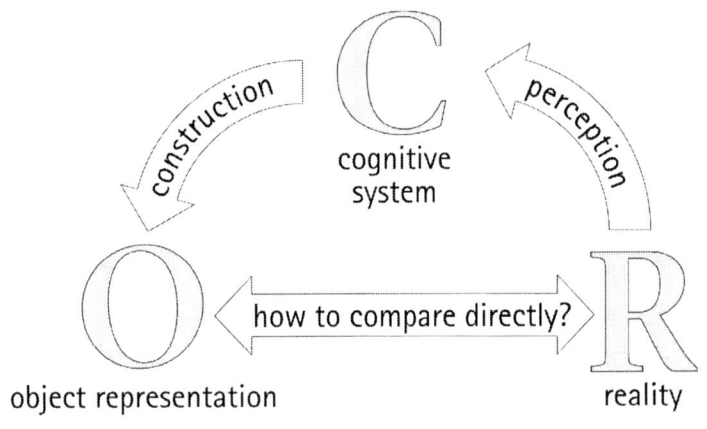

Figure 2. The skeptical dilemma

Q3. What is information at all?

It can be argued that information has to be distinguished from data, which is unstructured, lacks context and may not be relevant to the receiver. Only when data gets organized, filtered and accompanied by context it can become information. However, if human cognition is bad at coping with information and if we cannot validate the origin of information, perhaps there is something wrong with the notion of 'information' in the first place? Etymologically, the word information has its origin in the Latin verb *informare*, to give form to, to form an idea of. Taking this literally, the question arises: To form an idea of what?

At least from a neuropsychological perspective it is clear what sort of 'information' nervous signals carry from the sensory surfaces to the brain: nervous signals are just electrochemical impulses void of meaning. This century-old insight let Foerster formulate the *principle of undifferentiated encoding*: 'The response of a nerve cell does not encode the physical nature of the agents that caused its response. Encoded is only 'how much' at this point on my body, but not 'what'' (Foerster, 1973, pp. 214–215; Figure 3). In this perspective, there is no information about entities in the world, no information that could be processed by human cognition.

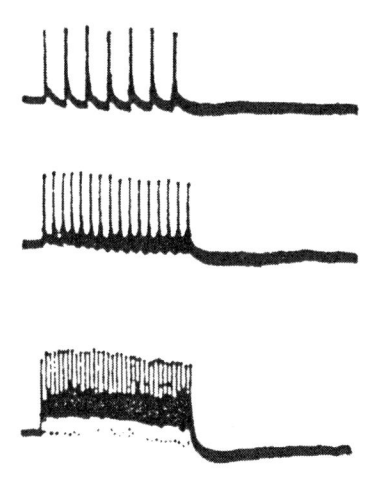

Figure 3. The principle of undifferentiated encoding: The pulse frequency represents the stimulus intensity, but the intensity only. (Foerster 1973/2003, pp. 219f.)

However, since 'the physical nature of the stimulus—its *quality* —is not encoded into nervous activity, the fundamental question arises as to how does our brain conjure up the tremendous variety of this colorful world as we experience it any moment while awake, and sometimes in dreams while asleep.' (Foerster, 1973/2003, p. 215). Foerster calls his perspective 'second-order cybernetics'. It transcends first order cybernetics, which describes observed systems in terms of regulatory mechanisms, and moves the focus of attention from the observed object to the *observing* subject.

Q4. Is cognition the manipulation of propositional knowledge?
The classical understanding of representation is largely based on the idea that propositions (e.g., Fodor, 1981) represent the (internal and external) environment in a more or less linguistically transparent way. Pylyshyn (1984) claims that cognition was computation, and since computation was symbol manipulation, cognition must be propositional. By distinguishing 'cognitive penetrability' from 'impenetrability' he defined the criterion for what was to be considered as cognitive. In other words, cognitive is what can be modified by what we know explicitly. That which eludes modification was 'subcognitive', and therefore not part of cognitive research. For example, habits and hormonal changes do not meet this criterion.

As pointed out in the beginning, propositions lend themselves conveniently to computer implementations. However, what is referred to as a proposition is the result of extremely complex processes occurring in neural dynamics and leading to the externalization of 'propositional categories', e.g., in form of symbols and language (Peschl & Riegler, 1999).

From the psychological literature it is known that cognitively sophisticated activities such as problem-solving do not depend on propositional representations. Even worse, such propositional knowledge may even make finding the solution more difficult. For example, Knowlton, Mangels, and Squire (1996) describe the 'weather prediction' experiment where subjects are asked to figure out the link between a configuration of cards with geometrical figures and a weather situation. As the authors point out, the mapping between the cues and the outcomes is too complex for the hippocampus, which is usually responsible for learning such propositional representations. Therefore the success of the subjects in this experiment must be attributed to unconscious and therefore non-propositional mechanisms.

Generally, in large propositional spaces, each experiential element has the potential of being linked with almost any other but only a very few of these connections make sense. For example, it is quite senseless to assume that the color of the walls in your room influences the weather. Tracking down all possible causal links would render taking actions impossible. Ignoring links altogether would make us superstitious neurotics who practice elaborate rituals and ceremonies to invoke magical powers for safety and protection (Malinowski, 1948). The complexity of the problem is demonstrated by Varela (1988) who compares the crystalline structure of the game of chess, in which entities and relations are clearly defined, with the rather chaotic network of a car driver's knowledge which quickly dissolves into the ambiguities of common sense (Figure 4). If formally well-defined areas such as chess already lead to vast combinatorial possibilities how much more complicated must the propositional description of common sense be?

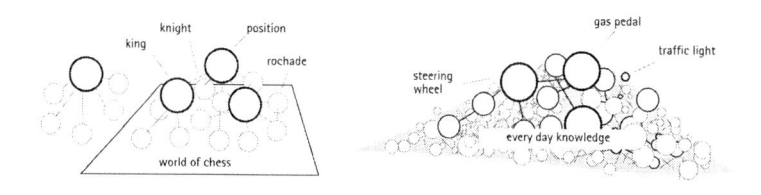

Figure 4. The crystalline structure of the world of chess and the ambiguous world of common sense. Redrawn from Varela (1988)

Q5. What is knowledge?

If there is no information which could inform cognition about the mind-independent reality, what does human knowledge consist of? Mainstream philosophy defines knowledge as justified true beliefs (JTB). This traditional perspective suffers from the problem that its three components—justification, truth, and belief—do not seem to be sufficient to account for knowledge, as demonstrated by Edmund Gettier (1963) and others who further extended Gettier's original counter examples. From the angle of post-cognitivist approaches, the difficulties of the conventional definition of knowledge can be traced back to at least two elementary problems:

1. The lack of a proper definition of 'truth' (i.e., when is a given proposition true?). As we noticed above, the verification of whether a given statement is true seems problematic due to the skeptical dilemma.

2. The restriction of the notion of knowledge to human cognition based on the assumption that knowledge must be formulated in the

form of propositions. For example, young blackbirds open their beaks if simple dummies are presented. Juvenile gulls mistake a pointed stick for an adult bird. Dummies that do not even closely resemble the appearance of the animal cause aggressive behavior in male sticklebacks. In all these cases, the dummies, although they do not resemble the 'real thing,' have a meaning for the animal (Figure 5). From the perspective of conventional philosophy, however, the young birds do not know anything although they may believe that they are approached by the parenting bird, and this belief is certainly justified by the fact that hungry young birds usually get food. But then, given the evolutionary success of their behavior, what else if not knowledge has been transmitted from generation to generation? Despite the animals' susceptibility to rather inaccurate stimuli their knowledge is successful on an evolutionary scale.

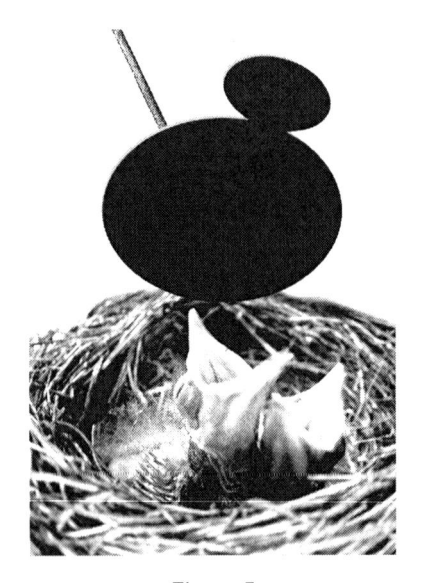

Figure 5.

Dummies as counterexample for knowledge as justified true belief

It is evident that correspondence with the real environment is not required for the generation of knowledge. For example, Keil (2003) points out that proponents of the phlogiston theory were not a bunch of cranks. They seriously tried to give coherence and sense to their observations and created the first comprehensive chemistry theory. But as careful experimentation revealed, they did not arrive at 'accurate' knowledge about combustion. They happened to try one of the virtually infinite possible mappings from sensory data to explanatory mechanisms but they were as wrong as a randomly guessing amateur. So is knowledge nothing but an accidental correspondence between the structure of the cognitive apparatus and the phenomenon in question?

Radical constructivism

The core problem of finding an appropriate account for cognition and knowledge arises from confusing two perspectives P1 and P2 (cf. Riegler, 2005, for an in-depth discussion).

P1. Observers such as scientists focus on the (measurable) output of an individual. Even worse, they attribute goals to the measured behavior without being able to know the intentions which are at the base of the behavior.

P2. In contrast to the observer, humans (and animals) control their input (perception) rather than their output (behavior), or as Powers (1973) put it, 'behavior is the process by which organisms control their input sensory data' (cf. also Porr & Wörgötter, 2005, who discuss input control in more technical terms). This perspective is based on the concept of homeostasis (Cannon, 1932), which says that a living organism has to keep its intrinsic variables within certain limits in order to survive. Such 'essential variables' (Ashby, 1952) include body temperature, levels of water, minerals and glucose, and similar physiological parameters, as well as other proprioceptively or consciously accessible aspects in higher animals and human beings. Consequently, individuals execute certain actions in order to control and change their input state, such as avoiding the perception of an obstacle or drinking to quench their thirst. The state of homeostasis is reached by the process of negative feedback. As in a thermostat, a given parameter is kept under control by appropriate counteractions. As is well known, the thermostat adjusts the temperature by turning off the heating as soon as a certain temperature is reached and turning it on as soon as the temperature drops below a certain reference value. While such a simple feedback loop may suffice for primitive intrinsic variables, higher order goals are accomplished in a *hierarchical structural-dynamic assemble* of feedback loops in which each level provides the reference value for the next lower level: 'The entire hierarchy is organized around a single concept: control by means of adjusting reference-signals for lower-order systems' (Powers, 1973). So at higher levels the system controls the output of lower levels, at the bottom, however, it controls its perceptual input.

P2 suggests that post-cognitivist accounts must not be behavioristically guided by copying observable behavior of existing natural systems. Rather, we need a deeper structural insight. The radical constructivist notion of organizational closure is a good point to start with. It is a necessary quality of the nervous system, and is based on the principle of undifferentiated encoding of nervous signals, as described above. In the case of the example of blackbirds presented in Q5, the nervous signals in the young birds that open their beaks at the sight of simple dummies do in no way convey the information of seeing a dummy (or the genuine parent bird it substitutes). Philosophically speaking, the cognitive system is in a brain-in-a-vat situation (Putnam 1982) as it has no independent reference to what has caused the incoming electro-chemical signals. With Maturana and Varela (1987), we can compare the situation with that of the navigator in a submarine. He avoids reefs and other obstacles by simply maintaining a certain dynamic relationship (homeostasis) between levers and gauges *inside* the vessel.

Radical constructivism (RC, Glasersfeld, 1995) is the conceptual framework that builds on this insight. According to the *radical constructivist postulate* (Riegler, 2001a) the cognitive system (mind) is organizationally closed. It necessarily interacts only with its own states. Or, as Winograd and Flores (1986) put it, the nervous system is 'a closed network of interacting neurons such that any change in the state of relative activity of a collection of neurons leads to a change in the state of relative activity of other or the same collection of neurons' (p. 42). Cognition is, therefore, a continuously self-transforming activity. There is no purpose attached to this dynamics, no goals imposed from *outside* the cognitive apparatus. According to Rodolfo Llinás (2001) the nervous system is able to generate sensory experiences of any type. Therefore, we are facing the fact that 'we are basically dreaming machines that construct virtual models' (p. 94). Llinás's closed-system hypothesis describes the mind primarily as a self-activating system, 'one whose organization is geared toward the generation of intrinsic images' (p. 57). The global picture is that cognition acts independently of the environment. It merely requests confirmation for its ongoing dynamical functioning and works autonomously otherwise: 'Although the brain may use the senses to take in the richness of the world, it is not limited by those senses; it is capable of doing what it does without any sensory input whatsoever' (p. 94).

As a result, cognition must be considered a *closed-loop* system whose primary goal is to regulate its input. This definition refers to Maturana and Varela's (1980) concept of *autopoietic* systems, which have to be distinguished from *allopoietic* ones. Autopoiesis refers to mutually chained processes that produce the components necessary to run these processes. Evidently, in the physical space of living systems, autopoiesis is instantiated by material processes, which produce, as it were, material and behavioral by-products visible to an observer. However, these 'outputs' do not define the autopoietic system.

Knowledge and Information

Evidently, in cognitively closed systems, knowledge cannot refer to mapping between an external state of affairs and cognitive structures. The conventional JTB definition of knowledge can no longer be applied in this context: Either the truth of propositions cannot be specified or there are no propositions at all. Following Glasersfeld's characterization of RC, knowledge must not be considered to be passively received but actively built up by the cognizing subject because the 'function of cognition is adaptive and serves the organization of the experiential world, not the discovery of ontological reality' (Glasersfeld, 1988, p. 83). This leads to an alternative understanding of knowledge that refrains from assuming that differently constructed conceptual frameworks in individuals gradually converge towards an 'objectively valid' knowledge system representing the 'reality.' Since from the perspective of RC no such convergence takes place, the emphasis is to be put on mechanisms of knowledge construction, and on the fact that cognitive systems actively construct their world rather than being passively flooded by information from the outside. Knowledge does not reside somewhere else and is not independent of the cognitive system that generates it. Hence, whatever it is that the cognitive apparatus picks up, it cannot be considered knowledge: 'The environment contains no information. The environment is as it is.' (Foerster, 1970b/2003, p. 189).

Neisser's (1975) schemata-guided pickup paradigm is one way to describe this matter of fact. By picking up sense data the perception-anticipating 'slots' in cognitive schemata change, which in turn changes the way in which they pick up further data. So what is being perceived (and taken in) at a given moment may not be perceived at a later instant. This accounts for the variation of meaning we and cognitive systems in general encounter over time. In Riegler (1994a,b) it is referred to as the 'constructivist-anticipatory principle'. It assumes that knowledge is implemented in the form of schemata, which consist of conditions and a sequence of actions. Schemata can be mutually embedded. So can conditions and actions. The purpose of the condition part is to provide context matching which allows the schema that best fits the present context to execute its action sequence. Since conditions can also be part of a sequence, they act as checkpoints for determining whether the anticipated meaning embodied by the schema is still on the right track. After a schema and all its subordinated elements finish, the cycle starts again. In this model, knowledge refers to the capability of the system to bridge between momentary perception and older experiences that are embedded in its schemata. (Further details are described in the next section.)

What are the consequences? Radical constructivism moves the focus of attention from defining a cognitive system as an information processor to describing it as an information *producer*.

That cognition excels at producing information becomes clear when we consider the phenomenon of superstitious perception that occurs for example when people see faces in clouds or figures in stellar constellations. In several experiments, Frédéric Gosselin and Philippe Schyns (2003) stimulated the visual system of test subjects with unstructured white noise, i.e., a static bit pattern that has equal energy at all spatial frequencies and does not correlate across trials. The subjects were asked to discriminate between a smiling and a nonsmiling face, which was allegedly present in 50% of the presentations. As a result, the subjects perceived the expected face. These findings confirm the information-producing view in the sense that the anticipated pattern was projected onto (i.e. partially correlated with) the perception of the white noise.

The information-producing view has gained great acceptance in the literature. For example. Susan Oyama (1985) and William Clancey (1991) also refer to the fact that information is not 'retrieved' but rather 'created' by the system. Dennett (1991) claims that the brain holds only a few salient details and fills in the rest from memory. Kevin O'Regan (1992) concludes that 'we only see what we attend to'. According to Gerhard Roth (quoted in Pörksen, 2001/2004, p. 121) the 're-enactment of the image, released by only a few sign stimuli, is far quicker than it would be if the eye had to scan the environment atomistically every single time.' However, radical constructivism goes an important step further. Due to the organizational closure of the cognitive apparatus it constructs its reality without 'knowing' that these inputs come from the sensory surface as there is no way to distinguish sensory signals from any other nervous signal. The idea of a sensory signal is only reconstructed a posteriori.

The information-producing perspective offers a crucial advantage over information-processing. As we can no longer speak of information input and the vicissitude of stimuli, organisms are no longer exposed to information overload as a result of processing the entirely available information. They no longer need to devote their cognitive resources to filter out irrelevant information in order to retain useful knowledge. It becomes clear that even insect brains can accomplish navigational tasks and sophisticated cognitive deeds in nontrivial environments without falling prey to the frame problem.

Therefore, cognitive research on perception should not focus on filtering mechanisms and data reduction. Information anxiety (Wurman, 1990) and cognitive overload (Kirsh, 2000) should not be considered a problem of the environment, as it is the case when talking, for example, about the overload that comes with the information flood on the internet. Instead, perception has to be explored in terms of the organism that performs the perceptive act.

Structure and dynamics

What do the structure and dynamics of such a radical constructivist cognitive system look like?

In order to remain explainable (but without forcing linguistic transparency by introducing propositional representations) the actual representational elements are schemata, which consist of conditions and actions.

Schemata work with nodes rather than propositions. However, in contrast to most artificial neural networks, which have several layers of discrete nodes, the apparatus uses only one layer that consists of a set S of discrete cells s. These *cells* can be modified, read, and compared with each other. The single-layer approach reduces the structural complexity in favor of a procedural hierarchy, as explained further below. The separation between cognitive apparatus and environment required by the cognitive closure of the cognitive system (cf. Q3) entails that all schemata deal with semantic- free states rather than with propositional representations. To bridge the gap between cognitive apparatus and environment, a 'transduction shell' is introduced, that is, a sensorimotor surface which takes over the function of nervous signals by mapping perceptive stimuli from the outside onto internal states S and vice versa. This 'anonymity' implements cognitive closure.

States are to be read and compared with each other in a fuzzy manner. Fuzzy means that the condition parts of schemata have smoothly varying, non-linear, interpolable classification boundaries comparable with the concept of partial membership described by fuzzy set theory (Zadeh, 1965). Therefore, the query response of conditions is defined over a continuous Gaussian curve rather than a discrete interval. That is, by querying a cell the extent is determined to which the value of the addressed cell s falls within the Gaussian interval defined by c.

Each fuzzy schema consists of an independent condition part and action part, which in turn may consist of single subcomponents and groups of subcomponents. For the condition part there are single queries and assemblies of queries, so-called *concepts*, which combine single conditions to represent composed entities. For the observer of the system, who can only access the system's output, such composed entities can be interpreted as multimodal perceptions, complex representations, composed hypotheses, etc.

As with single conditions, single actions, too, can be chained to form action sequences. Both condition and action chains can contain single and combined elements. There are two types of actions. The *set* action modifies the state of a particular cell. The *call* action can insert any arbitrary building block (i.e., primitive condition or action, concept or action sequence, or an entire schema) into the action part of a schema. From this description it follows that both the condition and action part form nested hierarchies in which encapsulations are re-used as building blocks. Elements can be functionally coupled as they make use of encapsulations and/or are part of encapsulations themselves. Therefore, the cognitive apparatus is a *hierarchical* system. (cf. Figure 6).

Finally, a single action may contain various flags such as stopping the current schema, or moving the execution of the current schema into the background such that the apparatus can start the concurrent execution of another schema.

How does the dynamics of the apparatus unfold? The algorithm uses the current *internal* context, i.e., the internal states S, which have partly been set by the transduction shell, to find a match among the condition parts of the existing rules. The matching is biased by the

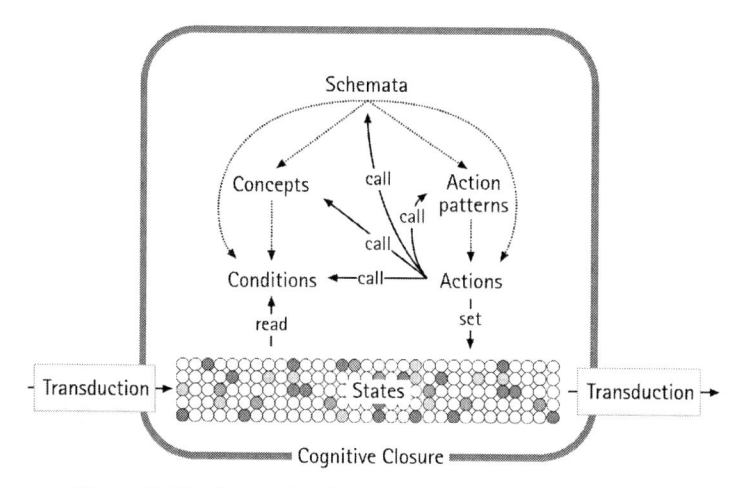

Figure 6. The hierarchical structure of the cognitive system

priority of the rules, which is inversely proportional to the length of the respective rule's condition part. These rules are at the lower end of the behavioral spectrum and could be anthropomorphically called 'reflexes.' The priority measure is motivated by the fact that reflexes are rather unspecific rules with low computational costs. It is also in alignment with the default hierarchy concept of Holland et al. (1986), where the most general elements have the shortest access path. Generally speaking, these reflex rules enable the apparatus to respond to critical events that endanger the existence of the cognitive system. Another conflict resolution criterion is the algorithm's preference for rules of low generality (as defined below).

At the other end of the behavioral spectrum are rules with long action parts and embedded conditions, which in the extreme case could make initial rule-triggering superfluous as they keep on branching to other action sequences and rules. They implement cognitive flexibility and dynamical continuity. However, an action sequence can come to a halt after the last action element is executed or if an embedded condition explicitly stops the execution of the current rule. In this case the algorithm again matches the current state against the condition parts to determine which rule may fire.

It is important to note that since the apparatus does not start with an a priori defined knowledge base but relies on various learning mechanisms as described below, it does not import the problems associated with the impossibility of making knowledge explicit

(Dreyfus & Dreyfus, 1986). In fact due to the learning component the initial set of rules in an individual can either be empty or inherited from ancestral individuals.

Learning is guided by maximizing two parameters. The *generality* of a schema is the weighted sum of the widths of the Gaussian intervals over all included conditions. It reflects the schema's specialization. The lower the generality the more specialized the schema is. The *importance* of a schema is the (weighted) sum of maximal degrees of membership over all included conditions. Rules with a higher importance are more likely to be carried out. Both these parameters enable the cognitive system to accommodate its schemata without reference to external entities and rewarding schemes (cf. Q2). The general idea is that the more often a schema has been carried out in the past, the higher its probability of being executed in the future. Ultimately, the success of cognition is defined in terms of success in the process of life (Heschl, 1990; Stewart, 1996). This definition extends the notion of cognition to animals: It is unlikely that the cognitive individual would have survived so far if frequently calling a particular schemata had a negative impact on its survival. Glasersfeld refers to this matter of fact as 'viability': '[W]e construct ideas, hypotheses, theories, and models, and as long they survive, which is to say, as long as our experience can be successfully fitted into them, they are *viable*' (Glasersfeld, 1981, p. 90, italics in the original).

In a population of reproducing individuals there is also *phylogenetic* learning which includes the application of genetic mutation and recombination. They can alter the composition of combined conditions and actions as well as schemata by adding, removing, or permuting their components. Compression and expansion are used to encapsulate such combined elements in order to increase the likelihood of being passed on to the next generation. Applying genetic operators to the compressed genotypes leads to functional couplings between control and structural genes as they implement homeotic mutations, which accelerate phylogenetic learning. Couplings enable coordinated development between structural elements of the cognitive apparatus in the sense that a *regulatory* element at a higher hierarchical level concurrently modifies elements at lower levels. Any mutation in a regulatory element simultaneously changes all connected elements as well. As a result, adaptability is increased because regulatory elements make synchronization possible among those dynamical elements which have to develop congruently as their proper functioning depends on each other.

Given the perpetual interplay of actions and conditions, which is rarely interrupted by initial rule firing, the system does not *compute* cognitive functions. Rather, it is a dynamical system that unfolds cognitive competence over time, as characterized by the dynamical approach to cognition (van Gelder, 1998).

Conclusion

Radical constructivism objects to considering knowledge as a justified belief that is true in the sense of referentially mapping propositional descriptions of the environment onto cognitive structures. Rather, knowledge must be *system-relative*. This term refers to situated cognitive processes, the dynamics of which are merely modulated by their environment on request of the cognitive apparatus rather than instructed by it. Furthermore, it becomes evident that knowledge is a relational dynamical structure rather than a set of propositions (cf. Q4). What a person knows today can have a completely different significance tomorrow. This dynamics cannot be captured in a static blueprint that we refer to as declarative or procedural knowledge. Rather, knowledge is the process of continuous constructions, the dovetailing of cognitive structures, which occasionally allow for assimilation of and accommodation to picked-up data from the environment (cf. Q5). These data (or signals) are neither computed nor do they constitute information (Q3). In the hierarchy of cognitive structures only the few schemata situated at the top can be isolated as propositions, since these are with a high degree of abstraction and distance from the lowest levels.

The radical constructivist information-producing paradigm emphasizes the primacy of the internal cognitive dynamics over influences from the outside. Therefore it negates Q1. Cognitive decisions are checkpoints embedded in action sequences. Both conditions and actions form schemata that populate the cognitive apparatus. Their dovetailing is continuously changing in the course of phylogenetic and ontogenetic learning. This leads to a hierarchical organization and, ultimately, to canalizations that force certain paths of schema execution (Riegler, 2001b), thereby foregoing external determination through reality (Q2). Interestingly, in this paradigm emotions do not play the role as arbiter because there is no need to cope with the computational costs of filtering and evaluating the flood of perceptual stimuli (Riegler, 2005).

In summary, the radical constructivist perspective points in the direction of a post-cognitivist psychology which (a) does not get stuck in perceptual overload, (b) does not run into epistemological problems of (propositional) knowledge representation, (c) takes the undifferentiated encoding of nervous signals into consideration, (d) does not exclude animals from being cognitive, and (e) accounts for implicit knowledge.

References

Ashby, W. R. (1952), *Design for a Brain* (London: Chapman and Hall).
Bradshaw, G. (1993), 'The airplane and the logic of invention', In: Giere, R. N. (ed.) *Cognitive Models of Science* (Univ. of Minnesota Press), pp. 239–250.
Broadbent, D. E. (1958), *Perception and Communication* (New York: Pergamon).
Cannon, W. B. (1932), *The Wisdom of the Body* (New York: Norton).
Carnap, R. (1932), 'Psychologie in physikalischer Sprache', *Erkenntnis* 3: 107–142. English Translation: Carnap, R. (1959) 'Psychology in physical language' (trans. by G. Schick). In: Ayer, A. J. (ed.) *Logical Positivism* (New York: Free Press), 165–197.
Chase, W. G. & Simon, H. A. (1973), 'Perception in chess', *Cognitive Psychology*, 4, pp. 55–81.
Chomsky, N. (1959), A review of B.F. Skinner's Verbal Behavior, *Language*, 35, pp. 26–58.
Clancey (1991), Review of Rosenfield's 'The Invention of Memory', *Artificial Intelligence*, 50, pp. 241–284.
Clancey, W. J. (1992), '"Situated" means coordinating without deliberation', *McDonnel Foundation Conference*. Santa Fe, NM.
Cook, S. A. (1971), 'The complexity of theorem proving procedures', *Proceedings of the Third Annual ACM Symposium on the Theory of Computing*. ACM, New York, pp. 151–158.
Dennett, D. C. (1984), 'Cognitive wheels', In: Hookway, C. (ed.) *Minds, Machines, and Evolution: Philosophical studies* (London: Cambridge University Press), pp. 129–151.
Dennett, D. C. (1991), *Consciousness Explained* (London: Little, Brown & Co.).
Dietrich, E. (2000), 'Cognitive science and the mechanistic forces of darkness, or why the computational science of mind suffers the slings and arrows of outrageous fortune', *Techné* 5(2).
Dörner, D. (1996), *The Logic of Failure* (New York: Metropolitan Books).
Duncker, K. (1945), 'On problem solving', *Psychological Monographs*, 58, pp. 1–112. German original published in 1935.
Dreyfus, H. & Dreyfus, S. (1986), *Man Over Machine: The Power of Human Intuition and Expertise in the Era of the Computer* (New York: The Free Press, Macmillan, Inc.).
Dreyfus, H. (1991), *Being-in-the-World: A Commentary on Heidegger's Being and Time, Division I* (Cambridge, MA: The MIT Press).
Foerster, H. von (1970a), 'Molecular ethology: An immodest proposal for semantic clarification', In: Ungar, G. (ed.) *Molecular Mechanisms in Memory and Learning* (New York: Plenum Press), pp. 213–248. Reprinted

in Foerster, H. von (1982), *Observing Systems*. Intersystems Publications: Seaside, pp. 149–188.

Foerster, H. von (1970b), 'Thoughts and notes on cognition', In: P. Garvin (ed.) *Cognition: A Multiple View* (New York: Spartan Books), pp. 25–48. Reprinted in: Foerster, H. von (2003) *Understanding Understanding* (New York: Springer), pp. 169–190.

Foerster, H. von (1972), 'Perception of the future and the future of perception', *Instructional Science*, 1, pp. 31–43. Reprinted in: Foerster, H. von (2003) *Understanding Understanding* (New York: Springer), pp. 199–210.

Foerster, H. von (1973), 'On constructing a reality', In: Preiser, F. E. (ed.) *Environmental Design Research*, Vol. 2. Dowden, Hutchinson & Ross, Stroudberg, pp. 35–46. Reprinted in: Foerster, H. von (2003) *Understanding Understanding* (New York: Springer), pp. 211–228.

Fodor, J. A. (1981), *Representations: Philosophical Essays on the Foundations of Cognitive Science* (Cambridge, MA: MIT Press).

Gettier, E. L. (1963), 'Is justified true belief knowledge?', *Analysis*, 23, pp. 121–123.

Gigerenzer, G. (2000), *Adaptive Thinking* (Oxford University Press).

Glasersfeld, E. von (1981), 'The concepts of adaptation and viability in a radical constructivist theory of knowledge', In: I. E. Sigel, D. M. Brodzinsky, and R. M. Golinkoff (eds.) *Piagetian Theory and Research* (Hillsdale, NJ: Erlbaum), pp. 87–95.

Glasersfeld, E. von (1988), 'The reluctance to change a way of thinking', *The Irish Journal of Psychology*, 9(1), pp. 83–90.

Glasersfeld, E. von (1995), *Radical Constructivism: A Way of Knowing and Learning* (London: Falmer Press).

Gosselin, F. & Schyns, P. G. (2003), 'Superstitious perceptions reveal properties of internal representations', *Psychological Science*, 14, pp. 505–509.

Heschl, A. (1990), 'L = C: A simple equation with astonishing consequences', *Journal of Theoretical Biology*, 145, pp. 13–40.

Keil, F. C. (2003), 'Folkscience: Coarse interpretations of a complex reality', *Trends in Cognitive Sciences*, 7, pp. 368–373.

Kirsh D. (2000), 'A few thoughts on cognitive overload', *Intellectica*, 30, pp. 19–51.

Knowlton, B., Mangels, J. & Squire, L. (1996), 'A neostriatal habit learning system in humans', *Science*, 273 (5280), pp. 1399–1402.

Kozhamthadam, J. (1994), *The Discovery of Kepler's Laws* (Notre Dame: University of Notre Dame Press).

Kuhn, T. S. (1962), *The Structure of Scientific Revolutions* (Cambridge, MA: Univ. of Chicago Press).

Lakoff, G. (1987), *Women, Fire and Dangerous Things* (Chicago: Chicago University Press).

Langley, P., Simon, H., Bradhaw, G. L. & Zytkow, J. M. (1987), *Scientific Discovery: Computational Explorations of the Creative Processes* (Cambridge, MA: MIT Press).

Llinás, R. R. (2001), *I of the Vortex* (Cambridge MA: MIT Press).

Malinowski, B. (1948), *Magic, Science and Religion and Other Essays* (Glencoe, IL: Free Press). Originally published in 1925.

Maturana, H. R. & Varela, F. J. (1980), *Autopoiesis and Cognition* (Dordrecht: Reidel).
Maturana, H. R. & Varela, F. J. (1987), *The Tree of Knowledge* (Boston MA: Shambhala).
Maturana, H. R., Uribe, G. & Frenk, S. (1968), 'A biological theory of relativistic colour coding in the primate retina: A discussion of nervous system closure with reference to certain visual effects', *Archiva de Biologia y Medicina Experimentales* (Suplemento Vol. 1), pp. 1–30.
McAllister, J. W. (1997), 'Phenomena and patterns in data sets', *Erkenntnis*, 47, pp. 217–228.
Merleau-Ponty, M. (1962), *Phenomenology of Perception*, trans. by C. Smith (London: Routledge & Kegan Paul).
Miller, G. A. (1956), 'The magical number seven, plus or minus two: Some limits on our capacity for processing information', *Psychological Review*, 63, pp. 81–97.
Nagel, T. (1974), 'What is it like to be a bat?', *Philosophical Review*, 83, pp. 435–450.
Neisser, U. (1967), *Cognitive Psychology* (New York: Meredith).
Neisser, U. (1975), *Cognition and Reality* (San Francisco: W. H. Freeman).
O'Donohue, W., Ferguson, K.E. & Naugle, A.E. (2003), 'The structure of the cognitive revolution: An examination from the philosophy of science', *The Behavior Analyst*, 26, pp. 85–110.
O'Regan, J. K. (1992), 'Solving the "real" mysteries of visual perception: The world as an outside memory', *Canadian Journal of Psychology*, 46, pp. 461–488.
Oyama, S. (1985), *The Ontogeny of Information: Developmental Systems and Evolution* (Cambridge University Press. Republished in 2000).
Peschl, M. & Riegler, A. (1999), 'Does representation need reality?', In: Riegler, A., Peschl, M. & Stein, A. von (eds.) (1999) *Understanding Representation in the Cognitive Sciences* (New York: Kluwer Academic / Plenum Publishers), pp. 9–17.
Pinker, S. (1997), *How the Mind Works* (New York: Norton).
Popper, K. (1979), *Objective Knowledge: An Evolutionary Approach*, rev. ed. (Oxford: Clarendon Press).
Pörksen, B. (2004), *The Certainty of Uncertainty* (Exeter: Imprint Academic). German original appeared in 2001.
Porr, B. & Wörgötter, F. (2005), 'Inside embodiment: What means embodiment to radical constructivists?', *Kybernetes*, 34 (1/2), pp. 105–117.
Powers, W. T. (1973), *Behavior: The Control of Perception* (New York: Aldine de Gruyter).
Putnam, H. (1982), *Reason, Truth, and History* (Cambridge: Cambridge Univ. Press).
Pylyshyn, Z. (1984), *Computation and Cognition: Toward a Foundation for Cognitive Science* (Cambridge, MA: Bradford Books/MIT Press).
Riegler, A. (1994a), 'Constructivist artificial life'. PhD Thesis, Vienna University of Technology.
Riegler, A. (1994b), 'Constructivist artificial life: The constructivist-anticipatory principle and functional coupling', In: Hopf, J. (ed.) *Proceedings of the 18th German Conference on Artificial Intelligence (KI-94)*

Workshop on Genetic Algorithms within the Framework of Evolutionary Computation. Max-Planck-Institute Report No. MPI-I-94-241, pp. 73–83.

Riegler, A. (1998), 'The end of science: Can we overcome cognitive limitations?', *Evolution & Cognition*, 4, pp. 37–50.

Riegler, A. (2001a), 'Towards a radical constructivist understanding of science', *Foundations of Science*, 6 (1–3), pp. 1–30.

Riegler, A. (2001b), 'The cognitive ratchet: The ratchet effect as a fundamental principle in evolution and cognition', *Cybernetics & Systems*, 32(3–4), pp. 411–427.

Riegler, A. (2002), 'When is a cognitive system embodied?', *Cognitive Systems Research*, special issue on 'Situated and embodied cognition', 3, pp. 339–348.

Riegler, A. (2005), 'Decision-making and anticipations: Why Buridani's ass is an unlikely creature', In: Smit, I., Wallach, W. & Lasker, G. E. (eds.) *Cognitive, Emotive and Ethical Aspects of Decision Making in Humans and in AI. Volume IV.* Windsor, Canada: The International Institute for Advanced Studies in Systems Research and Cybernetics, pp. 35–40.

Riegler, A. (2006), 'The paradox of autonomy: The interaction between humans and autonomous cognitive artifacts', In: Dodig-Crnkovic, G. & Susan Stuart, S. (eds.) *Computing, Philosophy, and Cognitive Science* (Cambridge: Scholars Press, in press).

Skinner, B. F. (1977), 'Why I am not a Cognitive Psychologist', *Behaviorism*, 5, pp. 1–10.

Stewart, J. (1996), 'Cognition = life: Implications for higher-level cognition', *Behavioural Processes*, 35, pp. 311–326.

van Gelder, T. J. (1998), 'The dynamical hypothesis in cognitive science', *Behavioral and Brain Sciences*, 21, pp. 1–14.

Varela, F. J. (1988), *Cognitive Science: A Cartography of Current Ideas* (Paris: CREA, Ecole Polytechnique).

Watson, J. (1930), *Behaviorism* (New York: Norton).

Winograd, T. (1972), *Understanding Natural Language* (New York: Academic Press).

Winograd, T. & Flores, F. (1986), *Understanding Computers and Cognition: A New Foundation for Design* (Norwood, NJ: Ablex).

Wittgenstein, L. (1922), *Tractatus Logico-Philosophicus* (London: Routledge).

Wurman, R. S. (1990), *Information Anxiety: What To Do When Information Doesn't Tell You What You Need To Know* (New York: Bantam Books).

Zadeh, L. (1965), 'Fuzzy sets', *Journal of Information and Control*, 8, pp. 338–353.

Susan A. J. Stuart

Unifying Experience: Imagination & Self-Consciousness

1. Introduction

There can be little doubt that there is something that it is like to have a perspective on the world, to perceive the world from the particular point of view of a human being, a weasel or a macaque monkey, that isn't simply its being that thing *qua* whatever it is, but which consists, at least in part, in its self-directed interaction with other things in its world, animate and inanimate, minded and non-minded. To have a perspective or point of view, from which the organism can identify and distinguish those things that have an affordance for it from those that do not, the system must be a perceiving and, even minimally, conceiving one that is embodied and embedded in its world (Dobbyn and Stuart, 2003). But perceptual and conceptual ability by itself is insufficient for experience to be rendered meaningful and, thus, useful to the organism. The elements of any experience need to be brought together if that experience is to be recognised by the organism as its own in some self-conscious reflective sense, or even if the organism is to have only some pre-reflective minimal sense of ownership of its experience.[1]

---

[1] *Contra* Carruthers (1996) I do not believe that 'self-awareness is a conceptually necessary condition for an organism to be a subject of phenomenal feelings, or for there to be anything that its experiences are like' [p.152]. In fact Carruthers gets this exactly the wrong way round claiming that self-awareness only emerges as the result of a developmental process that involves the acquisition of concepts and language. But without a pre-reflective self-awareness one could never embark on the kind of developmental process in question.

It is this capacity to integrate information that is stored across the brain into one unitary conscious experience which will be the subject of this article. In developing an overview of approaches to the problem, I will draw together the common strands from a diverse body of work; these will include Kantian metaphysics (Kant, 1929), Cotterill's neurophysiological approach (Cotterill, 1995; 1998), Sloman's cognitive architecture theory (Sloman, 2004; 2005), Aleksander's engineering approach that entails the integration of cognitive faculties into architectures (Aleksander and Dunmall, 2003), and two quite different approaches to robotics: the first from Brooks (1991), and the second from Bowling, Browning, and Veloso (2004).

Cotterill (1995) claims that consciousness is primarily associated with movement and response, with the necessary co-ordination of movement and response requiring a unity of conscious experience. In muscular movement, whether it is taking a step forward, reaching out with a hand, or simply looking around a room, we are asking — non-propositionalized — questions about our world. In the absence of kinaesthetic feedback — which we can see in people who have lost their proprioceptive sense — we rely on other forms of sensory feedback, and most often our dominant visual sense (Meijsing, 2000). Cotterill suggests that a master node draws together afferent and efferent information into coherent thought and action, and identifies the anterior cingulate as the possible location of consciousness where this activity might come together. Kant's critical philosophy focuses on describing the logically necessary prerequisites for a unity of consciousness, emphasising the role of the cognitive imagination in the act of synthesis. I will argue that, like Cotterill, Kant is committed to an active, sensorimotorily enmeshed view of consciousness, understanding the act of synthesis or binding to occur in some necessarily embodied enactive system.[2]

Early hybrid cognitive architectures represented knowledge symbolically as rules and facts but had a neurally-based activation process that determined which facts and rules got deployed in which situations.(Anderson, 1983; 1990; 1993) Sloman's Cog-Aff and H Cog-Aff architectures provide a more holistic approach, arguing that both cognitive and affective components must be brought together in one architecture. In the robotics work of Bowling, *et al.* (2004) the integration or synthesis of information operates on the basis of probability algorithms which must occur in both a temporal

---

[2] For an introduction and discussion of the notion of enactivism see Varela, Thompson & Rosch's *The Embodied Mind* (1991).

and a spatial framework if the system—in this case a robosoccer robot—is to act appropriately in real time. By examining, albeit briefly, Sloman's cognitive architecture theory, Aleksander & Dunmall's engineering approach, and the robotics work of Brooks (1991) and Bowling *et al.* (2004), we can see how the act of binding is being conceived and realised in a selection of artificial systems.

Fundamental to each of these approaches are the notions of engaged embodiment,[3] goal-directed animation, perception, and imagination, and, in turn, each of these notions requires a system that has (i) the ability to bind its experiences as experience for it, (ii) the ability to order and tag its experience temporally if it is to be able to plan ahead and direct its attention in an effort to sustain its existence, and (iii) some element of affective processing that enables the organism to establish a system of preferences and provides the system with a will to act.

2. Kant's Basic Architecture of the Mind

According to Kant we are logical subjects of thoughts, transcendental unities of apperception that are logically necessary for the very possibility of coherent cognition.

> That the 'I' of apperception, and therefore the 'I' in every act of thought, is one, and cannot be resolved into a plurality of subjects, and consequently signifies a logically simple subject, is something already contained in the very concept of thought, and is therefore an analytic proposition. (Kant, 1929, B407)

So, for Kant, a unity is already a condition of the possibility of experience. Thus, if an organism is capable of experience, it is capable of having even a minimal awareness of that experience as its own. In ourselves we look for a self, that which draws the perceptual data under some form of conceptual organisation, but find nothing substantial that could be the bearer of properties. In its absence we respond by conjuring up a unified self in the concept of a soul or mental thing (Descartes, 1968), in a bundle of discrete perceptions in a mental theatre (Hume, 1739), or we divert attention away from it by proposing a phenomenal unity at a much more fundamental level (Tye, 2003).

---

[3] By 'engaged embodiment' I have in mind an enactive system, but there is no reason to think there is anything especially privileged about being a physically embodied enactive system. The existence of self-aware animats acting and reacting within virtual environments is entirely plausible. (Dobbyn and Stuart, 2003)

Kant was content with neither Descartes' response [*viz.* The Paralogisms of Pure Reason, (Kant, 1929, A339/B397-A405/B432) nor Hume's [*viz.* The Refutation of Idealism, (Ibid. B275-94), and he would be unable to accept Tye's position because it emphasises phenomenal unity at the cost of subject unity. Kant's position would surely be that for phenomenal unity to take place, that is, to be located, subject unity must first be presupposed.

At first glance Kant's notion of the unified subject as simply a logical subject of thought, the vehicle of concepts (Ibid. B399 /A341), may not seem to be offering us anything more than we have already with Hume. But, firstly there is a subject in Kant and not merely a perception, and secondly, Kant's requirement that transcendental idealism and empirical realism are logically interdependent, *'The mere, but empirically determined, consciousness of my own existence proves the existence of objects in space outside me.'* (Ibid. B276) and his assertion that *'I am [necessarily] conscious of my own existence as determined in time'* (ibid.), commits to an embodied and embedded self, one that is dynamically and structurally coupled to its environment, and that is able to perceive itself as enduring through change.

Let's take this more slowly, so that we can see Kant's enactive agent emerge.

Kant's account of the mind has two fundamental elements:

1. perceptual awareness or *intuitions* of our world; they are (re)presentations of an object, material passively received by the mind through one's sense organs

2. conceptualisation of perceptual data through the active application of *a priori categories* or *concepts* by the faculty of Understanding

We can see exactly what Kant means when he claims that these elements are essential for experience by looking at two of his most famous phrases: 'Thoughts without content are empty, intuitions without concepts are blind' (Ibid. A52/B76). If our experience has no content, no experiential or perceptual input, our thoughts will be no thoughts at all for they will be empty. If we have perceptions or experience without any understanding to guide us in our organisation of the data of that experience, we will be as good as blind, for all we will experience, if experience is what we would want to call it, is chaos. So what makes this experience unchaotic? Well, two things: (i) the *a priori* concepts in our understanding that act in some way to synthesise it, drawing together the unity of self-consciousness and the unity of objective experience, and (ii) the power of the imagination. We need to unpack this a little further.

Experience is possible only if it refers to an objective world, that is, if we are embedded in an experientially rich and changing environment, for how else would our thoughts have content; except one might say through the imagination, but the content to be manipulated by the imagination cannot be conjured from nowhere. And, now it is possible to connect the following claims: 'Unity of diverse experiences in a single consciousness [a self] requires experience of objects' (Strawson, 1999, p.98) and, Kant's argument for the refutation of idealism, 'that there are things in space outside me' (Kant, 1929, B275). To demonstrate this latter claim Kant assumes Descartes' premise that I can determine my empirical consciousness in time without granting the existence of a physical world; but this will fail, for if inner experience is all I could have, then I could never arrive at a conception of myself as a temporally determined consciousness. The awareness of myself as temporally enduring is only possible through experience of change in things outside me: '...*the determination of my existence in time is possible only through the existence of actual things which I perceive outside me*'. (Ibid. B276) Thus Kant concludes that inner experience cannot be all there is; there must be an outside world.[4]

And now let's look again at the claim that unity of consciousness requires consciousness of unity, that is, to be able to attach the 'I think' to my thoughts they have to be ordered and unified by the application of the *a priori* concepts and synthesised by the power of the imagination. This requirement is a bi-directional logical requirement, an interdependence claim, not a contingent relation, and the nomological force of this claim clears the path for claiming that— because we have sensory awareness, understanding, a cognitive or productive imagination,[5] and a transcendental unity of apperception, it is possible to recognise our thoughts as our own, and all of this is made possible only because there is an external world with which

---

[4] It is really worth noting here that we see this most clearly set out in the argument for the second Analogy of Experience (Ibid. A189–211/B233–56) where Kant claims that in being able to distinguish surveys from events, that is, in being able to distinguish stasis from movement even when we ourselves are moving, we are aware of our subjective experience as distinguishable from objective fact. It is this capability that makes self-conscious experiences possible.

[5] I use productive or cognitive imagination here in opposition to creative or reproductive imagination which is the power to bring to mind something which is not wholly present.

we must engage if we are to have, even an illusory, sense of a continuing self. (Hume, 1739; Brook, 1994; Strawson, 1997 & 1999) There is a strong sense in which it is possible to accept that Kant is providing a notion of sensorimotorily enmeshed enactive agent that interacts with its, necessarily changing, world.

Thus, in ordinary cognitive judgement—the kind that, for Kant, involves the capacity for self-conscious reflection—the manifold of intuitions is 'synthesised' which involves it being brought under concepts to produce judgements. Synthesis occurs through the activity of the cognitive imagination which has three modes: apprehension, reproduction, and recognition. The synthesis of apprehension is *'of representations as modifications of the mind in intuition'*, sense impressions; the synthesis of reproduction is the *'merely empirical law, that representations which have often followed or accompanied one another finally become associated'*, the conjunction of contiguous impressions making possible the performance of inductive reasoning; and the synthesis of recognition which is the *'conscious that what we think is the same as what we thought a moment before ...[without which] ...all reproduction in the series of representations would be useless. For it would in its present state be a new representation'* and we would be where we were for Hume, the subject of discrete, synchronic experiences and nothing more. (Kant, 1929, A98-106) Hence ordinary cognition is a product of the interplay between the senses, the understanding, and the imagination; it is the conceptualisation and unification of experience with the potential—but only the potential—to be expressed in the form of a judgement beginning: 'I think'.

In unpicking the Kantian picture of the perceptual, conceptual and imaginative elements necessary for unifying experience we can begin to clarify what it is that must be resolved if we are to understand the binding problem in the more contemporary domains of neuroscience and robotics.

3. The Binding Problem

Information about the world and our bodily position in relation to the world is stored all over the brain and the central nervous system. How this information is integrated into one unitary perception to give us conscious experience is called the binding problem. Currently there are two main approaches to the resolution of this problem:

(i) Space-based binding which claims that there is a specific location or locations, perhaps clusters of neurons, in the brain where information is brought together.

(ii) Time-based binding which claims that there is no one place where binding happens, because integration can occur over the entire brain and is regulated by some process of synchronisation. Thus, time-based binding looks for when rather than where the binding occurs.

The Role of Attention and Synchrony in Binding

There has been much talk of central executives (Baddeley, 1986) and supervisory attentional systems (SAS) (Norman and Shallice, 1980; Shallice, 1982) and their role in marshalling perceptual input and cognitive processes into producing a unified experiential sense of the world; and a great deal has been said about the components that are being marshalled, for example, the visuo-spatial sketchpad and the phonological or articulatory loop; but very little has been said about the particular mechanism that must underpin the functioning of such executive or supervisory systems. In contrast to this Cotterill (1995; 1998) goes out of his way to specify, in some detail, the role of the *master node* in drawing together afferent/efferent information into coherent action and thought. Crucial to Cotterill's theory are synchrony and attentional processing. It is these we will concentrate on in analysing his theory.

Much of the sensory system works as an outer sense, enabling the organism to determine its external state, and links — directly or indirectly — to actuators, making action, and hence interaction with the world, possible. But in more complex organisms 'sensing' also comprises an 'inner sense', not only enabling the organism to determine its goal(s) and compare its sensory input with its internal state(s), but also to monitor its position, movement and actions in the world. This is the view, a sensorimotorily enmeshed view of conscious expeirence, to which I am committing Kant; it is also Cotterill's view. It is the unity of experience which co-ordinates information from the senses, including the proprioceptive sense — the ability to sense the position, location, orientation and movement of the body and its parts — with the agent's movement and appropriate responses.

In both Kant and Cotterill we see an emphasis on attention to movement for it is in attending to changes in our world, including changes in our body and position, being in a state of — what Cotterill describes as — 'plenisentience', where inputs can be consciously sensed and unconsciously processed, that with, for example, the proper functioning of cells in the visual cortex, we are able to distinguish movement from stasis.[6] But Cotterill adds to this that the position of our muscles and our subsequent muscular movements are what makes it possible for us to ask tacit, non-propositionalized questions about our environment and our position in our environment (Cotterill, 1995, p. 297). But we can go much further than this, for if we were unable to move or unable to receive feedback through our senses, our interaction and knowledge of our world would be extremely limited. If you are a tree this matters little, but if you are an animal that must avoid being on the menu for some predator it is essential. Thus, if our sensory system including our proprioceptive sense is working well, we will be in a position to receive and transduce afferent signals, and to produce appropriate efferent impulses in response. In this way we become aware of our world and, through the development of a body schema, are able to conceive of ourselves in relation to, whilst still being reasonably autonomous within, our world.

We have a ready made counter-example to any opposition to this claim in those individuals who have lost their proprioceptive sense, for without their internal feedback system they rely on the external feedback provided by, in most cases, their visual sense to regain their sense of selfhood or identity.

Miall and Wolpert (1993) state that the brain structure should

> ... receive as inputs an efferent copy of the motor command being sent to the ...limb, and also proprioceptive information about the current state of the body. The latter is needed for an accurate internal representation of the limb, as the arm's

---

[6] In humans and other primates, the vestibulo-ocular reflex (Churchland & Sejnowski, 1992) operates by direct feedback between sensory units (the semicircular canals) and actuators (motor neurons in the eye) with no 'inner' representational or cognitive system intervening. Light in the eye falls on the retina and, depending on its intensity and wavelength or colour, is translated by rod and cone cells into electrical impulses which are then transmitted along the optic nerves to the visual cortex at the back of the brain. It is in the visual cortex that this information is translated into perception of colour, depth, objects and movement. The lens and retina act in some ways like a camera but the information that is transferred onwards to the visual cortex is in a different form altogether. There is no single visual cortex, rather there are assemblies of discrete cells some dedicated to discerning edges, some to motion, some to colour, and so on. Neuropathological evidence shows us that damage to one batch of cells leaves others unaffected. For example, damage to the 'colour cells' will leave the individual able only to perceive in monochrome, and damage to the cells that determine objects might leave the individual able to perceive motion but without objects!

mechanical properties depend on its position and motion. Hence, the internal dynamic model must be updated by proprioceptors. (p.209)

Meijsing (2000) says of the patient, Ian Waterman, 'In the dark he did not know where his hand was; and even if he knew, he would not have been able to move it towards the bedside table without visual feedback' (p. 42). Yet, even this is insufficient for a fully unified sense of self.[7] Ian Waterman's sense of unity, his coherent sense of self, returned only when he had learned to move again with a great deal of concentrated visual feedback. Thus, it is is not just the passively received information about a changing environment, but the interplay between this information and active self-movement that places the self, a unity of experience, firmly at the centre of its environment. It is active self-movement which gives a sense of agency, as the perceived environment changes as a result of the agent's purposive action (Ibid., p. 46).

Cotterill suggests that there is a hierarchy of muscular control over which there is a global control mechanism – which he justifies on the grounds that there are limits to the amount of information that can be handled by the system at any one time (Broadbent, 1958) – and, in accordance with the spatial-based binding approach, he proposes that it be the anterior cingulate that acts in this way. It is neurally close to the higher motor hierarchical levels in the brain, and it is here – according to evidence from positron emission tomography [PET] scans (see Pardo, Pardo, Janer & Raichle [1990]) – that a response is translated into a physical or motor directive. For example,

> When I recognize a lemon, I am simultaneously detecting its pointed-oval shape, its dimpled skin, its yellow colour, and possibly also its relative softness and its characteristic citrus smell. The first three of these attributes are all detected by the visual system, but by different parts of it. The fourth feature is detected by touch, while the last one is discerned by my olfactory sense. And where is the logical conclusion, *lemon*, located? It is not deposited in some inner sanctum, farther up the hierarchy. On the contrary, its components are left in those same sensory modalities and areas. The concept *lemon* merely exists through the temporary binding together of its various attributes; and we are able to sense the lemon as a single unity because we can

---

[7] She goes on to note that this is the replacement of an inner sense with an outer sense, and these may not equate to the same thing since the inner sense is immune to error through misidentification (cf. Evans, 1982; Brewer, 1995) and the outer sense is not.

instantaneously detect what goes with what. (Cotterill, 1995, p. 305)

Thus, the anterior cingulate plays the role of, a kind of, central executive though not in any conscious sense.

Kant would echo the sentiment in this quotation but claim that '... and we are able to sense the lemon as a single unity because we draw together the intuitions under concepts and with the synthesising power of the apprehensive, reproductive, and recognitional imagination we are able to put together a thought which might be 'lemon' or, more complicatedly, 'I think it is a lemon' — though that would probably only arise if there was some doubt about the object's status. Being able to unite the disparate parts of my perceptual experience together into a thought is sufficient to reveal that the thought is being had in one head, that is, that it is 'my thought'.

In his emphasis on the synchrony of input and output Cotterill presents us with a temporal-based response to the binding problem, but only in some circumstances. In the process of object recognition there is a great deal of neural activity which is a result of the information received through the modalities involved in the perception of an object, and that neural activity is distributed across the parietal-temporal-occipital association cortex. But we have also seen that synchrony of input alone cannot be the complete or sole explanation for binding. The detection of movement, both internal to the system and external to it, and the co-ordination of sensory input, including the proprioceptive sense, with the agent's movement and responses, are essential if there is to be a unity of consciousness, and a unity of consciousness is necessary if we are to have coherent experience of our world. If Cotterill is right, this aspect of neural activity might well be located at the centre for determining muscular movement in the brain, for it is with the proper functioning of the anterior cingulate that we can ask questions about, and bring about changes within, our dynamically changing environment. Cotterill's picture is, then, of a hybrid model of how binding occurs; it is time-based in its synchrony and it is space-based in that it might be located in the anterior cingulate.

4. Cognitive Architecture Theories and Robotics

Early hybrid cognitive architectures, for example, ACT-R and SOAR, (Anderson, 1983; 1990; 1993), represented knowledge symbolically as rules and facts but had a neurally-based activation process that determined which facts and rules got deployed in different contexts. However, there are numerous reasons behind the move away from a computational approach of this kind. One of the most forceful is the claim that the agent and its environment are a whole with neither being isolable from the other if we want a full account of experience and consciousness. From this emerges the current emphasis on enactive agency whereby affective states are every bit as important as sensory and cognitive states and processes.[8]

Sloman's Cog-Aff and H Cog-Aff architectures (Sloman, 2004; 2005) provide a more holistic approach to the requirements for conscious experience, arguing that structural, cognitive and affective components must be combined in one architecture — perhaps as one subject of consciousness — consisting of physiological machine sub-architectures and virtual sub-architectures of mental states and mechanisms. Sloman distinguishes between three types of processing: perception, action, and central processing, each recognisable in Kant's and Cotterill's thinking, and three cognitive levels: reaction, deliberation and reflection. Reaction, he argues, and few would disagree, is the oldest and most fundamental part of any cognitive architecture,[9] with deliberative or inferential reasoning coming later, and finally, the 'meta-management' of reflection emerging much later still and, possibly, only in human conscious agents.

Unlike early architectures, H Cog-Aff is not algorithm- and representation-based, and this is bound to provide a distinct advantage when developing virtual architectures to specify mental states and mental state relations. However, even though Sloman raises numerous important questions about the nature and ontology of meta-management constraints like the emotions, he offers no account of the central processing element that acts to bind the perceptual information with other cognitive mechanisms and affective attitudes. In a contemporary version of the mind-body problem one might certainly wonder how the virtual architectures and machine sub-architectures would interact; so, what would be the virtual-mechanical equivalent of psycho-physical bridging laws? But criticism of this sort might be too hasty and too harsh, for it is clear

---

[8] A fine example of this is Damasio's work on the necessary role of affective processing in rational decision making. (Damasio, 1995)

[9] Corresponding to this claim is the physiological evidence that sensory signals are relayed from the sensory cortex to the thalamus and on to the brain stem, and it is the brain stem which controls various autonomic functions such as respiration and the regulation of heart rhythms as well as perceptual functions such as the primary aspects of sound localization. It is here that the fight/flight response (reaction) is triggered.

that the complexity of the cognitive system does not lend itself to easy explanations. As Sloman says, it isn't *'a single (atomic) state which switches when some input is received ...There may still be real, causally efficacious, internal virtual machine events and processes that cannot be directly observed and whose effects may not even be indirectly manifested externally'* (Sloman, 2004). In response he suggests that we might think about virtual architectures in terms of *'multiple concurrently active, interactive, sub-states changing on different time scales (some continuously) with varying complexity'* (Ibid.), and if he is right, then it will be some time before Cog-Aff and H Cog-Aff architectures have anything to say about their central processor and how a unity of consciousness might be achieved.

Aleksander and Dunmall (2003) present, in axiomatic form, a formal statement of five mechanisms that are thought minimally necessary to underpin consciousness and, thus, the creation of conscious machines. Theirs is an engineering approach that entails the integration of the cognitive faculties — perception, imagination, attention, prediction, and emotion — into computer-based depictions to create the sensation for the organism or system of being 'out-there'.[10] That these elements appear here as they have in Sloman and, to some extent, Kant and Cotterill is no surprise, but what is particularly novel about Aleksander & Dunmall's approach from the point of view of this paper is that it presents a sort of Kantian transcendental argument against the zombie theorists who argue that qualia or sensation cannot be supervenient on mechanism. They argue that mechanism is implied by the occurrence of sensation, that is, that a necessary condition for the occurrence of sensation is that there is some mechanism that underpins it. In short, mechanism may not imply sensation, but sensation implies mechanism. That we would find an argument of this sort in Aleksander's work is not surprising since he asks the same question Kant asks but from an implementational point of view; he asks 'What are the essential mechanisms for being conscious?'. And in another Kantian twist he concludes that the emergence of a subject or self, results from a combination of sensory, imaginational, attentional and (though Kant might be forgiven for excluding this element) affective depictions which can start with the logical subject 'I'. Neither Cotterill nor, I am sure, Sloman would disagree.

---

[10] There's possibly a rather interesting twist here in a comparison of Aleksander and Dunmall's 'being out there' and Heidegger's *Dasein* or 'being there' (Heidegger, 1962).

In contrast with Sloman's and Aleksander and Dunmall's heady brew, Brooks' work on cognitive architectures and robotics (Brooks, 1991) is rather flat, dealing with perceptual and reactive processes only.

> ... (the robots) are situated in the world – they do not deal with abstract descriptions but with the here and now of the world directly influencing the behaviour of the system ... (Brooks, 1991, p. 575)

Perception and action are connected directly; there is no central processing system, no central representation, and whatever binding there might be said to be must be temporally-based for there is no location or set of locations for information to come together. Where Sloman argues for a combination of physical and virtual architectures, and a move away from the image of a single state mechanism, Brooks' animat architectures have been strictly engineered: the finite state machines that govern their low-level behaviour have been carefully contrived; and the patterns of connection and message passing between these machines are the result of much experiment. These are behaviour-based machines and there is no role for affective states and processes that are so important in triggering thought and action in biological organisms. Nor is there any role for the imagination, though one might anticipate that the elements of the cognitive imagination that Kant specifies—apprehension, reproduction, and recognition—would be extremely useful for any artificial agent that is to not simply negotiate its world but to learn to negotiate and re-negotiate familiar terrain. In Brooks more recent work (Brooks, 2002), he is keen to emphasis mimesis and, thus, elements of reproduction and recognition. But in his claim that 'Kismet is alive. Or may as well be. People treat it that way.' (ibid. p.64) he is clearly more inclined to think of cognition in the observer than the robotic agent.

In contrast to Brooks' work is Bowling, Browning, & Veloso's robotics work (Bowling *et al.*, 2004). Their concern is with the use of neural networks to produce the kind of unpredictable behaviour involved in the dynamic environment of robot soccer; as they say:

> [The] challenge of controlling a team of robots within the context of robot soccer, a multi-robot, goal-driven, adversarial domain.

In many ways theirs is much more exciting work, for in a complex environment of this kind the binding of experiential input must occur within each individual as well as across the team if they are to achieve their end and score goals or, at the very least, block their opponents attempts at goal scoring. So,

Given a set of effective and parameterized individual robot behaviors, how do we select each robot's behavior (possibly using past execution experience) to achieve the team's goals?

The elements necessary for successful game play are perception, attention, reaction, coordination, and prediction, all of which are evident, to a greater or lesser extent, in Kant's, Cotterill's, Sloman's, and Aleksander and Dunmall's work. The 'afferent' input is synthesised or integrated with world/system state information, and possible 'efferent' feedback and action on the basis of probability algorithms. Such algorithms occur in both a temporal and a spatial framework in the *playbook* which is 'a method for seamlessly combining multiple team plans', if the robots are to act appropriately and effectively in real time. Thus, the Bowling et al. (2004) soccer robots[11] that are dynamically and structurally coupled to their world operate on a hybrid model of temporal and spatial binding.

5. Concluding Remarks

There are many common elements within these, at first glance, disparate approaches, with the exceptional case being Brooks. The others have at their core the notions of engaged embodiment, goal-directed animation, perception, and imagination, and for their instantiation they require a system that has the ability to synthesise its experiences and be able to recognise them as experiences for it. Without this there can be no urge to act, for unless I am aware of experiences being mine — whether rat, cat, badger, or soccer robot — I will have no desire to act to defend myself from predators or to act stealthily towards prey. For this reason I must be able to tag my experience temporally, not only to enable me to recognise that especially vivacious experiences are current and require immediate action, but also to make possible associationistic learning and the construction of preference models of those things which are desirable and those things which are not.

Cotterill's account of consciousness is primarily associated with movement and response, and the co-ordination of movement and response requires a unity of consciousness or subject unity. This is an

---

[11] The Bowling et al. (2004) soccer robots — the most sophisticated being the legged-teams using Sony AIBOs — have a variety of names from CMPack to CMDragons; information about them can be found at
http://www-2.cs.cmu.edu/~robosoccer/main/

interdependence claim not unlike Kant's claim that a unity of consciousness is possible only on condition that we have a consciousness of unity, and *vice versa*, and we have seen that Kant's argument for our being able to conceive of ourselves as unities of consciousness, that is, as temporally determined conscious agents, is based on our being able to discern and distinguish movement from stasis through the application of *a priori* concepts which order and unify our perceptual input. A great deal is implicit in Kant's notion of ordering and unifying, a great deal that is being excavated by current work in neurophysiology, robotics and cognitive architecture theories.

Cotterill's argument focuses on a neurophysiological approach to the problem and identifies the anterior cingulate as a possible 'site' of consciousness. Sloman's cognitive architecture theory is a model inspired by work in artificial intelligence. Aleksander & Dunmall's approach is combination of mathematics and engineering; and Bowling, Browning & Veloso's approach is based in Artificial Neural Networks (ANN). None of these approaches were available to Kant, yet in his metaphysical enquiry we find him committed to an active, sensorimotorily enmeshed view of consciousness, a view which is not just recognisable in, but there as an underpinning to, each of the very different frameworks of enquiry addressing the problems of consciousness and the integration of thought from beyond the constraints of our computational heritage.[12]

References

Aleksander, I. & Dunmall, B. (2003), 'Axioms and tests for the presence of minimal consciousness in agents', *Journal of Consciousness Studies*, 10(4-5), pp. 7–19.

Anderson, J. R. (1983), *The Architecture of Cognition* (Cambridge, MA: Harvard University Press).

Anderson, J. R. (1990), *The Adaptive Character of Thought* (Hillsdale, NJ: Erlbaum).

Anderson, J. R. (1993), *Rules of the Mind* (Hillsdale, NJ: Erlbaum).

Baddeley, A. D. (1986), *Working Memory* Oxford: Clarendon Press).

Bowling, M., Browning, B. & Veloso, M. (2004), 'Plays as effective multiagent plans enabling opponent-adaptive play selection', in *Proceedings of International Conference on Automated Planning and Scheduling (ICAPS'04)*.

Brewer, B. (1995), 'Bodily Awareness and the Self', in *The Body and the Self* (Cambridge, MA: MIT Press).

Broadbent, D. E. (1958), *Perception and Communication* (Oxford: Oxford University Press).

Brook, A. (1994), *Kant and the Mind* (Cambridge University Press).

---

[12] Some ideas in this chapter are further explored in Stuart (2007).

Brooks, R. (1991), 'Intelligence without representation', *Artificial Intelligence*, 47(1-3), pp. 139–159.
Brooks, R. (2002), *Flesh and Machines* (Pantheon Books).
Carruthers, P. (1996), *Language, Thoughts and Consciousness: An Essay in Philosophical Psychology* (Cambridge: Cambridge University Press).
Churchland, Patricia S. & Sejnowski, T.J. (1992), *The Computational Brain* (Cambridge, MA: MIT Press).
Cotterill, R. M. J. (1995), 'On the unity of conscious experience', *Journal of Consciousness Studies*, 2(4-5), pp. 290–311.
Cotterill, R. M. J. (1998), *Enchanted Looms: Conscious Networks in Brains and Computers* (Cambridge: Cambridge University Press).
Damasio, A. R. (1995), *Descartes' Error: Emotion, Reason and the Human Brain* (New York: Picador).
Descartes, R. (1968), *Discourse on Method, and the Meditations* (Penguin).
Dobbyn, C. & Stuart, S. A. J. (2003), 'The self as an embedded agent', *Minds and Machines*, 13(2), pp. 187–201.
Evans, G. (1982), *The Varieties of Reference* (Oxford: Clarendon Press).
Heidegger, M. (1962), *Being and Time*, trans. John Macquarrie and Edward Robinson (London: SCM Press).
Hume, David (1739), *A Treatise of Human Nature* (Oxford: Clarendon Press).
Kant, Immanuel (1929), *The Critique of Pure Reason*, translated by Norman Kemp Smith (London: Macmillan Press).
Meijsing, M. (2000), 'Self-consciousness and the body', *Journal of Consciousness Studies*, 7(6), pp. 34–52.
Miall, R. C. and Wolpert, D. J. (1993), 'Is the cerebellum a smith predictor?' *Journal of Motor Behaviour*, 25(3), pp. 203–216.
Norman, D. A. and Shallice, T. (1980), 'Attention to action: Willed and cutomatic control of behavior', CHIP Report 99, University of California, San Diego.
Pardo, J. V., Pardo, P. J., Janer, K. W. & Raichle, M. E. (1990), 'The anterior cingulate cortex mediates processing selection in the Stroop attentional conflict paradigm', *Proceedings of the National Academy of Sciences*, 87, pp. 256–9.
Shallice, T. (1982), 'Specific impairments of planning', *Philosophical Transactions of the Royal Society of London*, B 298, pp. 199–209.
Sloman, A. (2004), 'Varieties of affect and learning in a complete human-like architecture. Accessed online, July 2004. URL:
http://www.cs.bham.ac.uk/research/cogaff/talks/#talk24.
Sloman, A. (2005), 'What are information-processing machines? what are information-processing viitual machines?'. Accessed online, January 2005. URL: http://www.cs.bham.ac.uk/axs/misc/talks/information.pdf
Strawson, G. (1997), 'The "self"', *Journal of Consciousness Studies*, 4(5/6), pp. 405–428.
Strawson, P. F. (1966), 'Unity of diverse experiences in a single consciousness [a self] requires experience of objects', in *The Bounds of Sense* (London: Methuen).
Stuart, S. A. J. (2007), 'Machine consciousness: Cognitive and kinaesthetic imagination', *Journal of Consciousness Studies*, 14 (7) pp. 141–53.
Varela, F., Thompson, E. & Rosch, E. (1991/2003), *The Embodied Mind: Cognitive Science and Human Experience* (Cambridge, MA: MIT Press).
Tye, M. (2003), *Consciousness and Persons: Unity and Identity* (Cambridge, MA: MIT Press).

Pamela Lyon and Fred Keijzer

The Human Stain

Why Cognitivism Can't Tell Us What Cognition Is & What It Does

That the sciences concerned with cognition must move beyond cognitivism is not simply a good idea, it is a movement already well under way. Within a decade, perhaps sooner, few will disagree with the label 'first-generation cognitive science' used by Gallese and Lakoff (2005, p. 455) to describe the ultra-cognitivist period of this widely distributed, multidisciplinary enterprise. This suggests we already inhabit the second wave, whatever it is. By ultra-cognitivism we mean the thesis that the natural cognition of biological systems (the only kind we know so far) is meaningfully like what goes on inside a digital computer. That is, mental contents and processes are meaningfully thought of as symbolic (abstract, amodal) representations that combine according to formal syntactic rules, yielding language-like properties of thought such as productivity, compositionality and systematicity (Fodor, 1975). Because of these features ultra-cognitivism further proposed that cognitive processes — typically viewed as reasoning, in contrast to emotion and feeling — could themselves be considered abstractly, independent of their material context. Cognitivism can also refer generically, almost vacuously to an 'information processing' approach (cognitivism-lite), so we use the prefix 'ultra' to refer to the strong thesis that cognition is information processing of a particular type, which in its natural instantiation takes place in the brain of an agent, paradigmatically human.

Bechtel and colleagues (1998) locate the beginning of the end of first-generation cognitive science with an 'identity crisis' that began in the mid-1980s with the 'rediscovery' of neural networks, brain science, and the importance of the environment ('ecological validity' and 'situated action') to psychological processes (pp. 77–90). While the identity crisis has yet to fully play out, the parameters of the second generation are coming into focus (Winograd & Flores, 1986; Beer, 1990; Brooks, 1991; Varela *et al.*, 1991; Van Gelder, 1995; Clark, 1997; Keijzer, 2001). First and foremost, second-generation theoretical modelling can no longer operate purely in the abstract, divorced from how the brain works or the fact that cognition 'facilitates life in the real world' (Bechtel *et al.*, 1998, p. 91). Except perhaps in the narrowest circumstances, therefore, psychological explanations cannot bracket the rest of the body, mental features such as affect and feeling, and the fact that cognitive processes rely on phenomena outside the agent. Second-generation cognitive science thus is frequently referred to as 'embodied', 'embedded', 'situated', 'enactive', 'interactionist', and so on.

These developments are extremely positive, indeed, long overdue. However, we believe the post-cognitivist sciences of cognition will have to do much more than recognize the obvious: that natural cognition is a biological function which enables an organism to navigate an ecological niche the organism, in part, creates. A post-cognitivist science of cognition will have to do more, that is, if it truly aims to be a *natural* scientific enterprise, one capable of answering the three fundamental questions that Bechtel and colleagues (quite correctly) claim it must: *What is cognition? What does it do? How does it work?* So far, cognitivism has failed to provide sufficient traction on the first two issues (see, e.g., Neisser, 1976; Johnson and Erneling, 1997).

In this chapter we will argue there is a deeper issue that must be recognized if real progress is to be made toward understanding what we now think of as cognition, roughly: *the processes by which humans and other biological systems come to know the world*. Until this deeper issue is acknowledged and addressed, we suspect the best we can hope for is the continued accumulation of facts in disparate enterprises, despite an existing 'information overload that almost inhibits meaning' (Rose 1998, p. 87). The deeper issue revolves around the question of what sort of science the cognitive sciences, and psychology in particular, are supposed to be. Unlike any other science that has sought to understand a complex facet of the natural world, psychology and related disciplines have benchmarked their explanatory successes principally against a single organism: *Homo sapiens*.

This species-centrism, unique among the modern life-related sciences (Lyon 2006b), derives, naturally enough, from our understandable fascination with the (seemingly) peculiar human experience of being-in-the-world. However, it is also strongly supported by Anglo-European culture, in the context of which the so-called 'cognitive revolution' occurred. Judeo-Christian theology, which forms a major component of the cultural scaffolding, accords humans dominion over the rest of nature. This is the basis of the 'Great Chain of Being,' a concept that still haunts the Western imagination despite its comprehensive defeat by modern science. Many Asian cultures—for example, those influenced by Buddhism—have a much more egalitarian view of the distribution of cognition in nature. It is no accident that the first scientist to defend the once-heretical thesis that some nonhuman primates have 'culture,' an idea now the subject of much investigation, was Japanese (De Waal 2001). An equally titanic influence on the cognitive sciences' species-centrism is Cartesian psychology, which provided an 'enlightened' rationale for the theological picture by dividing the world into two stuffs, one exclusive to humans. Although dualism has long been a minority position among scientifically sophisticated moderns, the debt of cognitivism to Descartes—and the deleterious effects that intimate connection has wrought—is well known (for a recent critique in relation to neuroscience, see Bennett and Hacker 2003; to cognitive science generally, Wheeler 2005; but also Dupuy 2000; Gardner 1985).

Thus, while the great leaps of the 20th century in understanding human biology (e.g., genetics, development, physiology, pathologies) were made on the basis of experiments with simple model systems (e.g., bacteria, yeast, nematodes, fruit flies, frogs, zebrafish, mice, rats), cognitive psychology and related sciences largely focused on human intelligence—a highly complex and difficult to understand phenomenon—without much reliance on more simple animal model systems. In this chapter we will argue that, while not always overtly human-centred—although some comparative psychologists argue otherwise (e.g., Shettleworth, 1993; 1998)—cognitivism is, in fact, *anthropogenic*. It is so because it rests on the (usually implicit) assumption that the human case is the most fruitful, even necessary, starting point for extrapolating an ontology for the cognitive sciences, that is, for determining what the cognitive sciences are sciences *of* (Lyon, 2006a,b).

Biology often uses staining techniques in which a pigment is used to colour particular structures in a sample. The anthropogenic approach acts like a conceptual staining technique, which brings certain limited features of cognition into sharp relief. Using a 'human stain,' the sharp visibility of these artificially enhanced features makes them diagnostic or substantially indicative of cognition, to the exclusion of other processes that may be, and often are, more important. The pre-eminent use of a single technique is justified in a field of enquiry when it is the only or chief reliable method for investigation, but it can also mislead. The violet-coloured Gram stain revolutionized the field of bacteriology, for example, but also encouraged the postulation of a major taxonomic division that has not stood the test of time. The differential ability to retain the stain is the result of differences in cell-wall structure between Gram-positive and Gram-negative bacteria, differences once assumed to reflect a major natural division similar to that of animals and plants or, more recently, prokaryotes and eukaryotes. Just as sophisticated molecular biological techniques have blurred these other once-ironclad divisions, the Gram staining divide is now known to be highly permeable. It is no barrier to the exchange of genes (Ochman and Moran, 2001; Ragan, 2001), for example, or the marshalling of coordinated behaviour (Bassler and Losick, 2006). In other words, recent advances in microbiology suggest that bacteria are much more alike in general outline, and more different in detail, than the Gram stain shows.

Similarly, a major effect of cognitivism's 'human stain' has been the tendency to systematically underestimate the value of topics, such as 'basic behaviour' (Keijzer, 2001), which fall in the shadow of human cognition and/or consciousness. Whereas leading psychologists of the early decades of the 20th century assumed that the behaviour of even very simple creatures, such as amoeba and paramecia, were legitimate empirical avenues for understanding cognition (see in particular, Jennings, 1906; Washburn, 1936), scientists and philosophers in the revolutionary phase of ultra-cognitivism in the century's latter half largely rejected this work. Like little boys with their noses pressed against the window of a sweet shop, the cognitive revolutionaries waited for someone or something to break the window that separated them from the tantalizing goal they could intuit but not reach, while rejecting the option of searching for a door in the form of simple animal cases. The classic cognitivist's warrant for ignoring the behaviour of simple organisms in the quest to understand cognition, popularized by Dennett, is the putatively robotic provisioning behaviour of the well-known *Sphex* wasp. However, the *Sphex* example—originally published by Henri Fabre in 1879 —was in actuality a caricature of a behaviour that subsequent experiment revealed to be more complex and equivocal (Keijzer, 2001).

We believe the cognitivist tendency to neglect basic behaviour, which has proved surprisingly complex and resistant to easy explanation (Rosensweig *et al.*, 1996), has contributed to the cognitive sciences' failure to even *identify* their investigative target, much less explain it. After 150 years of scientific psychology and half a century of one of the most concentrated investigative efforts in human history, we still cannot agree what creatures exhibit cognition (Lyon, 2006b). Even non-human primates are not beyond doubt, as a former professor of animal behaviour states: 'If scientists, at least, finally cease to make the conscious or unconscious assumption that [non-human] animals have minds… [and] If the age-old mind-body problem comes to be considered as an exclusively human one, instead of indefinitely extended through the animal kingdom, then that problem too will have been brought nearer to a solution.' (Kennedy 1992:167-168). Comparing the state of his own discipline's theoretical armamentarium to that of the physical sciences, psychologist Christopher Green (2000, p. 5) concludes: 'To put it crudely…physics knows what it is talking about'—for example, electrons, quarks, pendula, falling bodies, turbulence in fluids, the behaviour of gases. '[T]o the extent these idealized entities correspond to real entities, physics works. Psychology does not, in this sense, know what it is talking about.'

This is not a trivial 'merely semantic' issue. At the very least the lack of agreement about basic theoretical constructs exacerbates commensurability problems already intrinsic to a multidisciplinary knowledge enterprise. Terminological confusion in psychology has been lamented since William James. The fact that this is still the case more than a century later, especially after five decades of extraordinarily intensive research, suggests to us that the subject matter of psychology is not only very complex but that the predominant manner of approaching it is also deeply flawed.

The shift away from cognitivism toward dynamic, embodied and situated approaches, however necessary and progressive, has so far left untouched the fundamental issues of a cognitive ontology, including the demarcation of the cognitive domain (although there have been some moves in that direction, particularly recently

(Moreno et al., 1997; Harnad, 2005; Lyon, 2006b; Van Duijn et al., 2006). We will argue that a truly post-cognitivist psychology will be impossible until we come to grips with the anthropogenic basis of the existing paradigm. What is required, we claim, is more attention to the deep biological context within which natural cognition arises. In contrast to the anthropogenic approach, a *biogenic* approach assumes that because natural cognition is first and foremost a biological function, which contributes to the persistence and wellbeing of an organism embedded in an ecological niche with which it must continually contend, then biological principles are the best guide to what cognition is and what it does. Like other biological functions (e.g., respiration, nutrient acquisition, digestion, waste elimination) the general outline may be broadly similar relative to the economy of an organism; some basic mechanisms may even be shared. On the other hand, the mechanistic details of how the function works are likely to differ from organism to organism, the result of making a living in a particular niche.

This chapter is structured as follows. First, we will sketch the characteristics of the anthropogenic and biogenic approaches to cognition[1] and point to some historical exemplars. Next we will explain why we think cognitivism is anthropogenic and outline some of the problems that arise for the paradigm for the very reason that it is so. Finally, we will show how biogenic theorizing is empirically constrained to a greater extent than are anthropogenic approaches to cognition, which provides advantages for addressing fundamental issues of scientific ontology. Basic forms of sensorimotor process are shown to be a principled starting point for demarcating the domain of cognitive phenomena, and although sensorimotor-based theories do not necessarily imply a form of experience, it is possible to address even such difficult topics as consciousness from a thorough-going biogenic perspective (e.g., Goodson, 2003).

It is important to stress that the anthropogenic and biogenic approaches are not mutually exclusive. Ideally, they are complementary. After all, we do want to know how the human mind works. However, if the cognitive sciences really do need a fundamental ontology—and there is growing sentiment that they do (Toulmin, 1972; Staats, 1983; 1999; Sternberg and Grigorenko, 2001; De Waal, 2002; Hartley, 2006), even in unrelated disciplines (Silver, 1998)—then we claim that the anthropogenic approach, of which

---

[1] The distinction was introduced in Lyon (2004) and developed in Lyon (2006a,b).

cognitivism is a prime example, is not likely to get us there. A biogenic approach is a more promising, potentially far less problematic vehicle.

The Anthropogenic Approach To Cognition

The choice of starting point for an inquiry into any phenomenon has important consequences for the ensuing science. It shapes the criteria by which the investigative target is identified, compared, described and explained, and has important consequences for the kinds of problems encountered and the permissible conclusions to be drawn. Fundamental conceptual matters present challenges in any discipline. The degree of difficulty is greater still in a multidisciplinary enterprise with varying explanatory agenda. Presuppositions about the starting point in the multidisciplinary cognitive sciences can be made explicit as an answer to a question. Do we begin with human cognition and work our way 'down' to a more general concept of cognition (if that is possible)? Or do we start from the facts of biology, derive a general concept, and then work our way 'up' to the human case, which we take (no doubt correctly) to be the most complex and sophisticated instance of cognition on this planet?

The terms *anthropogenic* and *biogenic* denote the different choices the answer to this question entails. The tradition of cognitive explanation that takes the human case as its starting point is called anthropogenic based on the Greek words for human (*anthropos*) and birth or origin (*genesis*). *Bios* is the Greek word for life, hence *biogenic* describes the cognitive approach that begins with biology. These adjectives are new only to the cognitive sciences. 'Anthropogenic' has long been used in plant ecology to refer to plants introduced by humans, and increasingly refers to global climate change associated with human activity. 'Biogenic' is employed in geology to refer to the origins of certain rock strata. Limestone is biogenic, for example, because its origin is material that once formed part of living organisms.

The important thing to keep in mind is that the anthropogenic/biogenic distinction refers to a methodological bias, a strategic calculation, not an ontological preference or belief. Of course, an ontological preference or belief may lurk behind the choice of methodology, but need not. The suffix is the key; *genic* is intended to convey the notion of a beginning or starting point. Thus, an investigator adopting an anthropogenic approach to cognition starts with the human case in the belief that the features of human cognition are the most plausible and potentially fruitful (possibly the only) guide to understanding the phenomenon of cognition generally. By contrast, an investigator adopting a biogenic approach assumes that the principles of biological organization present the most productive route to a general understanding of the principles of cognition because natural cognition is a biological process. Whether a machine can be engineered to either mimic or instantiate these processes is beside the point.

Assuming that the human case is the best starting point for an inquiry into mind is the oldest approach in the western philosophical and scientific tradition, and remains the dominant approach today. This is hardly surprising. We humans initially identify the features of the 'mental' domain as phenomena requiring description or explanation in the same way we identify spatial qualities and other features of the 'physical' world — through our experience of them (Fehr, 1991). Just as all human cultures appear to have words for 'big' and 'small', 'near' and 'far', so too do they have words for 'think', 'know', 'want', 'feel', 'see' and 'hear' (Wierzbicka 1996) — although it is important to remember that 'cognition' and 'mind' are not universal terms.

An argument in favour of the anthropogenic approach might run something like this. If cognition is a phenomenon amenable to scientific study and explication, then we would best profit by focusing our attention on the instance about which we are certain and with which we are most familiar. The most plausible (arguably the only) current candidate for a paradigmatic exemplar of cognition is human cognition. This is not to suggest that in the final analysis human cognition will prove to be the only or even the most typical example of the phenomenon. Indeed, it may prove to be quite atypical, depending on how a general concept of cognition shapes up. It is, rather, merely to point out the obvious: that human cognition is the sole example of the phenomenon upon which everyone can agree at this stage of investigation. Human beings, uncontroversially, are cognitive beings, however cognition ultimately may be cashed out scientifically. Cognition may not be an exclusively human phenomenon, but it nevertheless stands to reason that the properties of the human mind, which we know to a first approximation based on our own experience, will provide the best guide to developing a diagnostic criterion for determining which sorts of systems are cognitive and which are not.

Cognition not only is identified in the first instance as a describable phenomenon via human experience—the experience of thinking, feeling, wanting, believing, knowing, hearing, seeing, etc.—but also is apprehended elsewhere in the natural world, when it is so apprehended, based largely upon the prevailing understanding of the human case. This was so in pre-scientific times (Earle, 1881; Aristotle, 2001) and remains so today. This is not to imply that an anthropogenic approach to cognition is intrinsically anthropocentric; it need not be. Explanatory targets and starting points are not always identical. A researcher taking an anthropogenic approach might argue, however, that the only way cognitive features such as perception and memory can be identified in other animal species in the first instance is by virtue of their apparent similarity to the human exemplification of perception and memory. We have words for 'perception' and 'memory' to make sense of our own experience; they were not invented to account for non-human behaviours. We necessarily generalize from the human case; we cannot help but do so, as the anthropomorphism deeply embedded in ordinary language attests (Kennedy, 1992).

Contemporary theories of cognition need not explicitly take account of evolution (Fodor, 2005), but generally speaking, they aim to be consistent, more or less, with evolutionary theory. This means that features of human cognition are likely to be instantiated, to a greater or lesser extent, in our nearest primate relatives and, perhaps, other animals. Thus, the study of animal cognition, and primate cognition in particular, are potentially germane to the study of human cognition from the anthropogenic perspective. However, often an anthropogenic approach seems to presuppose a substantial, if not radical, cognitive discontinuity between humans (and perhaps their closest relatives) and other animals, which is how categorical concerns about anthropomorphism arise (Keely, 2004). An anthropogenic approach also is more likely to suggest that whether an animal can be said to be cognitive or not depends upon the degree of similarity its behavioural capacities bear to those of human beings (Shettleworth, 1993). Of course, estimations of which human cognitive features are most crucial for an ascription of mentality (e.g., consciousness, language, imagining the absent, 'theory of mind') vary widely. 'Similarity', too, is construed with varying degrees of liberality according to different criteria. Thus a worker adopting an anthropogenic approach could remain agnostic as to where on the phylogenetic bush cognition emerges—or even if it emerges solely in a biological context. (She could be a panpsychist, for example, or a worker in artificial intelligence.) Whether such agnosticism is found in practice is another matter.

The anthropogenic approach to cognitive explanation does not begin with René Descartes, but he is probably the best pre-20th century exemplar. Descartes' approach to cognition is anthropogenic because of its starting point (the human mind); his method of investigation (analytical introspection); and his assertion that a radical typological discontinuity exists between human beings and the rest of the natural world (Descartes, 1641/1986). Descartes conceived of thinking, as against perception or memory, as a capacity exclusive to humans, and the capacity for thought as dependent upon a special kind of substance (*res cogitans*), shared by no other living being.

The Biogenic Approach To Cognition

By contract, an investigator adopting a biogenic approach to cognition assumes that the properties and principles of biological organization present the most productive route to a general understanding of the properties and principles of what we now think of as cognition: the processes by which humans and presumably other biological systems come to know the world. The rationale behind this assumption is simple. Cognition as we know it—however we may conceive it in the future, and wherever else it may be found beyond the human domain—serves a biological function. Human beings are cognitive, and human beings are biological organisms. Cognition, however that ultimately may be characterized, exists because it makes a substantial contribution to the survival, wellbeing and reproduction of the human animal. For this reason, human cognition is still highly relevant to an investigator adopting a biogenic approach. After all, an adequate theory must account for the features of human cognition, and investigation of human cognitive capacities has generated a large amount of valuable data.

For the biogenic approach, however, human cognition is not the benchmark. While humans are obviously important to the study of cognition as a biological function—human traits typically are what we are most interested in—*Homo sapiens* is a privileged source of data only relative to human cognition. There is no assumption that human cognition is the 'most developed' or 'perfected' form of the biological function, however extraordinary and complex it may be. As modern biology moves ever further away from its essentialist roots in the *Scala naturae*, scientific justification for 'typological thinking' — the idea that a particular species or race is a 'generalized representative' of an entire order or class of phenomena — also diminishes (Hodos and Campbell, 1969/1996, p. 257). Thus even among closely related phyla, there are differences that reflect unique adaptive histories as well as shared features.

The second major difference between the biogenic and anthropogenic approaches is that evolutionary continuity, the idea that complex forms of life and organic process have evolved from simpler forms, is a *presupposition* of the biogenic approach, not an enforced necessity to accord with the current state of scientific theory. The principle of evolutionary continuity and the related principle of evolutionary convergence bear upon a biogenic approach to cognition in two ways. First, adaptations contributing to an organism's survival, wellbeing and reproduction tend to be conserved (positively selected) over evolutionary time. Molecular biology provides ample demonstration that this is overwhelmingly the case. Second, the repertoire of functional responses to identical or similar existential challenges tend to be rather more limited than mathematical possibility suggests (see, for example, Weinreich *et al.*, 2006), not least because new biological solutions to changing environmental conditions tend to be built on processes whose usefulness is already demonstrated. Because all animate systems must acquire energy from the environment, transform it into usable forms, discharge waste and reproduce they all also share certain generic functions, such as ingestion, digestion, circulation, respiration, elimination and replication. The heart of a leech and a human are neither homologous (descended from a common ancestor) nor do they bear much structural resemblance, but both organs pump blood to circulate oxygen and other nutrients and to remove wastes.

Finally, as the preceding discussion suggests, a biogenic approach must take seriously the material conditions within which cognition arises in a way an anthropogenic approach need not. Whereas an anthropogenic inquiry may proceed in utter disregard of the material instantiation of cognition, as we will see in the next section, a biogenic approach simply cannot. In biology, the elucidation of any type of function entails elucidation of a material mechanism.

In sum, a researcher who takes a biogenic approach assumes that the nature of cognition is best understood in the general context of biological organization and functioning, not in the specific context of the human instantiations of these functions. Cognition may prove to be a complex, multifaceted global function, like respiration, without which no organism can survive, or it may be a complex but more circumscribed trait, like avian song learning, that provides an adaptive advantage only for those lineages that possess it. Whereas an anthropogenic approach can more easily assume that cognition might be an example of the latter rather than the former, a biogenic approach is more likely to treat it as the open empirical question it is in actual fact.

Aristotle may not be the most unambiguous exemplar of the biogenic approach, but he is unquestionably its historical progenitor. Aristotle voices what could be termed 'the biogenic lament' in the opening chapter of *De Anima*, his treatise on *psuche*.[2] '[U]p to the present time,' he writes, 'those who have discussed and investigated [*psuche*] seem to have confined themselves to the human [case]' (Aristotle, 2001, p. 536). Aristotle is not concerned with delineating the conditions for applying mental and physical predicates. In fact, he draws no distinction whatsoever between the mental and the physical (Frede, 1992); thus it has been argued that Aristotle 'properly speaking ... does not have a philosophy of mind' (Nussbaum and Putnam, 1992, p. 28). Rather, Aristotle is concerned with answering the question *What is it?* and explaining how identity persists through change. His answer is form, or functional organization (Lennox, 2001). Functional organization, the pattern of interactive relations among the constituents of matter, is what differentiates one thing from another and maintains identity over time despite, in the case of animate things, continuous change. Functional organization, on this account, is importantly related to a thing's 'nature' or *telos* (purpose, goal), the ultimate realization toward which its development and maintenance tend (Charles, 1995, p. 56). For example, Aristotle (presciently) hypothesizes that the distinctive characteristics of human cognition, which he identifies as calculative reason and the ability to overcome desire, are largely determined by social living, which demands the capacity for weighing alternatives and behavioural restraint.

---

[2] This term, often rendered (wrongly, in terms of contemporary orthography) as *psyche*, has no English equivalent. Although frequently rendered by the medieval Scholastics as 'soul', it does not equate with that term. As the 'form' of a living being *psuche* is mortal. Thus it accounts both for the characteristics of vitality and of mind. *Nous*, the 'active intellect' that enables philosophical reason is immortal (following Plato, and in puzzling contrast to the rest of Aristotle's philosophy), and thus is more akin to the Christian notion of 'soul'.

The advent of modern scientific psychology provides another example of the anthropogenic/biogenic distinction in the approaches of Wilhelm Wundt and William James. Wundt regarded immediate human experience as the special subject of psychology; he neither conducted nor sponsored animal experiments at a time when comparative psychology was becoming an active field (Watson, 1978). Wundt's psychological pursuits began with measuring the voluntary control of attention and moved to measuring sensations and feelings, which he believed to be the elements of consciousness (Wade, 1995). Wundt's experiments depended on his subjects' introspective reports—for example, of their awareness of changes in light intensity, colour brightness and hue, sound volume and so on—so his approach was necessarily anthropogenic. He took the human case as his starting point and paradigm, and from this experimental platform was able to derive a number of law-like generalizations about human psychology, many of which apply to nonhuman cognition (Blumenthal, 1980).

James (1890), by contrast, was more deeply influenced by the biological psychology of Herbert Spencer and Darwin's evolutionary theory. Although James draws liberally on human experience in developing his psychological ideas—his description of the mental effort required to arise from bed on a cold morning and his proposals regarding the 'stream of consciousness' are classics of introspection—he relies on biological principles to suggest what he takes to be the most general, defining features of mind. The 'mark and criterion of the presence of mentality' for James is not consciousness but, rather, 'the pursuance of future ends and the choice of means for their attainment' (James, 1890/1950, Vol. 1, p. 8). James derived his criterion from zoological observation. Reliance on biological principles to arrive at generalizations about the nature of mind places James squarely in the biogenic camp. His emphasis on goal orientation, or teleology, in psychological explanation also makes him Aristotle's heir.

Finally, it is important not to conflate the anthropogenic/biogenic distinction with another methodological distinction commonly drawn in the psychological literature between a 'psychological' approach and a 'biological' approach. The two sets of distinctions are not co-extensive. The psychological approach typically focuses on broad behavioural response patterns characterized as mental that are based on the wants and needs of a whole subject—usually, but not always, human and often in a social context—rather than the physiological details and biological principles underwriting the behavioural responses (Zachar, 2000). The biological approach, by contrast, targets the physiological details. A psychological approach to the emotions, for example, might be concerned with how the emotions fit into the cognitive economy of an individual or group of individuals; how they vary in differing contexts; how patterns of dysfunction manifest; and how patterns of affective response might have evolved (Stein *et al.*, 1990). A biological approach, on the other hand, would be concerned with brain structures, neuronal firing patterns, molecular dynamics and the genetic, developmental and other biological factors involved in the generation or modulation of affect. The psychological approach is often construed as 'top down,' meaning the phenomenon of interest is a complex global pattern of activity exhibited by an entire system. 'Bottom-up' approaches attempt to understand complex global properties in terms of their microstructural constituents. The biological approach is frequently identified as 'bottom-up', or reductionist, but this characterization is also erroneous. Biological mechanisms come in global as well as microstructural varieties, and in every sort in between.

Whether one takes the human case or the living state as the starting point for an empirical investigation of mind, both approaches are by definition 'psychological', in the above sense. After all, the phenomenon to be described and explained is cognition, which until the advent of *in vivo* brain imaging techniques was typically inferred from whole-organism patterns of behaviour. The source of controversy is just what sorts of behaviour indicate cognition. Both approaches are also necessarily 'biological', in the sense described above. Human beings, whatever else they may be, are animals. Moreover, contemporary scientific and philosophical opinion is univocal in asserting that human psychological capacities must be explained in the context of their biological underpinnings. Contra Deacon (1997), human biology is not 'almost incidental' to human cognitive capacities; it is the matrix from which they arise. Thus, an anthropogenic approach can be psychological *or* biological, that is, concerned with global behaviour patterns or with the physiological mechanisms that underpin them. Ditto for a biogenic approach. Likewise, a psychological approach need not be anthropogenic, nor a biological approach biogenic.

Why Cognitivism Is Anthropogenic

Cognitivism is anthropogenic by virtue of the conceptual framework adopted by the early cognitivists, their guiding metaphor (the computer), and the major tests and explanatory goals they set for themselves. This might strike some as counter-intuitive. Through its close association with philosophical functionalism, cognitivism is typically regarded as an ontologically neutral paradigm for investigating cognition that does not play favourites with respect to material circumstances, much less species (Shapiro, 2004). The Turing machine, the mathematical idealization upon which the von Neumann computer was based, at its simplest is a device to transform an input (some state of affairs represented in symbolic form) into an output by virtue of a specified procedure or set of instructions, typically referred to as a computational function or algorithm. In behaviouristic terms, the input can be conceived of as a stimulus condition, the output a behavioural response, and the computational function the intervening variables, including previous conditioning, that specify the correct behavioural response given the current state of the system and the type of stimulus involved. On the face of it, there is nothing intrinsically human about this picture. Indeed, its supposed wide applicability was very much part of its attraction.

It is worth recalling, therefore, that the Turing machine was conceived by its inventor explicitly as the mechanization of deliberative mathematical computation (Turing, 1936; Copeland, 1996). At the time Alan Turing proposed his hypothetical device, legions of men and women known as 'computers' were carrying out complex mathematical calculations according to task-specific protocols all over the world, in a wide variety of fields. Turing was convinced, and many agreed, the Turing machine captured the key features of the human intellectual procedure of calculation. Thus the Turing machine was an intrinsically anthropogenic construct. Even if a specific application of the Turing machine idea might have nothing explicitly to do with human capacities, cognitive or otherwise, its inspiration was a behaviour believed to be distinctively human.

The earliest uses to which the Turing machine concept was put also explicitly involved human capacities, for example, code-breaking during World War II. The McCulloch-Pitts model of the neuron, which was directly inspired by Turing's work, suggested that neurons could act as 'logic gates' capable of manipulating symbols according to Boolean functions. That the neurons in question were assumed to be in human brains follows from the fact that McCulloch, whose early research was influenced by logical atomism, originally conceived of the symbols being processed as elements of linguistic propositions. Early artificial reasoning machines were based on human symbol use and problem-solving capacities. Some (e.g., Logic Theorist, General Problem Solver) employed abstract rules and rules-of-thumb (heuristics) believed to reflect those used by humans when they solve logical problems, practical problems, or play logic-using games such as chess (Dreyfus 1972). Moreover, these and other AI programs were tested mainly using problems typically faced by humans, such as language learning or translation, ordering food in a restaurant, and understanding a story.

The Turing Test, long the grail of AI, was also construed in anthropogenic terms. A machine could be said to be 'intelligent' if in the course of an electronic conversation it could deceive a human being into believing (s)he were conversing with another human being and not a machine . The goal of classical AI – 'to replicate human level intelligence in a machine' (Brooks, 1991, p. 139) – which powerfully shaped cognitive science in the early decades, thus was unambiguously anthropogenic and, indeed, anthropocentric. This meant that when the over-arching problem of intelligence was decomposed into specialized sub-problems (e.g., knowledge representation, natural language understanding, vision, truth maintenance) areas were typically defined in terms of, and system performance 'benchmarked against the sorts of tasks humans do within those areas' (ibid.). The human case thus was the starting point for understanding cognition and the inspiration for designing cognitive systems. Although some still defend their usefulness (e.g., French, 2000), sentiment seems to be growing that the Turing machine and Turing Test have proved to be something of a dead-end in AI, to say nothing of understanding natural cognition (Chomsky, 1997; Sloman, 2002; Eliasmith, 2002).

Another pillar of cognitivism was Claude Shannon's mathematical theory of communication (Shannon and Weaver, 1949), also known as information theory. Information theoretic terminology (e.g. encoding, decoding, input, output, signal transduction, noise) is ubiquitous in the life sciences, so the utility of information theory clearly transcends the human case. However, while Shannon's sender-message-channel-receiver model can be viewed in abstract terms of some generality there is no denying that Shannon's original theory was aimed at *human* communication and his theory fits in the anthropogenic mould. An engineer at Bell Laboratories, Shannon was concerned with measuring the efficiency of electronic signal transmission and quantifying information flows within human communications systems (e.g., telephony, radio, television). Shannon's concept of information famously is mute with respect to its biologically most salient feature: content, or meaning. Information theory has been applied to the study of cognition more broadly (e.g., Dretske, 1981; Godfrey-Smith, 1996), but the theory's presuppositions remain grounded in the human case.

Computational functionalism and the 'multiple realizability thesis' provided the philosophical justification for equating cognition and computation, mind and computer (Putnam, 1975). Computational functionalism holds that explanations of mental phenomena cannot be reduced to 'nothing-but' explanations of physical processes in a particular kind of system (e.g., a human brain). What matters is what a mental state does, what causal role it occupies in the system of which it is a part. A mental state is nothing over and above its causal role, which can be considered free of a particular material context, which theoretically could be many sorts of stuff. What makes computational functionalism anthropogenic is its tight linkage to AI and the common recourse to aspects of human experience (e.g., pain states, believing, desiring) or its science fiction equivalents (e.g., Martian pain, qualia-free zombies).

The psychology of language, especially Noam Chomsky's proposals, also contributed powerfully to the development of cognitivism by challenging the explanatory hegemony of Skinnerian behaviourism and suggesting causally efficacious internal mechanisms for language learning and use. Boldly for his time, Chomsky proposed that an innate mental ordering 'faculty' provides the syntactic structure in virtue of which children rapidly acquire language, despite the poverty of the stimuli with which they are presented. Fodor extended Chomsky's faculty approach to cognition more generally through his influential 'language of thought' hypothesis, which helped shape the agenda for classical cognitivism. Again, while aspects of the framework and its subsequent elaborations could be generalized to nonhuman species, the starting point (and indeed the focus) was human cognition.

The idea that the human mind has intrinsic power to structure experience and can know things prior to sensory experience is ancient, but its modern champion was Descartes, who as we have seen is the classical exemplar of the anthropogenic approach. Most significant for cognitivism is Descartes' view of what mentality crucially involves: *representation*, or the mind's capacity for making objects within itself both of things-in-the-world and of things-never-before-seen-in-the-world. Although he did not introduce the idea, mental representation was the 'core feature' of Cartesian psychology (Wheeler, 2005, p. 25) and became the core feature of 'the traditional cognitive science program' (Fodor, 1998, p. vii). Descartes claimed that perceptually guided intelligent action is a series of cycles in which some feature of the world is sensed, represented by the mind, the representation manipulated in some way, and action (including further representation) initiated (Wheeler, 2005). This putative cycle of sense-represent-plan-act was long the 'generic organizing principle' of classical AI (Putnam, 1975).

The nature of representational content and how it is acquired became the focus of much hypothesis and debate. Two aspects will serve to illustrate the anthropogenic bias of these explorations: the role of *inference*, long considered an exclusively human preserve, and the concern with *intentionality*. Inference, as used here, does not refer to deductive reasoning but, rather, to various forms of ampliative reasoning, inductive and abductive. Descartes suggested that an epistemic gap exists in human cognition between sensory perception, of which animals are capable, and the mental representation of a sensory object, which he believed only humans can do. An act of judgment 'essentially inferential in nature' was believed to fill the gap (Wheeler, 2005, p. 42). Helmholtz put psychophysical flesh on this idea with his hypothesis that human visual perception is a constructive process whereby the properties of objects are inferred on the basis of 'premises' supplied by the retinal image and unconscious 'assumptions' built into the structure of the perceptual apparatus (Rock 1983). The idea that mammalian behavioural outputs go beyond the information contained in stimulus inputs was the basis of the 'knowledge state' postulated to intervene between stimulus and response by 'cognitive' behaviourists like Tolman (Bindra, 1984).

Although their interpretations differed, philosophers in the Anglophone analytic and European phenomenological traditions were for years in unaccustomed agreement about the distinguishing characteristic of mentality: intentionality, or 'the mind's capacity to direct itself on things' (Crane, 1998). The term originated with the medieval Scholastic philosophers, was resurrected by Brentano in the late 19th century, and denotes 'concepts, notions or whatever it is before the mind in thought' (ibid.). 'Brentano's thesis' stimulated a huge and still expanding literature concerned (in the analytical tradition) with beliefs, desires and other so-called propositional attitudes. This licensed folk psychological 'intuitions' in cognitive theorizing in a way it never has been (or, arguably, could be) in any other science. The classic example is the 'intentional stance' (Dennett, 1987). Adopting an intentional stance means treating a system (any system) as a rational agent and figuring out what its beliefs and desires are likely to be. Thus we can often understand and predict what such a system will do without needing to know about its detailed physical makeup. Both the concept of intentionality and the intentional stance have been liberally applied to simple organisms and artefacts such as thermostats. Indeed, delineating 'genuine' from 'derived' or 'merely imputed' intentionality became something of a small cottage industry. Dennett (1994) himself suggests we 'don't ask' when it comes to determining where or when biological systems acquired 'genuine' intentionality. However, both concept and stance originate in an analysis of human mentality, and their only truly unproblematic applications are in the human domain.

Initially, the dominance of functionalism meant that recourse to brain science could be perfunctory or totally absent. When neurobiology began to figure in the design of computer architectures or theoretical speculations about the nature of mental content, however, reliance on the human or mammalian brain as the benchmark — 'brain chauvinism' — was never far away (Vertosick, 2002). The bias dates back two centuries to Lamarck, who dictated that 'no mental function shall be ascribed to an organism for which the complexity of the nervous system of the organism is insufficient' (Bateson, 1979, pp. 93–94). Lamarck's criterion was not seriously challenged until the latter 20th century (Maturana, 1970).

In sum, the disciplines that contributed significantly to the emergence of cognitive science — e.g., AI, linguistics, psychology, philosophy, neuroscience, anthropology — to a large extent assumed a human starting point. Cybernetics, or mathematical control theory, whose homeostasis-like feedback principles were critical to the project of designing a mind, was neither biogenic nor unambiguously anthropogenic, but it also was not especially influential in the formulation of cognitivism's central tenets (Dupuy, 2000; Bindra, 1984). The anthropogenic nature of cognitivism can also be seen in its would-be rivals, all of which were much closer to a biogenic approach, for example, the 'ecological approach' to perception (Gibson, 1979); evolutionary epistemology (Campbell, 1974); and the autopoietic theory of cognition (Maturana, 1970). Biogenic hypotheses remained fringe concerns until cognivitism's 'identity crisis' began in the mid-1980s.

Problems Associated with the Human Stain

Cognitivism has been hampered by all kinds of problems from its inception, most of them well known and some of them already mentioned. Lack of traction on these problems has been related to the neglect of action and emotion (Freeman and Nuñez 1999), and the ways in which the elements of human cognition, such as concepts, function in everyday life (Rosch 1999; Auyang 2000). Two of the major conundrums for cognitivism—the 'frame problem' and the 'symbol-grounding problem'—continue to be the subject of (diminishing) research, although they emerged decades ago.[3] Trying to solve some of these problems has led increasing numbers of researchers to diverge from the ultra-cognitivist approach.

The failures of the serial, symbol-processing, syntax-centric approach of classic AI, for example, led to rediscovery of neural networks and parallel distributed processing, and thus to connectionism. The impasse that resulted from trying to simulate human problem-solving led roboticist Rodney Brooks, for one, to strike out in a new direction. Turning for inspiration to 'the way in which Earth-based biological evolution spent its time' constructing intelligence, Brooks concluded that the hard part of intelligent behaviour—the bit that took the most time—was developing 'the ability to move around in a dynamic environment, sensing the surroundings to a degree sufficient to achieve the necessary maintenance of life and reproduction' (Brooks, 1991, p. 141). Brooks' suggestion that intelligence is possible without representation became something of a manifesto for the embodied cognition movement and led to an assault on this cornerstone of cognitivism that continues unabated (Van Gelder, 1995; Cliff and Noble, 1997; Keijzer, 2001; Beer, 1990; Haselager *et al.*, 2003).

[3] The frame problem relates to how a cognizer updates the parameters of a problem-solving context as result of an action, when the parameters that can change are potentially immense and the predictability of which ones will change rather limited. The symbol-grounding problem arises from the silence of information theory regarding semantic content, which raises the question how elements subject to computation come to mean anything at all if cognition is essentially syntactic.

Cognitive robotics and the goal of creating artificial intelligence remain a lively research area, but computational functionalism — the license for equating biological and machine cognition — has taken serious knocks. Denounced by its founder as 'utopian' and 'science fiction' rather than a 'serious empirical hypothesis' (Putnam, 1997, p. 38), computational functionalism appears to be experiencing a large-scale defection (see, for example, Shapiro, 2004; Churchland, 2005). Nevertheless, the explanatory agenda of computational functionalism — to explain cognition in humans (and any other species for which the attribution is justified) in such a way that the explanation also covers intelligent artefacts — appears to be largely intact.

The concern to be both a specialized science and an engineering science meant that cognitivist cognitive science sought to be a *naturalized* but not wholly *natural* science. Motivated in large part by philosophical concerns with metaphysical dualism, the naturalism project initiated by Quine deferred to natural science even as it failed to appreciate its method (Chomsky, 2000; Hacker, 2006). As Chomsky points out, naturalized cognitive science sought to build machines to meet performance criteria rather than to explain the natural phenomena the machines were designed to mimic. Moreover, they were designed largely in ignorance of the latest empirical data relating to cognitive processes. No other natural science has ever proceeded on such an abstract basis (Chomsky, 1997). No surprise, then, that agreement about the chief explanatory goals of the general enterprise remains highly elusive.

The deep problem of the cognitive sciences is that *there is no 'problem'*. Innumerable highly specialized problems exist but few of broad generality on which researchers agree. Although the three key questions set out by Bechtel and colleagues make sense, they are not pursued in any systematic way. Because the fundamental issues remain untouched, data continue to be churned out at a staggering rate in many hundreds of journals but with little means of making sense of them — as De Waal (2002, p. 187) puts it, 'thousands of ideas that are barely interconnected' (but see also Silver 1998; Staats 1999; Sternberg and Grigorenko, 2001). The history of science strongly suggests that systematic inquiry progresses most effectively, as distinct from merely expanding, when there is a certain degree of consensus at the foundations.[4] While disciplinary confusion is not new in the sciences concerned with cognition and human behaviour (Toulmin, 1972; Staats, 1983), the illumination provided by cognitivism during the four decades of its dominance appears to have been, for the most part, illusory.

The difficulties bequeathed by Cartesian psychology, although by now cliché, are worth rehearsing if only because some arguably arise from taking an anthropogenic approach. Two examples will suffice. First is the problem of metaphysical dualism. Studies with children suggest that dualism is the naïve human ontology; by the age of three children draw a fairly strong ontological distinction between mental and physical things (Bloom, 2004). This suggests that an alternative metaphysics must be acquired, either by enculturation or ratiocination. Thus, while an anthropogenic approach to cognition might assume a form of materialism, dualism is the more 'intuitive' metaphysical stance. If metaphysical dualism is false, then it is an error to which an anthropogenic approach leads quite naturally. A biogenic approach, by contrast, does not lead easily to dualism.

Second is the 'homunculus problem,' the idea that cognition is effected by a 'little man in the head' who interprets and uses mental representations in the generation of behaviour. The homuncular inference arguably is the common result of Descartes' chief method, analytical introspection.[5] The naïve felt human experience of the introspecting 'I' is of a place (e.g., head, heart) or a quasi-person (i.e., a faint reflection of the introspecting subject) where percept, concept, affect, drive and whatever else combine to make a mental state, although neurobiological evidence strongly suggests no locus exists where 'it all comes together' (Austin, 2000). It is hard to imagine how the homunculus problem could arise without introspection. Descartes' account of animal perception, memory and bodily movement, which was based on physiological investigation, has no use for a homunculus (Sutton, 1998).

[4] It is sobering to note that in the same time span that psychology has considered itself a science — 150 years — physics passed from the postulation of a heliocentric model of the solar system, which inspired Galileo to advance the mathematical model of physics, to the discovery of the three standard laws of motion, the law of universal gravitation and definition of the principal terms that would inform research for the next 300 years. All this was possible without benefit of mass publication, global electronic communication, computers, instruments of astonishing precision and large publicly and privately funded research teams.

[5] Certain deep states of meditation are known to yield a 'subject-less' or 'centre-less' experience (Austin, 2000).

In sum, while necessary for a complete understanding of cognition the anthropogenic approach appears ill-suited to the project of demarcating the cognitive domain, and cognitivism particularly so. The failure to do so despite centuries of anthropogenic theorizing and half a century of intensive research under the cognitivist paradigm supports this claim. Not only has cognitivism generated a number of problems that remain so-far intractable, it provided few empirical constraints to theorizing, another feature that differentiates the enterprise from other natural sciences. As we will see in the next section, the biogenic approach provides a substantial number of empirical constraints, which in our view is one of its great virtues for the ontological project.

Why a Biogenic Approach Is Suited to the Ontological Project

Lyon (2006b) sets out 17 empirical principles[6] that constrain biogenic theorizing about cognition. These principles both guide and set limits on hypotheses. As mentioned earlier, a biogenic approach presupposes that organisms are products of evolution by natural selection, and that complex biological functions, including cognition, have evolved from simpler forms of biological function. More important to biogenic theorizing about cognition, however, is the fact that organisms maintain themselves in a far from thermodynamic equilibrium by importing 'order' from their surroundings in the form of matter and energy, chemically transforming it to do work, and exporting 'disorder' in the form of waste products of various sorts. Living systems thus are forced to establish causal relations with features of their surroundings that lead to exchanges of matter and energy, which are essential to the organism's persistence, wellbeing and/or reproduction. Of necessity, then, organisms exhibit a wide variety of control and regulatory mechanisms, including multiple kinds of feedback mechanism, which maintain the system's fluctuating but steady state. Even in the simplest organisms (e.g., bacteria) control hierarchies regulate vital processes. Biological activities that have functions (e.g., homeostatic processes) operate within a range of values outside of which the organism's persistence or wellbeing is threatened. Essential functions thus are generally linked, directly or indirectly, strongly or weakly, to one another.

---

[6] Several additional principles were derived between publication of Lyon (2006a) and Lyon (2006b), the latter providing the most detailed treatment and the references for this summary.

Moreover, organisms are autopoietic; they are continually being produced by a network of components, which are themselves being continually produced by networks of components. At the same time that this continual production cycle is under way, the organism as a whole is interacting with a surrounding medium (as are the organism's constituent components within their local milieu). Because the features of its surrounding medium are constantly changing at varying time scales, an organism must have one or more mechanisms for reducing or managing the impact of environmental variability on its functioning. To persist, grow, thrive or reproduce, an organism must continually adapt to regular or stochastic fluctuations in the surrounding medium by altering its internal structure and/or its interactive relation to features of that medium. This is adaptive behaviour.

A state of affairs that stimulates an organism to adaptive behaviour (i.e., alteration of its internal structure and/or its interactive relation to environmental features) conveys information for that organism. Adaptive behaviour thus is dependent upon information. However, an organism is not capable of interacting profitably with all of the features of its environment, only some of them; hence not every state of affairs is information for that organism. Differentiation among states of affairs involves the comparison of what is happening now relative to what was happening at some moment in the past; this requires memory. Based on its evolutionary and interactive history and current needs, an organism responds to different states of affairs according to an internal projection of value—attractive, aversive or neutral salience—relative to its own persistence or wellbeing.

Finally, organisms are operationally closed, as well as open to flows of matter and energy. The activities that produce and maintain an organism take place within a semi-permeable boundary, which is the basis of its autonomy. As operationally closed (bounded) entities, organisms differentiate states of affairs that are permissible or belong within the boundary (self) from other phenomena (non-self). Although past events affect their adaptive behaviour, organisms are intrinsically oriented toward what happens next.

There are several things to notice about these constraints. First is that the options for theorizing remain wide open. Not as open across the material spectrum as computational functionalism would allow, perhaps, but more open along the biological spectrum than cognitivism typically admits. There is no *a priori* reason why data relating to, say, the learning and memory of the fruit fly *Drosophila melanogaster* has no bearing on an understanding of the biological function of learning and memory in humans, for example. Neither does a biogenic approach require that such data be taken into account. Remember, the biogenic approach is a methodological starting point, not a detailed prescription for conducting cognitive science, nor a prediction of what the results will be. However, a biogenic approach licenses the use of simple model systems of the sort that have been responsible for so much progress in the rest of the life sciences, without demanding tortuous explanations of why they might be useful, as is typically the case with an anthropogenic approach.

The second thing to notice about a biogenic approach is that it provides a wider range of properties and/or criteria for delineating the cognitive domain, such as the capacity to differentiate among and differentially value states of affairs within a context. Whereas cognitivism focused on rational problem solving as against emotion and feeling—which reflected the traditional 'trilogy of the mind' (Hilgard, 1980)—the biogenic principles do not provide *prima facie* justification for carving psychological nature at these particular joints. Indeed, they suggest what empirical evidence more than amply demonstrates: that the classic trilogy of cognition, emotion and motivation are principally heuristic, and at the level of physiology are more or less fictional (Lazarus, 1990).

The third thing to notice is that a biogenic approach allows a fundamental starting point for articulating what a minimal form of cognition might look like, more about which in a moment. It might seem that aligning the investigation of cognition so closely with that of the conditions of biological existence would lead to a potentially unproductive blurring of vital and cognitive processes. Indeed there are some biogenic approaches that emphatically claim that all life is cognition (Maturana & Varela, 1980; Stewart, 1996), or vice versa. This blurring can be avoided, however. The fundament of autopoiesis lies with self-producing metabolic interactions within a semi-permeable boundary. In addition there are systematic interactions between the autopoietic organization itself and its environment. These interactions can take many forms, some of which go beyond the fundamental level of molecular and energy exchanges. One important form can be described as sensorimotor coordination or basic behaviour. Basic behaviour is the sort that humans have in common with all animals, apes and insects alike (Keijzer, 2001). Examples include moving about over natural surfaces, using sensory stimulation to initiate, guide and terminate action, and performing behavioural sequences. Basic behaviour derives from the use of movements locked in step with sensory feedback resulting from these movements. The resulting sensorimotor couplings can modify environmental conditions in ways that enhance, overall, an organism's metabolic and reproductive success. For example, basic behaviour brings organisms into proximity with nutritive substances, lets them ingest these, enables the avoidance of predators, finding and courting mates, and so on.

We want to stress that basic behaviour is not defined in terms of these functional regularities, a strong tendency within behaviourism (Keijzer, 2005). Similar functionality is produced by very different means in organisms with varying body forms. Basic behaviour builds on a specific body structure—involving specific movement and sensing capabilities—as well as a dynamical structure provided by the sensorimotor couplings in which the organism takes part. The specifics of these sensorimotor couplings have their own information-processing characteristics influencing whole-system behaviour (Lungarella & Sporns, 2006). The focus on detailed morphological and sensorimotor organization makes basic behaviour a congenial domain for the investigation of minimal forms of cognitive phenomena in a way that is markedly different from sophisticated contemporary versions of behaviourism (Keijzer, 2005).

The structural organization of basic behaviour can already be differentiated from that of more fundamental metabolic processes in bacteria. The signal transduction pathways that underlie chemotaxis, movement toward or away from a feature of the environment, can be clearly differentiated from molecular pathways that underlie nutrient metabolism, although the two functions (chemotaxis, nutrient metabolism) are clearly structurally linked and both are subject, under stress conditions, to global regulatory control (Van Duijn *et al.*, 2006). Thus sensorimotor coordination sub-serves metabolism and reproduction, but is itself a different kind of process, which is played out at the global scale of a whole organism.

The recourse to a bacterial example is not facetious. Although typically regarded in the cognitive scientific literature as automata, bacteria display behaviour that is far more flexible, complex and adaptive—not merely adapted—than commonly believed (Lyon,

2006b, submitted).[7] Bacteria have memory, select actions based on the integration of multiple environmental cues sampled over time, amplify faint chemical signals by several orders of magnitude, 'tune' signal-to-noise ratios of their sensory perceptions, gain new behavioural competences to cope with changing environmental conditions via the acquisition of foreign DNA (including sex), and communicate with one another to effect complex behaviour, enabling populations to function as multicellular individuals. Some of the mechanisms that underlie these capacities in bacteria are also used in mammals, including humans. For example, the two-component signal transduction mechanism of bacterial chemotaxis involves a sensor and a response regulator that relies on the addition and subsequent removal of chemical moieties (e.g., phosphorylation, methylation). This mechanism is the basis of signal transduction within (not between) neurons, for example, in relation to neurotransmitters and neuromodulators such as serotonin and dopamine. Bacterial sensory perception is also subject to habituation and amplification, which are basic to the operation of human perception.

Casting basic behaviour and sensorimotor coordination as minimal forms of cognition provides a principled starting point for answering question concerning what cognition is. Moreover, it is a starting point that is organizationally separable from fundamental metabolic processes that constitute the heart of living organization (Van Duijn et al., 2006). Sensorimotor coordination sub-serves metabolism but is itself a different kind of process played out at a larger scale of whole organisms acting as a unity on its environment by physical displacements of this unity with respect to the environment. In other words, the key point is the switch from molecular interactions to whole organism motility. This issue is especially important as it dissociates cognition from any intrinsic connection with nervous systems. Sensorimotor coordination is essential, whether or not it involves a nervous system. The whole organism may be large with respect to metabolic processes, but as in the case of bacteria can still remain extremely small compared to us.

Sensorimotor coordination and basic behaviour also provide a principled starting point for explaining what features—behavioural, cognitive and experiential—the evolution of nervous systems add to this minimal set-up. Nevertheless, being a *nervous*

---

[7] See these two sources for a detailed treatment of and evidentiary support for these claims.

system is not necessarily what makes it special, but how it operates within a particular sensorimotor organization. Of course, the above is at present primarily the sketch of an option, but at the very least it gives an indication how a biogenic approach can turn into a very concrete project aimed at answering fundamental questions, such as what cognition is and what cognition does.

In sum, a biogenic approach provides a principled, specifically empirical rationale for taking sensorimotor coordination as a starting point for investigating the fundamental issues relating to cognition, but it also suggests that the historically necessary connection of cognition with a nervous system is less motivated than once it was, and thus may require justification in a way it previously did not.

Squinting against the Intentional Glare

Although the shape of second-generation cognitive science is coming into focus, we have argued that simply taking an embodied, embedded and situated approach will not be enough to eradicate the distorting residue of cognitivism's human stain. By acknowledging that the only cognitive mechanisms about which we are certain are those that have evolved in biological systems constantly engaged in body-world interactions, embodied cognition exhorts us to take prevailing biological knowledge and evolutionary theory seriously. But biology can be taken seriously in all sorts of ways. One need not *begin* with the principles of biology to ensure at a minimum that one's theory of mind does not *contravene* those principles. Whereas a biogenic approach to cognition is intrinsically embodied, an embodied approach need not be biogenic. Assuming that beliefs and desires are the *sine qua non* of cognition and then building a plausible biological case for how they function in the economy of an animal, and how they might have evolved, may be a thoroughly embodied approach, but it is not biogenic. Beliefs and desires derive their privileged status in cognitive science from folk psychology, and 'the folk' are necessarily human. It is quite another thing to derive a picture of what cognition is and what it does from the principles of biology and then see how beliefs and desires (such as we experience them) arise from that matrix.

The divergent concerns that flow from the usually tacit, possibly unconscious choice about starting points make addressing basic issues of discipline-related ontology in the cognitive sciences especially troublesome, in our view. But addressed they must be, if there is any hope of drawing together the disparate empirical strands of inquiry in the myriad disciplines concerned with cognition. The business of addressing these basic issues is complicated, not helped, by keeping one eye on the human case, as cognitivism has, not least because it licenses appeals to personal, culturally conditioned 'intuitions' in ways that are unsupportable in other natural sciences. What the natural sciences have generally taught us is that our untutored intuitions are almost always false. The world is not flat, the sun does not revolve around the earth, solid objects are mostly space, and the diverse kingdoms of life are vastly more similar than ordinary observation would suggest. To provide a credible answer to the basic ontological questions — what is cognition and what does it do — the cognitive sciences will have to become fully natural, not simply naturalized, sciences. Their best hope, we believe, is taking far more seriously than they have to date the over-arching knowledge enterprise in which they are embedded, the science of life.

References

Aristotle (2001), 'De Anima', in ed. R. McKeon, *The Basic Works of Aristotle* (New York: Modern Library Classics/Random House).

Austin, J.H. (2000), *Zen and the Brain: Toward and Understanding of Meditation and Consciousness* (Cambridge, MA: MIT Press).

Auyang, S.Y. (2000), *Mind in Everyday Life and Cognitive Science* (Cambridge, MA: MIT Press).

Bassler, B. and Losick, R. (2006), 'Bacterially speaking', *Cell*, 125(2), pp. 237–246.

Bateson, G. (1979), *Mind and Nature: A Necessary Unity* (New York: E.P. Dutton).

Bechtel, W., Abrahamsen, A. and Graham, G. (1998), 'The life of cognitive science', in ed. W. Bechtel and G. Graham, *A Companion to Cognitive Science* (Malden, MA and Oxford: Blackwell Publishers Ltd.), pp. 1–104.

Beer, R.D. (1990), *Intelligence as Adaptive Behavior: An Experiments in Computational Neuroethology* (San Diego: Academic Press).

Bennett, M.R. and Hacker, P.M.S. (2003), *Philosophical Foundations of Neuroscience* (Oxford: Blackwell Publishing).

Bickhard, M.H. (2001), 'Why children don't have to solve the frame problems: cognitive representations are not encodings', *Developmental Review*, 21, pp. 224–262.

Bindra, D. (1984), 'Cognition: its orgin and future in psychology', in ed. J.R. Royce and L.P. Mos, *Annals of Theoretical Psychology, Vol. 1* (New York: Plenum Press), pp. 1–29.

Bloom, P. (2004), *Descartes' Baby: How the Science of Child Development Explains What Makes Us Human* (New York: Basic Books).

Blumenthal, A.L. (1980), 'Wilhelm Wundt and early American psychology: a clash of cultures', in ed. R.W. Rieber and K. Salzinger, *Psychology: Theoretical-Historical Perspectives* (New York: Academic Press), pp. 25–42.

Boden, M.A. (2006), *Mind as Machine: A History of Cognitive Science* (Oxford: Oxford University Press).

Brooks, R. (1991), 'Intelligence without representation', *Artificial Intelligence*, 47(1-3), pp. 139–159.

Campbell, D.T. (1974), 'Evolutionary epistemology', in ed. P.A. Schlipp, *The Philosophy of Karl Popper, Vol. 1* (La Salle, Ill.: Open Court), pp. 413–463.

Charles, D. (1995), 'Aristotle', in ed. T. Honderich, *The Oxford Companion to Philosophy* (Oxford: Oxford University Press), pp. 53–57.

Chomsky, N. (1997), 'Language and cognition', in ed. D.M. Johnson and C.E. Erneling, *The Future of the Cognitive Revolution* (Oxford: Oxford University Press), pp. 15–31.

Chomsky, N. (2000), 'Naturalism and dualism in the study of language and mind', in ed. N. Chomsky, *New Horizons in the Study of Language and Mind* (Cambridge and New York: Cambridge University Press).

Churchland, P.M. (2005), 'Functionalism at forty: a critical retrospective', *Journal of Philosophy*, CII,(1), pp. 33-50.

Clark, A. (1997), *Being There: Putting Brain, body and World Back Together Again* (Cambridge, MA: MIT Press).

Cliff, D. and Noble, J. (1997), 'Knowledge-based vision and simple visual machines', *Philosophical Transactions: Biological Sciences (Royal Society of London)*, 352, pp. 1165–1175.

Copeland, B.J. (1996), 'What is computation?', *Synthese*, 108(3), pp. 335–359.

Crane, T. (1998), 'Intentionality: history of the concept of intentionality', in ed. E. Craig, *Routledge Encyclopedia of Philosophy* (London: Routledge), retrieved 28 November 2005, from
  http://www.rep.routledge.com.virtual.anu.edu.au/article/V019SECT1.

De Waal, F.B.M. (2001), *The Ape and the Sushi Master: Cultural Reflections by a Primatologist* (London: Allen Lane).

De Waal, F.B.M. (2002), 'Evolutionary psychology: the wheat from the chaff', *Current Directions in Psychological Science*, 11(6), pp. 187–191.

Deacon, T.W. (1997), *The Symbolic Species: The Co-Evolution of Language and the Brain* (New York: W.W. Norton & Company).

Dennett, D.C. (1987), *The Intentional Stance* (Cambridge, MA: MIT Press).

Dennett, D.C. (1994), 'Daniel C. Dennett', in ed. S. Guttenplan, *A Companion to the Philosophy of Mind* (Oxford: Basil Blackwell Ltd).

Descartes, R. (1641/1986), *Meditations on First Philosophy* (Cambridge: Cambridge University Press).

Dretske, F. (1981), *Knowledge and the Flow of Information* (Cambridge, MA: MIT Press).

Dreyfus, H.L. (1972), *What Computers Can't Do: A Critique of Artificial Reason* (New York: Harper & Row).

Dupuy, J-P. (2000), *The Mechanization of the Mind: On the Origins of Cognitive Science* (Princeton, N.J.: Princeton University Press).

Earle, J. (1881), 'The history of the word "mind"', *Mind*, 6(23), pp. 301–320.

Eliasmith, C. (2002), 'The myth of the Turing machine: the failings of functionalism and related theses', *Journal of Experimental and Theoretical Artificial Intelligence*, 14, pp. 1–8.

Fehr, E.S. (1991), 'Mind and body: an apparent perceptual error', *Journal of Mind and Behavior*, 12(3), pp. 393–406.

Fodor, J.A. (1975), *The Language of Thought* (New York: Thomas Y. Crowell).

Fodor, J.A. (1998), *In Critical Condition: Polemical Essays on Cognitive Science and the Philosophy of Mind* (Cambridge, MA: MIT Press).

Fodor, J.A. (2000), *The Mind Doesn't Work That Way: The Scope and Limits of Computational Psychology* (Cambridge, MA: MIT Press).

Fodor, J.A. (2005), 'Reply to Steven Pinker: So how *does* the mind work?', *Mind and Language*, 20(1), pp. 25–32.

Frede, M. (1992), 'On Aristotle's conception of the soul', in ed. M.C. Nussbaum and A.O. Rorty, *Essays on Aristotle's* De Anima (Oxford: Clarendon Press), pp. 93–107.

Freeman, W.J. and Nuñez, R. (1999), 'Restoring to cognition the forgotten primacy of action, intention and emotion', in ed. W.J. Freeman and R. Nuñez, *Reclaiming Cognition: The Primacy of Action, Intention and Emotion* (Thorverton: Imprint Academic), pp. ix–xix.

French, R.M. (2000), 'The Turing Test: the first 50 years', *Trends in Cognitive Sciences*, 4(3), pp. 115–122.

Gallese, V. and Lakoff, G. (2005), 'The brain's concepts: the role of the sensory-motor system in conceptual knowledge', *Cognitive Neuropsychology*, 22(3/4), pp. 455–479.

Gardner, H. (1985), *The Mind's New Science: A History of the Cognitive Revolution* (New York: Basic Books).

Gibson, J.J. (1979), *The Ecological Approach to Visual Perception* (Dallas: Houghton Mifflin).

Godfrey-Smith, P. (1996), *Complexity and the Function of Mind in Nature* (Cambridge: Cambridge University Press).

Goodson, F.E. (2003), *The Evolution and Function of Cognition* (Mahwah, NJ: Lawrence Erlbaum Associates).

Green, D.C. (1996), 'Where did the word 'cognitive' come from anyway?', *Canadian Psychology*, 37, pp. 31–39.

Green, D.C. (2000), 'Is AI the right method for cognitive science?', *Psycholoquy*, 11(061), pp. 1-7.

Hacker, P.M.S. (2006), 'Passing by the naturalistic turn on Quine's cul-de-sac', *Philosophy*, 81(2), pp. 231–253.

Harnad, S. (2005), 'To cognize is to categorize: Cognition is categorization', in ed. C. Cohen and C. LeFebvre, *Handbook of Categorization in Cognitive Science* (Amsterdam: Elsevier Science).

Hartley, T.A. (2004), 'Does cognitive neuropsychology have a future?', *Cognitive Neuropsychology*, 21(1), pp. 3–16.

Haselager, P., de Groot, A. and van Rappard, H. (2003), 'Representationalism vs. anti-representationalism: a debate for the sake of appearance', *Philosophical Psychology*, 16(1), pp. 5–23.

Hilgard, E.R. (1980), 'The trilogy of mind: cognition, affection, and conation', *Journal of the History of the Behavioral Sciences*, 16, pp. 107–116.

Hodos, W. and Campbell, C.B.G. (1969/1996), '*Scala Naturae*: why there is not theory in comparative psychology', in ed. L.D. Houck and L.C. Drickamer, *Foundations of Animal Behavior: Classic Papers with Commentaries* (Chicago: University of Chicago Press), pp. 246–259.
James, W. (1890/1950), *The Principles of Psychology, Vol. 1* (New York: Dover Publications Inc.).
Jennings, H.S. (1906/1962), *Behavior of the Lower Organisms* (Bloomington: Indiana University Press).
Johnson, D.M. and Erneling, C.E. (1997), *The Future of the Cognitive Revolution* (New York and Oxford: Oxford University Press).
Keely, B.L. (2004), 'Anthropomorphism, primatomorphism, mammalomorphism: Understanding cross-species comparisons', *Biology and Philosophy*, 19(4), pp. 489–520.
Keijzer, F.A. (2001), *Representation and Behavior* (Cambridge, MA: MIT Press).
Keijzer, F.A. (2005), 'Theoretical behaviorism meets embodied cognition: Two theoretical analyses of behavior', *Philosophical psychology*, 18(1), pp. 123-143.
Kennedy, J.S. (1992), *The New Anthropomorphism* (Cambridge: Cambridge University Press).
Lazarus, R.S. (1990), 'Constructs of the mind in adaptation', in eds. N. Stein, B. Leventhal and T. Trabasso, *Psychological and Biological Approaches to Emotion* (Hillsdale, N.J.: Lawrence Erlbaum Publishers), pp. 3–19.
Lennox, J.G. (2001), *Aristotle's Philosophy of Biology: Studies in the Origins of Life Science* (Cambridge: Cambridge University Press).
Lungarella, M. and Sporns, O. (2006). 'Mapping information flow in sensorimotor networks', *PloS Computational Biology*, 2(10), pp. 1301–1312.
Lyon, P. (2004), 'Autopoiesis and *knowing*: Maturana's biogenic explanation of cognition', *Cybernetics and Human Knowing*, 11(4), pp. 21–46.
Lyon, P. (2006a), 'The biogenic approach to cognition', *Cognitive Processing*, 7(1), pp. 11–29.
Lyon, P. (2006b), *The Agent in the Organism: Toward a Biogenic Theory of Cognition*, PhD thesis (Canberra: Australian National University).
Lyon, P. (submitted), 'The cognitive cell: bacterial behaviour revisited', *Biology & Philosophy*.
Maturana, H.R. (1970), 'The biology of cognition', in ed. H.R. Maturana and F.J. Varela, *Autopoiesis and Cognition: The Realization of the Living* (Dordrecht: D. Reidel Publishing Company).
Maturana, H.R. and Varela, F.J. (1980), *Autopoiesis and Cognition: The Realization of the Living* (Dordrecht: D. Reidel Publishing Company).
Moreno, A., Umerez, J. and Ibañez, J. (1997), 'Cognition and life: the autonomy of cognition', *Brain and Cognition*, 34(1), pp. 107–129.
Neisser, U. (1976), *Cognition and Reality: Principles and Implications of Cognitive Psychology* (San Francisco: W.H. Freeman and Company).
Nussbaum, M.C. and Putnam, H. (1992), 'Changing Aristotle's mind', in ed. M.C. Nussbaum and A.O. Rorty, *Essays on Aristotle's* De Anima (Oxford: Clarendon Press), pp. 27–56.
Ochman, H. and Moran, N.A. (2001), 'Genes lost and genes found; evolution of bacterial pathogenesis and symbiosis', *Science*, 292, pp. 1096–1098.

Putnam, H. (1975), *Mind, Language, and Reality: Philosophical Papers, Vol. 2* (Cambridge: Cambridge University Press).
Putnam, H. (1997), 'Functionalism: cognitive science or science fiction?', in ed. D.M. Johnson and C.E. Erneling, *The Future of the Cognitive Revolution* (Oxford: Oxford University Press), pp. 32-44.
Ragan, M.A. (2001), 'Detection of lateral gene transfer among microbial genomes', *Current Opinion in Genetics and Development*, 11(6), pp. 620-626.
Rock, I. (1983), *The Logic of Perception* (Cambridge, MA: MIT Press).
Rosch, E. (1999), 'Reclaiming concepts, in ed. W.J. Freeman and R. Nuñez, *Reclaiming Cognition: The Primacy of Action, Intention and Emotion* (Thorverton: Imprint Academic), pp. 61-78.
Rose, S. (1998), 'The rise of neurogenetic determinism', in ed. J. Cornwell, *Consciousness and Human Identity* (Oxford: Oxford University Press), pp. 86-100.
Rosenzweig, M.R., Leiman, A.L. and Breedlove, S.M. (1996), *Biological Psychology* (Sunderland, MA: Sinauer Associates Inc.).
Shannon, C.E. and Weaver, W. (1949), *The Mathematical Theory of Communication* (Urbana: University of Illinois Press).
Shapiro, L.A. (2004), *The Mind Incarnate* (Cambridge, MA: MIT Press).
Shettleworth, S.J. (1993), 'Where is the comparison in comparative cognition – alternative research programs', *Psychological Science*, 4(3), pp. 179-184.
Shettleworth, S.J. (1998), *Cognition, Evolution and Behavior* (New York and Oxford: Oxford University Press).
Silver, B.L. (1998), *The Ascent of Science* (New York and Oxford: Oxford University Press).
Sloman, A. (2002), 'The irrelevance of Turing machines to artificial intelligence', in ed. M. Scheutz, *Computationalism: New Directions* (Cambridge, MA: MIT Press).
Sorley, W.R. (1926), 'Fifty years of *Mind*', *Mind*, 35(140), pp. 409-418.
Staats, A. (1983), *Psychology's Crisis of Disunity: Philosophy and Method for a Unified Science* (New York: Praeger Press).
Staats, A. (1999), 'Unifying psychology requires new infrastructure, theory, method, and a research agenda', *Review of General Psychology*, 3(1), pp. 3-13.
Stein, N., Leventhal, B. and Trabasso, T. (1990), *Psychological and Biological Approaches to Emotion* (Hillsdale, N.J.: Lawrence Erlbaum Publishers).
Sternberg, R.J. and Grigorenko, E.L. (2001), 'Unified psychology', *American Psychologist*, 56(12), pp. 1069-1079.
Stewart, J. (1996), 'Cognition=life: implications for higher-level cognition', *Behavioural Processes*, 35(1-3), pp. 311-326.
Sutton, J. (1998), *Philosophy and Memory Traces: Descartes to Connectionism* (Cambridge: Cambridge University Press).
Toulmin, S. (1972), *Human Understanding, Vol. 1, General Introduction and Part I, The Collective Use and Evolution of Concepts* (Oxford: Clarendon Press).
Toulmin, S. (1998), *Cognition, Evolution and Behavior* (New York and Oxford: Oxford University Press).
Turing, A.M. (1950), 'Computing machinery and intelligence', *Mind*, 59(236), pp. 433-460.

Turing, A.M. (1936), 'On computable numbers, with an application to the *Entscheidungsproblem*', *Proceedings of the London Mathematical Society*, 42(2), pp. 230–265

Van Duijn, M., Keijzer, F.A.. & Franken, D. (2006), Principles of minimal cognition: Casting cognition as sensorimotor coordination. *Adaptive Behavior*, 14(2), pp. 157–170.

Van Gelder, T. (1995), 'What might cognition be, if not computation?', *Journal of Philosophy*, XCI(7), pp. 345–381.

Varela, F.J., Thompson, E. and Rosch, E. (1991), *The Embodied Mind: Cognitive Science and Human Experience* (Cambridge, MA: MIT Press).

Vertosick, F.T. (2002), *The Genius Within: Discovering the Intelligence of Every Living Thing* (New York: Harcourt, Inc.).

Wade, N. (1995), *Psychologists in Word and Image* (Cambridge, MA: MIT Press).

Washburn, M.F. (1936), *The Animal Mind: A Text-Book of Comparative Psychology* (New York: MacMillan Company).

Watson, R.I. (1978), *The Great Psychologists* (Philadelphia: J.B. Lippincott).

Weinreich, D.M., Delaney, N.F., DePristo, M.A. and Hartl, D.L. (2006), 'Darwinian evolution can follow only very few mutational paths to fitter proteins', *Science*, 312, pp. 111–114.

Wellman, H.M. (1990), *The Child's Theory of Mind* (Cambridge, MA: MIT Press).

Wheeler, M. (2005), *Reconstructing the Cognitive World: The Next Step* (Cambridge, MA: MIT Press).

Wierzbicka, A. (1996), *Semantics: Primes and Universals* (Oxford: Oxford University Press).

Winograd, T. and Flores, F. (1986), *Understanding Computers and Cognition: A New Foundation for Design* (Norwood, NJ: 1Ablex Publishing Corporation).

Zachar, P. (2000), *Psychological Concepts and Biological Psychiatry: A Philosophical Analysis* (Philadelphia: John Benjamins Publishing).

Alan Costall

How Will We Know When We Have Become Post-Cognitivists?

... subject and object antithetically defined can have logically no transactions with each other (Dewey, 1925/1958, p. 239).

once radically parted from the object, the subject reduces to its own measure; the subject swallows the object, forgetting how much it is an object itself (Adorno, 1982, p. 499).

Introduction

Some years ago, Arthur Still and I edited *Cognitive psychology in question* (Costall & Still, 1987) and a revised version, *Against cognitivism* (Still & Costall, 1991), in an attempt to bring together some of the main criticisms of cognitivism, as well as setting out some alternatives. These books were not widely read, but there were several reviews. One was sympathetic (Sternberg, 1988). The rest were negative, even hostile. We were accused of challenging a straw man. We were chastised for not acknowledging how cognitive psychology had liberated us all from behaviourism. We were even subject to diagnosis. According to Sharkey (1988, p. 340), Arthur Still and I 'must have both been bitten by rabid cognitivists in early childhood.' One reviewer, of an especially sensitive disposition, ended up completely beside himself:

> This book almost makes one envy the illiterate. Rarely has a work of such woolliness of thought, meandering prose, and gross self-congratulation appeared. ... I have tried long and hard, but cannot think of anything complementary [sic] to say about this book (Stuart-Hamilton, 1988, p. 411).

But what would happen if things got *really* nasty, and a committee of *un*cognitivist activities was set up to track down dissenters, and investigate whether we were (or ever had been) post-cognitivists? How would they know? How would *we* know? How could we tell if we had finally put cognitivism behind us?

At the time that Arthur Still and I published our books, the critics of 'cognitivism' seemed to have a reasonably definite target: *representationalism*, the general and fundamental appeal within psychological theory to rules and representations that are supposed to underlie, and generate, behaviour. However, as I will be arguing in this chapter, there is much more to 'cognitivism' than 'representationalism'. Representationalism is just the *surface* of cognitivism.

'Cognition' and 'Cognitivism'

Although 'cognitivism' is a relatively recent term, it is closely linked to 'cognition', a term with a long history. Cognition had a central place in scholastic thought, with its three-fold division of cognition, conation, and emotion. For many centuries, cognition has figured in a theoretical framework that I have come to call 'the schema of perception-and-cognition' (Costall, 2006a), where 'the deliverances of the senses' are supposed to be disorganized and meaningless, and only become coherent and meaningful through the intervention of the intellect which imposes form upon our otherwise chaotic experience (Hatfield & Epstein, 1979). This ancient schema remains central to modern cognitive theory, although now 'the deliverances of the senses' are rebranded as 'sensory input', and the 'intellect' as 'cognitive processing and enrichment'.

The term 'cognition' was certainly used within mainstream psychology long before the rise of modern cognitive psychology, as in Charles Spearman's *Nature of intelligence and principles of cognition* (1923).[1] However, according to Moroz (1972, p. 178), the first mention of 'cognition' in the introductory textbooks of psychology was as recent as 1966, in McKeachie & Doyle's *Psychology*. Even in the 1970s, some mainstream psychologists were still protesting that they had no idea what this now fashionable term actually *meant*:

---

[1] The first English-language textbook with the title, *Cognitive Psychology*, was written by Dom Thomas Verner Moore (1939), a Benedictine monk, but the approach adopted links back to the tradition of scholastic philosophy rather than anticipating the forthcoming 'cognitive revolution' (see Knapp, 1986).

> Querying colleagues about its meaning, I received a response direct but confusing (as that a child might receive when asking where he came from) or operationally precise but circular ... (Brown, 1976, p. 357)

> What makes the current high popularity of cognition especially astounding is that even its most dedicated advocates seem unable to provide us with a clear or consistent definition of exactly what is meant by or encompassed under the cognitive label, or how it is to be distinguished from the allegedly noncognitive character of whatever is (or was) not described as cognitive psychology (Battig, 1975, p. 195).

Moroz (1972) attempted to arrive at a definition of cognition appropriate for contemporary psychology, but had to admit he found it remarkably difficult. Instead, he referred to Robert Leeper's chapter on 'cognitive processes' in Stevens' prestigious *Handbook of Experimental Psychology* (Leeper, 1951). Leeper began his chapter by raising the issue of whether cognition should be defined in terms of particular psychological processes, or in relation to what he called an '*approach*'. In terms of processes, he considered whether the scope of the definition should be restricted to thinking or even specific kinds of thinking, or else be more inclusive to cover perception and remembering. Leeper wondered whether 'consciousness' should figure in the definition of cognition, but, drawing upon the early introspective research on imageless and sensationless thought, he concluded that cognition could indeed be unconscious. The definition Leeper finally settled upon sounds surprisingly modern:

> ... cognitive processes include all the means whereby the individual represents anything to himself or uses these representations as a means of guiding his behavior. It is in this broader sense that the term 'cognitive processes,' after virtually disappearing from the vocabulary of psychology, has been reappearing in the writings of [some] psychologists. ... (Leeper, 1951, p. 737).[2]

Leeper's definition of cognition in terms of representation embodies the source of our later perplexities. For his definition is ambiguous. It can be taken as based either upon *a field of inquiry* or else upon *a theoretical, indeed metatheoretical, approach*. Regarded as a field of inquiry,

---

[2] Leeper then cites the work of Heidbreder (1945) on thinking and Tolman (1932) on purposive behaviour, but, curiously, also the work of Adams (1931) and Hilgard (1948) on learning, the main field of behaviourist psychology. In fact, the new cognitive approaches of the 1950s and 1960s made some of their earliest appearances in the textbooks in the field of 'learning theory' [e.g. the chapter on 'information processing models' in Hilgard & Bower, (1966)].

the study of cognition would be reasonably restricted to those limited but important areas of human life where people manifestly engage in representation of various kinds as a general way of guiding their activities. However, as an 'approach' there is, in principle, no limit to the application of the term 'cognition' well beyond the restricted realm of thinking, planning, classifying, and so on. Already by the 1980s, psychology had almost entirely redefined itself as the science of 'cognition'. As William Kessen complained:

> Friendship has become social cognition, affect is seen as a form of problem-solving, new-born perception is subsumed under a set of transforming rules, and psychoanalysis is reread as a variant of information processing. Cognition, the feeble infant of the late Fifties and early Sixties, has become an apparently insatiable giant (Kessen, 1981, p. 168).

The computer is often supposed to have provided the first existence proof for the viability of representation as a respectable basis of scientific explanation. Yet, we ourselves have surely already provided a closer to hand 'existence proof'. After all, we do, among many other things, engage in representation. Interestingly, when Simon and Newell first 'ran' their general problem solving system, they did not use a computer at all. Their family and students were enlisted to enact the various stages of processing (Gigerenzer & Goldstein, 1996).

Now the fact that we *sometimes* manifestly engage in representation does give representational*ism* a good deal of initial plausibility, even though one of the crucial claims of representationalism is that the majority of 'cognitive processes' are not manifest but hidden away in the 'cognitive unconscious' only to be revealed very indirectly by the methods of experimental research.

As Jerry Fodor has pointed out, although representationalism is now closely identified with the modern metaphor of the mind as computer software, 'insofar as the Representational Theory of Mind is the content of the computer metaphor, the computer metaphor predates the computer by about three hundred years' (Fodor, 1981, p. 140). However, Fodor made little mention of the fact that *fundamental* problems had already been identified with representationalism long before the rise of modern cognitive psychology. Representationalism cannot, in principle, explain how mental representations come to have meaning, or how mental representations and rules can be applied intelligently and flexibly to actual situations. These problems were raised in the early days of the new cognitivism (see Shaw, 2003), and there have been several important, sustained critiques of representationalism over the last few years (e.g. Bichard & Richie, 1983; Bichard & Teerven, 1995; Bichard, 1996; Buttone *et al.*, 1995; Bennett & Hacker, 2003; Coulter, 1983; Dreyfus, 1992; Lave, 1988; Shanon, 1993; Winograd & Flores, 1986).

Representationalism remains, nevertheless, the predominant game in town. This is not just the case for the mainstream of cognitive psychology. Representationalism is also promoted by those claiming to take seriously the problem of *grounding* cognition, and even by those setting out apparently radical, socio-cultural alternatives to the individualism of mainstream cognitive psychology:

> Successful interaction with objects in the environment is the precondition for our survival and for the success of our attempts to improve life by using artifacts and technologies to transform our environment. *Our ability to interact appropriately with objects depends on the capacity, fundamental for human beings, for categorizing objects and storing information about them, thus forming concepts, and on the capacity to associate concepts with names* (Borghi, 2005, p. 8; emphasis added).

> Where discursive and cultural psychology come together is in the recognition given to *the primacy of representation* (discourse, mediation, etc), and its location in situated social practices rather than abstracted mental models (Edwards, 1995, p. 63; emphasis added).

> Representation is a fundamental process of all human life; it underlies the development of mind, self, societies and cultures. … The reality of the human world is in its *entirety* made of representation; in fact there is no sense of reality for our human world without the work of representation (Jovchelovitch, 2006, p. 10; emphasis added).

There is, however, much more to cognitivism than representationalism, including the dualisms of the subjective and objective, of matter and mind, of body and mind, and of meaning and materiality.

The dualism of the subjective and the objective

Few psychologists really appreciate the fundamental role that subject-object dualism played in the rise of classical physical science. The remarkable successes of the new physical science—its wide application to the 'heavens', to earthly events, and even to the understanding of the human body—encouraged its proponents to make highly ambitious claims on its behalf. Thus, according to Descartes, the new physics was nothing less than an all-embracing science of nature. However, the implication of this claim was that anything failing to figure within that science *must exist beyond the realm of the natural* (Wilson, 1980, pp. 41–42).

Despite all of his solitary cogitation, Descartes was not acting alone. Galileo and Kepler, among many others, also engaged in a similar 'ontological fix' to save the universal claims of the new physics (Burtt, 1969; Whitehead, 1926; Young, 1966). Their general line was that the new science was in the business of explaining *everything—and* hence everything the new science failed to explain was not *really* real.[3] Within this scheme, therefore, psychology's eventual subject became radically subjectivized, as that which *eludes* scientific methods. As Alexandre Koyré put it:

> [Modern science] broke down the barriers that separated the heavens and the earth …. [But] it did this by substituting for our world of quality and sense perception, the world in which we live, and love, and die, another world - the world of quantity, of reified geometry, a world in which, though there is a place for everything, there is no place for man (Koyré, 1965, p. 24).

Classical science 'set up' psychology to be a very odd kind of enterprise. Once physical science had promoted its methodology (of atomism, mechanism, and quantification) to the status of an exclusive ontology, psychology was a pretty obvious mistake just waiting to be made, a science that would take on the awkward residue of the 'subjective' which classical science had already defined in opposition to the 'objective' and hence beyond the reach of scientific method.

Most modern cognitive psychologists would protest that they are certainly not dualists in the sense of retaining an *ontological* opposition between mind and matter. Yet stark dualisms keep showing up in their theory and practice, the first of these being the closely allied dualism of *meaning* and *materiality*.

The dualism of meaning and materiality.

One important implication of the dualist ontology of classical science is that the world is devoid of significance, and that meaning and qualities (such as colour and warmth) are purely subjective, disconnected from the material nature of things (see Costall & Dreier, 2006). Thus meaning and quality are supposed to be projected onto the world in the form of individual or collective representations. Here is Stuart Hall, a sociologist actually concerned with 'material

---

[3] For example, Galileo's treatment of the 'secondary qualities' (Burtt, 1932), and the strict bounds that Kepler put upon his mechanistic account of vision, based on the analogy of eye and camera (Straker, 1976).

culture', and someone who would hardly count as a cognitive psychologist, nevertheless restating the basic idea:

> According to [our constructivist approach], we must not confuse the material world, where things and people exist, and the symbolic practices and processes through which representation, meaning and language operate. Constructivists do not deny the existence of the material world. However, *it is not the material world which conveys meaning: it is the language system or whatever system we are using to represent our concepts* (Hall, 1997, p. 25; emphasis added).

This assumption that meaning resides exclusively within us, either individually or in our shared systems of representation, is widespread within the human sciences, and fundamental to representationalism.

The dualism of mind and body.

The dualism of subject and object also appears in a more specific form as mind-body dualism. Curiously many psychologists regard the classic computer metaphor of cognitive theory as undermining *mind-body* dualism, since 'brain and mind are *bound* together as computer and program,' (Johnson-Laird, 1988, p. 23, emphasis added). In fact the computer metaphor represents a remarkable 'condensation' of most of the important problems behind representationalism. First of all, knowledge and meaning are *identified* with representation: there is no meaning beyond the realm of *re*-presentation. And then the computer metaphor, far from being anti-dualistic, implies two different dualisms: (1) the antithesis of mind and matter, since the software is separable from *any* hardware, and (2) the antithesis of meaning and materiality, since meaning is located exclusively within the software as self-enclosed symbols. As Pylyshyn revealingly put it, cognitive psychology is 'a science of structure and function *divorced from material substance*' (Pylyshyn, 1986, p. 68; emphasis added).

The Cartesian *ontological* dualism of *body* and *mind* has a further important implication. According to this scheme, the mind is supposed to be the only *active* principle in the universe, and hence the body (along with the rest of physical nature) must be regarded as essentially passive. Despite its claimed rejection of mechanistic behaviourism, and the new emphasis upon the highly active nature of 'cognition,' cognitive psychology blatantly retains this passive schema of the body as a reactive mechanism.

Curiously, a commitment to a stimulus-response conception of the body is restated every time cognitive psychologists try to explain how they have rejected mechanistic behaviourism. Here are Baars and McGovern (1994, p. 370), in their review of *Against Cognitivism*, patiently setting out the case for the necessity of cognitivist theorizing:

> scientific psychology, contrary to behavioristic doctrine, *must* make inferences beyond the bare observable *stimuli and responses* (emphases added).

Turn the pages of any text on cognitive psychology, and you will find passages such as the following where stimulus-response psychology is reinstated in the very act of pretending to reject it:

> [...] the dramatic shift away from behaviorism, which dominated the field for over thirty years, to cognitivism, ... [has] allowed one to study not just learning but memory, not just speech but language, and *not just stimulus and response but the processes that mediate them* (Hirst, 1988, p. vii, emphasis added).

Here is Rom Harré (2002, p. 104) appearing to reject stimulus-response psychology, while actually presenting us with a more elaborate version. He is using the specific example of word recognition to make a much more general point about how we should theorize in psychology:

> Instead of the behaviorist pattern:
>
> Stimulus (retinal sensation)
> → Response (perception of word)
>
> we must have:
>
> Observable stimulus (retinal sensation) together with unobservable Cognitive process ('knowledge utilization')
> → Observable response (recognition of word)

Donald Hebb remains an exception among mainstream psychologists in taking any notice of the fundamental commitment to stimulus-response thinking within the new cognitivism. In his presidential address to the American Psychological Association, he identified the *intimate connection* between cognitive theorizing and stimulus-response behaviorism:

> ... the whole meaning of the term 'cognitive' depends on [the stimulus-response idea], though cognitive psychologists seem unaware of the fact. The term is not a good one, but it does have meaning as a reference to features of behavior that do not fit the S-R formula; and no other meaning at all as far as one can discover. The formula, then, has two values: first, it provides a rea-

sonable explanation of much reflexive human behavior, not to mention the behavior of lower animals; and secondly, it provides a fundamental analytical tool, by which to distinguish between lower (noncognitive) and higher (cognitive) forms of behavior (Hebb, 1960, p. 737).

Far from challenging this dualism of a highly active mind, and a completely inert stimulus-response body, the computer metaphors of cognitive theory not only reformulate this dichotomy in seemingly modern ways, but in a form that would have made even Descartes protest (see Costall, 2007). For, according to the ideal of a computer as a 'general purpose machine', the body as 'hardware' could have absolutely no significance in psychological theory other than as an uninteresting input-output 'interface' (see Brooks, 1991). This is because the software alone is supposed to be the sole constraint upon the functioning of the hardware. Thus modern cognitive theorizing has been based upon *two* machine metaphors, that of an active computer ('mind' or that strange hybrid 'mind/brain'), and a passive stimulus-response interface ('body').

The dualism of mind and 'behaviour'.

In addition to the retention of the mechanistic stimulus-response formula, modern psychology has also taken over other important features of the methodology of neo-behaviourism, not least 'methodological behaviourism'.

Fundamental continuities between cognitive psychology and behaviourism have, however, been obscured by the hype about a 'cognitive revolution' (see Leahey, 1992). The 'textbook' histories of psychology typically present us with the following three stages:

1. Introspectionist psychology, established by Wilhelm Wundt, which defined psychology as a science of the *mind*, based almost exclusively upon the method of introspection.

2. Behaviourism, instigated by J.B. Watson, which rejected the method of introspection as unreliable, and consciousness as a proper object of scientific study. Instead, psychology was redefined as the science of behaviour.

3. Cognitive psychology, pioneered by a host of characters, which rejected behaviourism's limited agenda, and restored psychology's status as a science of *mind*.

As I have argued elsewhere, this three-stage history is largely mythical (Costall, 2006b). In particular, the rise of cognitive psychology did not herald a radical break with the behaviourist past (cf. Miller, 2003).

Interestingly, even the textbooks themselves acknowledge the serious methodological debt that cognitive psychology is supposed to owe to behaviourism. Here is an example from Hebb's early textbook:

> If Watson's work is seen as [a] house-cleaning operation ... , its importance becomes clearer. ... In 1913 the whole case for mental processes seemed to depend on introspection; if it did, the case was a bad one, and 'mind' had to be discarded from scientific consideration until better evidence could be found. ... Paradoxically, it was the denial of mental processes that put our knowledge of them on a firm foundation, and from this approach we have learned much more about the mind than was known when it was taken for granted more or less uncritically (Hebb, 1966, p. 5–6).

Here is a much more recent example, again presenting cognitive psychology as a *synthesis*, based on the methodology developed by the behaviourists:

> Because psychologists were growing impatient with introspection, the new behaviorism caught on rapidly ... . The modern cognitive perspective is in part a return to the cognitive roots of psychology and in part a reaction to the narrowness of behaviorism and the S-R view ... . Like the 19th century version, the modern study of cognition is concerned with mental processes such as perceiving, remembering, reasoning, deciding, and problem solving. Unlike the 19th-century version, however, modern cognitivism is not based on introspection. Instead, it assumes (1) only by studying mental processes can we fully understand what organisms do, and (2) we can study mental processes in an objective fashion by focusing on specific behaviors (*just as behaviorists do*) but interpreting them in terms of underlying mental processes (Atkinson *et al.*, 2000, pp. 12–13; emphasis added).

What the textbooks, and indeed most of the psychological literature, fail to note is that the conception of behaviour, as it was reformulated within mainstream behaviourism, was as dualistic as the conceptions of mind and consciousness Watson and his followers rejected. Many of Watson's contemporary critics were well aware of his commitment to a *dualism* of mind and behaviour:

> ... in so far as behaviorists tend to ignore the social qualities of behavior, they are perpetuating exactly the tradition against which they are nominally protesting. To conceive behavior exclusively in terms of the changes going on within an organism physically separate in space from other organisms is to continue the conception of mind which Professor Perry has well termed 'subcutaneous'. This conception is appropriate to the theory of existence of a field or stream of consciousness *that is private by its*

very nature; it is the essence of such a theory (Dewey, 1914/1977, p. 445, emphasis added; see also Carr, 1915, p. 309; Heidbreder, 1933, pp. 267–68; Rubinstejn, 1937/1987, p. 13).

In their classic text, *Plans and the structure of behavior,* Miller, Pribram, and Galanter (1960) make a nice joke about having talked themselves into becoming 'subjective behaviorists' (p. 211). They were, nevertheless, concerned that the subject matter of the new cognitive psychology was 'distressingly invisible,' and that 'a science with invisible content is likely to become an invisible science' (p. 6). In contrast most psychologists are quite untroubled by the 'occult' status of their subject. They point to the fact that many well established sciences, such as atomic physics and genetics, are also, in effect, sciences of the *invisible*. Yet, there is crucial difference. According to the official, decontextualized, desubjectivized, *behaviouristic* conception of behaviour that persists in modern cognitive psychology, the evidential link between behaviour and mind is deeply problematic.

Curiously this fundamental problem of evidence is emphasized, even celebrated, in the context of Theory of Mind, where 'people' (i.e. non-psychologists) are supposed to face a *big* problem of bridging the supposed chasm between what they can *know* about another person (namely, their behaviour) and their 'psychological states', including their intentions, feelings, and beliefs. The 'theory-theory' approach to this problem has been to suppose that 'people' go about making sense of other people by engaging in inferences about their hidden mental states.

Historians of psychology have examined the many ways in which psychology has drawn upon its own methodological procedures for its theories. The theory-theory approach to Theory of Mind has taken this process to its extreme, where the *psychologists'* own conception of behaviour as *antithetic* to mind is projected onto people in general, and then *they* are supposed to deal with the profound problem of knowing other minds, by resorting to the kind of theoretical work undertaken by cognitive psychologists.

Although the mysterious gulf between observable behaviour and unobservable mental state is presented as an intriguing and fundamental research 'problem' *within* psychology, there is seldom any serious discussion of the methodological implications *for* psychology. How are *psychologists* themselves supposed to deal with this same, supposedly awesome gulf. It is certainly not enough to point to other sciences of the invisible, such as atomic physics or genetics.

For there is a crucial difference between those other sciences and the new cognitivism. Given the retention of a thoroughly behaviouristic, and hence dualistic, conception of 'behaviour', any logical connection between the behavioural data and 'other minds' is completely undermined (see Costall & Leudar, 2004; Leudar & Costall, 2004 a&b).[4]

Intellectualism and the Spectator Theory of Knowing

There are two further important schemas that underlie modern cognitivism. Although these are entangled with the dualisms I have already discussed, they also have their own distinctive histories. First of all, there is what John Dewey has called the fallacy of 'intellectualism,' the identification of human experience with reflective and abstract thought. The primacy of theoretical knowledge over practical skill runs deep within the Western tradition. But, as Dewey put it:

> The assumption of 'intellectualism' goes contrary to the facts of what is primarily experienced. For things are objects to be treated, used, acted upon and with, enjoyed and endured, even more than things to be known. They are things *had* before they are things cognized (Dewey, 1925/1958, p. 21).

A specific example of such intellectualism in psychological theory concerns the way that *classification* has come to be regarded as the fundamental and exclusive way in which people, and perhaps other animals too, are supposed to relate meaningfully to their surroundings. Although there have been some valuable attempts to situate classification socially (Bowker & Leigh Star, 2000), the primacy of classification has hardly been questioned. James Gibson seems to be almost unique in trying to develop a concept of meaning not restricted to our various practices of classification and representation; as Gibson put it, 'to perceive an affordance is not to classify an object' (Gibson, 1979, p. 134; see also Costall, 1995).

---

[4] The dark menace of behaviourism has discouraged serious explorations of alternatives to what Solomon Asch long ago characterized as 'cognitive behaviourism'. But there are alternatives, as proposed, for example, by the Dutch phenomenologist, Buytendijk (1950), and the Belgian psychologist, Nuttin (1955). 'Animals and men are observable subjects, when we understand behavior as a system of intentional acts' (Buytendijk, 1950, pp. 127–8).

Intellectualism is closely connected with the 'spectator theory of knowledge' (Dewey, 1969). Within the western tradition, there has long been the conviction, deriving from rationalism, that 'reality is ready-made and complete from all eternity', rather than 'still in the making' (James, 1907/1955, p. 167). Consequently, the differences made through our own presence and activities *in* this world are relegated to some other realm beyond the 'material world'. We thus end up as mere onlookers, positioned outside of the world to be known in a 'cultural world' constituted entirely of symbols. Within this perspective, of course, knowing could be nothing other than representation. Furthermore, as Dilthey stressed, both intellectualism and the spectator theory of knowledge go back a long way together, and have deeply affected the Western 'outlook':

> Dilthey repeatedly criticized what he termed 'ocularism' or 'opsis,' that is, an excessively detached and 'spectatorial' account of our relation to reality. Modern thought tended to conceive of the human subject as pure thought for which the known world is not the perceived world of lived experience but a logico-mathematical construct endowed with pure and timeless certainty. The paradoxical result of this disjunction between abstract reason and concrete experience was that 'since Descartes we have been taken up in building bridges to the external world'. ... (Emarth, 1978, p. 118).

Life After Cognitivism

In this chapter, I have tried to show that there is much more to 'cognitivism' than representationalism. It involves a complicated network of more fundamental assumptions. Furthermore, representationalist theory far from being the 'essence' of cognitivism is just the proliferation of attempts to 'solve' the deep problems posed by these more basic assumptions. For example, representations are invoked, among many other things, to 'solve' the following supposedly fundamental problems: how, despite our embodiment as stimulus-response machines, we respond flexibly and appropriately to stimuli; how, despite living in an inherently meaningless world, we experience our surroundings as apparently replete with significance; and how, despite the dualism of behaviour and mind, we nevertheless can make sense of other people.

Over a period when both physics and biology were both forced to rethink their foundations, modern psychology has become increasingly entrenched within a set of very old-fashioned assumptions, many connected with subject–object dualism. However, becoming post-cognitive involves a complicated agenda, since there are many fundamental issues at stake. But let us assume that we eventually do manage to become post-cognitivists. What then? First of all we should *not* attempt to set ourselves up as providing a post-cognitivist science of *cognition*. The term cognition is not only ambiguous but its various meanings are all theoretically loaded. Cognition can refer, firstly, to the 'cognitive approach' itself, secondly, to the so-called 'higher mental functions', and, finally, to 'knowing' in a general epistemic sense. Now this third sense of 'cognition' might seem to be entirely theoretically neutral, and yet it is not. To repeat Dewey's crucial point, we do not live our lives on this earth solely as knowers:

> ... things are objects to be treated, used, acted upon and with, enjoyed and endured, even more than things to be known. They are things *had* before they are things cognized (Dewey, 1925/1958, p. 21; see also Ingold, 2000).

Finally, and more radically, I want to suggest that in going beyond cognitivism we should *not* aspire to becoming post-cognitivist *psychologists*. A post-cognitive *psychology* is surely a serious contradiction in terms. The term 'psychology' over the last century or so, has served as a 'place holder' for an autonomous discipline (variously defined) which has sought anxiously to set itself apart from wider concerns and most other disciplines, such as philosophy, theology, ethics, politics, sociology, anthropology, biology, physiology, and the material sciences. The disjunctions between modern disciplines not only reflect the dualisms central to the Western intellectual tradition, they also perpetuate them. So, in the end, part of becoming post-cognitivists might require redefining the boundaries between existing disciplines, and, perhaps, rethinking disciplinarity itself.

References

Adams, D.K. (1931), 'A restatement of the problem of learning' *British Journal of General Psychology,* 22, pp. 150–178.

Adorno, T. (1982). Subject and object. In A. Arato & E. Berghardt (Eds.), *The Essential Frankfurt School Reader* (New York: Continuum), pp. 497–511.

Atkinson, R. L., Atkinson, R. C., Smith, E. E., Bem, D. J., & Nolen-Hoeksema, S. (2000). *Hilgard's Introduction to Psychology,* 13th ed. (Fort Worth, TX: Harcourt College Publishers).

Baars, B.J. & McGovern, K. (1994), 'How not to start a scientific revolution', *Contemporary Psychology,* 39, pp. 370–71.

Battig, William. (1975), 'Within-individual differences in "cognitive" processes', In R.L. Solso (Ed.), *Information Processing and Cognition* (Hillsdale, NJ: Lawrence Erlbaum Associates).

Bennett, M.R. & Hacker, P.M.S. (2003), *Philosophical Foundations of Neuroscience* (Oxford: Blackwell).

Bickhard, Mark H. (1996), 'Troubles with computationalism', In W. O'Donohue & R.F. Kitchener (Eds.), *The Philosophy of Psychology* (London: Sage), pp. 173–183.

Bickhard, M. H. & Richie, D. M. (1983), *On the Nature of Representation* (New York: Praeger).

Bickhard, M. H. & Terveen, L. (1995), *Foundational Issues In Artificial Intelligence and Cognitive Science: Impasse and Solution* (Amsterdam: Elsevier Scientific).

Borghi, Anna M. (2005), 'Object concepts and action', In Diane Pecher, & Rolf A. Zwaan (Eds.), *Grounding Cognition: The Role of Perception and Action In Memory, Language, and Thinking* (Cambridge: CUP), pp. 8–34.

Bowker, Geoffrey C. & Leigh Star, Susan (2000), *Sorting Things Out: Classification and its Consequences* (Cambridge, MA: MIT Press).

Brooks, R.A. (1991), 'Intelligence without representation', *Artificial Intelligence*, 47, pp. 139–159.

Brown, A.S. (1976), 'Review of Information Processing and Cognition: The Loyola Symposium', edited by Robert L. Solso. *American Journal of Psychology*, 89, pp. 357–361.

Burtt, E. A. (1923/1954), *The Metaphysical Foundations of Modern Physical Science* (New York: Anchor Books).

Button, G., Coulter, J., Lee, J. & Sharrock, W. (1995), *Computers, Minds and Conduct* (Oxford: Polity).

Buytendijk, F. J. J. (1950), 'The phenomenological approach to the problem of feelings and emotions', In M. L. Reymert (Ed.), *Feelings and Emotions: The Mooseheart Symposium* (New York: McGraw-Hill), pp. 127–8.

Carr, H. A. (1915), Review of J.B. Watson (1914). Behavior: an introduction to comparative psychology, *Psychological Bulletin*, 12, pp. 308–312.

Costall, A. (1995), 'Socializing affordances', *Theory and Psychology*, 5, pp. 467–481.

Costall, A. (2006),' Perception and cognition', In B.D. Midgley & E.K. Morris (Eds.), *Modern Perspectives on J.R. Kantor and Interbehaviorism* (Reno, NV: Context Press), pp. 205-18).

Costall, A. (2006b), 'Introspectionism and the mythical origins of modern scientific psychology', *Consciousness and Cognition,* 15, pp. 634-654.

Costall, A. (2007), 'Bringing the body back to life: James Gibson's ecology of agency', In J. Zlatev, T. Ziemke, R. Frank, & R. Dirven (Eds.), *Body, Language and Mind: 1: Embodiment* (The Hague: de Gruyter), pp. 241–270.

Costall, A. & Dreier,O. (2006), *Doing Things with Things: The Design and Use of Everyday Objects* (London: Ashgate).

Costall, A. & Still, A. (Eds.) (1987), *Cognitive Psychology In Question* (Brighton: Harvester Press).

Coulter, J. (1983), *Rethinking Cognitive Theory* (London: Macmillan).

Dewey, J. (1914/1977), 'Psychological doctrine and philosophical teaching', In S. Morgenbesser (Ed.), *Dewey and His Critics*. (New York: Journal of Philosophy, Inc.), pp. 439–445. [First published in the Journal of Philosophy Psychology and Scientific Methods, 1914, 11(19).]

Dewey, J. (1925/1958), *Experience and Nature* [Based on the Paul Carus lectures of 1925] (New York: Dover).

Dewey, J. (1969), *The Quest For Certainty* (New York: Putnam Pub Group).

Dreyfus, H. (1992), *What Computers Still Can't Do* (Cambridge, MA: MIT).
Edwards, D. (1995), 'A commentary on discursive and cultural psychology', *Culture and Psychology*, 1, pp. 55–65.
Ermarth, Michael (1978), *Wilhelm Dilthey: The critique of Historical Reason* (Chicago: University of Chicago Press).
Fodor, J. A. (1981), *Representations* (Cambridge, MA: MIT Press).
Gibson, J. J. (1979), *The Ecological Approach To Visual Perception* (Boston, MA: Houghton Mifflin.)
Gigerenzer, G. & Goldstein, D. G. (1996), 'Mind as computer: birth of a metaphor', *Creativity Research Journal*, 9, pp. 131–144.
Hall, Stuart (1997), 'The work of representation', In Stuart Hall (Ed.) *Representation: Cultural Representations and Signifying Practices* (London: Sage), pp. 13–64.
Harré, Rom (2002), *Cognitive Science: A Philosophical Introduction* (London: Sage).
Hatfield, G. C., & Epstein, W. (1979), 'The sensory core and the medieval foundations of early modern perceptual theory', *ISIS*, 70, pp. 363–84.
Hebb, Donald (1960), 'The American revolution', *American Psychologist*, 15, pp. 735–745.
Heidbreder, E. (1933), *Seven Psychologies* (New York: Century).
Heidbreder, F. (1945), 'Toward a dynamic psychology of thinking', *Psychological Review*, 52, pp. 1–22.
Hilgard, E.R. (1948), *Theories of Learning* (New York: Appleton-Century-Crofts).
Hilgard, E.R. & Bower, G.H. (1966), *Theories of Learning*, 3rd. edition (New York: Appleton-Century-Crofts).
Hirst, W. (1988), Preface. In W. Hirst, Ed. *The Making of Cognitive Science: Essays in Honor of George A. Miller* (Cambridge: CUP).
Ingold, T. (2000), *The Perception of the Environment: Essays in Livelihood, Dwelling and Skill* (London: Routledge).
James, W. (1907/1955), *Pragmatism* (Cambridge, MA: Harvard Univ. Press).
Johnson-Laird, P. (1988), *The Computer and the Mind* (Cambridge, MA: Cambridge University Press).
Jovchelovitch, Sandra. (2006), *Knowledge in Context: Representations, Community and Culture* (Hove, East Sussex: Routledge).
Kessen, W. (1981), 'Early settlements in New Cognition', *Cognition*, 10, pp. 167–171.
Knapp, T.J. (1986), 'The emergence of cognitive psychology in the latter half of the twentieth century', In T.J. Knapp & L.C. Robertson (Eds.), *Approaches to Cognition: Contrasts and Controversies* (Hillsdale, NJ: Erlbaum), pp. 13-35.
Koyré, A. (1965), *Newtonian Studies* (London: Chapman & Hall).
Lave, J. (1988), *Cognition in Practice* (New York: Cambridge University Press).
Leahey, T. H. (1992), 'The mythical revolutions of American psychology', *American Psychologist*, 47, pp. 308–18.
Leeper, R. S. (1951), 'Cognitive processes', In S. S. Stevens (Ed.), *Handbook of Experimental Psychology* (New York: Wiley), pp. 730–757.
Leudar, I. & Costall, A. (Eds.) (2004a), Special issue: Theory of mind. *Theory & Psychology*, 14(5), pp. 571–752.

Leudar, I. & Costall, A. (2004b), 'On the persistence of the "problem of other minds" in psychology: Chomsky, Grice and "theory of mind"', *Theory and Psychology*, 14, pp. 603-623.

McKeachie, W.J. & Doyle, C.L. (1966), *Psychology* (Reading, MA: Addison-Wesley).

Miller, G. A. (2003), 'The cognitive revolution: a historical perspective', *TRENDS in Cognitive Sciences*, 7, pp. 141-144.

Miller, G.A., Pribram, K. & Galanter, E. (1960), *Plans and the Structure of Behavior* (New York: Holt).

Moore, T.V. (1939), *Cognitive Psychology* (Lippincott: Philadelphia).

Moroz, Myron (1972), 'The concept of cognition in contemporary psychology', Royce & W.W. Rozeboom (Eds.), *The Psychology of Knowing* (New York: Gordon and Breach), pp. 177-205.

Nuttin, J. (1955), 'Consciousness, behavior, and personality', *Psychological Review*, 62, pp. 349-55.

Pylyshyn, Z. (1986), *Computation and Cognition* (Cambridge, MA: MIT Press).

Rubinstejn, S. L. (1937/1987), 'Problems of psychology in the works of Karl Marx', *Studies in Soviet Thought*, 33, 111-130 [First published in Sovetskaja psichotechnika, 7(1), 1934. Trans. T.J. Blakeley].

Searle, J. (1989), *Minds, Brains and Science* (London: Penguin).

Shanon, B. (1993), *The Representational and the Presentational* (New York: Harvester-Wheatsheaf).

Sharkey, N. (1988), Review of 'Cognitive psychology in question', edited by A. Costall & A. Still, *Current Psychological Research and Reviews*, 6, pp. 339-340.

Shaw, R. E. (2003), 'The agent-environment interface: Simon's indirect or Gibson's direct coupling', *Ecological Psychology*, 15, pp. 37-106.

Spearman, C. (1923), *Nature of Intelligence and Principles of Cognition* (New York: Arno Press).

Sternberg, R.J. (1988), 'Questioning cognitive psychology: Review of Alan Costall and Arthur Still (Eds.) Cognitive psychology in question', *Contemporary Psychology*, 33, pp. 206-207.

Still, A. W. & Costall, A. (Eds.) (1991), *Against Cognitivism* (London: Harvester).

Straker, S. (1976), 'The eye made "other": Durer, Kepler, and the mechanisation of light and vision', In L. A. Knafla, M. S. Staum, & T. H. E. Travers (Eds.), *Science, Technology, and Culture in Historical Perspective*. University of Calgary Studies in History, No. 1, pp. 7-25.

Stuart-Hamilton, I. (1988), Review of Costall & Still (1987) 'Cognitive psychology in question', *Quarterly Journal of Experimental Psychology*, 40A, 411-412.

Tolman, E.C. (1932), *Purposive Behavior in Animals and Men* (New York: Appleton-Century-Crofts).

Winograd, T. & Flores, F. (1986), *Understanding Computers and Cognition: : A new foundation for design* (Norwood, NJ: Ablex).

Wilson, M. D. (1980), 'Body and mind from the Cartesian point of view', In R. W. Rieber (Ed.), *Body and Mind: Past, Present, and Future* (New York: Academic Press), pp. 35-55.

Whitehead, A.N. (1926), *Science and the Modern World* (Cambridge: CUP).

Young, R. M. (1966), 'Scholarship and the history of the behavioural sciences', *History of Science*, 5, pp. 1-51.

Section Two

LANGUAGE

Steve Croker

Symbols Without Rules
A Computational Model of Language Acquisition Using Distributional Analysis

Introduction

There has been much debate over the ability of computational models to explain various aspects of cognition. Such discussions have tended to focus on connectionist or subsymbolic models. Symbolic models, typically characterised as production systems with a fixed database of rules, have not received as much attention. However, there is a family of symbolic computational models, based on Feigenbaum & Simon's (1984) EPAM (Elementary Perceiver And Memorizer), which represents knowledge in long-term memory as a discrimination network, rather than as a list of declarative statements or procedural rules. The CHREST (Chunk Hierarchy and REtrieval STructures) family of models (Gobet *et al.*, 2001), add to the basic EPAM architecture with a mechanism for representing semantic associations between nodes in the hierarchical network. CHREST has been used to model various cognitive phenomena, including aspects of the development of language.

Language has proved to be a very rich domain for computational modelling, particularly aspects of language acquisition and development. There tend to be two types of computational approaches to language—those that attempt to solve a particular problem within the domain and those that attempt to inform our knowledge of the empirical data. The former often deal with small-scale data sets, such as Elman's (1993) simple recurrent networks that show that the problem of learning complex sequential relationships is soluble. The latter, such as Redington, Chater & Finch's (1993) hierarchical cluster analysis, use large corpora and, in this case, tells us that the English language is a rich source of statistical information to be utilised by the language-learning child. This distinction can be described in terms of *weak* and *strong* approaches to modelling. A weak approach (such as Redington et al.'s) uses a model to explore the data without claiming to explain the cognitive processes used in producing the data. A strong approach (such as Elman's) tries to build a model of language acquisition using psychologically plausible structures. In the latter case, the human data is used as a constraint upon the model and can be used to refine it. MOSAIC (Model Of Syntax Acquisition In Children) is a variant of the CHREST architecture used to model early grammatical development and represents both approaches.

MOSAIC embodies a constructivist theory of language acquisition and there is, therefore, no linguistic knowledge built into the model. Instead, MOSAIC extracts distributional information from large naturalistic datasets; the only information received by the model is that present in the transcribed adult speech presented as input. This enables, at the least, an understanding of the data and additionally provides a learning mechanism that can go some way toward explaining how children acquire language. The model constructs a network consisting of nodes that represent words or sequences of words present in the input. It is sensitive to the distributional properties of items occurring in the input and is able to create 'generative' links between words that occur frequently in similar contexts, building pseudo-categories. Some of the errors children make in their early multi-word speech can be explained by rote learning. Other errors can be simulated by utilising the generative links to create novel utterances. One aim of this chapter is to show how the pattern of children's speech errors can be explained without assuming domain-specific knowledge of linguistic structure, suggesting that any claim that this pattern can be taken as evidence for innate grammatical knowledge is too strong, and that at least some aspects of children's early language can be explained in terms of a distributional analysis of the statistics of the language being learned. A second aim is to show that symbolic computational models can be useful tools within contemporary psychology. Although this type of use of computational models is clearly 'cognitivist' to some degree, I hope to demonstrate that this tool is not inextricably bound to rationalist accounts of cognition and, further, that many of the dichotomies within psychology are not always useful when attempting to understand cognition. More specifically, we need to look beyond the dichotomies of rationalism/empiricism, cognitivism/post-cognitivism and symbolic/connectionist models of cognition. I will start by offering a brief overview of the nativist/constructivist debate within language acquisition before moving on to a discussion of computational modelling. I will then describe MOSAIC and show how it has been used to model specific phenomena in child language.

Language Acquisition

The basic problem of grammatical acquisition is for language-learning children to be able to successfully manipulate grammatical categories. This is not a trivial problem, as more than four decades of theorising, experimentation and no small amount of argument will attest to. Theories of grammatical acquisition fall broadly into two categories: nativist theories and constructivist theories. The basic argument of nativists is that children are born with innate knowledge of grammar, whereas constructivists argue that language is learned via a process of extracting information available in the linguistic environment. These two positions represent a highly polarised community of language researchers. Whereas some deplore the polarisation (e.g. Rispoli, 1999), Maratsos (1999b) is swift to point out that many of these differences are non-negotiable.

Nativism

In response to Skinner's (1957) claims that language is learned by imitation, Chomsky (1957; 1959) published the original nativist account of language acquisition. Various modifications and updates have been made to basic nativist theory, however, there are three main arguments used to justify an approach that specifies innate linguistic knowledge. First, the *poverty of the stimulus* argument states that the language heard by children does not contain all the information necessary to 'decode' it or interpret it correctly. Any given word may have a number of different interpretations, depending on context. The Chomskyan argument is that this information is not present in the stimulus itself, so therefore must be present in the child (Maratsos, 1999a). In addition children are exposed to poor, incorrect grammar; how do children, in the face of complex spoken language, decide which utterances are grammatical and which are not?

Second, children make *overgeneralisation errors*; they create words such as 'runned' or 'goed' that follow the rules of grammar for regular verbs, but are extremely unlikely to have been heard by the child. This suggests that rather than simply imitating the language they hear, children are attempting to utilise rules in their language production (Pinker, 1979). Third, the problem of *no negative evidence* — children do not generally receive feedback regarding the grammaticality of their speech and, even in cases where they do, they do not seem to incorporate this information into their speech (Bowerman, 1988). This suggests that children are not being 'taught' language by their elders. Related to both this point and the poverty of the stimulus argument is the work of Gold (1967), who uses a formal theoretical proof to assert that no natural human languages are learnable as they contain a massive amount of positive examples but no negative examples. The basis of Gold's argument is that if a language-learning child has a set of possible solutions to the problem of identifying the grammar of the target language which includes at least one incorrect non-finite grammar (in addition to all possible finite grammars), then the child will not be able to learn the target grammar, as an incorrect non-finite grammar can be used to generate illegal strings — and the child is never given feedback regarding the illegality of these strings.

Gold's work is repeatedly used to support the notion of innate knowledge as necessary for language learning. However, MacWhinney (2004) notes seven possible solutions to Gold's problem. First, there have been a number of studies that demonstrate that complex non-finite languages *can* be learned from positive examples alone (e.g. Kanazawa, 1998; Shinohara, 1994; Jain, Osherson, Royer, & Sharma, 1999). Second, Gold's proof requires that the end-state criterion is that the grammar is identified such that there is no possibility of an alternate solution. However, we can assume that a probabilistic identification of the target grammar is made, rather than a completely certain identification — 'asymptotically correct but somewhere short of perfect' (Bates & Elman, 1996). In this case, Gold's argument no longer applies, according to a proof by Horning (1969; cited in MacWhinney, 2004). Third, if children use an item-based approach to learning grammar, in which they utilise the conservative rule of never hypothesising a more powerful grammar than is necessary for dealing with the input, they will never (or at least rarely) overgeneralise, which obviates the need for negative evidence. Children do of course produce errors, though, and the final four solutions discussed by MacWhinney all deal with error recovery. First, a 'competition' mechanism can be invoked, whereby incorrect forms (e.g. 'goed') compete with correct forms (e.g. 'went'). As the correct form will be of higher frequency than the incorrect form, its representation will grow in strength and it will override and eventually displace the competing incorrect form. Some errors, such as those made when a verb is extended by analogy and placed inappropriately (e.g. 'she ate her plate clean', derived from 'she licked her bowl clean') are more subtle and will not be solved by simple competition. The second error-recovery mechanism discussed by MacWhinney is Bowerman's (1988) 'cue construction', which deals with these sorts of errors. The child will block overgeneralisations by representing additional features of lexical items so that they are not permitted (on the basis of these features) to be used with an incorrect argument structure. An additional strategy is children's self-monitoring, the third error-recovery strategy. By comparing their own output with their internal representations of input they have received, children can self-correct when a 'weak' incorrect form is produced, replacing it with the 'strong' competing form. Finally, MacWhinney discusses 'indirect negative evidence' — a mechanism whereby a child computes the likelihood of a particular form of a particular word, given the frequency of that form for other words. For example, 'runned' has a vanishingly low frequency which we would not expect given the prevalence of items such as 'walked' and 'jumped'; we can therefore conclude that 'runned' is probably not the correct form.

Constructivism

The fundamental argument of constructivist accounts of language acquisition is that the input received by children is not impoverished — rather, it contains all the information necessary for language learning (Snow, 1977). Snow (1995) argues that child-directed speech is different to adult-directed speech in that it is simpler and 'cleaner', therefore easier to learn language from, though it is still complex and consistent with 'full' adult speech. In addition to the arguments against Gold (1967) presented above, the learnability issue has been questioned by many including Chater & Vitányi (2001) and Rohde & Plaut (1999), who suggest that statistical learning techniques provide evidence that natural languages are learnable. Chater & Redington (1999) argue that a lot of information is present in the distributional information present in language;

Cartwright & Brent (1997) propose a strategy with which children can make use of this information. Distributional accounts, in conjunction with the rise of computational modelling techniques, have become increasingly popular. In a move away from the previous reliance on abstract categories necessary for both nativist and earlier constructivist accounts (e.g. Bates & MacWhinney, 1982; Schlesinger, 1982), this approach has as its core thesis the idea that grammatical rules and categories are implicit in the distributional characteristics of language. Children attend to the patterns present in language and are able to form syntactic categories on the basis of positional commonalities between syntactically similar items, using general cognitive tools. This idea of the domain-generality of mechanisms involved in language acquisition highlights a debate in the psycholinguistic field which is generally subsumed by the nativist/constructivist debate—do we possess specific cognitive mechanisms for comprehending and producing language or are these capabilities achieved using general cognitive tools? Broadly speaking, the former tends to be favoured by nativist theorists and the latter by constructivists—if one posits innate grammatical knowledge, it almost certainly has to be domain-specific; likewise, a move away from such knowledge implies a reluctance to grant language some special cognitive status. Sabbagh & Gelman (2000) note that general learning mechanisms are undoubtedly powerful (and necessary), but query whether they are sufficient. They ask how we are able to classify words in terms of abstract categories, unless we already have knowledge of these categories. Similarly, Pinker (1987) notes that distributional learning can explain the identification of items with respect to their syntactic categories on the basis of context, but identifies this as problematic as these contexts have to already exist. A strong constructivist perspective, such as the emergentist school of thought (MacWhinney, 1999), argues that this is something of a red herring—there is no need for abstract categories to exist prior to language learning. These can emerge from the information present in the linguistic environment, when coupled with powerful, yet constrained, learning mechanisms.

Regardless of the specific theory used to describe the process of acquisition, what becomes clear is that there is much evidence in support of the general constructivist paradigm. With regard to lexical learning, Huttenlocher, Haight, Bryk, Setzer & Lyons (1991) demonstrated that there is a relationship between individual differences in vocabulary growth and the amount of parental speech input children receive. Aslin, Saffran & Newport (1999) argue that the transitional probabilities between sounds heard by children are 'logically sufficient' for some aspects of word segmentation. Redington et al. (1993), who utilise cluster analysis techniques to examine a large corpus of speech data, show that grammatical categories are implicit in the linguistic input children receive. The results of this cluster analysis, based on the distributional statistics of language provided by local context, provide evidence that syntactic categories are clearly differentiated in adult speech.

Cognitive Modelling

Members of the cognitive science community have modelled various aspects of language comprehension and production. The types of architecture used vary immensely, but they generally fit into categories of either 'symbolic' or 'subsymbolic' models. The former, which represent information in terms of discrete symbols, include production systems and semantic networks. The development of symbolic systems has largely been driven by Newell and Simon's (1976) *Physical-Symbol System Hypothesis* – the idea that intelligence occurs as a result of symbol manipulation. The essence of this hypothesis is that a symbol system, which must be expressed in a physical medium such as a brain or a computer, is both necessary and sufficient for intelligent behaviour.

Connectionist models of language offer a subsymbolic alternative explanation to traditional symbolic models, which are often characterised by explicit rule systems. Connectionist models consist of a number of layers of units with a set of interconnections of varying and variable weights. Input signals are multiplied by the weight of a connection between the input node and another node in the next layer. Each node has a threshold; if the incoming signal value is above the threshold, that node is activated. Complex information can be represented as a pattern of activation across the network. With respect to language, connectionist models offer an explanation that rests on associationism rather than combinatorial rules (Pinker, 1999). The inherent sensitivity to the input of neural networks makes them appealing to empiricist language theorists, although Plunkett (1995) notes that connectionist architectures can be defined in such a way that the role of pre-existing structures can be examined. Although the distinction between rationalist-symbolic models and empiricist-connectionist models is widely accepted, critics of cognitivism such as Cisek (1999) and Freeman & Núñez (1999) argue that connectionism is not a radical break with cognitivism, merely a different implementation to symbolic models.

Westermann (1999) describes three, largely binary dimensions along which models and theories can be classified. First, *fixed structure vs. emergent structure.* The structure of a cognitive system can either be completely predetermined or can be added to as learning takes place. Second, *homogeneous architecture vs. modular architecture.* A system can have interdependent data structures or can be composed of independent modules where deletion of a structure has no impact on the rest of the system. In reality, the distinction is not always so clear (hence the reference to 'largely' binary dimensions). Gobet (2001) points out that there may be interdependence between structures in what appears to be a modular system and there may be emergent modularisation in an initially heterogeneous system. The third dimension is *single mechanism vs. multiple mechanisms.* Input to the system may be processed differently according to the nature of each input item. In terms of the nativist/constructivist debate it would seem that a nativist theory will commonly imply a fixed-structure, modular, multiple-mechanism system, whereas a constructivist theory is likely to necessitate an emergent-structure, homogeneous-architecture, single-mechanism system. Many nativist theories are based on innate knowledge consisting of a set of abstract rules. A system of innate rules implies a predetermined fixed structure composed of modules for dealing with separate rules and elements in memory, which in turn implies multiple mechanisms. In many constructivist theories, the system is data-driven, possessing no language-specific innate knowledge or rules, which implies (but does not necessitate) an emergent structure derived from the input and a homogeneous, single-mechanism system, with no *a priori* distinctions between classes of input data. This, however, is a broad generalisation; it is possible to have either nativist or constructivist accounts which occupy any point in the space defined by this scheme of classification, although the distinction does seem to hinge on whether the system is rule-based or not. If we consider the symbolic/subsymbolic distinction mentioned above, a commitment to a rule-based system is arguably a commitment to a symbolic system, although a non-rule-based system could be implemented in either a symbolic or subsymbolic model. In favour of a symbolic approach, Hahn (1999) argues that it may be a better research strategy to implement high-level (i.e. symbolic) models, due to the inherent transparency of such architectures. Ling & Marinov (1994) provide evidence that tasks involving non-conscious processes do not need to be modelled in subsymbolic architectures and argue for the psychological plausibility of symbolic models.

MOSAIC

MOSAIC (Model Of Syntax Acquisition In Children; Gobet & Pine, 1997) is a symbolic computational model based on the CHREST architecture (Gobet et al., 2001). CHREST is, in turn, a member of the EPAM family (Feigenbaum & Simon, 1984). Variants of CHREST have been used to model various areas of human cognition such as chess expertise (Gobet & Simon, 2000), diagrammatic reasoning (Lane, Cheng & Gobet, 1999) and computer programming (Gobet & Oliver, 2002), as well as a number of phenomena in language acquisition. These include the acquisition of vocabulary (Jones, Gobet & Pine, 2000; Jones, this volume), verb islands (Jones, this volume) subject omission in child language (Freudenthal, Pine & Gobet, 2002), case-marking errors (Croker, Pine & Gobet, 2001), negation errors (Croker, Pine & Gobet, 2003), optional infinitive errors in English (Croker, Pine & Gobet, 2000) and a cross-linguistic examination of optional infinitive errors in English and Dutch (Freudenthal, Pine & Gobet, 2006).

Input to the model

An important feature of MOSAIC is its ability to deal with semi-naturalistic data. Cognitive models of aspects of language acquisition are often criticised for producing output that looks very little like natural language, derived from input that has been transformed into an abstraction of language. The input given to MOSAIC is *semi-* or *pseudo-naturalistic* data, taken from maternal speech. This input consists of transcribed speech presented as text (e.g. 'he liked it'). Whilst not *fully* naturalistic (i.e. an unsegmented audio stream), this input representation is more 'naturalistic' than the representations used by other models. The output produced by MOSAIC also appears in this form. This means that the predictions made by the model can be feasibly compared to child speech data, transcribed similarly. For the simulations described in this chapter, the model was given input data from the mother of one of the children (Anne) in the CHILDES database (MacWhinney & Snow, 1990), collected in the same sessions as the children's speech. This consisted of 33,390 utterances.

Network formation

MOSAIC consists of a hierarchical discrimination network. The network is grown as input is presented to the model. When an utterance is presented, each word in the utterance is considered in turn. If the word currently considered has not previously been seen by the model, a new node corresponding to that word is created. The new node is created at the first layer of the network, just below the root node. This first layer may be seen as the layer where the 'primitives' of the network (i.e., the individual words that have been seen by the model) are learned and stored. The model learns the distributional statistics of both words that follow and words that precede a given word - the network contains information about which words have been presented as occurring immediately before a particular item and which words have been presented as occurring immediately afterwards (see the chapter by Jones for a more detailed account of learning in MOSAIC). Figure 1 depicts a fragment of a network created in this manner.

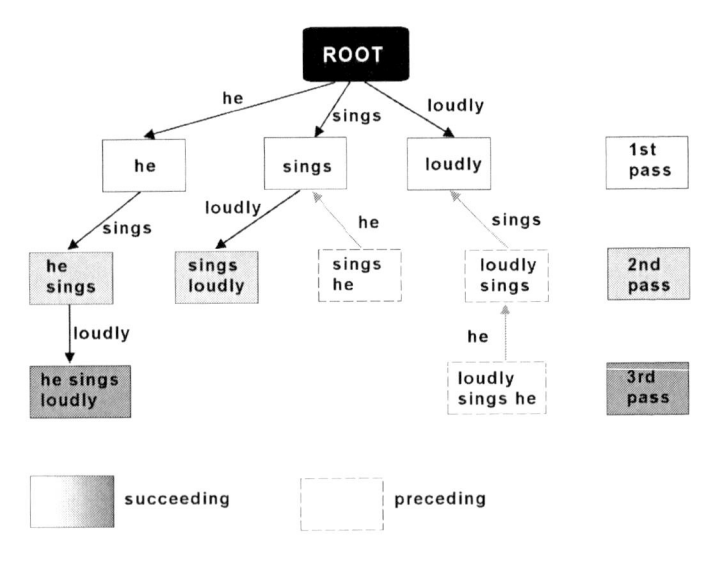

Figure 1. Network formed after the utterance 'he sings loudly' is presented 3 times to the model.

Generative Links

As well as learning utterances by rote, MOSAIC is able to generate novel utterances using *generative links*, an important feature of the model. Generative links are 'lateral' links between nodes that have contextual similarities. If two words in the network occur frequently in similar contexts (e.g. they are preceded and succeeded by the same items), then a generative link can be made between these items. The number of common features needed to create a generative link (the similarity measure) is the degree of overlap between items that precede and succeed any two nodes. This is calculated by taking all the 'children' and 'parents' of any two nodes and assessing whether the proportion of children and parents shared by both nodes exceeds a certain threshold with respect to the total number of child nodes. The value used to obtain the data presented below was 8%; this value is the same in both directions (i.e. 8% is the critical value for shared nodes both above and below the nodes under consideration). Figure 2 contains an example of generative link creation. In this figure, 'sings', 'goes' and 'likes' all succeed 'he' and 'she'. A generative link is formed between 'he' and 'she' as a result of this contextual similarity.

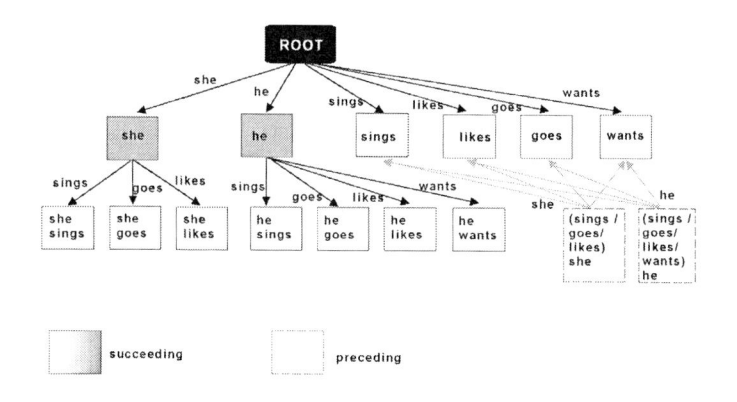

Figure 2. Generative link formation: 'he' and 'she' are linked by virtue of possessing child nodes in common.

Probabilistic Learning

Another feature of MOSAIC is probabilistic learning. There is a parameter which determines how likely it is that any given word in the input is learned. This parameter was set to 0.1. This means that, on average, a word must be seen 10 times before it is added to the network. This form of learning gives a positive bias to words and phrases that occur many times in the input corpus. The output is therefore a reflection of the frequency with which words occur, rather than a reflection of which items are present in the input. To offset the fact that little is learned from one presentation of the input corpus, the input is presented several times before an output is produced. The data presented below were produced by MOSAIC after the input set had been presented 5 times.

Production of Utterances

Once a network has been created, it can be used to produce utterances in two ways: by *recognition* and by *generation*. Utterances produced by recognition are essentially rote-learned, i.e. they are utterances or portions of utterances presented to the model in the input corpus. These are produced by starting at each node in turn, and following the links down the network. For example, from the fragment of a network shown in Figure 2, utterances such as 'she sings' and 'he wants' could be produced by recognition. Production by generation utilises the generative links to create utterances not seen in the input. This occurs in a similar way to production by recognition, the difference being that lateral generative links can be traversed as well as vertical links, although only one generative link can be followed per generated utterance. Thus, from the network in Figure 2, the utterance 'she wants' could be produced by generation. It is possible for some utterances to be produced in either of the two ways in cases where there are identical tests below both the nodes connected by a generative link. 'He goes' can be produced by following the 'goes' link down from the 'he' node or by following the generative link to 'she' and then taking the 'goes' link below 'she'. When all possible utterances are generated from a completed network, there may be many instances of a particular utterance in the output corpus, of which there may be any number produced by recognition and any number produced by generation. The frequency of information in the input is therefore reflected in the output. This information may be highly frequent word pairs or even complete sentences. The output produced by MOSAIC consisted of 98,533 utterances, of which 8,794 were produced by recognition and 89,559 by generation. Samples of this output were taken for analysis.

Modelling optional infinitive phenomena

To illustrate the use of MOSAIC, I will briefly describe a nativist account of the development of grammar and show how the model supports an alternative explanation. The optional infinitive hypothesis (Wexler, 1994, 1996) is an attempt to provide a unified nativist account of young children's knowledge of verb inflection and verb movement across a variety of different languages. According to this view, by the time that children begin to produce multi-word utterances they have already correctly set all the basic inflectional/clause structure parameters of their language. However, there is an initial stage—the optional infinitive stage—during which they lack the knowledge that tense is obligatory in finite clauses; knowledge which matures at a later stage of development. Children in the optional infinitive stage are thus assumed to know about tense and agreement, and to know verb movement and all the morpho-syntactic conditions associated with verb movement (both the Universal Grammar conditions and the language-particular conditions). The only piece of knowledge that they are assumed to lack is the knowledge that tense is obligatory in finite clauses. This leads them to treat non-finite tense as if it can be fixed by context, rather than as being necessarily dependent on a higher tense (i.e. the tense of the matrix verb), and hence to show tense optionality in their speech. Tense refers to verb morphology used to situate the verb in time (e.g. -s as in 'she goes' or -ed as in 'they walked'). Agreement refers to the form of the verb with respect to the subject (e.g. 'I run', 'he runs', 'they run'). Finite verb forms are those tensed as above; non-finite forms are the infinitive, progressive and perfect tenses, e.g. 'go', 'going', 'gone'.

Key Phenomena

1. Optional Infinitives

When applied to children learning English, the optional infinitive hypothesis can be used to explain a variety of phenomena in their early multi-word speech. First, it can be used to explain why children sometimes fail to use appropriately tensed forms in finite clauses (e.g. 'that go in there' instead of 'that goes in there' or 'that going in there' instead of 'that's going in there'). Such errors are interpreted not as the dropping of inflections or auxiliaries, but as the use of untensed forms in contexts where tensed forms are obligatory. Wexler makes very clear predictions about what a child in the optional infinitive stage of development should and should not say. Children may produce forms such as 'she hide', previously viewed as a process of -s dropping, and also forms in which the -s is present ('she hides') as tense is optional; tensed forms are thus predicted to co-exist with untensed forms. Wexler also predicts that utterances such as 'she is going' (grammatically correct) or 'she going' (tense omission) can be legitimately produced by the child, whereas 'she be going' should not be. This is because 'is' is only included as a tense carrier. In this example, 'be' does not carry tense therefore the child should not include 'be' in the utterance.

2. Case-Marking Errors

Children in the early stages of language development are known to make case-marking errors. These errors are utterances in which a nominative pronoun (e.g. 'he') has been replaced with a non-nominative pronoun, such as the accusative (e.g. 'him'), resulting in utterances such as 'him does it' instead of 'he does it', and 'her get it' instead of 'she gets it'. There are a number of possible explanations for this phenomenon. According to Schütze and Wexler's (1996) ATOM (Agreement/Tense Omission Model) (see also Wexler, 1998, for an overview of this model), pronoun case-marking errors occur because the child produces the accusative form of the pronoun as a default when the abstract features of agreement (which are necessary for correct case assignment) are absent from the child's underlying representation of the sentence. The reason for considering both tense and agreement as optional features, and not just tense, is that tense omission is acknowledged by Wexler, Schütze & Rice (1998) to be insufficient for a full explanation of case development.

3. Agreement

The optional infinitive hypothesis can be also be used to explain the pattern of subject-verb agreement in children's speech. Thus, even though English-speaking children do not always use tensed forms in obligatory contexts, the tensed forms that they do use tend to agree in person and number with their subjects (e.g. 'I am', 'she is', but not 'I is' or 'she are'). This is taken as evidence that English-speaking children know about agreement (though this knowledge only surfaces in the child's speech when tense and agreement are present in the underlying representation of the sentence). As only tense is optional and agreement is assumed to be known by the child, agreement errors such as 'he are' and 'you runs' are predicted *not* to occur.

4. Verb-Raising Over 'Not'

Even in the earliest stages of multi-word speech, English-speaking children's use of tensed and untensed forms tends to pattern correctly with respect to placement of the negative particle 'not' (e.g. 'he does not go', 'he not go' but not 'he goes not' or 'he not goes'). This is taken as evidence that English-speaking children know that finite verbs do not raise to the left of negation.

An Alternative Explanation

An alternative explanation for the phenomena described by Wexler is that the formation of syntactic relationships in children's speech can be accounted for in the input the child receives from external sources, in particular parental input. In the account proposed here, the child's use of lexical forms is a result of the distribution of these forms in the input. The predicted speech patterns all have models in the speech of adults, which acts as the linguistic input to the child. For example, a child may produce the utterance 'she going' which is accounted for in the optional infinitive hypothesis as the use of an untensed form in a position where tense is required, rather than the omission of an auxiliary. Obviously, a child should not hear her mother saying 'she going' however, she will hear utterances such as 'where is she going?' and 'is she going to the shops?'. Similarly, utterances such as 'look at him go' provide a model for the case-marking error observed in child-produced utterances like 'him go'. Types of utterances predicted not to occur in the optional infinitive hypothesis do not have models in the input. For example 'it are' is predicted not to occur as part of a child's speech and does not occur as a fragment of a correctly formed adult utterance.

Child Data

Data was obtained from several children, taken from the Manchester corpus (Theakston, Lieven, Pine & Rowland, 2000) of the CHILDES database (MacWhinney & Snow, 1990). Tape transcripts were made twice every three weeks for a period of 12 months, between the ages of 1;10 and 2;9 (Anne), 1;11 and 2;10 (Aran), 2;0 and 2;11 (Becky) and 1;11 and 2;11 (Gail) . Each session consists of two half-hour transcripts, one taken during free play and the other during structured play. The data used in analysing both human performance and the performance of the model consists of types, not tokens. Much of the research in children's speech is based on analysis using tokens as the entire corpus is considered. Here it is necessary to only use types as MOSAIC does not produce multiple instances of utterances in the same way that a child does. The model produces all the utterances it is capable of producing whereas a child produces speech in response to the context in which the child is situated. Any duplicates of utterances in the children's data sets were removed so as to be in line with the simulation data. For the analyses of optional infinitives, agreement errors and case-marking errors, the only utterances analysed were those produced by each child which started with the pronouns 'he', 'him' and 'his' (presented here as 'he' utterances); 'she' and 'her' (presented as 'she' utterances) and 'I', 'me' and 'my' (presented as 'I' utterances) which contained a verb of which that pronoun was the subject. For the analysis of negation errors, only utterances containing negation and a verb were analysed.

Results from child data and MOSAIC

1. Optional Infinitives

Table 1 shows the rate at which Anne, Aran, Becky and MOSAIC made optional infinitive errors. The rates of error of this type are fairly similar with respect to masculine 3psg utterances. The rate for feminine utterances is more variable across children, although should be noted that the error rate for Aran's feminine 3psg utterances may not be reliable, as it is based on a sample size of just 6 — all the utterances commencing with 'she' that Aran makes. The main difference between the children lies in the error rate for 'I + infinitive' errors. Anne makes 38 errors in 633 utterances and Becky makes 87 errors in 1007 utterances, whereas Aran only makes 7 in 1583 utterances. Although it *could* be argued that these rates appear negligible, Becky's error rate is 19 times that of Aran. The data in Table 1 illustrates three things: First, children make optional infinitive errors in conjunction with both first- and third-person-singular subjects; second, the error rates are much higher for 3psg subjects — this is largely due to the fact that for most verbs in English the correct form of a present-tense verb for the first (and second) person is identical to the uninflected infinitival form, making it impossible to distinguish between correct usage and an 'optional infinitive' type error (if, indeed, such a distinction has any meaning); third, the rate at which such errors are made is not consistent across children, although there may be a similarity in this rate. The number of errors produced by MOSAIC is comparable to the error rates of the children.

Table 1: Optional infinitive errors (%)

	Anne	Aran	Becky	MOSAIC
He	17.09	12.68	17.89	20.4
She	24.39	33.33	9.26	13.6
I	6.00	0.44	8.64	1.6

2. Case-Marking Errors

Table 2 shows the number of case-marking errors Anne, Becky, Gail and MOSAIC make with respect to 3psg subjects (Aran makes no case-marking errors). The figures for Anne and Becky are very similar, but Gail produces a much greater number of errors — over half of her feminine-subject utterances contain case-marking errors. However, the pattern is very similar across all three children: They are all more likely to overextend 'her' for 'she' than 'him' for 'he'. Although the difference between masculine and feminine in not so large in the data produced by MOSAIC, the same pattern is observed.

Table 2: Case-marking errors (%)

	Anne	Becky	Gail	MOSAIC
He	1.13	1.24	5.38	5.08
She	16.28	12.04	52.78	11.97

3. Agreement

The optional infinitive hypothesis predicts that children will not make agreement errors of the form 'singular subject + agreeing verb' where the agreement is inappropriate to the person, e.g. 'I goes' or 'she am'. The data from Anne, Aran and Becky, presented in Table 3, show this is possibly true for third-person-singular subjects, but not for the first-person-singular subject 'I' — Anne makes four such errors, Aran makes one and Becky makes two. The fact that no agreement errors are made with 3psg subjects does not, of course, mean that children are not capable of making them, but rather if the phenomenon exists, it is rare and is not caught in the samples analysed. As almost all agreeing verbs (goes, was, looks etc.) can be used grammatically in conjunction with 3psg subjects (the only exceptions are 'are' and 'were'), a lack of errors is not surprising. MOSAIC produces more agreement errors than the children, although it must be noted that the error rate is still very low — only 1.8% of utterances commencing with 'he' have the wrong agreement, 0.6% of utterances commencing with 'she' have agreement errors and 5.6% of 'I' utterances contain a verb that carries agreement for the second- or third-person. Although the fit is not superb, MOSAIC does correctly predict that errors are more likely to occur with 'I'.

Table 3: Agreement errors (%)

	Anne	Aran	Becky	MOSAIC
He	0	0	0	1.8
She	0	0	0	0.6
I	0.63	0.06	0.2	5.6

4. Verb-Raising Over 'Not'

All of Anne's, Aran's and Becky's utterances containing both a verb and the word 'not', or one of its contractions ('shouldn't', 'won't' etc.), were analysed for the presence of various patterns. These are 'correct' (grammatical) utterances such as 'doesn't go' or 'hasn't gone', optional infinitive errors (e.g. 'not go'), 'inflected verb + not' ('goes not') and 'not + inflected verb' ('not goes'). The former two are predicted to occur by Harris & Wexler (1996), whereas the latter two are not. It was found to be necessary to include a further category — 'uninflected verb + not' ('go not') — as Aran makes errors of this type. The children's usage of verbs and negation is shown in Table 4; grammatically correct utterances have been omitted from the table. The analysis of these data shows that all three children use infinitival verbs following negation. In addition, Anne and Becky produced errors in which an inflected verb is used after negation and Aran produced the negative particle *preceded* by an inflected verb — errors which are predicted *not* to happen in the optional infinitive hypothesis. The frequency and types of error made by MOSAIC are very similar to those produced by the children. Importantly, neither the children or MOSAIC make errors in which an inflected verb immediately precedes the negative particle.

Table 4: Negation errors (%)

	Anne	Aran	Becky	MOSAIC
OI-not go	11.72	16.39	6.28	10.0
goes not	0	0	0	0
not goes	0.42	0	0.18	0.4
go not	0	0.28	0	0

Conclusion

The results presented above, combined with the results from simulations of other linguistic phenomena, suggest that the constructivist theory embodied by MOSAIC can go some way towards explaining the acquisition of language. Children's speech errors can be explained without assuming any domain-specific knowledge of linguistic structure. Therefore such errors cannot, by themselves, be taken as evidence for innate grammatical knowledge on the part of the child.

MOSAIC differs from many previous models of language acquisition in two major ways. First, it utilises a discrimination network rather than a production system or a connectionist network. Second, it is 'situated' in that the form of the network (and hence the output it produces) are contingent upon context – the linguistic input given to the model, a large corpus of pseudo-naturalistic input which is not pre-digested or recoded in any way. The architecture of MOSAIC means that although it is symbolic in the sense of having representations, no explicitly specified rule-set is necessary and the network is free to grow as input is received. Production systems require a comprehensive set of instructions and connectionist architectures need a pre-defined space of operation. As a result, most models of language have necessarily been subsets of what is, after all, a very large and complex domain. Rumelhart and McClelland's (1986) past tense acquisition model, for example, is very limited in scope. The fact that relatively 'naturalistic' input can be given as input and the same pseudo-naturalistic output can be generated is quite a useful accomplishment. Arguments such as Pinker and Prince's (1988) claim that output is shaped by the input are no longer relevant as the input to the model is similar to that heard by children. MOSAIC is an implementation of CHREST designed specifically with language in mind, but is does not represent a 'language module' as one facet of cognition; the same basic mechanisms are used to explain computer programming, diagrammatic reasoning and chess ability.

References

Aslin, R. N., Saffran, J. R. & Newport., E. L. (1999), 'Statistical learning in linguistic and nonlinguistic domains', in *The Emergence of Language*, ed. B. MacWhinney (Mahwah, NJ: Erlbaum).

Bates, E., & Elman, J. (1996), 'Learning rediscovered: A perspective on Saffran, Aslin, and Newport', *Science*, 274, pp. 1849–1850.

Bates, E., & MacWhinney, B. (1982), 'Functionalist approaches to grammar', in *Language Acquisition: The State of the Art*, eds. E. Wanner & L. Gleitman (New York: Cambridge University Press).

Bowerman, M. (1988), 'The "no negative evidence" problem: How do children avoid constructing an overly general grammar?', in *Explaining Language Universals*, ed. J. A. Hawkins (Oxford: Blackwell).

Cartwright, T. A. & Brent, M. R. (1997), 'Syntactic categorization in early language acquisition: formalizing the role of distributional analysis' *Cognition*, 63, pp. 121–170.

Chater, N. & Redington, M. (1999), 'Connectionism, theories of learning, and syntax acquisition: where do we stand?', *Journal of Child Language*, 26, pp. 226–232.

Chater, N. & Vitányi, P. (2001), 'A simplicity principle for language learning: re-evaluating what can be learned from positive evidence' (Manuscript submitted for publication).

Chomsky, N. (1957), *Syntactic Structures* (The Hague: Mouton).

Chomsky, N. (1959), 'A review of B.F. Skinner's "Verbal Behavior"', *Language*, 35, pp. 26–58.

Cisek, P. (1999), 'Beyond the computer metaphor: Behaviour as interaction', in *Reclaiming Cognition*, eds. R. Núñez & W. J. Freeman (Thorverton: Imprint Academic).

Croker, S., Pine, J. M. & Gobet, F. (2000), 'Modelling optional infinitive phenomena', in *Proceedings of the 3rd International Conference on Cognitive Modeling* (Veenendaal: Universal Press).

Croker, S., Pine, J. M. & Gobet, F. (2001), 'Modelling children's case-marking errors with MOSAIC', in *Proceedings of the 2001 4th International Conference on Cognitive Modeling* (Mahwah, NJ: Erlbaum).

Croker, S., Pine, J. M. & Gobet, F. (2003), 'Modelling children's negation errors using probabilistic learning in MOSAIC', in *Proceedings of the 5th International Conference on Cognitive Modeling* (Bamberg: Universitäts-Verlag).

Elman, J. L. (1993), 'Learning and development in neural networks: the importance of starting small', *Cognition*, 48, pp. 71–99.

Feigenbaum, E. A. & Simon, H. A. (1984), 'EPAM-like models of recognition and learning', *Cognitive Science*, 8, pp. 305–336.

Freeman, W. J. & Núñez, R. (1999), 'Beyond the computer metaphor: Behaviour as interaction', in *Reclaiming Cognition*, eds. R. Núñez & W. J. Freeman (Thorverton: Imprint Academic).

Freudenthal, D., Pine, J. M. & Gobet, F. (2002), 'Subject omission in children's language: The case for performance limitations in learning', in *Proceedings of the 24th Meeting of the Cognitive Science Society* (Mahwah, NJ: Erlbaum).

Freudenthal, D, Pine, J. M. & Gobet, F. (2006), 'Modelling the development of children's use of optional infinitives in Dutch and English using MOSAIC', *Cognitive Science*, 30, pp. 277–310.

Gobet, F. (2001), 'Is experts' knowledge modular?', in *Proceedings of the 23rd Meeting of the Cognitive Science Society* (Mahwah, NJ: Erlbaum).

Gobet, F., Lane, P. C. R., Croker, S., Cheng, P. C-H., Jones, G., Oliver, I. & Pine, J. M. (2001), 'Chunking mechanisms in human learning', *Trends in Cognitive Sciences*, 5 (6), pp. 236–243.

Gobet, F. & Oliver, I. (2002), 'A simulation of memory for computer programs', *CREDIT Technical Report* 74 (University of Nottingham).

Gobet, F. & Pine, J. M. (1997), 'Modelling the acquisition of syntactic categories', in *Proceedings of the 19th Annual Meeting of the Cognitive Science Society* (Hillsdale, NJ: Erlbaum).

Gobet, F. & Simon, H. A. (2000), 'Five seconds or sixty? Presentation time in expert memory', *Cognitive Science*, 24, pp. 651–682.

Gold, E. M. (1967), 'Language identification in the limit', *Information and Control*, 10, pp. 447–474.

Hahn, U. (1999), 'Language acquisition also needs non-connectionist models', *Journal of Child Language*, 26, pp. 245–248.

Harris, T. & Wexler, K. (1996), 'The Optional-Infinitive Stage in Child English', in *Generative Perspectives in Language Acquisition*, ed. H. Clahsen (Philadelphia: John Benjamins).

Huttenlocher, J., Haight, W., Bryk, A., Setzer, M. & Lyons, T. (1991), 'Early vocabulary growth: Relation to language input and gender', *Developmental Psychology*, 27 (2), pp. 236–248.

Jain, S., Osherson, D., Royer, J. & Sharma, A. (1999), *Systems That Learn* (Cambridge, MA: MIT Press).

Jones, G., Gobet, F., & Pine, J. M. (2000), 'Learning novel sound patterns', in *Proceedings of the 3rd International Conference on Cognitive Modeling* (Veenendaal: Universal Press).

Kanazawa, M. (1998), *Learnable Classes of Categorial Grammars* (Stanford, CA: CSLI Publications).

Lane, P. C. R., Cheng, P. C-H., & Gobet, F. (1999), 'Learning perceptual schemas to avoid the utility problem', in *Proceedings of the 19th SGES International Conference on Knowledge Based Systems & Applied Artificial Intelligence* (Cambridge: Springer-Verlag).

Ling, C. X. & Marinov, M. (1994), 'A symbolic model of the nonconscious acquisition of information', *Cognitive Science*, 18, pp. 595–621.

MacWhinney, B. (1999), *The Emergence of Language* (Mahwah, NJ: Erlbaum).
MacWhinney, B. (2004), 'Multiple solutions to the logical problem of language acquisition', *Journal of Child Language*, 31 (4), pp. 883–914.
MacWhinney, B., & Snow, C. (1990), 'The Child Language Data Exchange System: An update', *Journal of Child Language*, 17, pp. 457–472.
Maratsos, M. (1999a), 'Some aspects of innateness and complexity in grammatical acquisition', in *The Development of Language*, ed. M. Barrett (Hove: Psychology Press).
Maratsos, M. (1999b), 'A sunny view of polarization', *Journal of Child Language*, 26, pp. 239–242.
Newell, A. & Simon, H. A. (1976), 'Computer science as empirical enquiry: Symbols and search', *Communications of the ACM*, 19 (3), pp. 113–126.
Pinker, S. (1979), 'Formal models of language learning', *Cognition*, 7, pp. 217–283.
Pinker, S. (1987), 'The bootstrapping problem in language acquisition', in *Mechanisms of Language Acquisition*, ed. B. MacWhinney (Hillsdale, NJ: Erlbaum).
Pinker, S. (1999), *Words and Rules* (London: Weidenfeld & Nicolson).
Pinker, S. & Prince, A. (1988), 'On language and connectionism: Analysis of a parallel distributed processing model of language acquisition' *Cognition*, 28, pp. 73–193.
Plunkett, K. (1995), 'Connectionism and language acquisition', in *The Handbook of Child Language*, eds. P. Fletcher & B. MacWhinney (Oxford: Blackwell).
Redington, M. & Chater, N. (1997), 'Probabilistic and distributional approaches to language acquisition', *Trends in Cognitive Sciences*, 1 (7), pp. 273–281.
Redington, M., Chater, N. & Finch, S. (1993), 'Distributional information and the acquisition of linguistic categories: a statistical approach', in *Proceedings of the 15th Annual Conference of the Cognitive Science Society* (Hillsdale, NJ: Erlbaum).
Rispoli, M. (1999), 'Review of Elman et al. Rethinking innateness', *Journal of Child Language*, 26, pp. 217–225.
Rohde, D. L. T. & Plaut, D. C. (1999), 'Language acquisition in the absence of explicit negative evidence: How important is starting small?', *Cognition*, 72, pp. 67–109.
Rumelhart, D. & McClelland, J. L. (1986), *Parallel Distributed Processing Vol. 2* (Cambridge, MA: MIT Press).
Sabbagh, M. A. & Gelman, S. A. (2000), 'Buzzsaws and blueprints: What children need (or don't need) to learn language', *Journal of Child Language*, 27, pp. 715–726.
Schlesinger, I. M. (1982), *Steps to Language* (London: Erlbaum).
Schütze, C. & Wexler, K. (1996), 'Subject case licensing and English root infinitives', in *Proceedings of the 20th Annual Boston University Conference on Language Development*, eds. A. Stringfellow, D. Cahma-Amitay, E. Hughes & A. Zukowski (Somerville, MA: Cascadilla Press).

Shinohara, T. (1994), 'Rich classes inferable from positive data: length-bounded elementary formal systems', *Information and Computation*, 108, pp. 175–186.

Skinner, B.F. (1957), *Verbal Learning* (New York: Appleton-Century-Crofts).

Snow, C.E. (1977), 'Mother's speech research: From input to interaction', in *Talking to Children: Language Input and Acquisition*, eds. C. E. Snow & C. A. Ferguson (Cambridge: Cambridge University Press).

Snow, C.E. (1995), 'Issues in the study of input: Finetuning, universality, individual and developmental differences, and necessary causes', in The *Handbook of Child Language*, eds. P. Fletcher & B. MacWhinney (Oxford: Blackwell).

Theakston, A. L., Lieven, E. V. M., Pine, J. M., & Rowland, C. F. (2000), 'The role of performance limitations in the acquisition of 'mixed' verb-argument structure at stage 1', in *New Directions in Language Development and Disorders*, eds. M. Perkins & S. Howard (New York: Plenum).

Westermann, G. (1999), 'Single mechanism but not single route: Learning verb inflections in constructivist neural networks. Commentary on "Lexical entries and rules of language: A multidisciplinary study of German inflection", by H. Clahsen', *Behavioral and Brain Sciences*, 22, pp. 1042–1043.

Wexler, K. (1994), 'Optional infinitives, head movement and the economy of derivations in child grammar', in *Verb Movement*, eds. D. Lightfoot & N. Hornstein (Cambridge: Cambridge University Press).

Wexler, K. (1996), 'The development of inflection in a biologically based theory of language acquisition', in *Toward a Genetics of Language*, ed. M.L. Rice (Hillsdale, NJ: Erlbaum).

Wexler, K. (1998), 'Very early parameter setting and the unique checking constraint: A new explanation of the optional infinitive stage', *Lingua*, 106, pp. 23–79.

Wexler, K., Schütze, C. T. & Rice, M. (1998), 'Subject case in children with SLI and unaffected controls: Evidence for the Agr/Tns model', *Language Acquisition*, 7(2–4), pp. 317–344.

Gary Jones

Distributional Accounts of Language

Explaining Key Phenomena in Child Language Acquisition Using a Distributional Account of the Input the Child Receives

Chapter Abstract

One of the simplest methods of examining language acquisition is to see to what extent child language phenomena can be explained solely from the input the child receives. This approach works on the premise that mechanisms need only be created for phenomena that lie outside what can be explained by the input. MOSAIC represents a constructivist computational model of such an approach, utilising very simple mechanisms to provide what is largely a simple distributional account of the input. In contrast to many computational models of language acquisition, MOSAIC is trained on large-scale realistic speech (the mother's utterances from mother-child interactions), producing child-like utterances that enable easy comparison to the data. Two areas of language acquisition are compared here: verb learning and vocabulary acquisition. For verb learning, simulations of the verb-island hypothesis are presented. The verb-island hypothesis (Tomasello, 1992) states that children's early grammars consist of sets of lexically-specific predicate structures (or verb-islands). However, Pine, Lieven and Rowland (1998) have found that children's early language can also be built around lexical items other than verbs, such as pronouns (contradicting a strict version of the verb-island hypothesis). Simulations show that the output from MOSAIC more closely resembles the child's data than the child's mother's data on which MOSAIC is trained, and MOSAIC can readily simulate both the verb-island and other-island phenomena which exist in the child's data. For vocabulary acquisition, simulations of the nonword repetition test are presented. The acquisition of vocabulary represents a key phenomenon in language acquisition, but is still poorly understood. Gathercole and Baddeley (1989) claim that the phonological store, one of the components of working memory, offers a critical mechanism for learning new words. Nonword repetition tests mimic the learning of new words by asking the child to repeat nonsense words that will not be known in the child's vocabulary. Simulations show that MOSAIC-VOC can account for the nonword repetition task described by Gathercole and Baddeley (1989), a task often presented as a powerful diagnostic of vocabulary learning. Taken as a whole, MOSAIC provides a powerful distributional account of the data that is able to simulate several key phenomena in language acquisition.

Introduction

The predominant explanation for how children learn language is the nativist approach that asserts that children are born with innate mechanisms that predispose them to acquire language. For example, the Language Acquisition Device (e.g. Chomsky, 1969) is one such mechanism by which the child is able to ascertain certain key components of the language they hear. However, why should intricate mechanisms of language acquisition be created without first assessing the extent to which the language the child produces can be explained from the language that the child actually hears? An alternative view of language acquisition has thus been proposed that suggests that there may be a large amount of child language phenomena that can be explained solely from the language input the child receives. This 'constructivist' approach works on the premise that mechanisms need only be created for phenomena that lie outside what can be explained by the input (see the Croker chapter for a detailed discussion of the nativist and constructivist approaches). MOSAIC (Model of Syntax Acquisition in Children) represents a constructivist computational model utilising very simple mechanisms to provide what is largely a simple distributional account of the input. In contrast to many computational models of language acquisition, MOSAIC is trained on large-scale naturalistic speech (the mother's utterances from mother-child interactions), producing child-like utterances that enable easy comparison to the data. In order to illustrate how key child language phenomena can be explained solely from the input the child receives, two key areas of language acquisition will be examined — verb learning and vocabulary acquisition. It will be shown that the simple distributional account of the input that MOSAIC produces is able to account very well for the child language phenomena examined. First the workings of the model are detailed before showing how well the model performs for the two key areas of language that are the focus of this chapter.

The Model

MOSAIC is a variant of EPAM/CHREST (De Groot & Gobet, 1996; Gobet, 1993; Gobet & Simon, 2000; Gobet *et al.*, 2001) which creates a discrimination network (a hierarchical structure of nodes which are linked together) based on a given input. Discrimination networks have a root node at the top of the hierarchy, with all other nodes cascading from the root node (see Figure 1 for an example of the concepts of the network). Nodes are connected to each other by links. EPAM-based models have been used to explain a wide-range of psychological phenomena, such as learning, memory, and perception in chess (De Groot & Gobet, 1996; Gobet, 1993; Gobet & Simon, 2000;

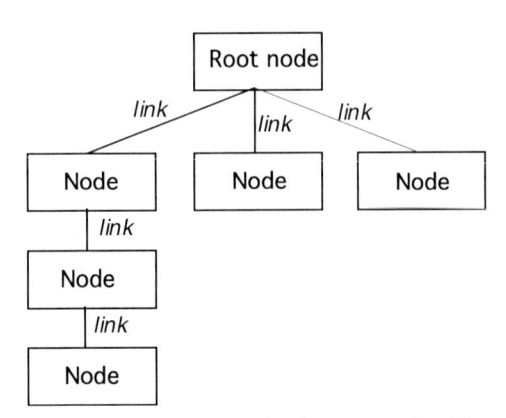

Figure 1. A simple discrimination network with concepts labelled. The network always has an empty root node. Links descend from nodes to other nodes.

Simon & Gilmartin, 1973), the digit span task (Richman, Staszewski & Simon, 1995), and verbal learning behaviour (Feigenbaum & Simon, 1984). EPAM therefore provides an ideal environment to examine further psychological processes, in particular that of language learning. This section will describe the basic working of MOSAIC, and then give an example of MOSAIC's learning mechanisms using mother's speech as input.

A general overview of MOSAIC

MOSAIC's discrimination network starts with a root node that always contains no information. Consistent with other models of the EPAM family (Feigenbaum & Simon, 1984), learning occurs in two steps. The first step involves traversing the network as far as possible with the given input, taking each individual feature of the input in sequence. This is done by starting at the root node and examining all the links from the root node, selecting the first link that matches the first feature of the input (when beginning learning, only the root node will exist and therefore no matches can be made). The node at the end of the link now becomes the current node and the next feature of the input is applied to all the links immediately below this node. The traversal continues until a node is reached where no further traversing can be done (either because the current input feature could not be matched to any links below the current node, or the current node has no test links below it). Traversing the network in this way is also how information can be output from the network.

The second step involves adding new information in the form of a node and link. A link to a new node is created that contains the next feature of the input. The actual contents of the new node contain the information that led up to the new node plus the next feature from the input. The amount of information stored at nodes increases with their distance from the root, because each node contains the accumulation of information of all the nodes that were accessed in traversing to the node.

There are two constraints that are imposed when learning information in the network. First, before creating a node containing more than one input feature (i.e. a sequence of features), the individual features in the sequence must have been learned (each input element is said to be a *primitive*). Second, all nodes containing just one input feature are linked to the root node (i.e. all primitives are immediately below the root node; in this way all sequences of input features are below the node which represents the initial feature in the sequence).

Learning can also occur *whilst* traversing the network. MOSAIC compares each node traversed with other nodes in the network to see if they are used in a similar context. Similar context here is defined as two nodes sharing common information in the links below the nodes. When this is the case, a generative link is created between the nodes (this is explained further in the following section).

An example of MOSAIC learning an utterance

The input given to MOSAIC consists of a set of mother's utterances. Each line of input corresponds to a single utterance (delimited by an END marker which signifies the end of the utterance), and each word in the utterance is an input feature. The example utterance 'Who ate cakes?' will be used as input to illustrate how MOSAIC learns.

The first input feature ('who') is analysed and MOSAIC attempts to match this feature to any of the links that are immediately below the root node. As the network is empty, there are no links. At this point MOSAIC learns something about the input feature. A new node is created that contains 'who', and a link from the root node to the new node with the information 'who'. MOSAIC then reverts back to the root node and proceeds to the next feature of the input. There are no links below the root node that match 'ate' and so again, MOSAIC learns a new node and link below the root node, both of which contain the information 'ate'. The next input feature 'cakes' is similarly learned below the root node (see Figure 2).

When encountering the same input for a second time, the link 'who' can be taken, and the input can move to the next feature, 'ate'.

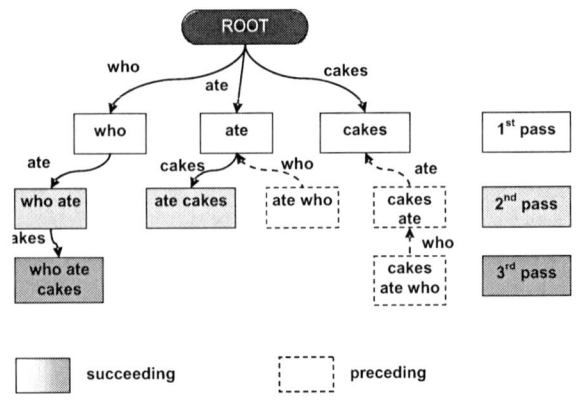

Figure 2. Structure of the MOSAIC network after three presentations of the input 'Who ate cakes?'.

No further links are available below the 'who' node, so MOSAIC can learn something about the next input feature 'ate'. The primitive for this feature already exists and so a new node and link can be created below the 'who' node (if the primitive did not exist then a new node and link for 'ate' would be created below the root node). The link contains the information 'ate' and the node contains the information 'who ate' i.e., the accumulation of the information leading up to the new node (see Figure 2). Something has been learned for the first feature of the input and so the input now becomes 'ate cakes' and processing reverts to the root node. The first feature of the input 'ate' is applied to all links below the root node. A link matching the input feature exists, and so the 'ate' link is traversed and the input moves on to the next feature 'cakes'. In the same way as the 'who ate' node was created, MOSAIC learns a new node below the 'ate' node containing the information 'ate cakes' with the link containing 'cakes'. Processing then reverts to the root node and the input moves on to the remaining input feature 'cakes'. As this has already been learned below the root node, no learning takes place.

When 'who ate cakes' is presented a third time, the first input feature 'who' is matched to a link below the root node, and the 'who' node becomes the current node. The next feature of the input is then processed, and because 'ate' exists as a link below the current node this can be traversed such that the node 'who ate' becomes the current node. The next feature of the input, 'cakes' is then processed. As this does not exist as a link below the current node but the primitive for 'cakes' has been learned, a new node 'who ate cakes' can be learned with the link information being 'cakes'. Thus after three presentations of the input, the phrase 'who ate cakes' has been learned. (see Figure 2). This simple example serves to illustrate how MOSAIC works; in the actual learning phase each utterance is only used once, encouraging a diverse network of nodes to be built.

The method by which MOSAIC learns means it is sensitive to the distributional properties of the input. First, a large amount of input means that MOSAIC will build a deep network of nodes and links that contain various multi-word phrases. Second, words and phrases that occur frequently within this input have more information learned for them within the network e.g. they are more likely to have a variety of links below their respective nodes. The learning in MOSAIC shares great similarities with the concept of chunking (Miller, 1956) — each node represents a chunk of knowledge.

Generative links in MOSAIC

During traversal of the network, generative links can be created. A generative link is a link between any two nodes in a MOSAIC network (excepting the root node). Generative links are designed to link together nodes which are used in a similar manner. Usage is based on the links that are immediately below a particular node such that generative links will be made between nodes that are used in the same context.

In language, context can be defined both by words that succeed a particular word and words that precede a particular word. For example, classic SVO word order has subjects that precede the verb and objects that succeed the verb. For this reason, MOSAIC not only learns utterances in the left-to-right fashion as illustrated in the previous section, but it also processes the same utterance in a right-to-left fashion in order to establish contextual information. Processing a right-to-left utterance occurs in exactly the same way as the previous section (see Figure 2). Importantly, the processing means that links below a node contain words that occurred both before and after the word or phrase contained in the node.

All the links that are below a particular node will consist of the word or words that preceded or succeeded that node in the input. For example, in Figure 3, the words 'cries' and 'can' followed 'baby' in the input, meaning sentences such as 'baby can go' must have been seen in the input. The word 'how's' preceded 'baby' in the input (e.g. an utterance such as 'how's baby gonna sit down' was seen in the input). Similarly, the words 'cries', 'can' and 'goes' must have followed 'he' in input utterances, and 'how's' must have preceded 'he' in input utterances. Note that for ease of explication, Figure 3 does not label the links between nodes.

When there is a significant amount of overlap between words or phrases that are used in similar contexts (i.e. there is significant overlap between the links that are below two particular nodes) then the two nodes can be linked by a generative link. The minimum number of links which must overlap for a generative link to be created is determined by an *overlap parameter*. Using the network in Figure 3 as an example, with the overlap parameter set to 3, 'he' and 'baby' will have a generative link between them because at least 3 of the links below 'he' and 'baby' are shared ('can', 'cries' and 'how's'). Novel utterances can be produced in the network by traversing using generative links.

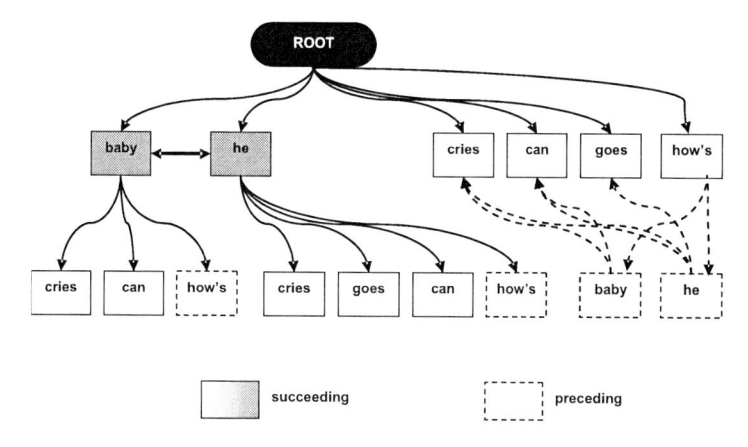

Figure 3. Example of how generative links are created. The word 'how's' appears before both 'he' and 'baby', and the words 'cries' and 'can' appear after both 'he' and 'baby'. This means a generative link can be made between 'he' and 'baby'.

Generating utterances from a MOSAIC network

Utterances can be generated from MOSAIC by beginning at the root node and traversing down until encountering a node which contains an END marker (i.e. the last word in the utterance must be one which ended an utterance in the input). Whilst traversing down the network, both standard links and generative links can be taken. Note that only links that were produced when processing the input in a left-to-right fashion are considered for generating utterances.

To help explain how utterances are generated from the network, the normal links created when processing utterances in a left-to-right manner will be called *rote links* hereafter, because these links are created from rote learning (whereas generative links are created from overlap in node use). When traversing the network, if only rote links are taken then the resulting utterance must have been present in the input (because of the dynamics of the creation of the discrimination network, traversing down from the root node using rote links will always produce a phrase that existed as a full utterance or part of an utterance in the input). That is, an utterance created from only rote links must be a rote-learned utterance. However, when a generative link is taken, the resulting utterance may never have been seen before in the input.

When generative links exist, MOSAIC can take these links as part of the traversal of the network. For example, in the network shown in Figure 3, the generated utterance could begin with 'baby', take the generative link across to 'he', and then continue the utterance with any phrase that follows 'he' (i.e. the remainder of the phrase is built up by traversing the nodes below 'he'). This produces novel utterances that were not seen before in the input, such as 'baby goes'. This is important because when simulating phenomena like the learning of verbs, children's use of verbs becomes productive (i.e. generative) at an early age.

Verb Learning: Simulating the Verb-Island Hypothesis

The verb-island hypothesis

One of the most influential recent constructivist accounts of early grammatical development is Tomasello's (1992) verb-island hypothesis. Tomasello argues that children's early language is built up around lexically-specific predicate-argument structures that are based on the child's experience with particular predicates. For example, arguments to the predicate 'Hit' would be 'Hitters' and 'Hittees' rather than (for example) subjects and objects. The notion of 'verb-island' arises because verbs usually form the relational structure of sentences (i.e. the majority of predicates are verbs), and arguments are specific to the verb (e.g. 'walkers' and 'walkees'), thus forming islands. Children's acquisition of syntactic and morphological marking is assumed to proceed on a verb-by-verb basis, with verb-general marking awaiting the formation of a paradigmatic verb category.

For Tomasello, the definition of verb is functionally equivalent to the definition of predicate: a verb is 'any word that the child uses to predicate a process of something' (Tomasello, 1992, p.11). A verb is therefore synonymous with a predicate and can include lexical items that, in adult language, are not categorised as a verb.

Following Ninio (1988), it is argued that children will only start to construct paradigmatic categories such as noun and verb when they begin to operate on instances of these categories as the arguments of predicates. The implication is that children learning English will form a paradigmatic noun category relatively early, because nouns are used as arguments of predicates at an early stage of development. On the other hand the formation of a paradigmatic verb category will only occur later when children begin to use verbs as the arguments of other predicates, for example in double-verb constructions such as 'Want to + V' or 'Can't + V'.

The verb-island hypothesis can account for a number of phenomena in children's early multi-word speech. First, it can explain the lexically-specific patterning of children's early verb use. For example, Tomasello (1992) has shown that in the early stages of grammatical development his daughter's ability to generate longer sentences built up piecemeal around particular verbs, and failed to generalise to new verbs which typically entered her speech in very simple structures. Second, it can explain the restricted nature of children's early word order rules. For example Akhtar and Tomasello (1997) have shown that young children not only fail to generalise SVO word order knowledge from one verb to another, but are also unable to use it as a cue for sentence comprehension with novel verbs. Third, it can explain differences in the flexibility with which children use nouns and verbs in their early multi-word speech. For example, Tomasello and his colleagues have shown that young children will readily slot novel nouns into familiar verb structures but tend to restrict their use of novel verbs to the structures in which they have heard those same verbs modelled in the input (Akhtar & Tomasello, 1997; Olguin & Tomasello, 1993; Tomasello & Olguin, 1993).

Although the verb-island hypothesis fits the developmental data reasonably well, it also has one major weakness. Verbs are defined within the theory as 'anything in the child's language that functions as a predicate' (Tomasello, 1992, p. 11) suggesting that children will not show lexically-specific structures based around other categories such as pronouns. Pine, Lieven and Rowland (1998) have shown that such phenomena exist in children. For example, many children acquire lexically-specific structures based around case-marked pronouns such as 'I' and 'He' and proper-nouns such as 'Mummy' and 'Anne', items which would not normally be defined as predicates. Moreover, these pronoun and proper-noun islands not only seem to be functioning as structuring elements in children's speech, but as structuring elements for which verbs act as slot-fillers. These data suggest that the lexical specificity of children's early multi-word speech is not always 'verb-specificity', or even 'predicate-specificity', as such, and hence verb-island effects may simply be a special case of more general frequency effects on children's acquisition of lexically-specific structures.

Simulating verb-islands and other-islands

The verb-island hypothesis can be confirmed if the language data contains verbs which exist as frames (i.e. verbs which take several different items as slot fillers), and contains *very few other lexical items* which exist as frames. To examine this, MOSAIC was trained on mother's utterances and the output from the model (i.e. generating all possible utterances the model could produce using generative links) was examined for the existence of verb-islands and also other predicate structures that did not involve verbs (i.e. 'other' islands). The utterances generated from the model were analysed by extracting verb+common-noun sequences (common-noun+verb sequences were also extracted to ensure that common-noun islands did not exist). Common-nouns, rather than all lexical items, were examined for three reasons. First, they are the most common category in children's speech. Second, Tomasello (1992) predicts that children form noun categories earlier than verb categories based on their use as slot fillers (i.e. they should be used often as the slot fillers of verb frames). Third, the analysis was more tractable with only two lexical items.

To investigate whether other-island phenomena exist, pronoun+verb and proper-noun+verb combinations were extracted and analysed. Pronouns were used because a strict version of the verb-island hypothesis does not allow pronouns to act as islands. Also, pronouns occur with high frequency in the child's data and are often followed by a verb (i.e. they may show verbs being used as slot fillers to other frames). Proper-nouns were used for an additional test of other-islands.

Three sets of data were compared for the verb-island phenomena: the utterances from one child, Anne; the utterances from Anne's mother; and the utterances from MOSAIC when trained using Anne's mothers utterances as input. The utterances for Anne and her mother were taken from the Manchester corpus (Theakston, Lieven, Pine & Rowland, 2001) of the CHILDES database (MacWhinney & Snow, 1990). The corpus consists of transcripts of the mother-child interactions of twelve children over a period of twelve months. The transcripts contain both the utterances and the syntactic categories (e.g. noun, verb) of all words in the utterances. The child focused on

Distributional Accounts of Language

here, Anne, began at age 1;10.7 and completed the study at age 2;9.10. Her starting MLU was 1.62 with a vocabulary size of 180.

For Anne there were 17,967 utterances (i.e. utterance tokens), of which 8,257 utterances were unique (i.e. utterance types). There were 7,331 multi-word utterance types. For Anne's mother, there were 33,390 utterance tokens, 19,358 utterance types, and 18,684 multi-word utterance types. A random sample of 7,331 of Anne's mother's multi-word utterance types was taken to match Anne for quantity of data.

MOSAIC was trained on the full 33,390 utterance tokens of Anne's mother in chronological order, one utterance at a time (as a list of words). MOSAIC's overlap parameter was set to 15. The input to MOSAIC did *not* contain any coding information. This means that MOSAIC was not presented with any information about the categories of words (e.g. that 'dog' was a noun or 'go' was a verb) or about noun or verb morphology (e.g. 'going' was seen rather than the morpheme '-ing' attached to the root form of the verb 'go').

After MOSAIC had seen all of the input utterances, every possible utterance that could be generated was output. This resulted in 178,068 utterance types (21,510 produced by rote and 156,558 produced by generation). Note that any generated utterances that also existed as rote-learned utterances were discarded. Examples of the utterances generated from MOSAIC are shown in Table 1.

Table 1. Sample of the utterances generated from MOSAIC.

MOSAIC utterance
I forgotten
That's my toes again
Where's the magic bag
And she like them
Baby put the sheep in the farmyard
What about the camel
All on the settee
Who can you see on here
He didn't catch me

The analyses of the data from MOSAIC is based on a random sample of 7,331 (i.e. matching Anne for quantity) of the multi-word utterance types produced by *generation*, because these are the novel utterances that will not have existed as part of the mothers' input.

The utterances for both the child and mother included the syntactic category for each word in an utterance. The codings for the child's utterances were used to determine the categories of words in the utterances of the child; the codings for the mother's utterances were used to determine the categories of words in the utterances of the mother. Some words (such as 'fire') belong to more than one category. In these cases, a category was only assigned if the word was used as that category in at least 80% of the instances in which the word was used. For MOSAIC's utterances, the categories were calculated based on the codings from the mother's utterances.

The three sets of data were analysed in the same way. The method of extracting verb+common-noun combinations is detailed here but the method is the same for the extraction of common-noun+verb, pronoun+verb, and proper-noun+verb combinations.

Each utterance was searched for a word which was categorised as a verb. The two words following the verb-category word were examined to see if either occurred as a common-noun. If so, the verb+common-noun pair was stored for analysis. Verbs were then converted to their root form (e.g. 'going' and 'goes' both become 'go') and common-nouns to their singular form (e.g. 'dogs' becomes 'dog'), and any duplicate pairs were removed. Analysis was therefore conducted on types, not tokens. The number of slot fillers for a verb is the number of different common-noun types that were paired with that verb.

Results

As explained earlier, the data is expected to show that verbs act as frames (taking lots of different common-nouns as slot fillers) whereas common-nouns are not expected to act as frames. Whether this is true can be examined by looking at the number of common-noun types that follow verb types, and vice versa. We operationalise the concept of an 'island' as a lexical item which acts as a frame for at least ten different slot fillers (e.g. a verb type would have to have ten different common-noun types as slot fillers). For example, for Anne, the verb 'Find' is an island because it is followed by ten common-noun types ('Dolly', 'Plate', 'Seat', 'Welly-boot', 'Baby', 'Ribbon', 'Hat', 'Duck', 'Pen', and 'Bird'). Table 2 shows these data for Anne, Anne's mother, and MOSAIC. This shows that there are many verb-islands for all three sources of data, but very few common-noun islands. In both cases, MOSAIC provides an identical match to Anne for number of islands.

Table 2. Number of nominal+verb and verb+nominal combinations accounted for by pronouns, proper-nouns, and common-nouns, based on the 7,331 multi-word utterances from Anne, Anne's mother, and MOSAIC. The mean is the mean number of slot fillers for each lexical item. The islands are the number of that lexical item that have ten or more unique slot fillers.

Data Source	Mean	Islands	Islands having the most slot fillers
VERB+COMMON-NOUN (frame=verb; slot filler=common-noun)			
Anne	6.24	10	Get, Put, Want, Go, Need, Make
Mother	5.97	13	Get, Put, Want, Need, Have, Find
MOSAIC	9.74	10	Get, Put, Eat, Think, Want, Find
COMMON-NOUN+VERB (frame=common-noun; slot filler=verb)			
Anne	1.51	1	Baby
Mother	2.08	4	Baby, Animal, Dolly, Penguin
MOSAIC	1.57	1	Baby
PRONOUN+VERB (frame=pronoun; slot filler=verb)			
Anne	21.69	10	I, You, He, It, That, They, We
Mother	27.65	11	You, I, He, We, She, They, It
MOSAIC	25.20	12	You, It, That, I, He, We, She
PROPER-NOUN+VERB (frame=proper-noun; slot filler=verb)			
Anne	5.65	3	Anne, Mummy, Daddy
Mother	3.23	3	Anne, Mummy, Daddy
MOSAIC	6.67	2	Anne, Mummy

Table 2 also shows that both pronoun-islands and proper-noun islands exist for Anne, Anne's mother, and MOSAIC. The pronoun-islands are particularly strong (the mean number of slot fillers for pronouns is more than 20 for all three sets of data) and because pronouns take verbs as slot fillers, these islands are problematic for a strict version of the verb-island hypothesis which predicts that only verbs are initially used as frames. These 'other-islands', as Table 2 shows, are readily simulated by MOSAIC.

Summary

The output from MOSAIC more closely resembles the child than the child's mother, demonstrating that MOSAIC is doing more than just a straightforward distributional analysis of its input. In fact, it is a combination of the performance-limitations imposed on the model (e.g. learning one word at a time), and the frequency of occurrence of items in the input, that enable MOSAIC to match the child data. MOSAIC seeks to maximise the information held at nodes in the network, but can only do so for input sequences that occur frequently (e.g. due to limitations in only learning one item at a time). MOSAIC therefore offers a process-based explanation of why some lexical items come to function as 'islands' in children's grammar and others do not: children are also maximally sensitive to the high frequency lexical items that exist in their input.

The results show that the combination of naturalistic input and a simple distributional learning mechanism are able to provide an effective simulation of child language data. The simulations show that it is possible to model verb-island phenomena as the product of a frequency-sensitive distributional analysis of the child's input, and, second, that the same mechanism can also simulate other-island patterns which are problematic for a strict version of the verb-island hypothesis.

Vocabulary Acquisition: Simulating the Nonword Repetition Test

The nonword repetition test

The acquisition of vocabulary represents a key phenomenon in language acquisition. After an initial slow period from about 12 to 16 months when most children learn around 40 words, the learning rate increases such that in the next four months children will have learned 130 more new words (Bates *et al.*, 1994). A major part of learning new words is learning the novel sequences of sounds that represent the word. However, it is difficult to directly examine the processes involved in learning the sound patterns of new words because it is impossible to be certain that the new sound pattern has never been encountered before. The use of *nonwords* (e.g. *nate*) which conform to the phonotactic rules of English provides a good test of vocabulary learning because it ensures that the (non)word to be learned is novel.

The nonword repetition (NWR) test (Gathercole, Willis, Baddeley & Emslie, 1994) involves the experimenter speaking aloud a nonword and the child attempting to repeat the nonword. The test involves two sets of nonwords, one set having single consonants (e.g. *rubid*) and one set having clustered consonants (e.g. *glistow*). There are twenty nonwords in each set, divided into four groups of five based on the number of syllables in the nonword (two to five). Studies using these types of nonwords have found that repetition accuracy decreases as the number of syllables in the nonword increases (e.g. Gathercole & Adams, 1993; Gathercole, Willis, Emslie & Baddeley, 1991), accuracy is better for single consonant nonwords over clustered consonant nonwords (e.g. Gathercole & Baddeley, 1989) and accuracy improves with age (Gathercole & Baddeley, 1989). Furthermore, Gathercole and Baddeley (1989) found that NWR was the best predictor of vocabulary size in 4 and 5 year old children even when compared to specific language-based abilities such as sound mimicry, and memory-based abilities such as digit span. NWR is also highly predictive of vocabulary in 2-3 year old children (Gathercole & Adams, 1993), illustrating the test to be suitable for assessing young children's vocabulary knowledge. Moreover, NWR performance was seen as indicating phonological working memory as a mediator in vocabulary learning (Gathercole, Willis, Baddeley & Emslie, 1994).

However, Gathercole, Willis, Emslie, and Baddeley (1991) found better NWR performance on nonwords that were rated high in wordlikeness than nonwords rated low in wordlikeness. Such findings illustrate the influence that vocabulary knowledge has upon the learning of new words. In fact, rather than phonological working memory mediating vocabulary knowledge, it could be that vocabulary knowledge itself mediates the amount of information that can be stored in phonological working memory. The latter view is consistent with the ideas presented in this chapter where the language input governs performance. This is what will be explored in the simulations of NWR performance.

Simulating the nonword repetition test

A simplified version of the MOSAIC model presented earlier will be used to simulate NWR. First, the concept of generative links that were used to capture context are dispensed with. Second, rather than use words as input, each utterance is recoded into its phonemic equivalent. The same hierarchical nature of the model is therefore maintained but the contents of nodes will now be phonemes and phoneme sequences rather than words and parts of utterances. Third, the model parses the input in a slightly different way — when something is learned about a feature in the input, processing continues after the feature that was learned rather than beginning with the learned feature.

An example of the model learning a word will be given in order to illustrate how learning differs from that of the standard MOSAIC model. Let us assume the network is empty (i.e. just having the root node that always contains no information) and the utterance 'What?' (phonemic equivalent 'W AH1 T') is presented. As with MOSAIC, the network is traversed by examining the input in sequence. The first input feature, the phoneme 'W', is examined. The network has no links below the root node, so no traversing can be accomplished. The network therefore creates a 'W' node and link below the root node. The input then moves on to the next feature ('AH1'), traversal reverts back to the root node, and the process begins again. No links below the root node match 'AH1' and so the node and link 'AH1' are learned below the root node. The phoneme 'T' is learned in the same way.

When 'W AH1 T' is presented a second time to the network, the 'W' link can be taken and the node 'W' becomes the current node. The next input feature is then examined ('AH1'). As 'AH1' exists as a primitive, it can be learned below the 'W' node (resulting in a 'W AH1' node with the link containing the information 'AH1'). The network reverts back to the root node and the input then moves onto 'T'. Note that in standard MOSAIC, the input would first process the feature 'AH1' and hence learn a node 'AH1 T'. In this version of the model, learning is slowed by processing the input in a more piecemeal fashion. The input feature 'T' has already been learned and so processing ends. Presenting 'W AH1 T' a third time leads to the 'W' and 'AH1' links being taken, with learning placing a 'W AH1 T' node below the 'W AH1' node, with a link of 'T'. Thus, after three presentations of 'W AH1 T', the model learns the word as a complete phoneme sequence (as shown in Figure 4). Further details of the specifics

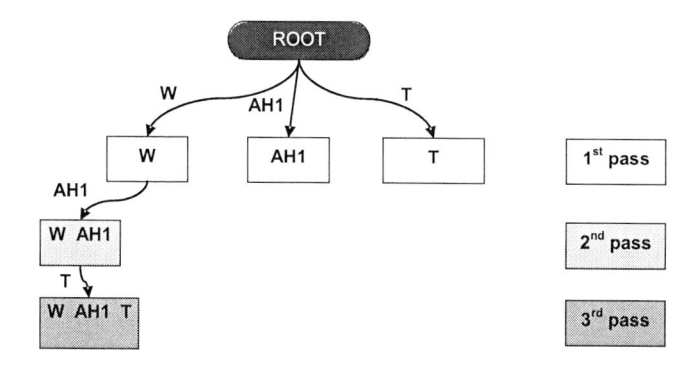

Figure 4. Structure of EPAM-VOC after receiving the input 'W AH1 T' three times.

of the model (hereafter named EPAM-VOC) can be found in Jones, Gobet and Pine (in press).

The NWR test involves both long-term phonological knowledge and phonological working memory. Incoming speech enters phonological working memory and after analysis phonological knowledge is learned in long-term memory. The network as described above serves as long-term phonological knowledge because it specifies the phoneme sequences known by the model. EPAM-VOC now requires a specification of phonological working memory (PWM). When PWM is described (e.g. Gathercole & Baddeley, 1989), it is normally equated to the phonological loop component of the working memory model (Baddeley & Hitch, 1974). The phonological loop contains a phonological store (where speech heard by the listener is stored in phonemes) and a sub-vocal rehearsal mechanism. The phonological store has a limited duration of 2,000 ms (Baddeley, Thomson & Buchanan, 1975) but the sub-vocal rehearsal mechanism can be used to enable items to remain in the store.

EPAM-VOC suggests that long-term knowledge mediates PWM. Rather than placing the input directly into PWM, EPAM-VOC first re-codes the input as much as possible by matching it to phonological knowledge that exists in the network. Re-coding the input will allow long-term phonological knowledge to influence how much information can fit into PWM. Let us examine how this works. PWM has a capacity of 2,000 ms. EPAM already has timing estimates for matching nodes in the network (400 ms) and items within a node excepting the first item (30 ms per subsequent item in a node) (timing estimates are from Zhang & Simon, 1985). With an empty network, an utterance such as 'What is that?' (phonemic equivalent 'W AH1 T IH1 Z DH AE1 T') would be limited by PWM to the phonemes 'W AH1 T IH1 Z' (as no phonemes exist in the network, the maximum 400 ms is assumed as the time taken to represent each phoneme in PWM). However, with the network as shown in Figure 4, 'W AH1 T IH1 Z DH' could be represented in PWM capacity within the 2,000 ms time duration. The sequence 'W AH1 T' can be matched to a single node, so it is allocated a time of 460 ms — 400 ms to access the node and a further 30 ms for each phoneme bar the first. The remaining phonemes in the input are assumed to have a time of 400 ms (the total time for the phonemes in PWM is 1,660 ms).

It is only after re-coding of the input that the network learning process in EPAM-VOC takes place. That is, the input is re-coded into PWM by matching it as much as possible to nodes in EPAM-VOC, and then learning occurs on the information that resides in PWM to create new nodes and links.

Long-term phonological knowledge interacts with PWM such that when the network of nodes is small, long-term phonological knowledge does not aid PWM a great deal. When the network is large, long-term phonological knowledge can be used to fit much more of the input into PWM and thus there is more opportunity for the subsequent learning of phonemic knowledge.

The model was compared to the NWR performance of Gathercole and Adams' (1993) 2-3 year old and Gathercole and Baddeley's (1989) 4 and 5 year old children. Children of five years of age and below do not rehearse, or are inconsistent in their rehearsal (Gathercole & Adams, 1994), and so no rehearsal mechanism was defined in PWM. The network was again trained on the utterances from Anne's mother (33,390 utterances in total, converted to their phonemic equivalent using the CMU Lexicon database, available at http://www.speech.cs.cmu.edu/cgi-bin/cmudict). To compare to 2-3 year olds, 4 year olds, and 5 year olds, a NWR test was taken after 37.5%, 75% and 100% of the models input respectively.

In order to estimate the type of input a 5 year old child may receive, the input was doubled. That is, the first 50% of the input was mother's utterances, and the remainder of the input consisted of random phonemic words from the CMU Lexicon. The NWR tests consisted of presenting each phonemic nonword to the model in turn, and seeing if the nonword could be represented in PWM within the 2,000 ms duration. However, because young children make errors based on incorrect encoding or articulation (processes not simulated in the model), a probability of making an incorrect traversal in the network was imposed. This was set at 10% (based on the one syllable nonword errors of Gathercole & Adams, 1993 and Jones, Gobet & Pine, in press) and was reduced over time under the assumption that with age, children become more adept at encoding and articulating spoken material. Given two random elements in the model (random lexicon words and the probability of a traversal error when performing NWR), ten simulations were run and two rather than one NWR test was taken at each relevant point.

Results

The NWR test for the 2-3 year olds used different nonwords to the standard NWR test in order to be suitable for young children and so the 2-3 year olds are analysed separately. The central NWR findings in the two studies used are: a decline in performance as nonword length increases (Gathercole & Adams, 1993; Gathercole & Baddeley, 1989); improved performance with age (Gathercole & Baddeley, 1989), and improved performance for single consonant nonwords over clustered consonant nonwords (Gathercole & Baddeley, 1989). In order for the model to provide a good explanation of NWR performance, it must at least be able to simulate these phenomena.

2-3 year old simulation

Figure 5 shows the performance for the 2-3 year old children compared with EPAM-VOC. The simulations show a good correlation to the child data ($r=.99$). A one-way ANOVA was performed on the data with nonword-length as the within-subjects factor. A significant effect of nonword-length was found ($F(2,38)=26.78$, MSE=23.4, $p<.001$). Post-hoc Bonferroni tests indicated that three syllable nonwords were repeated less accurately than both one and two syllable nonwords ($p<.001$ in both cases). The data not only match the children well but also support the finding that NWR performance declines as nonword length increases.

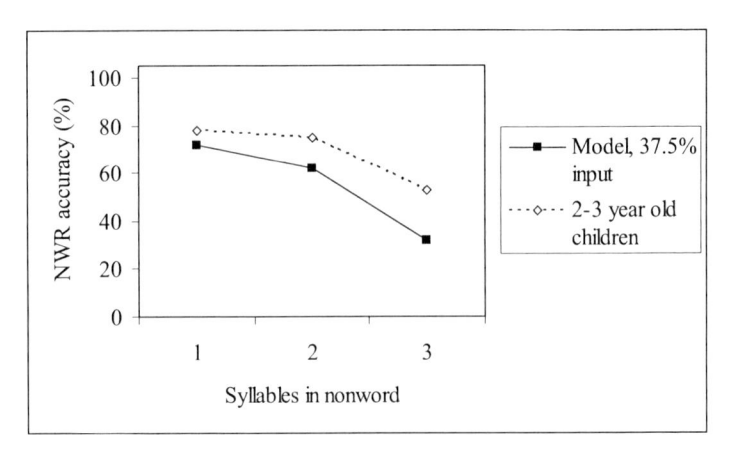

Figure 5. NWR performance for EPAM-VOC after 37.5% of the input is seen compared with 2-3 year olds from Gathercole and Adams (1993).

4 and 5 year olds simulation

The nonword test used for the 4 and 5 year olds in Gathercole and Baddeley (1989) contained the 2-4 syllable nonwords of the standard NWR test because children at this age had difficulty with 5 syllable nonwords (the test also included 1 syllable nonwords though these are discarded here because of accepted problems with the nonwords, see Gathercole & Baddeley, 1989). Figure 6 shows the performance for 4 and 5 year old children compared with EPAM-VOC after 75% and 100% of its learning for *single* consonant nonwords. The 75% input simulations show a good correlation to the 4 year old children ($r=.96$) and the 100% simulations show a good correlation to the 5 year old children ($r=.99$). Figure 7 shows the performance for 4 and 5 year old children compared with EPAM-VOC after 75% and 100% of its learning for *clustered* consonant nonwords. Again, both the 75% input and 100% input simulations show good correlation to the 4 and 5 year old children ($r=.99$ and $r=.93$ respectively).

A 2 (input: 75% or 100%) x 2 (nonword-type: single or clustered) x 3 (nonword-length: 2, 3, or 4 syllables) repeated measures ANOVA was carried out on the data. There was a significant main effect of input ($F(1,19)=17.08$, MSE=12.15, $p<.001$), showing that with more language input, NWR performance improved. There was a significant main effect of nonword-type ($F(1,19)=7.58$, MSE=9.60, $p<.02$)

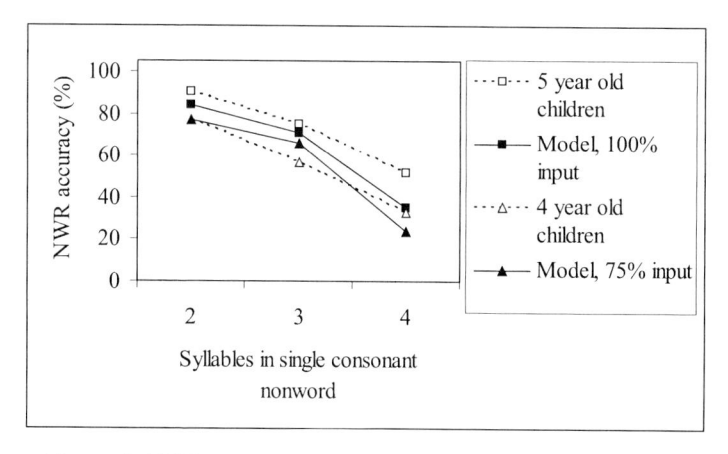

Figure 6. NWR performance for single consonant nonwords for EPAM-VOC after 75% and 100% of the input is seen, and the 4 and 5 year old children of Gathercole and Baddeley (1989).

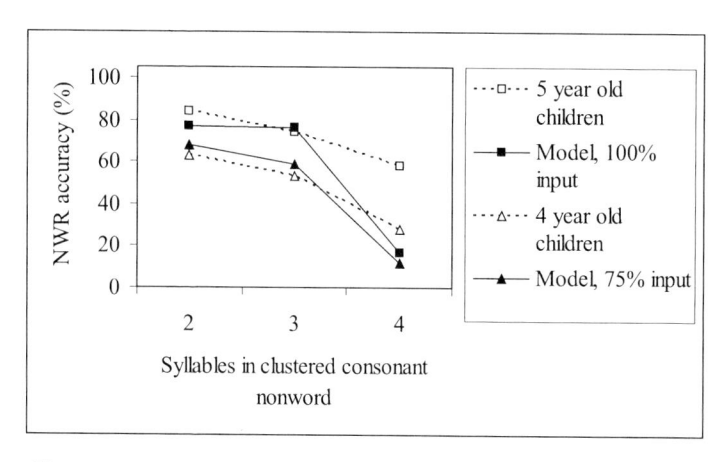

Figure 7. NWR performance for clustered consonant nonwords for EPAM-VOC after 75% and 100% of the input is seen, and the 4 and 5 year old children of Gathercole and Baddeley (1989).

showing that NWR performance was better for single consonant nonwords over clustered consonant nonwords. There was also a significant main effect of nonword-length ($F(2,38)=176.92$, MSE=171.95, $p<.001$) showing that as nonword length increased, performance decreased. Performance declined for three syllable nonwords over two syllable nonwords ($p<.05$) and for four syllable nonwords over three syllable nonwords ($p<.001$). The model shows exactly the same differences in performance as the children: performance improves with age and performance declines with the complexity and length of the nonword.

Summary

The model was able to show exactly the same differences as the children on three key NWR performance criteria: improvement with age, and a decline in performance with nonword complexity and length. EPAM-VOC achieves these performance differences from an interaction between a fixed capacity phonological working memory and the learning of phonemic knowledge, together with variation in the amount of input.

EPAM-VOC also makes two key theoretical contributions. First, the simulations presented illustrate that developmental increases in NWR performance can be obtained primarily from the increase in linguistic input the child receives. Note that throughout the simulations, PWM capacity remained constant at 2,000 ms. This suggests that, for nonword repetition at least, capacity differences are not necessary to explain performance differences across age. Such a finding is important because it suggests that children's development may be primarily due to experience rather than any developmental increases in concepts such as capacity.

Second, EPAM-VOC explains how PWM interacts with long-term knowledge. The model gradually builds up a network of phonological knowledge that enables more information to be stored in PWM capacity over time. The model presents a parsimonious account of how PWM and long-term knowledge interact that has been lacking in the literature. Such an account also fits in with existing ideas of vocabulary acquisition (e.g. Metsala, 1999).

Chapter summary

MOSAIC and its simplified variant EPAM-VOC provide a simple distributional account of the mother's utterances that is able to simulate key child language phenomena using what is almost wholly a constructivist account of language acquisition. The set of simulations presented suggests that a fruitful approach to child language acquisition is to see the extent to which child language phenomena can be explained solely from the input the child receives. Accomplishing this will then provide researchers with a set of phenomena that require more than just the input as an explanation—and that is where innate mechanisms will arise.

References

Akhtar, N., & Tomasello, M. (1997), 'Young children's productivity with word order and verb morphology', *Developmental Psychology*, 33, pp. 952–965.

Baddeley, A. D. & Hitch, G. J. (1974), 'Working memory', In G. Bower (Ed.), *The Psychology of Learning and Motivation: Advances In Research and Theory* (New York, NY: Academic Press), pp. 47–90.

Baddeley, A. D., Thompson, N. & Buchanan, M. (1975), 'Word length and the structure of short-term memory', *Journal of Verbal Learning and Verbal Behaviour*, 14, pp. 575–589.

Bates, E., Marchman, V., Thal, D., Fenson, L., Dale, P., Reznick, J. S., Reilly, J. & Hartung, J. (1994), 'Developmental and stylistic variation in the composition of early vocabulary', *Journal of Child Language*, 21, pp. 85–123.

Chomsky, N. (1969), *Aspects of the Theory of Syntax* (Cambridge, MA: MIT Press).

De Groot, A. D. & Gobet, F. (1996), *Perception and Memory In Chess: Studies In the Heuristics of the Professional Eye* (Assen: Van Gorcum).

Feigenbaum, E. A. & Simon, H. A. (1984), 'EPAM-like models of recognition and learning', *Cognitive Science*, 8, pp. 305–336.

Gathercole, S. E. & Adams, A-M. (1993), 'Phonological working memory in very young children', *Developmental Psychology*, 29, pp. 770–778.

Gathercole, S. E. & Adams, A-M. (1994), 'Children's phonological working memory: Contributions of long-term knowledge and rehearsal', *Journal of Memory and Language*, 33, pp. 672–688.

Gathercole, S. E. & Baddeley, A. D. (1989), 'Evaluation of the role of phonological STM in the development of vocabulary in children: A longitudinal study', *Journal of Memory and Language*, 28, pp. 200–213.

Gathercole, S. E., Willis, C. S., Baddeley, A. D. & Emslie, H. (1994), 'The children's test of nonword repetition: A test of phonological working memory', *Memory*, 2, pp. 103–127.

Gathercole, S. E., Willis, C. S., Emslie, H. & Baddeley, A. D. (1991), 'The influence of number of syllables and wordlikeness on children's repetition of nonwords', *Applied Psycholinguistics*, 12, pp. 349–367.

Gobet, F. (1993), 'A computer model of chess memory', In W. Kintsch (Ed.), *Proceedings of the Fifteenth Annual Meeting of the Cognitive Science Society* (Boulder, CO: Erlbaum), pp. 463–468.

Gobet, F. & Simon, H. A. (2000), 'Five seconds or sixty? Presentation time in expert memory', *Cognitive Science*, 24, pp. 651–682.

Gobet, F., Lane, P. C. R., Croker, S., Cheng, P. C. H., Jones, G., Oliver, I. & Pine, J. M. (2001), 'Chunking mechanisms in human learning', *Trends in Cognitive Sciences*, 5, pp. 236–243.

Jones, G., Gobet, F. & Pine, J.M. (2005), 'Modelling vocabulary acquisition: An explanation of the link between the phonological loop and long-term memory', *Artificial Intelligence and Simulation of Behaviour Journal*, 1, pp. 509–522.

Jones, G., Gobet, F. & Pine, J.M. (in press), 'Linking working memory and long-term memory: A computational model of the learning of new words', *Developmental Science*.

MacWhinney, B. & Snow, C. (1990), 'The Child Language Data Exchange System: An update', *Journal of Child Language*, 17, pp. 457–472.

Metsala, J. L. (1999), 'Young children's phonological awareness and nonword repetition as a function of vocabulary development', *Journal of Educational Psychology*, 91, pp. 3–19.

Miller, G. A. (1956), 'The magical number seven, plus or minus two: Some limits on our capacity for processing information', *Psychological Review*, 63, pp. 81–97.

Ninio, A. (1988), 'On formal grammatical categories in early child language', In Y. Levy, I. M. Schlesinger, & M. D. S. Braine (Eds.), *Categories and Processes in Language Acquisition* (Hillsdale, NJ: Lawrence Erlbaum Associates).

Olguin, R. & Tomasello, M. (1993), 'Twenty-five-month-old children do not have a grammatical category of verb', *Cognitive Development*, 8, pp. 245–272.

Pine, J. M., Lieven, E. V. M. & Rowland, C. F. (1998), 'Comparing different models of the development of the English verb category', *Linguistics*, 36, pp. 807–830.

Richman, H. B., Staszewski, J. & Simon, H. A. (1995), 'Simulation of expert memory with EPAM IV', *Psychological Review*, 102, pp. 305–330.

Simon, H. A., & Gilmartin, K. J. (1973), 'A simulation of memory for chess positions', *Cognitive Psychology*, 5, pp. 29–46.

Theakston, A. L., Lieven, E. V. M., Pine, J. M. & Rowland, C. F. (2001), 'The role of performance limitations in the acquisition of Verb-Argument structure: An alternative account', *Journal of Child Language*, 28, pp. 127–152.

Tomasello, M. (1992), *First Verbs: A Case Study of Early Grammatical Development* (Cambridge: CUP).

Tomasello, M. & Olguin, R. (1993), 'Twenty-three-month-old children have a grammatical category of noun', *Cognitive Development*, 8, pp. 451–464.

Zhang, G., & Simon, H. A. (1985), 'STM capacity for Chinese words and idioms: Chunking and acoustical loop hypothesis', *Memory and Cognition*, 13, pp. 193–201.

Paul Vogt

Variation, Competition and Selection in the Self-Organisation of Compositionality

Abstract

This chapter discusses how Darwin's theory of evolution can be applied to explain language evolution at a cultural level. So, rather than viewing language evolution as a process in which the users adapt biologically to learn language, languages themselves adapt to the learning abilities of individuals. Within this framework, languages evolve through variation, competition and selection. Invention and learning are identified as the mechanisms producing variation; learnability, transmission bottlenecks and stability are pressures for competition; and optimising for success is a good selection mechanism. Rather than studying language development in individual users, this chapter illustrates how artificial multi-agent systems equipped with these principles can self-organise a compositional language from scratch. It is argued that this model offers a good alternative to many standard approaches in linguistics.

1. Introduction

Language is possibly the most complex form of cognitive behaviour displayed by humans and may well have laid the foundation for the high level of intelligence that we generally attribute to the human species. Not surprisingly, we have great difficulties understanding exactly how we acquire and process language. One recent trend is to view languages as self-organising systems that organise on a global scale as the result of local interactions (Croft, 2002; Steels, 1997; De Boer, 2005).

This view contrasts with the idea that language has evolved into a genetically encoded Universal Grammar (Chomsky, 1956; Pinker & Bloom, 1990), which suggests that humans are innately endowed to acquire the grammatical structures of language constrained and formed by UG. One problem with this approach is that it is only concerned with the *perfect* competence of an *idealised* speaker, rather than with the performance of real speakers (see, e.g., Croft, 2002, for a discussion).

Accounts of the self-organising nature of language (not to be confused with the nature of its speakers) are more concerned with performance and thus regard languages the way they are used, rather than the way they are represented in an idealised manner. Regarding languages as self-organising systems allows us to investigate the origins of languages (e.g. Steels, 1997) and the evolution of languages (e.g. Croft, 2000) as dynamical processes at a cultural instead of a genetic level. These aspects further suggest that it is more profitable to study language development and evolution at a population level, rather than at the individual level.

An important mechanism that has often been proposed is Darwinian selection, though not on genetic material, but on *linguemes* (Croft, 2000; Mufwene, 2002). According to this view, language users replicate parts of the language (e.g., speech sounds, words or grammar) with various modifications. As a result, a lot of variation tends to arise among which speakers have to select, either consciously or unconsciously, what variant they produce. This way, a global pattern (i.e. language) self-organises as the result of variation, competition and selection.

In the past decade or so, an increasing number of studies have simulated the origins and evolution of language computationally (see, e.g., Cangelosi & Parisi, 2002; Steels, 1997; Vogt, 2006b, for overviews). Most of these studies regard languages as self-organising systems (De Boer, 2005). In this chapter, I will briefly review a few recent studies using a computational model that simulates the emergence of compositional structures in language (Vogt, 2005a, 2005b).

Building further on these studies, the objective of this chapter is to illustrate how the interaction between variation, competition and selection can explain the emergence of compositionality. The next section will briefly discuss the idea of Darwinian selection in language evolution. I will then present and discuss the computational studies on the emergence of compositionality.

2. Variation, Competition and Selection

Darwin's theory of natural selection (Darwin, 1959) has not only found its way in biology, but also in other disciplines such as social science (Dawkins, 1976), linguistics (Croft, 2002) and even the philosophy of science (Hull, 1988). Let me briefly summarise the essence of Darwinian evolution. At its heart lies the principle of *variation*. Elements such as DNA molecules are replicated and during this process errors or mutations occur. These mutations cause variations in the gene pool. Some variations are more adaptive in the current environment and tend to survive; others are not so adaptive and fail to replicate further. This process is called *selection*. The reason there has to be selection is *competition*. The different genes (or replicated individuals, i.e. offspring) compete for their suitedness in the environment. Some variations that occur may not be well adapted to the environment, so the organism having this variation may not survive long enough to pass over their genes.

Following Hull (1988), who has proposed the *general analysis of selection* theory for processes applicable to biological, social and conceptual development, Croft (2000) has proposed to apply these Darwinian mechanisms to explain language evolution and language change. In Croft's model, the replicators are called lingemes, which include elementary units in language such as speech sounds, syllables, morphemes, words and grammatical units. Linguemes are acquired by individuals primarily based on what they hear in their environment. Since different speakers use different variants of a lingueme or because some linguemes are transmitted with noise, a hearer will acquire a variety of linguemes. In order to produce or interpret an utterance, individuals select linguemes from this pool. Selection can — possibly unconsciously — be based on the social status of the speaker or the hearer, but may also be based on a drive to communicate effectively.

Just as each individual acquires a lingueme pool, the entire speech community forms a lingueme pool. As linguemes have been produced by a variety of speakers, the pool contains a lot of variation, from which certain linguemes are selected by the same or new speakers and possibly undergo further mutations. The evolution of this lingueme pool marks language change. A good theory of language evolution according to this line of thinking will need a number of mechanisms that cause variation, competition and selection on all types of linguemes. Mechanisms causing variation include invention and mutation. Invention is typically necessary when the current language (of an individual) is insufficient for communicating something. For instance, when a new product is invented and put on the market, this may require the invention of a new word. Sounds can mutate due to noisy transmission and word-meaning mappings can also mutate due to errors in learning. Word-meanings, however, can also change by reusing an existing word to refer to a new product. Language contact is, of course, another source for variation (Mufwene, 2002). As we shall see, variations may also occur through the creative productivity of individuals through newly discovered generalisations.

Since an uncontrolled growth of the lingueme pool causes unstable communication systems to emerge, competition is required. Stability is considered to be one of the major pressures for competition (Cavalli-Sforza & Feldman, 1981), which may relate to particular pressures regulating understandability, learnability (Deacon, 1997) or social status (Croft, 2002). To facilitate competition, one or more selection mechanisms are required. One mechanism that seems plausible is optimisation of understandability. With such a mechanism, individuals tend to select elements that have been used successfully in the past. In addition, this may be achieved by individuals aligning their communication to what they expect their speech partners will most likely understand (Pickering & Garrod, 2004).

Based on such mechanisms, De Boer (2001) has convincingly shown how a population of simulated agents equipped with a quasi-realistic model of the human vocal tract and auditory system could develop human-like vowel systems. Interactions among agents were modelled by means of imitation games, where an imitator tried to imitate the vowel produced by a speaker. If the imitated vowel was perceived by the speaker as the one it produced, the game was considered successful and the imitator would shift this vowel closer to the vowel perceived. Occasionally, the agents invented new random vowels and when two vowels came very close to one another, they were merged. As a result of the population playing many imitation games, De Boer showed that, under certain conditions, the distribution of different vowel systems that arose in different runs of the simulations were highly similar to the distribution of human vowel systems across the world's languages as reported in Maddieson (1984).

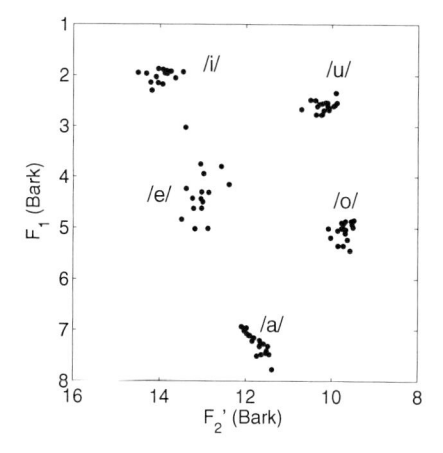

Figure 1. An example of the type of vowel systems that evolved in De Boer's simulations. The figure shows 5 clusters of vowels. In each cluster, one dot represents the vowel of one agent. Clearly, there is quite some variation in the system, though at this stage, the system is quite stable. (Reprinted with permission from De Boer, 1999.)

De Boer's model fits well with the theory of variation, competition and selection. Variation in his model was introduced in three ways: random insertion of new vowels, noise in transmission and shifting vowels toward physically heard ones. As a result of the random insertion, vowels were introduced in different areas of the vowel space. Due to the attraction of vowels (through shift), clusters were formed in different regions. Because an agent could have several vowels near one cluster, different vowels in the system competed for occupying a region in the vowel space. The individual selection mechanism, of taking the nearest neighbouring vowel to the one heard, caused vowel systems to evolve towards relatively stable systems, such as shown in Figure 1. So, the agents' tendency to imitate each other as closely as possible was the main selection mechanism in De Boer's model.

This type of approach has not only been applied to the evolution of vowel systems, but also to the evolution of lexicons (Oliphant, 1996), lexicon grounding (Steels & Vogt, 1997), syntax (Kirby, 2001) and grammar (Steels, 2005; Vogt, 2005a). In the remainder of this chapter, I will discuss how the principles of variation, competition and selection can be used to study the self-organisation of compositionality in languages.

3. The Emergence of Compositionality

Before presenting the computational studies, a definition of compositionality is required. *Compositionality* refers to a representation (e.g. an utterance) where the meaning of the whole is a function of the meaning of its parts and the way they are combined. An example of a compositional utterance is 'green square', where the part 'green' refers to the colour green and the part 'square' to a rectangular shape with equal sides. Combined they form the whole meaning referring to a green square. One important aspect of compositionality is that parts can be recombined with different parts, referring to different things. For instance, 'green' can be combined with 'triangle' to form the utterance 'green triangle'. In contrast, a holistic expression is an expression of which the meaning of the whole is not a function of its parts. An example would be idiomatic expressions like 'kick the bucket' whose meaning is not the sum of the meaning of the individual words that compose it; there is no part of the expression that refers to the meaning 'died'.

It has been shown that if an initially holistic language is transmitted iteratively over subsequent generations, this system can transform into a compositional one if the language is transmitted through a *transmission bottleneck* (i.e. learners only observe a small subset of the language), provided that learners are equipped with a mechanism to acquire compositional structures (Kirby, 2001). This is consistent with Wray's (1998) hypothesis that complex languages evolved from holistic protolanguages. The model I will discuss is based on Kirby's model, though changed in a number of crucial ways, which allows compositionality to arise under different conditions as well.

3.1 Modelling language games

This model is based on the language game model (Steels, 1997) in combination with the iterated learning model (Kirby, 2001). It is implemented in a simulation of the Talking Heads experiment (Steels, Kaplan, McIntyre, & Van Looveren, 2002).[1] The simulation implements a multi-agent system in which the population evolves a communication system from scratch to describe coloured geometrical shapes. Each agent starts to 'live' without any categories or linguistic knowledge; these are all constructed during their lifetimes by engaging in a series of interactions, called language games. It is

[1] This implementation is freely available at http://www.ling.ed.ac.uk/~paulv/thsim.html.

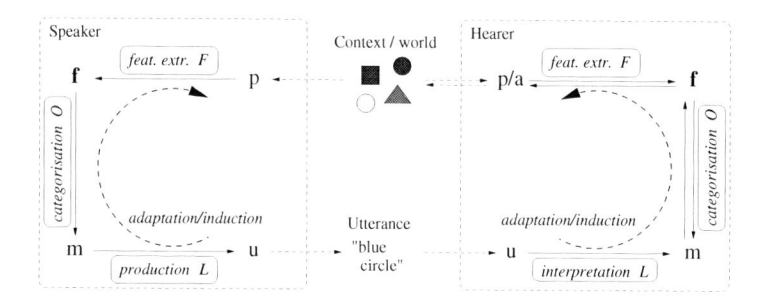

Figure 2. This figure shows a coupled semiotic square that summarises the guessing game. See the text for details.

beyond the scope of this chapter to present the model in detail, and in the following some explanations are simplified to benefit the readability without doing away with the general principles of the model. Full details are in Vogt (2005a).

One type of language game implemented is the *guessing game*, which is summarised in Figure 2. This game is played by two agents: a speaker and a hearer, who are presented a context that contains a given number of coloured shapes. Both agents extract perceptual features from each object and categorise these. The speaker selects one object as the topic of communication and encodes an utterance by searching his grammar for the best way to express the object. In turn, the hearer decodes the utterance by searching her grammar for the best way to parse the expression such that it is consistent with one of the objects in the context. This way, the hearer guesses the speaker's intention and subsequently points at this object. The speaker verifies whether this is the intended object and if it is, he acknowledges the hearer's success; if not, the speaker points to the topic, thus providing corrective feedback on the utterance's reference. At the end of the game (or in some cases during the game), the agents adapt their memories.

There are two types of knowledge agents acquire during their lifetimes. The first type are prototypical categories, acquired whenever the categorisation of objects fail. Objects are categorised with prototypes nearest to the objects' features representing colours and shapes. Each agent is forced to categorise each object such that its category distinguishes this object from the rest of the context. If this fails, the agent will add a new prototype to its memory for which the object's features serve as an exemplar. This categorisation scheme is called a *discrimination game* (Steels, 1997). So, early during an agent's development, the discrimination games will fail frequently, but the agent will rapidly develop an ontology that allows successful categorisation. The second type of knowledge is the grammar, which consists of rules that associate expressions with meanings (or *categories*)[2] either holistically or compositionally.

An example grammar is shown in Figure 3. In this example, rule 1 is holistic and rule 2 is compositional with terminal rules 3 and 4 as possible fillers. The grammar is constructed by invention or acquisition. If the speaker fails to encode an utterance (i.e. no rule combination matches the topic's category), he will invent a new random string either to be associated with the part of the meaning that does not match, or with the whole meaning — in which case a holistic rule is created. For instance, if the speaker of the example grammar wants to communicate about a red square categorised with (1,0,0,1), only the part (1,0,0,?) matches rule 3, so rule B → x/(?,?,?,1) is invented, where x is a random string constructed from a limited alphabet. If this string is, e.g., 'toma', the speaker can now produce the utterance 'redtoma' to convey the meaning of red square.

1	S → greensquare/(0,0,1,1)	0.2
2	S → A/rgb B/s	0.8
3	A → red/(1,0,0,?)	0.6
4	B → triangle/(?,?,?,0)	0.7

Figure 3. An example grammar fragment. The grammar contains rules that rewrite a non-terminal into an expression-meaning pair (1, 3 and 4) or into a compositional rule that combines different non-terminals (2). The meanings are 4-dimensional vectors where the first three dimensions relate to the RGB colour space and the fourth relates to the shape feature. The question marks are wild-cards. Each rule has a rule score that indicates its effectiveness in past language games.

If the hearer fails to decode the utterance or guesses the wrong referent, she will acquire one or more new rules. While doing that, she will try to generalise her language by searching for similarity patterns that allow her to form compositional rules in a usage-based

[2] Meaning in this study is represented by a category. I will use the term meaning if the category is associated with an expression.

fashion, such as that proposed by, e.g., Lieven, Behrens, Speares, and Tomasello (2003); Tomasello (2003). As in human speech, utterances are transmitted without directly observable word boundaries, nor do agents have prior knowledge how to break up the meaning space.

If a part of the received utterance can be decoded correctly, the rest of the utterance will be associated with the rest of the meaning. For instance, suppose the hearer of the example grammar heard the utterance 'redsquare', and that she knows, through corrective feedback, that the utterance refers to the object categorised as (1,0,0,1). Since the part 'red' can be correctly decoded with meaning (1,0,0,?), the part 'square' can be associated with meaning (?,?,?,1) resulting in the newly acquired rule B → square/(?,?,?,1). When the hearer fails to perform such an acquisition, she will see if there are any similarities between the heard utterance-meaning pair and previously heard utterance-meaning pairs stored in the agent's memory. Suppose the hearer heard 'greencircle' meaning (0,0,1,0.5), then there is a regular pattern when comparing it to 'greensquare' meaning (0,0,1,1), namely 'green' and (0,0,1,?). This allows the agent to break up these utterances into the parts 'green', 'circle' and 'square' with corresponding meanings, forming the terminal rules A → green/(0,0,1,?), B → circle/(?,?,?,0.5) and B → square/(?,?,?,1). If the corresponding compositional rule, such as rule 2 in Figure 3, does not yet exists, this will also be constructed. If this acquisition mechanism also fails, the hearer incorporates the utterance-meaning pair holistically.

If new knowledge is acquired, old knowledge is not thrown away (which is the case in Kirby's, 2001, model). This is important, because it allows different variants to compete with each other. In principle, each meaning can be associated with different utterances and each utterance can be associated with multiple meanings. Also compositional rules may compete with each other. Competition is regulated primarily with the rule score σ_r. Every time a rule is used to encode or decode an utterance successfully, its score is increased by

$$\sigma_r = \eta \cdot \sigma_r + 1 - \eta \quad (1)$$

where $\eta = 0.9$ is a constant learning parameter. At the same time, competing rules (i.e. those rules that either match the meaning or the utterance) are laterally inhibited by

$$\sigma_r = \eta \cdot \sigma_r \quad (2)$$

If a rule is used unsuccessfully, its score is decreased by this same equation. Given that initial scores are between 0 and 1, these updates make that the rule score is always a value between 0 and 1.

When a speaker or hearer has to select between two or more competing compositions of rules when decoding or encoding an utterance, they will always select the rule with the highest combined score. The combined score is the product of all scores used in a composition. If the utterance is formed from a holistic one, the composition contains one rule, otherwise it contains three rules.[3] This way, selection is biased towards holistic rules. However, a compositional rule can be used in novel situations (e.g., to talk about a red circle without ever having talked or heard this before). Moreover, compositional rules can be used in more situations than a single holistic rule. When this occurs frequently enough, the score of the compositional rule may become so high that a combination of scores using this rule can exceed the score of a holistic rule, so that the holistic rule would lose the competition.

Note, by the way, that applying a compositional rule in a novel situation does not only yield a new variation in the individual's language, but may also introduce a new variation in the global language. Hence, learned generalisations may provide new variations that could compete with other variations.

All simulations discussed below were carried out with a population of which half were 'adult' agents and the other half were 'children'. After a given number of language games, all adults were removed, the children became adults and new children were added to the simulation. This type of population dynamics is similar to the *iterated learning model* (Kirby, 2001), which is a standard model for studying language evolution computationally.

The world in all experiments contained 120 different objects (10 shapes times 12 colours) and each guessing game was played in a context of 8 objects randomly sampled from the world. Each different experiment was replicated 10 times (i.e. 10 runs) with different random seeds.

3.2 Transmission bottlenecks

Before reviewing some of the results, it is important to note that complex dynamical systems such as the one presented here tend to evolve toward *stable states* (Cavalli-Sforza & Feldman, 1981). As mentioned, it was shown by Kirby (2001) that compositional sys-

[3] In the current model, compositions are formed from two constituents at most, thus using three rules (the compositional rule and the two terminal rules).

tems can emerge from holistic ones, provided children are equipped with acquisition mechanisms to discover and acquire compositional rules and provided the language is transmitted through a bottleneck. This transmission bottleneck means that children only observe a small subset of the adults' language. This transition from holistic to compositional languages can be understood by realising that only compositional languages can be transmitted stably through a bottleneck. If a language is holistic, learning from observing only a subset requires the invention of new utterances for the elements not observed.

Consider, for example, this simple language with four holistic utterance-meaning pairs: *toma-[red,square]*, *tupa-[green,triangle]*, *bulo-[green,square]* and *rino-[red,triangle]*. If you only see the first three instances, you need to create a new utterance for meaning *[red,triangle]* when you wish to convey it. However, if the language is compositionally structured, such as *toma-[red,square]*, *bulo-[green,triangle]*, *buma-[green,square]* and *tolo-[red,triangle]*, then learning from the first three instances allows you to recreate the entire language. Hence, compositional languages are stable under the transmission of a bottleneck, whereas holistic languages are not. However, when the holistic language has some fortuitous pattern in some utterance-meaning pairs, these may be extracted and have a higher chance to survive the bottleneck. This then increases the chance that a new variation that has a regular pattern may enter the global language by combining extracted patterns, thus increasing the amount of compositionality in the language.

This is all very well, but using the model explained above and with a population size of 1 adult and 1 child, and considering only *vertical transmission* (which are the same conditions as in Kirby, 2001), it has been shown that compositionality can emerge stably without a bottleneck (Vogt, 2005a). Vertical transmission means that the language is transmitted from one generation to the next. In such a protocol all speakers are adults and all hearers are children. Why is that the case? First, recall that agents can form new compositional rules if they find a similarity in two utterance-meaning pairs. The chance that this happens in this model is quite large. Second, once compositional rules exist, they apply to more situations than a holistic rule and are therefore used more frequently. If rules are used more frequently, their scores tend to increase more strongly than those of rules used less frequently. So, the competition between holistic rules and compositional ones will be won by the compositional ones. In Kirby's model there is no competition between different rules, because his learning mechanism only allows one-to-one mappings between utterances and meanings. In that case, there is no need to form compositional rules when there is no bottleneck. Some will emerge, but holistic rules have a good chance to survive.

When, however, the population size is increased from 2 to 6 agents (3 adults and 3 children), transmission through a bottleneck is required for stable compositional systems to emerge (Fig. 4). This is because there are more agents in each generation and agents of one generation do not communicate with each other in this vertical transmission protocol (all speakers are adults and all hearers are children), so there arises much ambiguity in the input to the children, which — in this case — leads to instability of compositionality (note that communicative success is hardly affected). Moreover, it has been shown that in this model the incremental development of categories can cause words to be associated with very broad categories in early stages of development, leading to overextensions and eventually to dramatic changes of a word's meaning (leading to meaning drift) when they are narrowed down, which also leads to unstable solutions (Vogt, 2006c). Since ambiguities or meaning drift have more impact on compositional languages than on holistic ones[4], the competition is won by holistic rules. So, in the case with larger populations and vertical transmission with a bottleneck, variation is not good for compositionality as it leads to unstable systems. What seems to be lacking is an effective type of competition pressure.

The transmission bottleneck turns out to be an effective type of pressure, because with a bottleneck, agents will tend to use compositional rules more frequently when they need to communicate about previously unseen meanings. Consequently, such rules will be reinforced and thus tend to win the competition. In a way, the bottleneck tightens the competition, which triggers the selection of more compact and combinatorial languages.

Up to now, I have discussed only simulations with a vertical transmission of language. However, children in our society do not start speaking when they are grown up; they start speaking from the age

[4] Imagine what will happen if the meaning of 'red' will change into green in comparison to changing the meaning of 'kicked the bucket' to lived. The former change will definitely have a larger impact on the language as a whole than the latter.

of one or even before. In a *horizontal transmission* scheme, where both speakers and hearers are randomly selected from the entire population (including both adults and children), communication goes in all directions within the population.[5] In such a case, compositionality does evolve to a stable state, even in the absence of a transmission bottleneck (see, Fig 4, Vogt, 2005b).

The reason why in the absence of a transmission bottleneck compositionality evolves to a stable state is that for horizontal transmission children sometimes need to speak about things they have never encountered before. They, thus, face the consequences of the

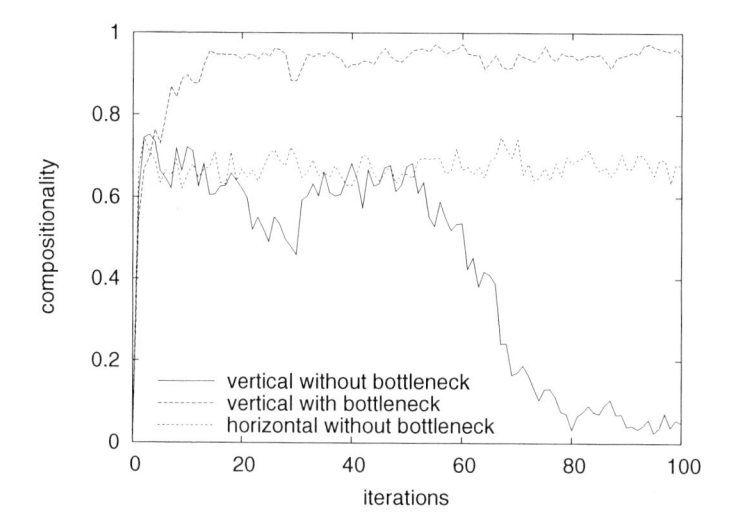

Figure 4. Compositionality as a function of the number of iterations (or generations). Compositionality is measured as the proportion of utterances produced or interpreted using a compositional rule, rather than a holistic one. In each iteration 3 adults and 3 children engaged in 3,000 guessing games, after which the adults are replaced by the children and new children entered the population. Results are provided for the cases where there was no bottleneck (solid line), with a bottleneck (dashed line) – both with vertical transmission – and one without a bottleneck, but with horizontal transmission (dotted line). This figure is adapted from Vogt (2005b).

[5] This definition of horizontal transmission is consistent with the one used in epidemiology, where it relates to a transmission between all members of a population irrespective of their generation. This is different from the definition given by Cavalli-Sforza and Feldman (1981) who consider horizontal transmission only within one generation.

bottleneck, even though this bottleneck is not imposed by the experimenter (which was necessary in the case of vertical transmission). As explained before, when the child needs to communicate about a meaning it has not encountered before (e.g., meaning *[red,triangle]*), while it did learn the utterance-meaning pairs of this meaning's parts (e.g., it learned from hearing *toma-[red,square]*, *bulo-[green,triangle]*, *buma-[green,square]*), the child does not need to invent a new word, but can select a compositional rule to express the meaning. This *implicit bottleneck* effect is a natural consequence of the normal development and interactive communication of the child. Again, when compositional rules are used more frequently, they are reinforced more strongly (at least when they are used successfully), and consequently more likely to be reselected, thus forming a positive feedback loop.

3.3 Population size effects

So far, all simulations were carried out with a very small population size (starting with only 2 agents — 1 per generation — and then with 6 agents). Vogt (2005c) investigated what happens if we increase the population size. Interestingly, after a first decline for populations up to 30 agents, the level of compositionality increases up to around 95% when the population further increases to 100 agents — at least for those runs that yielded compositionality higher than 50% (Fig. 5, top). Interestingly, only those simulations with a population size larger than 30, yielded compositionality of levels higher than 90%, while the simulations with 100 agents performed best (Fig. 5, bottom). More precisely, for a population size of 100, 7 out of 10 different runs yielded compositionality higher than 0.9.

The reason for this increase in compositionality is to be sought in the increased level of variation and competition. As there are more agents in the population, each starting without any linguistic knowledge, more new words will be invented. This will increase the chance that different utterance-meaning pairs will find a similarity that allows agents to break up utterances and form compositional rules. As a consequence, the chance is also increased that good (i.e. effective) compositions are formed. However, having a larger population also makes it is harder to achieve communicative success (the level of communicative success increases more slowly for larger populations). There is more competition (due to more variation), but it is also harder for all agents to understand each other agent. This competition makes the selection more crucial. It appears that compositionality does help in this, as in consecutive generations learning appears to become more and more effective (i.e. higher levels of success are reached, while similar levels are reached faster).[6] So, it seems that the language evolves to become more learnable; a conclusion that was also reached by Kirby (2001), though for slightly different reasons.

3.4 Population dynamics

The learnability of the language becomes more apparent when looking at the population dynamics of the system, which has been studied in Vogt (2006a). This study started from the observation in Vogt (2005b) that the evolution across generations does not seem to change a lot when the language is transmitted horizontally. So, to what extent does it not change and what is the added value of a population turnover — if any? To study this question, a comparison was made between a simulation that contained only one generation and one in which, halfway during the simulation, half of the population was replaced by children. So, in effect in the first case there was only one iteration and in the second case there were two. The total population size in these simulations were 50 agents. The results, reported in Vogt (2006a), are summarised in Fig. 6.

The graphs show that for compositionality (top) and communicative success (middle) there are similar evolutions for both conditions, though the simulation considering two generations (right) showed a short discontinuity when the population was changed. The two bottom graphs show the relative frequencies with which different rule types are used and need a bit more explanation.

The agents can form holistic rules (rule type I) and compositional rules by breaking apart the 4-dimensional conceptual space in different ways. They can form rules by combining colour and shape (rule types IV and V), but they can also combine, for instance, the red component of the RGB colour space with the blue and green components together with shape (i.e. red vs. blue, green and shape — rule types II and III).[7] The 10 other ways to combine the different dimensions of the meaning space do occur, but with negligible frequencies.

---

[6] A more extensive study on population size effects has recently been published in Vogt (2007).
[7] For each way of breaking up the 4 dimensional space, there are two types indicating word order: e.g., IV is colour first and V is shape first.

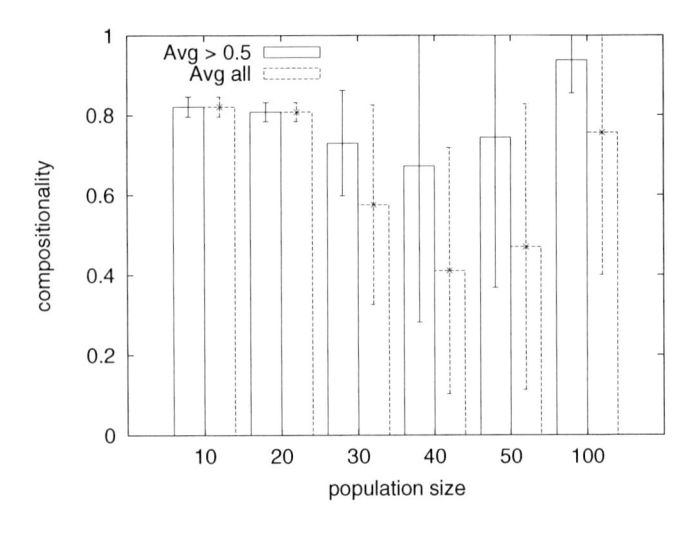

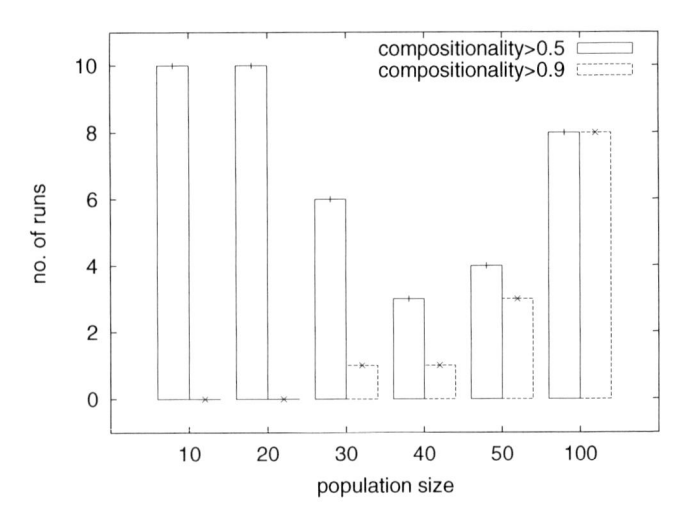

Figure 5. (top) The level of compositionality reached at the end of simulations with different population sizes. The solid boxes give the results averaged for only those runs that yielded compositionality higher than 0.5 and the dashed boxes give the averages for all 10 different runs per condition. The error-bars indicate standard deviations. (bottom) This graph shows the number of runs out of 10 that yielded compositionality higher than 0.5 and those higher than 0.9.

Self-Organisation of Compositionality

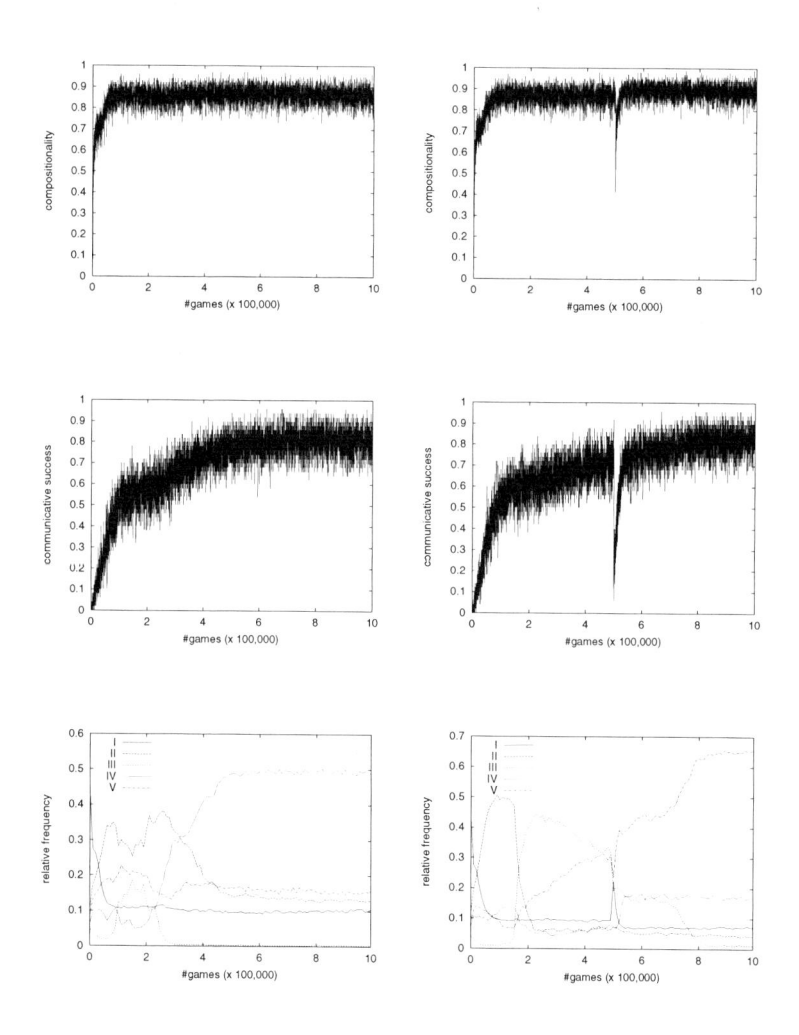

Figure 6. Comparing the evolution of one generation playing 1 million guessing games (left) with two generations playing a total of 1 million guessing games in two iterations (right). The graphs show compositionality (top), communicative success (middle) and rule frequencies (bottom). All results relate to one simulation run for both conditions.

Figure 6 (bottom left) shows that initially, there is a lot of competition among the different rule types, but that around game 500,000 a more or less stable system has developed. In this system, there is a relatively high incidence of rule types IV and V, but rule types I and II also occur quite frequently. So, this language has stabilised more or less in a sub-optimal system in the sense that the grammar is not in the most compact form, which requires the language to be formed of rules combining colours with shapes only (i.e. rule types IV and V). Nevertheless, communicative success is quite high.

When after the initial competition the adults are removed and new children are introduced, the language changes rapidly and rule types IV and V start to dominate while others tend to die out (Fig. 6, bottom right). This happens because the new agents rapidly learn these rules and tend to reuse them in cases where they have to communicate about previously unseen meanings due to the implicit bottleneck. The reason for the fact that these rules are rapidly learnt and used is that they apply in all possible situations, whereas all other rule types are less optimal. (Combining each colour with each shape relates to all objects in the world, but combining, e.g. each value of the red component with all possible values in the other dimensions may give descriptions of objects that do not exist in the virtual world.) This allows the children to form new combinations of words that can effectively convey their referents. So, where the older generation may express a number of meanings using holistic rules or compositional rules of type II and III, children tend to introduce novel combinations (i.e. variations) in the language using mainly rule type IV and V.

The chance that such new variations become rapidly successful is quite high, because part of the older generation will have acquired similar rules, even though they may not actively use them for certain situations. As a result, the uses of these rules are reinforced by all agents (young and old), so they tend to be reused more frequently. Simulations over more than two generations have shown that eventually the language evolves to an almost entire use of rule types IV and V (Vogt, 2006a). Moreover, similar results have been achieved in simulations where the population change is more natural, in contrast to the presented catastrophic population change at the end of each iteration (Tamariz & Vogt, in prep.).

4. Implications

This chapter has reviewed a number of recent studies regarding the evolution of compositional structures in language using computer simulations (Vogt, 2005a,b,c; 2006a,c). This review places these studies in the context of a neo-Darwinian usage-based approach to language evolution, similar to those proposed by, e.g., Croft (2000); Mufwene (2002); Tomasello (2003). It shows that the neo-Darwinian approach to language evolution is a fruitful approach that can explain, at least, the evolution of communicatively successful languages which have a limited level of compositionality in a population. Crucial to this approach is to study language development and use in populations, rather than to study the language competence of individuals as is done in the Chomskyan tradition and many (if not most) psychological studies on language development.

The model with which the simulations were carried out implement learning mechanisms that allow the development of a constructive grammar similar to those described by Lieven et al. (2003); Tomasello (2003) and which are general enough to count as a general learning mechanism that need not have evolved specifically for language. Although all individuals in all generations started with these learning mechanisms, transitions from initially holistic languages to well structured compositional languages have been shown. Moreover, simulations have shown that the languages themselves evolve to become learnable, rather than that the individual language users evolve to learn the languages as an innate theory such as that proposed by Pinker and Bloom (1990) would predict.

The simulations discussed do not provide unequivocal evidence that language has evolved this way, however, they do illustrate a clear alternative to the nativist theories advocated by, e.g., Chomsky (1956); Pinker and Bloom (1990). Assuming the origins of language coincides with the appearance of Homo Sapiens, language arose some 250,000 years ago and given the—on an evolutionary time scale—short time it took for modern languages to have evolved from their precursors, cultural evolution seems a more likely candidate to explain a transition from holistic protolanguages to modern languages. Certainly, a number of major biological adaptations, such as adaptations relating to our speech organ (Fitch, 2000) or the emergence of Theory of Mind related issues (Tomasello, 2003), must have facilitated language evolution, but whether there were language specific adaptations as proposed by Chomsky or Pinker and Bloom is questionable. For instance, the ability to acquire compositional structures (e.g., predicate logic) could have evolved for more general cognitive abilities such as vision and can even be found in certain other species (Hurford, 2004). In addition, Parker (2006) has argued that the same could even hold for what Hauser, Chomsky, and Fitch (2002) have called the *narrow language faculty* that has recursion as its hallmark and which they hypothesise is what makes homo sapiens unique regarding their language abilities.

So, I argue that having non-domain specific learning mechanisms which try to extract regular patters from the speech input in relation to regular patterns in their meanings, such as proposed by Lieven et al. (2003); Tomasello (2003), could be sufficient to explain the transition from holistic languages to compositional or even syntactic recursive languages (Kirby, 2002). One reason why such an explanation is to be favoured is that such a fast process is possibly more easy to achieve than a slow biological evolution. However, such a cultural cumulation of complexity in language (and perhaps culture in general) seems only to be possible if (see also, Vogt, 2006a, for a related discussion):

1. language is transmitted repeatedly from one generation to the next,
2. there is sufficient variation in the language for novel traits to be discovered,
3. language is sufficiently well-structured so that the cost of learning is lower,
4. there is room for cognitive development, and
5. there is an ecological niche that attracts further development.

As the final set of experiments showed, the structure of language can evolve towards a local maximum, which may be sufficient for communication, but not for cumulating knowledge. The new generation introduces new variation that triggers the system to get out of the local maximum (in a way, this is similar to simulated annealing used in many AI systems to get out of local maximums). In addition, these children face an implicit bottleneck that serves as a competition pressure for selecting compositional structures. For complexity to cumulate, the language must also evolve so that it becomes easier to learn, which frees time for the population to create new structures. Though in the simulations discussed this only happens early in evolution (i.e. first few iterations), decreasing the cost of learning will be a prerequisite to understand the explosive growth in cultural knowledge and possibly also for explaining the complexification of language (see also, Boyd & Richerson, 2005).[8]

Of course, in order to increase the complexity of language, there must be enough room for cognitive development. In the current set up, agents are restricted to form only two word sentences. However, if the cognitive architecture would allow more complex sentences, such sentences would evolve, though maybe these will not be very efficient. In addition, the language development could face another limit, namely that of the environment. In the model the environment only provides four perceptual features with a limited number of objects. If the language has evolved such that it reflects those features and those objects, there is no possibility to become more complex as the language can then describe all possible aspects of the environment. So, there must be an ecological niche that attracts further development. Of course, our natural environment is far more complex than that of the model, but it may be that our contemporary language surpasses the relevant structure of the ecological niche from, say, 250,000 years ago. However, humans not only observe the environment (which is what the agents in the model do), but also change it so there is ecological or cultural niche construction (Laland, Odling-Smee, & Feldman, 2001). Niche construction (be it ecological or cultural) can change the niche such that new targets arise to which our culture or language evolves.

5. Conclusions

In this chapter, I have discussed a Darwinian approach to explain language evolution. This approach was not on a biological level, but on a cultural, language level. In short, I have explained how variation, competition and selection can account for language change and I have reviewed a number of recent computational studies to show how these mechanisms can explain a self-organisation of compositional structures in languages.

The studies suggest that variation, competition and selection can explain how compositionality in languages can arise. Variation is crucial for setting the right conditions for competition and selection. Too much variation can harm the system if this leads to too much ambiguity. However, more variation can also lead to better performances if it increases the chance of finding good solutions. In addi-

---

[8] If languages become easier to learn, one may wonder if talking about complexification is justified.

tion, the creative process of recombining learnt parts when the consequence of transmission bottlenecks occur can also be seen as a vital selection mechanism.

Competition pressures are required to allow the system to self-organise toward a (quasi) stable state. (I use the term quasi, because the system keeps on evolving, i.e. changing, even though the level of compositionality or communicative success remains stable.) Language stability, transmission bottlenecks and learnability have been identified as possible pressures for competition. Selection processes are important ingredients that should serve the purpose of competition. In the current model, optimisation has proved to be a viable selection mechanism for stable languages to develop.

Concluding, Darwin's theory on variation, competition and selection can well be applied to explain how languages can evolve. It offers a powerful alternative to more traditional approaches taken in linguistics. Finally, the computational model presented is a starting point to investigate how (grammatically) more complex languages can evolve.

Acknowledgements

Most of the work presented in this chapter was carried out at the Language Evolution and Computation Research Unit of the University of Edinburgh. I am grateful to all of its members for their comments and suggestions on this work. The work has been financed by the EC through a Marie Curie Fellowship and by the Netherlands Organisation for Scientific Research (NWO) through a VENI grant.

References

Boyd, R. & Richerson, P. (2005), *The Origin and Evolution of Cultures* (Oxford: Oxford University Press).

Cangelosi, A. & Parisi, D. (Eds.) (2002), *Simulating the Evolution of Language* (London: Springer).

Cavalli-Sforza, L. L. & Feldman, M. W. (1981), *Cultural Transmission and Evolution: A Quantitative Approach* (Princeton, NJ: Princeton University Press).

Chomsky, N. (1956), 'Three models for the description of language', *IRE Transactions on Information Theory IT*, 2(3), pp. 13–54.

Croft, W. (2000), *Explaining Language Change: An Evolutionary Approach.* (Harlow: Longman).

Croft, W. (2002), 'The Darwinization of linguistics', *Selection, 3*, pp. 75–91.

Darwin, C. (1959), *The Origin of Species* (London: John Murray).

Dawkins, R. (1976), *The Selfish Gene* (Oxford: Oxford University Press).

Deacon, T. (1997), *The Symbolic Species* (New York: W. Norton and Co.).
De Boer, B. (1999), *Self-organisation in Vowel Systems*. Unpublished doctoral dissertation, Vrije Universiteit Brussels.
De Boer, B. (2001), *The Origins of Vowel Systems* (Oxford: Oxford University Press).
De Boer, B. (2005), 'Self-organisation in language', In C. Hemelrijk (Ed.), *Self-organisation and Evolution of Biological and Social Systems* (Cambridge: Cambridge University Press).
Fitch, W. (2000), 'The evolution of speech: A comparative review', *Trends in Cognitive Sciences*, 4 (7), pp. 258–267.
Hauser, M., Chomsky, N., & Fitch, W. (2002), 'The Faculty of Language: What Is It, Who Has It, and How Did It Evolve?', *Science*, 298 (5598), p. 1569.
Hull, D. (1988), *Science as a Process* (Chicago: Chicago University Press).
Hurford, J. (2004), 'The neural basis of predicate-argument structure', *Behavioral and Brain Sciences*, 26 (3), pp. 261–283.
Kirby, S. (2001), 'Spontaneous evolution of linguistic structure: an iterated learning model of the emergence of regularity and irregularity', *IEEE Transactions on Evolutionary Computation*, 5(2), pp. 102–110.
Kirby, S. (2002), 'Learning, bottlenecks and the evolution of recursive syntax', In T. Briscoe (Ed.), *Linguistic Evolution Through Language Acquisition: Formal and Computational Models* (Cambridge University Press).
Laland, K., Odling-Smee, J. & Feldman, M. (2001), 'Niche construction, biological evolution, and cultural change', *Behavioral and Brain Sciences*, 23 (01), p. 131–146.
Lieven, E., Behrens, H., Speares, J. & Tomasello, M. (2003), 'Early syntactic creativity: a usage-based approach', *Journal of Child Language*, 30(2), pp. 333–370.
Maddieson, I. (1984), *Patterns of Sounds* (Cambridge: Cambridge University Press).
Mufwene, S. (2002), 'Competition and selection in language evolution', *Selection*, 3, pp. 46–56.
Oliphant, M. (1996), 'The dilemma of saussurean communication', *Biosystems*, 1–2(37), pp. 31–38.
Parker, A. R. (2006), 'Evolving the narrow language faculty: Was recursion the pivotal step?', In A. Cangelosi, A. Smith, & K. Smith (Eds.), *The Evolution of Language: Proceedings of the 6th International Conference on the Evolution of Language* (World Scientific Press).
Pickering, M. & Garrod, S. (2004), 'Toward a mechanistic psychology of dialogue', *Behavioral and Brain Sciences*, 27, pp. 169–226.
Pinker, S. & Bloom, P. (1990), 'Natural language and natural selection', *Behavioral and Brain Sciences*, 13, pp. 707–789.
Steels, L. (1997), 'The synthetic modeling of language origins', *Evolution of Communication*, 1(1), pp. 1–34.
Steels, L. (2005), 'The emergence and evolution of linguistic structure: From lexical to grammatical communication systems', *Connection Science*, 17 (3–4), pp. 213–230.

Steels, L., Kaplan, F., McIntyre, A. & Van Looveren, J. (2002), 'Crucial factors in the origins of word-meaning', In A. Wray (Ed.), *The Transition to Language* (Oxford: Oxford University Press).

Steels, L. & Vogt, P. (1997), 'Grounding adaptive language games in robotic agents', In C. Husbands & I. Harvey (Eds.), *Proceedings of the Fourth European Conference on Artificial Life* (Cambridge, MA, and London: MIT Press).

Tamariz, M., & Vogt, P. (in prep.), 'A co-evolutionary framework for cultural transmission: Interactions between public and mental representations', *In preparation*.

Tomasello, M. (2003), *Constructing a Language: A Usage-Based Theory of Language Acquisition* (Harvard University Press).

Vogt, P. (2005a), 'The emergence of compositional structures in perceptually grounded language games', *Artificial Intelligence*, 167(1-2), pp. 206–242.

Vogt, P. (2005b), 'On the acquisition and evolution of compositional languages: Sparse input and the productive creativity of children', *Adaptive Behavior*, 13(4), pp. 325–346.

Vogt, P. (2005c), 'Stability conditions in the evolution of compositional languages: issues in scaling population sizes', In P. Bourgine, F. Képès, & M. Schoenauer (Eds.), *Proceedings of the European Conference on Complex Systems, ECCS'05*.

Vogt, P. (2006a), 'Cumulative cultural evolution: Can we ever learn more?', In S. Nolfi et al. (Eds.), *From Animals to Animats 9: Proceedings of the Ninth International Conference on Simulation of Adaptive Behaviour* (Berlin: Springer Verlag).

Vogt, P. (2006b), 'Language evolution and robotics: Issues in symbol grounding and language acquisition', In A. Loula, R. Gudwin, & J. Queiroz (Eds.), *Artificial Cognition Systems* (Idea Group).

Vogt, P. (2006c), 'Overextensions and the emergence of compositionality', In A. Cangelosi, A. Smith, & K. Smith (Eds.), *The Evolution of Language: Proceedings of the 6th International Conference on the Evolution of Language* (World Scientific Press).

Vogt, P. (2007), 'Group size effects on the emergence of compositional structures in language', In F. Almeida e Costa, L. M. Rocha, E. Costa, I. Harvey & A. Coutinho (Eds.) *Proceedings of the European Conference on Artificial Life, ECAL 2007* (Berlin: Springer Verlag).

Wray, A. (1998), 'Protolanguage as a holistic system for social interaction', *Language and Communication*, 18, pp. 47–67.

Yanna Popova

On Human Temporality – Time, Language, and a Sense of Self

> … we can, if we wish, close our eyes and think about what we did ten minutes ago, or how we celebrated our last birthday. And we can think about what we might be doing tomorrow, or next year. This kind of sense of time makes a huge difference to what we are and how we live. If we retained all our other mental capacities, but lost the awareness of time in which our lives are played out, we might still be uniquely different from all other animals but we would no longer be human as we understand it. (Tulving, 2002.)

> What is now clear and plain is, that neither things to come nor past are. Nor is it properly said , 'there be three times, past, present and to come:' yet perchance it might be properly said, 'there be three times; a present of things past, a present of things present, and a present of things future.' (Augustine, 1907.)

Introduction

The question of time and its significance for the human mind has been a major preoccupation for many thinkers working in diverse fields: physics, philosophy, psychology, linguistics, as well as newer fields such as neuroscience. Time and the nature of its relationship to human experience and behaviour is a topic most people find interesting and important. Yet, while a great deal of knowledge exists about how organisms perceive and adjust to space, much less is known about how the human mind constructs a notion of time. Despite its profound influence on human experience, time remains, in the words of one of its investigators, 'the familiar stranger' (Fraser, 1987).

This paper will argue that time should be seen as occupying a certain privileged position with respect to how human beings construe their world. The foundations for this privileged position are going to be examined in relation to language and linguistic expression; episodic memory construal; and a resulting sense of self or self-awareness. In purely linguistic terms I will use the work of Givon (1979, 1984) to underline the fact that the main grammatical classes in language reflect a scale of temporal stability from the most stable (nouns), to relatively stable (adjectives), to those denoting least stability and change (verbs). My claim, following Givon's ideas, is that in human conceptualization time occupies a position that space simply cannot: while temporal entities can exist outside of space, spatial entities exist in both time and space. Hence, contrary to more recent claims that the spatialization of time dominates the way we think and speak of it, I will argue that time is in fact a precondition for our understanding of entities and events (including motion events) and cannot be reduced to notions of space alone.

Time is also of crucial importance for the way we construct an 'objective' sense of self. Episodic memory or an ability to perform time travel to one's past or future (Tulving, 2002; 2005) is an integral component of human cognition and, according to some theorists, the unique component that makes us distinct from other species. On this view, the passage of time is not perceived directly but is constructed in memory as a result of the human mind's unique imaginative capacity to travel back into the past and project into the future. People with injuries to specific brain regions, as well as small children, have intact semantic memories but lack the ability to recollect personal autobiographical events or plan their own future. Not only are such individuals unable to experience the passage of time; importantly, they are also unable to construe a sense of self that endures beyond the present moment. Time, as such cases seem to suggest, is constitutive of consciousness itself.

Temporality and Language

When we look at the expression of time in language, i.e. temporality, a question of significant interest is to see if and how human experience of time can influence linguistic structure. While many linguists describe time as metaphorically derived from our notions of space, I consider this to be an oversimplification. Time, expressed linguistically, allows us to travel not just in a straight line to the past or the future, but to engage in situations that are possible, counterfactual, imagined or simply conditional on some other prior or future event. Space, with its rigid three-dimensionality, could not allow such a complex modelling of a situation because space helps us construe only the 'reality' of the world. Time, on the other hand, provides us with the novel ability to think about the irreality of that world, the mere possibility or even impossibility of an event or a future situation that we want to make happen. Thus, while it may be true that our notions of space have evolved before our notions of time, it does not follow that time is not directly perceived nor in some sense constituted by other kinds of subjective experience, like planning, imagining or thinking about the future.

There is a wide range of facts from diverse human languages which suggest that for human beings a basic way of classifying the world involves a hierarchical arrangement in which time is of crucial importance (Givon, 1979, p. 314). Things (entities in the world) exist in space (concrete), exist in time (temporal), and exist (abstract). More precisely, what exists in space must also exist in time and what exists in time must also exist, but not vice versa. There are a number of temporal predicates specific to temporal nouns, so that they can predicate neither concrete nor abstract nouns: e.g. 'happen', 'occur', 'take place', 'come about'. Following Givon, I assume that the first dimension necessary for cognition is the ordering dimension of time. This is because I assume time to be not some kind of an absolute quality of experience but an ordering relationship between things, places and events. As Givon observes, while 'it is possible to define the experiential uniqueness of entities by reference to time but without reference to space, it is impossible to define space-uniqueness of entities without reference to time' (Givon, 1979, p. 320). In other words, time and space are not interchangeable because temporal entities can exist outside of space but spatial entities exist in both time and space.

How does language structure reflect that observation? In general there are no languages without the two major grammatical classes, nouns and verbs. Nouns are those entities that are construed as generally time-stable. For example, the primary group of nouns in any language are the concrete nouns, i.e. ones that code entities which exist in both space and time. Because they are perceived to be time-stable, they are characterized primarily by spatial deixis, i.e. by space indicating demonstratives and prepositions. Moreover, while all languages have abstract nouns, the majority of abstract nouns are derived from verbs (or adjectives) (Givon, 1979, pp. 320–321).

On the opposite end of lexical coding in language are verbs, which most commonly denote actions or events, i.e. entities that are less concrete than nouns and exist only in time. These are grammatically marked by tense-aspect deixis, as well as mood and conditionality. Adjectives occupy the middle in the continuum of time stability in grammatical classes: they are less stable than nouns but more so than verbs. Importantly, the most likely qualities to be lexicalized as adjectives are the more stable or permanent qualities of entities such as size, length, width, gender, colour, texture, etc. (Givon, 1979, p. 321). Thus, if a language has only a small number of adjectives, those will be the properties construed as time-stable, while less stable qualities such as *hot-cold*, *happy-sad*, *calm-angry*, will be expressed as (mainly intransitive) verbs (Dixon, 1982). Overall, it can be said that instances of perceptual judgement receive cognitive-lexical coding in language as nouns, adjectives or verbs according to the criterion of temporal stability.

All this is to suggest that temporality inheres within the semantics of all linguistic classes, albeit with different degrees of explicitness. As already noted, abstract nouns in many languages are derived from verbs. Hence, not only is their temporality explicitly coded through the process of derivation, but their very meanings can be seen as inherently narrative (i.e. reporting a sequence of events). The meanings of such concepts cannot be explained without introducing a causally linked chain of the events that have produced them. There are many examples of this kind: for instance, *wedding*, *ransom*, *fishing* all describe narrative sequences of different complexity. This is certainly not a new observation: the semiotic theories of Greimas (1983) and Eco (1984) similarly propose that lexical units contain a condensed underlying narrative structure, that is, they are inherently temporal.

Psychological Time: How do we experience time?

When it comes to describing how the human mind perceives or experiences time directly, that is, in the process of our immediate perceptual interaction with the world, there are a number of approaches. On the one hand, we have psychologists and neuroscientists who focus on the relationships between experience and objectively measurable physical events. For these researchers time is primary and is given to us directly through the senses. The types of questions asked in these kinds of studies are: 'Is time a sense impression, measurable through 'observable' units at both the psychological and the neuronal levels?'; 'Is time perceptually real?'; 'What constitutes a temporal experience?' These questions have already received some satisfactory answers. On the other hand, we have long-standing research on memory that situates the experience of time in tight correlation with a continuous 'sense of self'. For these researchers, while human life is lived in the present, much of what is of great importance to the human mind is also linked to a lived past and a possible future.

One of the main representatives of the former line of research, Ernst Pöppel (following Ornstein, 1969), breaks down the vast question about temporal experience into smaller, constituent phenomena such as: the experience of simultaneity versus non-simultaneity, the experience of the present moment, and the experience of duration. In order to determine whether two perceptions are simultaneous or not, Pöppel uses a simple experiment with a headset (1988, p. 12). The ability to tell whether two objectively non-simultaneous events (two separate tones) are being judged by the subjects to be one (a single tone) depends crucially on the interval between them. Pöppel's experiments show that as the interval between the two signals increases (usually two to five thousandths of a second are needed, depending on the individual) the single tone is suddenly perceived as two distinct tones. Similar results have been obtained for other modalities: vision and touch, but interestingly, compared to hearing or touch, the human visual system is very slow. Pöppel estimates that between twenty to thirty thousandths of a second need to pass before two visual impressions can be judged to be non-simultaneous (p. 16).

Another major aspect of time experience that has been studied experimentally is the question of temporal duration. A number of scholars have suggested that human estimates of temporal duration are highly unreliable and subjective, and at best constitute rough estimates of the actual passage of time (James, 1962; Ornstein, 1969). In general, there is a consensus that a time filled with varied and interesting experiences appears to pass more quickly, while a period of time that is empty of experiences seems long in passing. Once committed to memory however, the flow of time is experienced according to whether time itself has entered conscious consideration. In retrospect, that which was boring in the present, becomes short (a month of sickness yields very few memories), while an apparently short and engrossing period of changes in the present (a week of travel), becomes lengthy in memory.

Possibly the most intriguing aspect of temporal experience is the experience of *'now'* or the present moment. When we are hearing a piece of music or touching an object, we are integrating sequential events (say, the individual tones) into units of perception. Conscious perception is thus temporal: there is a phenomenological continuity of experience whereby each instant becomes past as it gives way to the next one. Numerous philosophers, psychologists and more recently neuroscientists like Pöppel have puzzled over the mystery of the human 'now', the very boundary at which future somehow touches past. St Augustine in book 11 of his *Confessions* ([circa 397] 1907) was the first thinker to derive the notion of time from human conscious experience. He suggested that we can meaningfully speak not of three kinds of time: a past, a present and a future, but, rather, of three types of present: the present of things past (memory: *memoria*), the present of things present (on-going perception: *continuitus*), and the present of things to come (expectation: *expectatio*). Cognitive psychology in general is in agreement with such a triple distinction in perceptual processing, whereby on-going perception (the present) is viewed as referring back to schemata held in memory (the past), which in turn are used to predict and recognize new input (the future). A question of great interest here is the duration of the present moment, which has been experimentally proven to last about 2-3 seconds (Pöppel, 1988).

Pöppel approaches the question by analysing the perception of an ambiguous figure such as a Necker cube. This type of figure allows a double perspective, only one of which is initially perceived by a given subject. When both perspectives become easily perceivable, the subjects are instructed to try and let both perspectives of the cube flip back and forth. Most people are able to alternate perspectives of the cube at will and even accelerate the alternating views, but only up to a certain speed which cannot be exceeded. This speed illustrates, for Pöppel, the temporal range of the human attentional span, or willpower. To test the limit of the attentional span in the opposite direction, he then asks his subjects to try and intentionally not allow the cube to flip-flop between perspectives. Yet, as long as the cube remains the centre of our attention, no matter how hard we try to hold a single perspective, it will inevitably flop back to the other perspective after just a few seconds. Hence, Pöppel's conclusion that a single content of consciousness persists up to three seconds before being replaced by another. The *now* has a temporal extension of maximally three seconds. Another important issue, that becomes evident in the experiments, is the fact that only one perspective is possible to maintain at any given moment. We see the cube either this way or that way, but we can never see both perspective simultaneously. A related interesting discovery concerns the fact that periodic division in spontaneous speech (individual consecutive units of utterance or phrases) also last on average about three seconds. Each phrasal unit is concluded with a short pause, followed by the next unit, a fact observable across languages and thus not dependent on language specific syntactic structure. That the three-second rhythm of natural speech mirrors (or even determines) the chronological adjustment of a rhythm of attentional span of equivalent duration in a listener, may be seen as a great facilitator of successful communication. As Poppel suggests, if speakers were to produce phrase units each of arbitrary duration and listeners were unable to predict the expected course of what was said, the possibility of communication would be greatly diminished. Most interestingly, Turner and Poppel have shown that fundamental units of metered poetry, what they term 'the line', containing between four and twenty syllables depending on the original language, also take about three seconds to recite. This is based on a wide survey of languages from different families (Turner and Poppel, 1983). The upshot of all this is of course, what interpretation can be given to the remarkable relationship that exists for Poppel among line length in poetry, durations of utterance in language and the subjective experience of the present moment. One valid conclusion appears to be that, despite being given in the senses, the basis of time experience is internal (i.e. mind and brain-driven) rather than external.

In summary of this section, it can be said that Pöppel's experiments contribute to the view that the human mind construes time in highly unreliable ways. If two signals separated by an interval of up to thirty thousandths of a second blur for us into a single event, then the human experience of temporal simultaneity is an illusion. With longer intervals, we are often able to distinguish the signals but not the order in which they come. Duration is also judged on the basis of interest and involvement in the particular experience we are attending to and does not reflect the actual duration of an act or event. Duration hence, is similarly an illusion. Most startlingly, if the extent of consciousness at any given moment is never more than three seconds, the apparent continuity of time (and consciousness) that we experience is also an illusion. The human subjective stream of time, however, is characterized not by a succession of discrete moments but by continuity. How is this sense of continuity, i.e. identity, from one moment to the next, realized in conscious experience? The answer provided by Pöppel is that it is given by the content of consciousness itself. Because consciousness is always a consciousness of something, each subsequent content of consciousness is provided by the preceding one (Pöppel, 1989, p. 230). What we are attending to at any one moment provides the semantic connection which in turn serves as the basis for the experience of temporal continuity. For Pöppel, this illusory continuity is constituted by a mind that looks beyond itself to what currently engages its attention. There exists another line of research, which looks at the human experience of temporal continuity not as illusory, but, rather, as constitutive of consciousness and a sense of self. To this view I turn now.

Time, Memory and Consciousness

Memory is a fundamental aspect of human cognition. Psychologist Endel Tulving distinguishes among three main types of memory and links them to three respective kinds of consciousness (1985). First, human beings possess procedural (implicit) memory, such as is given in the knowledge of how to drive a car, which correlates with basic awareness or anoetic (non-knowing) consciousness. Secondly, we have semantic memory, which is linked to representations or knowledge of facts, and implies a noetic (knowing) consciousness. Finally, episodic memory (mental time travel to the personal past or future) implies autonoetic (self-knowing) consciousness or an awareness of a sense of self.

According to Tulving, the order of the types of memory presented above reflects the order of their emergence in evolution. Importantly, episodic memory and autonoetic consciousness are uniquely human. Semantic memory precedes episodic memory both in phylogenetic evolution and in ontogenetic human development. It is also a memory system that deteriorates early with age. The crucial distinction between semantic and episodic memory is that the former describes an individual's knowledge of the world, while the latter describes the same knowledge in relation to that individual's sense of self. Hence, unlike all other forms of biological memory, episodic memory is oriented to time: it allows people to consciously re-experience the past (Tulving, 2005, p. 16) or imagine a personal future. In terms of the neural components of episodic memory, Tulving and colleagues have suggested that damage to the frontal lobes (pre-frontal cortex) of the brain has been shown to be linked to loss in episodic memory, while leaving other types of memory intact (Wheeler, Stuss, Tulving, 1997).

The conjunction of the three aspects of the human mind: sense of self, autonoetic consciousness and the experience of time in the theory, proposed and elaborated by Tulving and colleagues, necessarily invites the question what will happen if one of these aspects is suddenly missing due to brain damage or other form of pathology. Is it possible to lose the ability to engage in episodic remembering or future thinking, while retaining semantic knowledge of the past? Numerous cases from development (childhood amnesia) and from brain-damaged individuals confirm that a sense of self and the experience of time are indeed inextricably linked.

Tulving and his team have studied K.C., who suffered frontal parietal damage during an accident, has his previously acquired knowledge of the world (his semantic memory) undamaged, while his ability to recollect personal autobiographical events is completely lost (Tulving 2005, p. 22). K.C.'s intelligence, language ability, imagery, mathematical skills and knowledge of objective, publicly shared facts from his own past (like his date of birth, home address, the make and colour of his car, etc.) are all normal. His major deficit is that he cannot remember anything that has happened to him. However hard he tries, he cannot bring into his conscious awareness a single event or situation in which he has been involved. This global episodic amnesia covers the whole of his life, both before and after the accident, including highly traumatic personal events (p. 24).

What appears even more striking is that K.C. cannot think about his own personal future and cannot ever say what he is going to do later on that day or at any time in the rest of his life. He cannot project into the future or anticipate any future event. Observations of other patients with specific brain damage have shown that lack of episodic memory means also a lack of the ability to plan, or experience future events. Patient D.B. (Klein et al, 2002) suffers severe retrograde episodic amnesia. He performs well on semantic memory tests, but cannot remember a single experience of his 'lived' past. He can answer questions about the world's 'known' future, but is completely unable to imagine his own personal future.

The awareness of self that K.C. or D.B. possess does not stretch beyond the present moment, beyond the not-now. This is very similar to the cognitive status of the very young child (less than 4–5 years old), who is yet unable to represent her own act of experiencing continuity of self through time. This inability to remember events as experienced can explain adults' inability to have memories of childhood events before that age (a phenomenon called 'childhood amnesia'). Both the child and the amnesic patient have no episodic memories, hence, no experience of time and autonoetic awareness. Extensive work from clinical studies (on depersonalization, acute depression, schizophrenia) also points in the direction of a strong correlation between a sense of self and a sense of time. Importantly, temporal perspective, especially future time perspective, is seen as foundational for a sense of self (Melges, 1990). Similarly to patients with frontal lobe lesions, people with acute psychiatric disorders show a pronounced indifference toward the future (Melges, 1982). For example, schizophrenics have difficulties with temporal continuity (Poppel, 1994) and with thinking about the future (Minkowski, 1970). In all these cases a sense of self or, rather, the lack of it, clearly relates to a lack of experience of 'felt' time. All these patients (and small children) are missing is a fundamental aspect of conscious experience: the feeling that they are continuous and temporally extended beings. They live literally in the discontinuous moments of three seconds that constitute Poppel's idea of the quantum nature of conscious experience.

Conclusion: Recent Brain Studies and 'the Sense of Self'

Very recent fMRI studies have examined brain activity patterns produced by demanding sensory categorization exercises and compared them to patterns created during self-reflective introspection. The results show a complete segregation between the two patterns of activity in the two respective tasks (Goldberg, Harel, Malach, 2006). During intense sensorimotor processing the self-related cortical regions (medial prefrontal cortex) get inhibited and activation there is suppressed. In the words of the authors, during demanding perceptual tasks the self-related cortex (the self) is inactive, i.e. is actually 'being lost' (p. 337).

Another recent set of PET and fMRI studies compare activation patterns in undirected task states (the so-called 'default mode' of brain activation during passive thought) with activation patterns during directed activities that depend on episodic memory and self-projection (Buckner and Carroll, 2006). The implicated regions are the frontal regions and the medial temporal lobe structures, both of which show remarkable similarity of activation patterns during the 'default mode' and the self-projection tasks. The authors raise the possibility that default modes of cognition (the brain's passive state) are characterized by a shift from perceptual tasks to internal modes of thought related to a sense of self.

If this is the case, both Pöppel and Tulving are right in their conclusions. In active sensorimotor processing, temporal integration is achieved by semantic binding, i.e. by what is provided by the external world. When not otherwise engaged in demanding sensory-perceptual tasks, temporal integration results from a sense of subjective, felt continuity or, in other words, from a sense of self. Even if time is an illusion, it permeates language, constitutes memory and establishes a sense of self without which human life is greatly diminished. It is the illusion that makes us who we are.

References

Augustine (1907), *The Confessions* (London: J. M. Dent and Son).
Buckner, Randy L. and Daniel C. Carroll (2006), 'Self-Projection and the Brain', *Trends in Cognitive Sciences*, 11, pp. 49–57.
Dixon, R. H. W. (1982), *Where Have All the Adjectives Gone* (Berlin and New York: Mouton Publishers).
Eco, Umberto (1984), *Semiotics and the Philosophy of Language* (Bloomington: Indiana University Press).
Fraser, J. T. (1987), *Time: The Familiar Stranger* (Amherst, MA: University of Massachusetts Press).
Givon, Talmy (1979), *On Understanding Grammar* (New York: Academic Press).
Givon, Talmy (1984), *Syntax: A Functional–Typological Introduction* (Amsterdam: John Benjamins).
Greimas, A.-J. (1983), *Structural Semantics: An Attempt at a Method* (Lincoln and London: University of Nebraska Press).
Goldberg, Illan I., Harel, Michal, Malach, Rafael (2006), 'When the Brain Loses Its Self: Prefrontal Inactivation during Sensorimotor Processing', *Neuron*, 50, pp. 329–339.
James, William (1962), *Psychology: Briefer Course* (New York: Collier Books).
Klein, S., Loftus, J., Kihlstrom, J. F. (2002), 'Memory and Temporal Experience: The Effects of Episodic Memory Loss on an Amnesic Patients's Ability to Remember the Past and to Imagine the Future', *Social Cognition*, 20, pp. 353–379.
Melges, Frederick Towne (1982), *Time and the Inner Future: A Temporal Approach to Psychiatric Disorders* (New York: John Wiley & Sons).
Melges, Frederick Towne (1990), 'Identity and Temporal Perspective' in *Cognitive Models of Psychological Time*, ed. Richard A. Block (Hillsdale, NJ: Lawrence Erlbaum Associates), pp. 253–266.
Minkowski, Eugene (1970), *Lived Time: Phenomenological and Psychological Studies* (Evanston: Northwestern University Press).

Ornstein, Robert (1969), *On the Experience of Time* (Boulder, CO: Westview Press).

Pöppel, Ernst (1988), *Mindworks: Time and Conscious Experience* (Boston: Harcourt Brace Jovanovich Publishers).

Pöppel, Ernst (1989), 'Taxonomy of the Subjective: An Evolutionary Perspective' in *Neuropsychology of Visual Perception*, ed. Jason W. Brown (Hillsdale, NJ: Lawrence Erlbaum Associates), pp. 219–232.

Pöppel, Ernst (1994), 'Temporal Mechanisms in Perception', *International Review of Neurobiology*, 37, pp. 185–202.

Tulving, Endel (1985), 'How Many Memory Systems are there?', American Psychologist, 40, pp. 385–398.

Tulving, Endel (2002), 'Chronesthesia: Awareness of Subjective Time', in *Principles of Frontal Lobe Functions, eds. D. T. Stuss and R. C. Knight* (New York: Oxford University Press), pp. 311–325.

Tulving, Endel (2005), 'Episodic Memory and Autonoesis: Uniquely Human?' in *The Missing Link in Cognition: Origins of Self-Reflective Consciousness*, eds. Herbert S. Terrace and Janet Metcaffe (New York: Oxford University Press), pp. 3–56.

Turner, Frederick, Pöppel, Ernst, (1983), 'The Neural Lyre: Poetic Meter, the Brain and Time', *Poetry*, 142, pp. 277–303.

Wheeler, Mark A., Stuss, Donald T., Tulving, Endel (1997), 'Toward a Theory of Episodic Memory: The Frontal Lobes and Autonoetic Consciousness', *Psychological Bulletin*, 121, pp. 331–354.

Michael Wheeler

Is Language the Ultimate Artefact?

Abstract[1]

Andy Clark has argued that language is 'in many ways the ultimate artifact' (Clark, 1997, p. 218). Fuelling this conclusion is a view according to which the human brain is essentially no more than a pattern-completing device, while language is an external resource which is adaptively fitted to the human brain in such a way that it enables that brain to exceed its unaided (pattern-completing) cognitive capacities, in much the same way as a pair of scissors enables us to 'exploit our basic manipulative capacities to fulfill new ends' (Clark, 1997, pp. 193-4). How should we respond to this bold reconceptualization of our linguistic abilities? First we need to understand it properly. So I begin by identifying and unpacking (and making a small 'Heideggerian' amendment to) Clark's main language-specific claims. That done I take a step back. Clark's approach to language is generated from a theoretical perspective which sees cognition as distributed over brain, body, and world. So I continue my investigation of Clark's incursion into linguistic territory by uncovering and illustrating those key ideas from the overall distributed cognition research programme which are particularly relevant in the present context. I then use this analysis as a spring-board from which to examine a crucial issue that arises for Clark's account of language, namely linguistic inner rehearsal. I

[1] This paper was originally published in the journal *Language Sciences*, 26:6, 2004, pp. 693–715, special issue on Distributed Cognition and Integrational Linguistics, Edited by D. Spurrett. The text of this reprinted version has been revised in the following respect: a number of bibliographical entries and associated textual references have been changed to give up-to-date publication details. This explains how a paper published in 2004 contains references to material published in 2005!

argue that while there is much to recommend in Clark's treatment of this issue, some significant difficulties remain to be overcome. Via this critique of Clark's position, alongside some proposals for how the revealed problems might be addressed, I hope to edge us that bit closer to a full understanding of our linguistic abilities.

1. Introduction

Towards the end of his highly influential 1997 book, *Being There: Putting Brain, Body, and World Together Again*, the philosopher Andy Clark unveils a rich and challenging account of language.[2] My intention in this paper is to interrogate certain key moments in Clark's account. I should say at the outset that I am in deep sympathy with Clark's fundamental approach to the issue. This is unsurprising, perhaps, since he and I share a range of gut intuitions, philosophical assumptions, and science-driven thoughts about the essential nature of mind, cognition and intelligence (more on this in section 3 below). Nevertheless, one consequence of this large measure of agreement is that any readers out there who find themselves hankering after a blanket demolition of Clark's position will, I wager, be sorely disappointed by what follows. Indeed, it seems to me that something like Clark's view of language must be right, even if, as I shall argue, the details of his own particular treatment stand in need of some significant clarifications and revisions. My ultimate goal then is not to scupper the ship that Clark launches, but rather to enhance its philosophical and scientific sea-worthiness.

2. Cognitive Scissors

Let's begin by laying out Clark's account. Clark's first major claim is that language is best viewed not—or, to be more accurate, not merely—as a medium of communication (which is how it is standardly and most readily conceived). Language is equally (perhaps even primarily) 'a tool that alters the nature of the computational tasks involved in various kinds of problem solving' (Clark, 1997, p. 193). The idea here is that public language is a resource that enables human beings (or their brains) to restructure certain problems so that (as we shall see later) those problems are rendered amenable to the kinds of systems that we (or our brains) most funda-

---

[2] See also (Clark, 1998; 2001; 2003). Clark would be the first to remind us that his work on language draws and builds on a number of previous treatments by others (for discussion, see Clark, 1997, pp.194-200).

mentally are. Intertwined with this quite radical rethinking of the functional role of language in human cognition is a further claim. Linguistic competence is often paraded as requiring a revolution in psychological innards, with the upshot being that the linguistic-haves and the linguistic-have-nots are held to possess fundamentally different brains. On this view, the brains of the former (but not those of the latter) are typically thought to contain some sort of domain-specific language processing system, one whose elements are organized, at a fundamental level, so as to encode the structural properties of natural language (e.g. a Chomskyan language acquisition device; see e.g. Chomsky, 1986). But Clark rejects the need for any such drastic inner discontinuity at the threshold of language. His striking alternative proposal is that language is 'an external resource that complements but does not profoundly alter the brain's own basic modes of representation and computation' (p. 198).

This further claim has three components. The first two are explicit in the immediately preceding quotation, while the third needs to be teased out. The first (explicit) component, which dovetails neatly with Clark's opening claim that language is a tool which humans exploit, is to promote the externality of language as a phenomenon. Like more familiar tools—hammers, compasses, computers and so on—language is part of the external supporting environment in which our brains and bodies mature and work. The second (explicit) component trades on the thought that the biological brain has certain generic forms of inner state and mechanism ('the brain's own basic modes of representation and computation') that, from both an evolutionary and a developmental perspective, precede linguistic competence. The idea, then, is that when language comes onto the cognitive scene, it heralds not a transformation in those generic types of inner resource, but rather an augmentation of them.

In developing this picture, Clark explores an analogy with a more mundane external tool, namely a pair of scissors (Clark, 1997, p. 193). Scissors allow human beings to exceed their unaided manipulative capabilities by, for example, enabling us to make straight cuts in paper. It is here that the third component of Clark's external scaffolding claim comes out of the shadows. Part of the reason why scissors are such powerful augmenters of our unaided manipulative capabilities is that scissors are adaptively fitted to the shape and the capacities of the human hand (its ability to grip in a certain way, and so on). This important moral transfers to the case of language. Thus part of the reason why language is so effective in enabling the language-exploiting brain to exceed its unaided psychological capacities is that language is adaptively fitted to that kind of brain. Of course, scissors have been adapted to the hand largely through the conscious and deliberate efforts of human design, whereas (the thought is) language has become adapted to the brain through the blind and unintelligent engine of Darwinian selection, but that difference is not, in and of itself, a difference that makes a difference to the present point which concerns the end result of the adaptive process.[3]

In sum, then, Clark urges us to take seriously the thought that language is an externally located tool that boosts the unaided psychological capacities of the human brain, in part by being adaptively fitted to that brain. One might say that linguistic systems are like cognitive scissors. This vision bequeaths two immediate interpretative questions: 'What exactly are the unaided cognitive capacities of the human brain?' and 'What exactly are the extra cognitive achievements that language makes possible?'. The answer that Clark gives to the first of these questions (an answer which reveals his broadly

[3] In Clark's treatment, the claim that language is itself a system evolving under selection pressures — pressures established principally by the character of its evolutionary conduit, the human brain — is left somewhat skeletal. However, the idea is given compelling theoretical and experimental flesh by, for example, the Language Evolution and Computation Research Unit at the University of Edinburgh (see http://www.ling.ed.ac.uk/lec). As just one example of the exciting work coming out of this group, consider the following: Simon Kirby and his colleagues have used computer simulations to show that if (a) one places language in its learning context, that is as being passed on from one generation to the next by cultural transmission, (b) one begins, as seems evolutionarily likely, with a holistic language (one in which there is no systematic mapping from the structure of the symbols used to the structure of the meanings conveyed), (c) there is, as many have suggested, a transmission bottleneck in the language learning process (such that learners are exposed only to some impoverished subset of the language), and (d) language learners have a rudimentary domain-independent generalization capacity, then the language in question will evolve compositional structure. The reason for this is that compositional languages are generalizable languages, and generalizable languages can be recreated in each generation without exposure to the whole language. This makes such languages more evolutionarily stable, so that once a generalizing learner, by chance, stumbles across compositional structure, such structure will spread throughout the population. (For the details, see e.g. Kirby, 2002; Brighton, 2002; Kirby & Christiansen, 2003; Smith et al., 2003) This result is exciting because, among other things, it sees the poverty of the stimulus as a force that drives the evolution of linguistic structure, rather than as a problem to be overcome by some Chomskyan innate language acquisition device.

connectionist perspective) is that the human brain is essentially a device for pattern-association, pattern-completion and pattern-manipulation. (Henceforth I shall speak simply of the 'pattern-completing brain' and assume that we mean to include the other, closely related capacities.) Thus Clark's claim is that our language-involving behaviour is to be explained by an all-conquering partnership between, on the one hand, a pattern-completing brain and, on the other, an external storehouse of rich linguistic structures.

In order to appreciate just how radical Clark's position here is, we need to disentangle its evolutionary dimension from its developmental one. And we can do that by noting the way in which Clark distances his position from a view (putatively) held by Dennett (1991). On an interpretation that Clark himself admits is tentative (Clark, 1997, p. 197), Dennett argues that our innate neural hardware may differ from that of our non-linguistic evolutionary near-neighbours (such as chimpanzees) in only relatively minor ways. Nevertheless, it is precisely these relatively minor hardware differences that constitute the evolutionary source of the human ability to create, learn and use public language. According to Clark, this part of Dennett's story is correct: there is no mandate to attribute human beings with the kind of innate language processing mechanism whose design would mean that our brains, compared with those of our evolutionary near-neighbours, contain a fundamentally different kind of neural device. However, when we enter the developmental arena, Clark jumps the Dennettian train. Dennett's further proposal, as Clark explains it, is that developmental exposure to a linguistic environment results in a subtle reprogramming of the computational resources of the human brain, such that our innate pattern-completing neural architecture comes to simulate a kind of logic-like serial processing device. Clark, by contrast, resists the idea of any extensive ontogenetic reprogramming phase driven by language. Thus, we are told, developmental exposure to and use of language brings about no *significant* reorganization of the brain's processing architecture. In that sense, language remains external and the brain remains a pattern-completing machine (more on this in a moment).

Now let's turn to our second interpretative question: what are the extra cognitive achievements that language makes possible? This is where Clark's first major claim re-surfaces and assumes its full importance. We can all agree that language enables sophisticated communication, but, as we have seen, Clark alerts us to a rather different functional contribution that language may make to our lives, namely its power to transform the character of certain problems so that those problems are rendered amenable to the pattern-completing strengths of the biological brain. Clark explicates this thought using a host of examples (see Clark, 1997, especially pp. 200–11). For present purposes we can make do with a representative sample of illustrative cases (some of which I have adapted for local effect).

One simple manifestation of the phenomenon of interest is that we sometimes use concrete linguistic artefacts in the world (notebooks, shopping lists, memo boards etc.) as data stores (especially where the body of data is large and/or complex), thereby reducing the demands on our limited and overworked biological memory. More impressively, we sometimes use linguistic structures to organize actions, of both an individual (writing yourself a note to record Buffy the Vampire Slayer) and a collective (sending group e-mails to organize a celebratory drink) kind. Furthermore, instantiations of language in external media may themselves be non-trivial factors in a distributed reasoning or creative process that flows between and through both the inner resources of the brain and the external resources of the outer environment (more on this sort of thing in the next section). Thus chunks of printed or electronic text may be used to preserve half-baked ideas, or moved around so as to be juxtaposed in newly suggestive ways, or stored for later recall and remanipulation, and so on. And even where the straightforwardly communicative function of language is in the frame, it may still be the case that one thing that public language is doing is enabling individual human minds to overcome certain blockages in their local cognitive trajectories. Thus it seems to be a fact about human cognition that it is heavily path-dependent (i.e., where one can get to in cognitive space depends on where one is and where one has been in that space). But, given the differences between human brains, it is plausible that 'one agent's local minimum [may be] another's potent building block' (Clark, 1997, p. 206), so communal idea-sharing through linguistic communication may help groups of cognizers to transcend the limitations of individual path-dependence.

The foregoing examples lend powerful support to Clark's claim that language may extend our unaided cognitive capacities by acting as an external resource that beneficially alters the basic shape of certain problem-solving scenarios. However, other examples that Clark gives of the transformational and augmentational power of language seem, at first sight, to reinvite a vision of language as being, in some sense, inner. For example, he notes that self-directed speech (whether silent or aloud), especially in the form of repeated instructions to oneself, sometimes sets up a control loop that enhances (novice or expert) problem-solving performance. (Think of the squash player silently telling herself over and over again in between shots that she really must get to the 'T'.) And even more suggestive of an essentially inner aspect to language, one might think, is our introspectively manifest ability to run through sentences 'in our heads'.

Interlude: Clark suggests that our ability for linguistic inner rehearsal may be a crucial psychological stepping stone, since it may be precisely this ability which enables us to think about our own thinking (in the sense of spotting a problem with one of our judgments or beliefs, uncovering the logical or illogical transitions in our arguments, etc.). The idea (Clark 1997, p.209) is that the very process of formulating a thought in words effectively creates that thought as a stable object available for evaluation. That is, thinking in language fashions thoughts as the sort of thing that the thinker can have thoughts about. The fact that words bestow this kind of stability can be traced, Clark argues, to the communicative function of language, on the grounds that successful communicative interactions (of the kind that language supports) require a code that is (a) context neutral (or largely so), (b) modality independent (e.g., linguistic inputs and outputs may be visual, auditory or tactile), and (c) supportive of the relatively easy learning of simple linguistic structures.

Now, depending on how one thinks about language, one might be tempted to challenge Clark's confident espousal of (a)-(c) as necessary conditions for successful linguistic communication. However, let's allow that at least some forms of ordinary linguistic communication bear these hallmarks. That would be enough for Clark to run his suggestion concerning the linguistic source of second-order thinking (having thoughts about thoughts). A second challenge to this aspect of Clark's account is less easily deflected. One might wonder whether language really is the *only* route to the kind of cognitive stability that, on Clark's view, supports the presence of second-order thinking. Indeed, consider the kind of systematic behaviour observed in many non-linguistic animals, according to which a creature capable of responding selectively to one input is capable of responding selectively to many semantically related inputs. Fodor (1987) has argued that this behavioural systematicity is good evidence for some kind of combinatorial structure in the causally efficacious inner states involved, such that those states are constructed out of the same or overlapping simpler recurrent elements. Let's say that Fodor is right, *in principle*, that is, that it *could in principle* be the case that rats and pigeons have a combinatorially organized system of thought. Given that one standard condition on a system being combinatorial is that for any recurrent element within that system, that element must make approximately the same contribution to each of the many different larger structures in which it figures, there seems to be no obvious reason why, in principle at least, a combinatorial system of non-linguistic inner states couldn't deliver the kind of stability which Clark reserves for language.[4] Of course, that isn't to say that combinatorially endowed rats and pigeons would thereby enjoy thoughts about their own thoughts. Such creatures presumably lack the additional cognitive machinery required to turn that impressive psychological trick. However, it does cast Clark's speculation that 'public language … is responsible for … the ability to display *second-order cognitive dynamics* [second-order thinking]' (Clark, 1997, p. 208) in a different light. Language may very plausibly be *one possible* source of such second-order thinking; but it may not be the *only possible* source. In other words, language isn't strictly necessary for second-order thinking.

Let's say that the foregoing argument is sound. Would conceding the conclusion do serious damage to Clark's position? I don't think so. It seems to me that Clark could simply retreat to the weaker claim

[4] For Fodor, of course, the behavioural systematicity in play here indicates that animals such as rats and pigeons have a language of thought. I have avoided putting things this way. For one thing, I am not claiming that rats and pigeons *in fact* have a language of thought, only that we can make sense of the idea that they might. More importantly, in the present context, I am trying to distance the kind of combinatorially organized system of inner states that may possibly be present in such animals from public language. So describing such a system as a language of thought would simply muddy the waters (and they're murky enough already). To be clear, however, a Fodorian language of thought is not a public language. Indeed, for Fodor, it couldn't be. This is because, according to Fodor, learning a natural language is a species of concept acquisition, and concept acquisition works by a method of hypothesis and test. This in turn requires the existence of a language-like system in which candidate hypotheses may be expressed. Thus, Fodor concludes, for us to learn our natural language, we must already have a prior (indeed, to avoid an infinite regress, an innate), in-the-head, language-like system in place; hence the language of thought (Fodor 1975). What all this means is that as long as we reserve the term 'linguistic' for public language, it is correct to speak of non-human animals as, in principle, having a non-linguistic but combinatorially organized system of inner states.

that, as a matter of contingent empirical fact, it's language that provides the route to second-order thinking in humans. Indeed if, as a matter of contingent empirical fact, no other animals realize second-order thoughts, the claim that language has played such a role would look to be plausible, or at least to be an idea worth pursuing. In any case, for present purposes we need not get overly hung up on this issue, since while the underlying phenomenon of linguistic inner rehearsal will exercise a good deal of our critical attention in what follows, the second-order thinking that such rehearsal may possibly support will be of only secondary interest.

Interlude over: let's get back to the main plot, which at this point concerns the worry that the very fact of linguistic inner rehearsal (in particular) seems to demand that we think of language as having a robustly internal dimension. This seems to be in conflict with Clark's claim that language is an external resource. And the whiff of inconsistency here becomes stronger in the wake of the following remark that Clark makes: 'the mere fact that we often mentally rehearse sentences in our heads and use these to guide and alter our behavior means that one cannot treat language and culture as wholly external resources' (Clark, 1997, p. 198). What is going on? As it happens, the apparent tension in Clark's account may be relieved if we interpret him as being implicitly sensitive to two different senses in which language may be inner, only one of which we have met already. According to the first (newly exposed) sense, language is inner just so long as there are private thought processes which are formulated in language.[5] This is a sense in which Clark would, I think, be happy to say that language is, in part, an inner resource. According to the second sense in which language may be inner (scouted earlier), language is inner just so long as there is, in the brain, a domain-specific language processing system, one whose elements are organized, at a fundamental level, so as to encode the structural properties of natural language. This is a sense in which Clark would, I think, want to reject the claim that language is inner. And crucially, according to Clark, the phenomenon of linguistic inner rehearsal does not force this unwanted vision upon us. As he himself puts the point, citing connectionist research on language processing in support, 'it remains possible that … [inner linguistic] rehearsal does not involve

---

[5] 'Private' here means 'unvocalized in public earshot by the thinker when thought (plus non-auditory equivalents)' not 'inaccessible to others in principle'.

the use of any fundamentally different kind of computational device in the brain so much as the use of the same old (essentially pattern-completing) resources to model the special kinds of behavior observed in the world of public language' (p. 198). So, to recall a quotation from earlier, Clark's claim is that linguistic competence, even of the mental rehearsal kind, does not require a transformation in 'the brain's own basic modes of representation and computation.' As we noted last time around, it is this claim which provides a sense in which, for Clark, language remains external.

We shall be returning to the issue of linguistic inner rehearsal and exactly what it tells us about the externality or otherwise of language later. Right now I want to round off my preliminary analysis of Clark's view with a few critical remarks about where he ends up. The final twist in the plot is Clark's claim that once we have signed up for the image of our linguistic abilities that he has advocated, the very ideas that have been used to construct that image come under critical pressure. Thus the illuminating power of a term such as 'tool,' as well as the distinctive interlocking suggestion that language must be conceived as externally located, are seemingly placed in question when Clark concludes that language is 'in many ways the ultimate artifact: so ubiquitous it is almost invisible, so intimate it is not clear whether it is a kind of tool or a dimension of the user' (p. 218). It is important to note here that in claiming (a) that the intimacy between language and user means that there is a mandate to conceive of language as a dimension of the user, Clark is not claiming (b) that the intimacy between language and user means that there is a mandate to conceive of language as inner (in the previously rejected sense of that term). Clark's point, as I read him, is that for the purposes of conceiving the relationship between the language-user and her language, the boundary between what we have previously been thinking of as two systems may sometimes collapse, such that there is really just a single system, one dimension of which is language. So the ultimate artefact is one that rebels against any separation between it and its user. But it is not as if we should, in the end, shift language from the external to the internal side of some persisting agent-environment boundary. Rather, the local agent-environment boundary is itself in danger of disappearing, which is why terms such as 'tool' (conceived as something in the environment which agents use) and 'external' become problematic.

Despite appearances, this is not quite a case of early-Wittgensteinian ladder dumping.[6] To see why, we need only plug in a piece of thinking by a philosopher whom Clark (2003) has described as a subterranean influence on his own work, namely Heidegger. If there's one bit of Heidegger that's passed into mass philosophical and cognitive-scientific consciousness, it's his phenomenological analysis of tool-use (Heidegger, 1926).[7] According to Heidegger, when skilled tool-use is smooth and uninterrupted, the human agent has no conscious experience of the tools in question *as independent objects*. Thus, to use Heidegger's most famous example, while engaged in trouble-free hammering, the skilled carpenter has no conscious recognition of the hammer, the nails, or the work-bench, *in the way that one would if one simply stood back and thought about them* (Heidegger, 1926). Considered as independent objects these tools-in-use become, as it were, phenomenologically transparent. Moreover, Heidegger observes, not only are the hammer, nails, and work-bench in this way not part of the engaged carpenter's phenomenal world, neither, in a sense, is the carpenter! The carpenter becomes absorbed in his activity in such a way that he has no awareness of himself as a subject over and against a world of objects. So, in the domain of smooth and uninterrupted skilled tool-use there are, phenomenologically speaking, no subjects and no objects; there is only the experience of the ongoing task (e.g., hammering).

So what? The message is that hammers too are, or rather under the right circumstances can be, ultimate artefacts. Of course, Heidegger's example turns on phenomenological analysis rather than any hypothesis about the causal mechanisms involved, but given the (in my view) highly plausible principle that phenomenological experience will often reflect its causal underpinnings, not much may hang on that difference.[8] In any case, we're surely in the

---

[6] For the uninitiated, the penultimate proposition of Wittgenstein's *Tractatus Logico-Philosophicus* contains the following, eminently quotable remark: 'My propositions are elucidatory in this way: he who understands me finally recognizes them as senseless, when he has climbed out through them, on them, over them. (He must so to speak throw away the ladder, after he has climbed up on it.)' (Wittgenstein, 1922).

[7] In actual fact, Heidegger was concerned to give an analysis of our skilled dealings with *equipment*, where the term 'equipment' has a special, technical meaning, but tool-use is close enough.

[8] For an extended discussion of the principle in question, plus a defence of the idea that Heidegger signed up for it, see (Wheeler, 2005b).

same ballpark. Once again the key claim is that the intimacy between user and tool collapses the local agent-environment boundary, leaving behind just one system. But that means that with respect to the present point, and pace Clark, there's nothing special about language when compared with more familiar tools and artefacts. Any tool can meet the condition of intimacy required of an 'ultimate artefact.' It simply needs to be used skillfully in a hitch-free manner, such that user and tool are best conceived as a single system. This is, of course, a temporary status achieved by a tool when the dynamics of use are of a certain fluid and undisrupted kind. And crucially, for any tool, there will be other contexts of activity in which the condition of intimacy will fail to be met. Heidegger identified two broad categories of such contexts—*disturbances*, in which, for example, a tool breaks, and *detached reflection*, in which, for example, we consider the tool as an object for scientific or philosophical investigation. In such contexts, a kind of distance is established between the agent and the tool.[9]

One might think that this is the moment where my attempt to lump language in with other tools breaks down. 'Surely,' I hear you say, 'there is a dimension of intimacy that is particular to language, namely that we humans are *always* in intimate contact with language.' (This might be the way to read Clark's remark that language is ubiquitous.) However, if we continue to draw on a Heideggerian analysis, the force of this objection is blunted. As I interpret him, Heidegger too thought that language was a cognitive tool.[10] Indeed, he argues explicitly that we encounter words and sentences in all the modes in which we encounter other tools (Heidegger, 1926). Thus, in free-flowing conversation, we employ words in appropriate ways without being aware of those words as objects to be manipulated. However, there are situations of disturbance in which language-use breaks down and the right words become difficult to find. Finally, we sometimes remove language from its everyday contexts of use, and treat it as an object of scientific or philosophical study, as in formal linguistics or philosophy of language. Where language-use is

---

[9] For much more by way of exegetical discussion, see, for example, Dreyfus (1991) and Wheeler (2005b).
[10] I should confess that while I believe that this is precisely how Heidegger thought of language, it is a far from uncontroversial interpretation. Guignon (1983), for example, explicitly rejects the tool interpretation in favour of an alternative reading according to which, for Heidegger, language is a constitutive precondition for meaningful experience.

disturbed, or language becomes the object of detached scientific or philosophical reflection, the condition of intimacy fails to be met.

Given this Heideggerian amendment, the target of my critical pressure in what follows will not be Clark's inference from the conceptualization of language as cognitive scissors to the suspicion that the agent-environment boundary between language-user and language may collapse. If tools in general (cognitive or otherwise) facilitate such boundary-collapsing events, and if language is indeed best conceived as a tool, then language will facilitate such boundary-collapsing events. Given that I accept the boundary-collapsing power of smooth and uninterrupted skilled tool-use, what I think stands in need of careful evaluation here are some of the details of Clark's vision of language as a (cognitive) tool. If language is incorrectly conceived as an artefact, it certainly can't be the, or even an, ultimate one.

3. Distributed Cognition

Time to take a step back. Clark's approach to language reflects a more general perspective on mind, cognition and intelligence, one which has been gaining ground recently in cognitive science, and of which Clark is a prominent advocate. In order to clear the way to the difficulty that I want to raise for Clark's account of language, we need to make contact with that wider framework. In the contemporary philosophical and cognitive-scientific literature, it trades under a bewildering plethora of different names, including situated cognition, embodied cognition, embedded cognition, embodied-embedded cognition, active externalism, vehicle externalism, the extended mind and (the moniker we'll be using) distributed cognition. In fact there are almost certainly subtle nuances of approach here which someone with an over-enthusiasm for drawing distinctions and too much time on their hands might exploit to divide these various trends from each other. This is not the place to play that particular game, however, since we'll be concerned with a specific proposal about psychological phenomena that has purchase across the board. The proposal in question is that, under certain conditions, the

> organism is linked with an external entity in a two-way interaction, creating a *coupled system* that can be seen as a cognitive system in its own right. All the components in the system play an active causal role, and they jointly govern behavior in the same sort of way that cognition usually does. If we remove the external component the system's behavioral competence will drop, just as

it would if we removed part of its brain. Our thesis is that this sort of coupled process counts equally well as a cognitive process, whether or not it is wholly in the head (Clark & Chalmers, 1998, p. 7).

Notice that the claim on the table here is that there are conditions under which something which counts as a single cognitive system or as a single cognitive process contains some elements which are agent-internal and some which are agent-external. It is *not* the claim that I deliberately sidelined a little earlier, namely that there are conditions under which the very idea of an agent-environment boundary becomes misleading. What seems likely is that unless we have a case of the former, we wouldn't even be tempted to say that we have a case of the latter; but that doesn't make the two cases equivalent.

For our purposes, Clark and Chalmers' proposal may be unpacked as follows: we have a case of genuinely distributed cognition where (i) the source of intelligent action is to be found not purely in the inner activity of neural states and processes, but rather in complex causal interactions between neural factors and additional (extra-neural) elements located in the non-neural body and the environment, and (ii) the behaviour-generating causal contribution of the additional elements is of the same kind as the corresponding contribution of the brain, in that those additional elements account directly for some of the distinctive adaptive richness and flexibility of the observed behaviour.[11] Elsewhere, Clark and I have played out what amounts to the same idea in terms of what we have dubbed *non-trivial causal spread* (Wheeler & Clark, 1999). One has a case of non-trivial causal spread when (a) some phenomenon of interest (e.g., intelligent behaviour) turns out to depend, in unexpected ways, upon causal factors external to the system previously or intuitively thought responsible, and (b) the newly discovered additional causal factors reveal themselves to be at the root of some distinctive target feature of the phenomenon of interest (e.g., the adaptive richness and flexibility of intelligent behaviour). (If condition (a) alone is met, then the causal spread will be trivial in character. In such cases, while we may find it surprising that certain additional factors turn out to play some supporting causal role in generating the phenome-

[11] In another context (Wheeler forthcoming), I've described this proposal as specifying the conditions for *extended cognition*, so that's another label for the list. In the wider philosophical literature, the target position (or something very close to it) is defended, in different ways, by (among others) Haugeland (1995/1998), Hurley (1998), Rowlands (1999) and Wheeler (2005b).

non of interest, the distinctive character of that phenomenon will still be correctly traced to the system previously or intuitively thought responsible.) Where one's best cognitive science displays a case of non-trivial causal spread, one will have a case of distributed cognition.

So, if we go looking for non-trivial causal spread, where will we find it? Consider the following problem.[12] A robot with a control system comprising an artificial neural network and some rather basic visual receptors is placed in a rectangular dark-walled arena. This arena features a white triangle and a white rectangle mounted on one wall. The task is to set up the robot's control system so that, under wildly varying lighting conditions, it will approach the triangle but not the rectangle. The specific architecture of the neural network, the way in which the network is coupled to the visual receptors, and the field-sizes and spatial positions (within predetermined ranges) of those visual receptors are all to be determined. That's the design specification; so why don't you play along by taking a moment now to think about the general kinds of states and structures that you believe will be needed ...

Finished? OK. If you are a cognitive-scientifically minded individual who has not been exposed to the delights of distributed cognition, then I'm prepared to bet that your rough design looks something like this: The robot will need a way of internally representing triangles, rectangles and the spatial layout of its environment. Its strategy should be to build the best map it can of its environment, locating the triangle and the rectangle as accurately as possible on that map. The robot should then plan a path to the triangle and follow it. You might have decided to trade in reliability for speed, and thus to compensate for both the fact that the robot's visual receptors are pretty simple and the fact that the lighting conditions will be changing radically. If so, you will probably have built in a number of 'stop-and-check' stages in which the robot pauses to assess the accuracy of its map and (if necessary) to adjust that map and revise its path.

That's certainly one way to go. But here's an alternative, computationally cheaper (and thus adaptively more efficient) strategy, revealed when Harvey *et al.* (1994) presented the self-same problem to a design methodology known as *evolutionary robotics*. In evolutionary robotics, algorithms inspired largely by Darwinian

[12] I have used this example before. The present analysis draws directly on the treatments to be found in Wheeler (2001; 2005a, b).

evolution are used to automatically design the control systems for (real or simulated) robots.[13] The solution arrived at in this manner was canny, to say the least. Two visual receptors were positioned geometrically such that visual fixation on the oblique edge of the triangle would typically result in a pair of visual signals (i.e., receptor 1 = low, receptor 2 = high) which was different from such pairs produced anywhere else in the arena (or rather *almost* anywhere else in the arena; more on this shortly). The robot would move in a straight line if the pair of visual signals was appropriate for fixation on the triangle, and in a rotational movement otherwise. Thus if the robot was fixated on the triangle, it would tend to move in a straight line towards it. Otherwise it would simply rotate until it did locate the triangle. Occasionally the robot would fixate, 'by mistake,' on one edge of the rectangle, simply because, from certain angles, that edge would result in a qualitatively similar pair of visual signals being generated as would have been generated by the sloping edge of the triangle. Perturbed into straight line movement, the robot would begin to approach the rectangle. However, the looming rectangle would, unlike a looming triangle, produce a change in the relative values of the visual inputs (receptor 1 would be forced into a high state of activation), and the robot would be perturbed into a rotational movement. During this rotation, the robot would almost invariably refixate on the correct target, the triangle.

This is a demonstration of non-trivial causal spread. The systematic activity of inner maps, route-planning algorithms and so on (as present in our cognitive-scientifically intuitive solution) has been replaced by a suite of organized interactions involving significant causal contributions not only from states and processes in the robot's brain, but also from certain additional bodily factors and from the

[13] Roughly speaking, the evolutionary robotics methodology is to set up a way of encoding robot control systems as genotypes, and then, starting with a randomly generated population of controllers, and some evaluation task, to implement a selection cycle such that more successful controllers have a proportionally higher opportunity to contribute genetic material to subsequent generations, i.e., to be 'parents.' Genetic operators analogous to recombination and mutation in natural reproduction are applied to the parental genotypes to produce 'children,' and (typically) a number of existing members of the population are discarded so that the population size remains constant. Each robot in the resulting new population is then evaluated, and the process starts all over again. Over successive generations, better performing controllers are discovered. For useful introductions to evolutionary robotics, see Husbands and Meyer (1998) and Nolfi and Floreano (2000).

environment. It is true, of course, that the robot's artificial brain contributes to the observed adaptive success (although it is worth noting that the evolved neural network was, structurally speaking, quite simple). But a further agent-side factor that plays a non-trivial part in the story is the spatial organization of the robot's visual morphology. Indeed, one might well think that it is this geometric fact about the agent's bodily periphery that principally explains the robot's ability to become, and then to remain, locked onto the correct figure. The crucial role played by the environment becomes clear once one realizes that it is the specific ecological niche inhabited by the robot that enables the selected-for strategy to produce reliable triangle-rectangle discrimination. If, for example, non-triangle-related sloping edges were common in the robot's environment, then although the evolved strategy would presumably enable the robot to avoid rectangles, it would no longer enable it to move reliably towards *only* triangles. So adaptive success depends not just on the work done by the agent-side mechanisms, but also on the tight coupling between those mechanisms and certain specific structures in the environment which can be depended upon to be reliably present.

About now, Clark and Chalmers' words should be ringing in our ears: 'if we remove the external component the system's behavioral competence will drop, just as it would if we removed part of its brain ... this sort of coupled process counts equally well as a cognitive process, whether or not it is wholly in the head.' With this principle back in full view, it seems clear that we can understand Harvey *et al.*'s triangle-rectangle discrimination robot as realizing a distributed-cognition-style adaptive solution. Moreover, the robot illustrates an important feature of such solutions, a feature that bears emphasis now because it will turn out to be crucial to my argument later. In paradigmatic cases of distributed cognition, adaptive success ensues because, during the actual run-time of the behaviour, the internal elements become *directly causally locked onto* the contributing external elements. That's the nature of the coupling relationship. And that's why the removal of the external elements results in significant behavioural degradation or collapse. Notice that the same run-time dependence does not exist for more traditional cognitive architectures which deal in detailed (or relatively detailed) internal representations of the environment. In these architectures, once the salient internal surrogate has been built, it's *that* structure (rather than its external source) with which the other inner elements enter into direct causal commerce, in run-time, in order to guide behaviour.[14]

Still, while Harvey *et al.*'s robot helps to illuminate the key principles of distributed cognition, the adaptive problem it solves seems to be a long way from anything like language-use. So here's another example of those key principles at work, one which is intuitively closer to our primary target. In a passage written long before the distributed cognition paradigm emerged as a well-formed cognitive-scientific research programme, but in which there appears the prescient phrase 'the external environment becomes a key extension to our mind,' Rumelhart *et al.* note that most of us solve difficult multiplication problems by using 'pen and paper' as an external resource. This environmental prop enables us to transform a difficult cognitive problem into a set of simpler ones, and to temporarily store the results of those intermediate calculations (Rumelhart *et al.*, 1986, quote from p. 46). Thus, as we might now put it, the externally located pen-and-paper resource makes a non-trivial causal contribution to the observed problem-solving behaviour, and the distributed combination of this resource and certain inner psychological processes constitutes a cognitive system in its own right.

It is by way of Rumelhart et al.'s compelling example that Clark introduces the following thought: the agent-internal contribution to

---

[14] To be clear, I am not intending to suggest that fans of distributed cognition must eschew any concept of internal representation. The status and character of representational explanation in distributed cognition is a complex and subtle issue, and this paper is certainly not the place to explore it. For my own thoughts, see (Wheeler and Clark 1999; Wheeler 2001, 2005a, b, forthcoming). However, put briefly (and thus inadequately), one general message is that where a representation-exploiting control strategy is an example of distributed cognition, the kinds of representations paradigmatically deployed will make their contribution to adaptive success not by internally specifying, in any detailed way, the objective properties and relations of the external environment, but rather by coding, sparsely and temporarily, only for certain context-specific properties (often defined in an egocentric manner), and by working in close and ongoing interaction with the environment itself. The reliance on regular sensing here is more fundamental than in the 'stop-and-check' strategy mentioned earlier, since there will be no sense in which the distributed solution involves the construction, abandonment or re-construction of an overall plan for achieving the intended goal. Goal-achieving behaviour emerges out of the pattern of ongoing interactions between the inner and outer elements in the distributed cognitive system, without the need for any internally maintained global plan. For a distributed solution that features this kind of representational contribution, see e.g. Franceschini *et al.* (1992, discussed in Wheeler, 2001; 2005b).

mathematical problem-solving is likely to be 'just' a matter of pattern completion, and so will be amenable to connectionist modelling (Clark, 1997, pp. 61–2). This is the mathematics-specific version of a more general claim that we can understand Clark as making, namely that the agent-internal contribution to the kind of distributed problem-solving that turns on the active exploitation of external symbols is likely to be 'just' a matter of pattern completion, and so will be amenable to connectionist modelling. Of course, as we have seen already, Clark applies this same reasoning to another specific case of external symbol exploitation — language-use. Indeed, we might strengthen the link here further by saying that systems of mathematical symbols, like language, are external cognitive tools that augment and extend the unaided psychological capacities of the human brain.

I could go on all day giving intriguing examples of distributed cognition. There's a lot of it around. (For many more examples see Clark, 1997; Wheeler, 2005b, among other treatments.) For the purposes of the present paper, however, we have now learned enough about the general form of the phenomenon to turn our attention back to Clark's distributed-cognition-style vision of language. So what exactly is wrong with the idea that language is an external tool which augments the pattern-completing activities of the human brain? In the next section I shall explore some problems faced by Clark's account.

4. Off-Line Language

It seems clear that the natural home of non-trivial causal spread, and thus of distributed cognition, is in the domain of what might be called *on-line intelligence* (Wheeler & Clark, 1999). A creature displays *on-line intelligence* just when it produces a suite of fluid and flexible real-time adaptive responses to incoming sensory stimuli. Examples might include escaping from a predator, catching a prey, tracking a mate, taking a catch in cricket or baseball, manipulating written mathematical symbols to solve a complex multiplication problem, or holding a lively conversation. By contrast, a creature displays *off-line intelligence* just when it disentangles itself in some way from the ongoing perception-action cycle. Examples might include wondering what the weather's like in Durban now, mentally planning that imminent trip to London, or *doing complex multiplica-*

tion in one's head.[15] The fact that I have emphasized the final example here is not idle, because the counterbalance to the unquestionable observation that most of us solve difficult multiplication problems by using the external prop of pen and paper is that some lucky souls can solve difficult multiplication problems in their heads without the use of such cognitive scaffolding. In the latter case it seems fair to say that the inner mechanisms involved are functioning in an off-line way. Given the thought that, as we noted above, mathematical symbol systems may, in the present context, be treated as close-cousins of language, we can beat a path back to language by examining the distinction between on-line and off-line mathematical reasoning.

What kind of cognitive innards might plausibly support off-line mathematical reasoning? Drawing again on Rumelhart *et al.*'s rich discussion, Clark suggests that this is a case of learning 'to manipulate a mental model in the same way as we originally manipulated the real world' (Clark, 1997, p. 61). In other words it's another instance of inner rehearsal. So how does the mechanics of this process work? Here Clark offers the following argument (again using Rumelhart *et al.*'s treatment as a source of insights): 'experience with drawing and using Venn diagrams allows us to train a neural network which subsequently allows us to manipulate imagined Venn diagrams in our heads... there is no reason to suppose that such training results in the installation of a different *kind* of computational device. It is the same old process of pattern-completion in high-dimensional representa-

---

[15] Recently, some thinkers (e.g., Esther Thelen and Andy Clark, both in seminar discussion) have raised doubts about the on-line/off-line distinction, on the grounds that no intelligent agent is (they claim) ever wholly on-line or wholly off-line. On this view, intelligence is always a dynamic negotiation between on-line and off-line processes. I have no doubt that this interactive view is true for many cases of (at least) human intelligence. Producing this paper, for example, has been an unfolding interplay between off-line reflection and on-line activities such as cutting and pasting text (cf. Clark, 1997, pp. 206–7). However, even if such composite or intermediate cases abound, there are also cognitive achievements that seem to fall squarely into one category or the other. Moreover, even where we judge an observed behaviour to be a composite case — one in which there is an interaction between off-line and on-line components processes — the on-line/off-line distinction is in fact still being used as a way of classifying those component processes and we can still ask meaningful questions about their character as members of one category or the other; so the distinction remains conceptually and explanatorily useful at that level.

tional spaces, but applied to the special domain of a specific kind of external representation' (p. 199).

There is something odd about Clark's final remark here, in that it seems to run together the learning and the performance phases of the target behaviour. To be sure, the particular external representations in question must provide the source domain for a process in which certain inner mechanisms learn how to be sensitive to and then how to manipulate certain patterns, in the correct way. However, once that training phase is complete, and we thus have the inner resources to perform off-line mathematical reasoning (conceived as the inner rehearsal of a process that previously involved external symbol manipulation), there is a straightforward mechanical sense in which, during such off-line reasoning, the 'process of pattern-completion in high-dimensional representational spaces' must be 'applied to' certain inner states and structures. After all, the whole point about off-line cases is the absence of any ongoing interaction with the environment. That's how the representations in which we are interested here earn their adaptive keep, by standing in, within the inner processing economy, for certain absent environmental factors. But Clark's treatment leaves the structure of those inner surrogates awkwardly mysterious.

Why awkwardly so? It is here that our foray into the general character of distributed-cognition-style adaptive solutions yields dividends. There we learned that, in paradigmatic cases of distributed cognition, adaptive success ensues because, during the actual run-time of the behaviour, certain internal elements become directly causally locked onto the contributing external elements. This general principle produces the following local picture. When the mathematical reasoning in which we are interested is a case of on-line distributed cognition, the inner pattern-completing mechanism will be directly causally locked onto certain properties of mathematical symbols located in the environment. But when our mathematical reasoning is off-line, there are, by hypothesis, no such environmental factors onto which the mechanisms concerned could be locked. However, we can easily hold onto the Clark-inspired thought that fundamentally the same kind of processing mechanism (perhaps even the very same pattern-completing mechanism) may still be deployed, just so long as there are in place certain inner surrogates for those missing environmental factors, surrogates which recapitulate certain structural properties of those factors, viz the ones, whatever they may be, to which the mechanisms concerned are designed so as to be mechanically keyed. So what we need are inner surrogates that realize certain structural properties of mathematical symbols. That's what the inner models that support off-line mathematical problem-solving will be like.

Clark's account of mathematical reasoning may be summarized as follows: (i) on-line mathematical reasoning essentially involves the manipulation of external symbols; (ii) off-line mathematical reasoning is a case of mathematical inner rehearsal; and (iii) fundamentally the same inner processing mechanisms are active in both cases. This account shapes his view of language-use. To see this, we merely need to restage some of the core aspects of Clark's view of language using the on-line/off-line distinction. Thus (i) on-line language-use essentially involves the manipulation of external symbols (words, sentences etc.); (ii) off-line language-use is a case of linguistic inner rehearsal (so it requires the internal modelling of certain external symbolic elements); and (iii) fundamentally the same inner processing mechanisms are active in both cases. But, given this, our recent moral ought to transfer too. Thus just as off-line mathematical reasoning requires inner representations that recapitulate certain structural properties of external mathematical symbol-systems, namely those structural properties which are non-trivial contributing factors in on-line distributed mathematical problem-solving, so off-line language-use requires inner representations that recapitulate certain structural properties of external linguistic symbol systems, namely those structural properties which are non-trivial contributing factors in on-line distributed linguistic performance. Exactly what those properties are is a matter for theoretical debate and for interdisciplinary empirical investigation. That they need to be internally recapitulated is an unavoidable consequence of the basic logic of the distributed cognition paradigm.

'So what?' you might be thinking. 'Wheeler has agreed, hasn't he, that the computational process active in off-line mathematical problem-solving, and now by extension the computational process active in off-line language-use, may remain one of pattern-completion? Therefore the shortfall identified in Clark's account of the inner models required fails to damage Clark's view that neither the capacity for off-line mathematics nor the capacity for off-line language-use demands the installation of a different kind of computational device.' So much is true. But now let's return to one of Clark's position-defining remarks about language. Clark argues that language is 'an external resource that complements but does not profoundly alter the brain's own basic modes of *representation* and computation' (p.198, emphasis added).[16] As far as I can see, while the sub-claim concerning the neutral effects of language on the brain's own basic mode of computation can still be sustained following my critical comments, the sub-claim concerning the neutral effects of language on the brain's own basic mode of representation cannot.

It is here that we need, perhaps belatedly, to try to say exactly what Clark means by the phrase 'the brain's own basic mode of representation'. We know that the computational counterpart to this notion identifies pattern-completion in the style of connectionist networks. So it seems reasonable to infer (and there is plenty of textual evidence to back up the inference; see e.g. Clark, 1997, p. 141) that, for Clark, the brain's own basic representational format is broadly connectionist in form. Thus it will be one of distributed (in the connectionist sense of that term), multi-dimensional patterns of activation and similarity metrics. Having said that, it should be noted that Clark sees these patterns and metrics through the lens not of traditional connectionism, but of contemporary neuroscience, dynamical systems approaches to cognitive science and, of course, the distributed cognition paradigm (see e.g. Clark, 1997, p. 174). So the brain's own basic mode of representation is a substantially recontextualized, broadly connectionist one. The claim of interest, then, is that language-use, on-line or off-line, does not require any radical changes to this format.

At this juncture we need to tread with care. One might be tempted to think that Clark's persistence claim amounts only to the demand that any new structural properties which we are compelled to introduce into our inner processing story, in order to account for linguistic competence, must be *implemented* in a distinctively brain-like form, that is, in terms of high-dimensional patterns of activation and similarity metrics in connectionist-style networks. This requirement, however, is too weak for what Clark wants. After all, even Fodor and Pylyshyn, those arch enemies of everything connectionist, agree that connectionist-style states and processes may be used to implement classical systems, systems whose funda-

[16] Clark gives the putative persistence of the brain's own basic representational format far less prominence during his discussion of mathematical reasoning. But it is there. Consider, for example, the claim that off-line mathematical reasoning is 'the same old process of pattern-completion in *high-dimensional representational spaces*' (Clark, 1997, p. 199, emphasis added). More on high-dimensional representational spaces in a moment.

mental structural properties include a language-like combinatorial syntax (Fodor & Pylyshyn, 1988). So if what Clark's claim required were nothing weightier than the persistence of the brain's own basic representational format at an implementational level, his position would be consistent with the following suggestion: the kinds of phenomena that we standardly take to be realized by language—infinite productivity, overwhelming systematicity and so on—can be accounted for only if a classical representational format (one which features a language-like combinatorial syntax) is understood to be a fundamental feature of the neural economy at some 'higher,' non-implementational level. But any such suggestion is surely at odds with Clark's more radical intended message, which (it is now clear) must be that the inner processing story that we need to tell, in order to account for linguistic competence, may be couched *exhaustively* in terms of the structural properties which define the brain's own characteristic style of representation (at root, high-dimensional patterns of activation and similarity metrics).

From what we have seen, on-line language-use (as conceived within the distributed cognition paradigm) may pass Clark's more-than-implementation persistence test, since it involves an interactive real-time combination of domain-general inner mechanisms and external linguistic symbol systems. Given such teamwork, the organizational properties (e.g. compositionality) that plausibly count as the source of the distinctive features of language mentioned above may be realized environmentally, in the external symbol systems, *without* being recaptured internally. So the inner states in play will not need to be reconfigured significantly to support successful performance in the linguistic domain. However, the fundamental logic of the general distributed-cognition framework in which Clark's view is embedded dictates that off-line language-use (linguistic inner rehearsal) requires the presence of inner surrogates that *do* recapture these organizational properties, or at least key aspects of them (see my closing thought below). Thus in the off-line case we confront nothing less than a profound transformation in the brain's own basic mode of representation, and that runs contrary to Clark's avowed view.[17]

[17] In this context it is interesting to note that in their treatment of mathematical problem-solving, Rumelhart et al. write of the 'internalization of an external representational format' (1986, p. 47). The closest Clark himself comes to opening up this issue is when, as we saw previously, he talks about using 'the same old (essentially pattern-completing) resources to model the *special*

5. The Stings in the Tale

I warned you at the outset that this wasn't going to be a blanket demolition of Clark on language. Still, it may seem that I have spent my time focussing on a rather narrow issue in Clark's account, to the exclusion of much that is rich and illuminating in the wider picture. To reassure you that the issue on which I have been concentrating is a far from minor one, I want to conclude by pointing out just how much hangs on it. First I shall identify the direct implications of the preceding reflections for Clark's account of language as a cognitive tool. Then I shall argue that what my argument about off-line language-use demonstrates is that in the case of a creature who has the capacity to engage in off-line thinking, one cannot argue for the distributed cognition perspective on grounds of adaptive efficiency.

Clark's account of language as a cognitive tool turns, in part, on the idea that language is an *external* resource which augments, rather than transforms, our unaided psychological capacities. Recall that a clear sense in which Clark rejects the claim that language is inner is the sense in which there exists some sort of domain-specific language processing system whose elements are organized, at basic level, so as to code for the structural properties of natural language. Now, the view for which I have argued does not herald the return of a Chomskyan in-the-head language device or even a Fodorian language of thought. For one thing there is no reason to think that the implicated inner structures will be innate (see footnote 4). It doesn't even amount to an endorsement of the 'reprogramming' view that Clark attributes to Dennett (see above), since, according to the tabled suggestion, (a) on-line language-use heralds no radical change of inner representational format, whereas, on the view of Clark's Dennett, it seems that exposure to language does, and (b) off-line language-use demands a change of inner representational format but not of inner computational process, whereas, on the view of Clark's Dennett, it seems that exposure to language produces changes of both. However, it does open up a conceptual space within which there emerges a robust third sense in which language may be inner. (Recall that Clark can live happily with the position according to which language is inner just when linguistically formed thoughts are expressed privately.) In the newly emerged sense in which lan-

---

kinds of behavior observed in the world of public language' (p. 198, emphasis added).

guage may be inner, language is inner if there exists, in the brain, representations which recapitulate the structural properties of natural language. Notice that this sense of language being inner doesn't require the presence of any domain-specific language processing system. The mechanisms which deal in the linguistically structured representations may themselves be domain-general in character (e.g. generic connectionist pattern-completers). What matters is the structure of the representations concerned.[18]

With this representation-oriented sense of 'language as inner' distinguished from its mechanism-oriented cousin, Clark's arguments concerning the nature of language are revealed as constituting a case against (i) the idea that language-use requires a domain-specific language processing mechanism, and not (ii) the idea that (some) language-use requires internal representations with specifically linguistic structure. So they do not constitute an argument against our newly emerged sense in which language may be inner. Indeed, as we have seen, in the particular case of linguistic inner rehearsal, the very logic of the theoretical perspective which Clark endorses demands that off-line language-use is supported by representations which encode linguistic structure. So there is, after all, a robust sense in which language may be inner. And note that Clark cannot accept this newly emerged sense in which language may be inner in the same way that he can accept the sense which turns on the private expression of linguistically formed thoughts. For what makes the sense that turns on the presence of a domain-specific language processing mechanism troublesome is the fact that the relevant language-based structures are to be found in the agent's brain, and that is equally true of our newly emerged sense. So if the key claim that language is a cognitive tool is interpreted as requiring the externality of language (which seems correct, at least within Clark's framework), then that claim is under serious threat.

Let me finish by leaving Clark himself behind, and by mining a general consequence of my critique of his account of language. To bring this consequence into view, we need to note that, according to the position I've defended, linguistic inner rehearsal is just one

---

[18] In effect, this is to exploit a strong distinction between mechanism and information (or computational process and representational state) that Tony Atkinson and I have used elsewhere to shape a critique of the evolutionary-psychological view that the human mind is a collection of domain-specific modules (see Wheeler and Atkinson, 2001; Atkinson and Wheeler, 2004).

species of inner rehearsal among others. Of course, we have already met a mathematically oriented kind of inner rehearsal. But there are others too, such as my mentally recalling a favourite walk along the Royal Mile up to Edinburgh Castle. Now notice that the general assumption here (an assumption which Clark shares; see his discussion of reasoning with Venn diagrams) is that we first perform a behaviour (language-use, mathematical reasoning, perceptually guided action etc.) on-line. Later we may rehearse the same movements and manipulations off-line, in our heads. Now, in each of the different contexts of off-line thinking, inner mechanisms which, in the on-line case, will have been in regular causal commerce with certain external elements are re-targeted on inner surrogates of those external elements, in order to support inner rehearsal. The content realized by the inner surrogates in play here will be determined by the nature of the domain in question.

So where do the crucial surrogates come from? Since, according to the distributed cognition perspective, they aren't causally necessary for on-line intelligent activity, they certainly won't have been built in order to enable such activity at the time of performance. One option here is to hold that such states are constructed in parallel with the action being performed, even though they play no direct causal role in enabling that performance. It is perhaps hard to see how such a system would ever be evolutionarily selected for. After all, if we assume, as we have been, that the on-line behaviour is in place ahead of the capacity for the inner rehearsal of that behaviour, why should Darwinian selection favour the diverting of resources to a model-building strategy when that strategy has no beneficial effects whatsoever on the behaviour itself? Perhaps, however, we are looking with too narrow a field of vision. After all, we know that skilled sportsmen and sportswomen may improve their athletic performance on the day of competition through a prior process in which key moves and techniques are visualized. This imaginative trick is surely based on inner rehearsal, and has adaptive pay-offs.

Whatever the prospects for such evolutionary explanations, however, the fact remains that the state of affairs suggested by the distributed cognition paradigm credits the agent with what seems to be a rather less efficient cognitive set-up than that attributed to her by a more orthodox cognitive science. After all, on a more orthodox story, not only off-line thinking but also real-time intelligent action is guided by, broadly speaking, the kinds of states and structures (structure preserving inner representations) that I have suggested are needed for off-line thinking. So the traditional theorist faces no mystery about how such states and structures get installed: on-line intelligent action demands their presence. Those very same elements are then simply re-used in the off-line case. So while we fans of distributed cognition often claim that the sorts of adaptive strategies we favour are more efficient than their traditional counterparts (since on our view there is no requirement for the agent to build or to maintain computationally costly detailed models of the world in order to generate on-line intelligent action; see e.g. Brooks, 1991), this really does look to be an unsupportable argument, in those cases where we are dealing with creatures who are also capable of off-line intelligence.

One closing thought: Perhaps this worry about the relative inefficiency of the kind of cognitive architecture that is authorized by the basic logic of the distributed cognition paradigm might be mitigated, if it could be shown that creatures who are capable of off-line cognition may not commit themselves to recapitulating all the relevant environmental and experiential structure present during real-time action. According to this proposal, which applies to linguistic inner rehearsal as much as to post-perceptual recall, at least some off-line thinking may, in truth, be the result of a sly alliance between sparse, just-good-enough memory (laid down as representations in parallel with real-time performance) and creative cognitive reconstruction. Like so many regions of the exciting terrain that is contemporary cognitive science (and the peak that corresponds to an explanation of our linguistic abilities is surely one of the hardest to climb in that terrain), this remains, I think, an open question ripe for further philosophical and empirical exploration. The distributed cognition paradigm may not have all the answers, but it has, I am convinced, made the problems all the more interesting.

Acknowledgements

Many thanks to the following audiences for invaluable feedback and discussion: the Mind AND World 2003 conference in Durban, the Mental Phenomena VII conference in Dubrovnik, the E-Intentionality Research Seminar at the University of Sussex, and the Language Evolution and Computation Research Seminar at the University of Edinburgh. Also, many thanks to the following individuals for specific critical responses: Henry Brighton, Seth Bullock, Stephen Cowley, Ezequiel di Paolo, Inman Harvey, Simon Kirby, Richard Menary, David Papineau, Don Ross and John Sutton.

References

Atkinson, A.P. and Wheeler, M. (2004), 'The grain of domains: the evolutionary-psychological case against domain-general cognition', *Mind And Language*, 19 (2), pp. 147–176.

Brighton, H. (2002), 'Compositional syntax from cultural transmission', *Artificial Life*, 8 (1), pp. 25–54.

Brooks R.A. (1991), 'Intelligence without reason', in *Proceedings of the Twelfth Joint International Conference On Artificial Intelligence* (San Mateo, California: Morgan Kauffman), pp. 569–95.

Chomsky, N.A. (1986), *Knowledge of Language* (New York: Praeger).

Clark, A. (1997), *Being There: Putting Brain, Body, And World Together Again* (Cambridge, MA. and London: MIT Press/Bradford Books).

Clark, A. (1998), 'Magic words: how language augments human computation', in *Language And Thought: Interdisciplinary Themes*, eds. P. Carruthers and J. Boucher (Cambridge: Cambridge University Press), pp. 162–183.

Clark, A. (2001), *Mindware: An Introduction To the Philosophy of Cognitive Science* (Oxford: Oxford University Press).

Clark, A. (2003), *Natural-Born Cyborgs: Minds, Technologies, and the Future of Human Intelligence* (Oxford: Oxford University Press).

Clark, A. and Chalmers, D. (1998), 'The extended mind', *Analysis*, 58 (1), pp. 7–19.

Dennett, D.C. (1991), *Consciousness Explained* (Boston: Little, Brown & Co.).

Dreyfus, H.L. (1991), *Being-In-The-World: A Commentary On Heidegger's Being and Time, Division 1* (Cambridge, MA. and London: MIT Press).

Fodor, J.A. (1975), *The Language of Thought* (New York: Thomas Cromwell).

Fodor, J.A. (1987), 'Why there still has to be a language of thought', in Fodor, J.A., *Psychosemantics: The Problem of Meaning in the Philosophy of Mind* (Cambridge, MA.: MIT Press), pp. 135–67.

Fodor, J.A. and Pylyshyn, Z. (1988), 'Connectionism and cognitive architecture: a critical analysis', *Cognition*, 28, pp. 3–71.

Franceschini, N., Pichon, J.-M. and Blanes, C. (1992), 'From insect vision to robot vision', *Philosophical Transactions Of The Royal Society, Series B*, 337, pp. 283–94.

Guignon C.B. (1983), *Heidegger and the Problem of Knowledge* (Indiana: Hackett).

Harvey, I., Husbands, P., and Cliff, D. (1994), 'Seeing the light: artificial evolution, real vision', in *From Animals To Animats 3: Proceedings of the Third International Conference on Simulation of Adaptive Behavior*, eds. D. Cliff, P. Husbands, J.-A., Meyer and S.W. Wilson, (Cambridge, MA.: MIT Press/ Bradford Books), pp. 392–401.

Haugeland, J. (1995/1998), 'Mind embodied and embedded', in Haugeland, J., *Having Thought: Essays in the Metaphysics of Mind* (Cambridge, MA., and London: Harvard University Press), pp. 207–37.

Heidegger, M. (1926), *Being and Time*, Translation: J. Macquarrie and E. Robinson (Oxford: Basil Blackwell).

Hurley, S. (1998), 'Vehicles, contents, conceptual structure, and externalism', *Analysis*, 58 (1), pp. 1–6.

Husbands, P. and Meyer, J.-A. eds. (1998), *Evolutionary Robotics: Proceedings of the First European Workshop, EvoRobot98. Vol. 1468 Of Lecture Notes In Computer Science* (Berlin: Springer-Verlag).

Kirby, S. (2002), 'Learning, bottlenecks and the evolution of recursive syntax', in *Linguistic Evolution Through Language Acquisition: Formal and Computational Models,* ed. E. Briscoe (Cambridge: Cambridge University Press), pp. 173–204.

Kirby, S. and Christiensen, M. H. (2003), 'From language learning to language evolution', in *Language Evolution*, eds. M.H. Christiansen and S. Kirby, (Oxford: Oxford University Press), pp. 272–294.

Nolfi, S. and Floreano, D. (2000), *Evolutionary Robotics: The Biology, Intelligence, and Technology of Self-Organizing Machines* (Cambridge, MA: MIT Press).

Rowlands, M. (1999), *The Body in Mind: Understanding Cognitive Processes* (Cambridge: Cambridge University Press).

Rumelhart, D.E., Smolensky, P., McClelland, J.L. and Hinton, G. (1986), 'Schemata and sequential thought processes in PDP models', in *Parallel Distributed Processing: Explorations in the Microstructure of Cognition, Vol. 2: Psychological and Biological Models*, eds. J.L. McClelland and D. Rumelhart (Cambridge, MA: MIT Press), pp. 7–57.

Smith, K., Kirby, S. and Brighton, H. (2003), 'Iterated learning: a framework for the emergence of language', *Artificial Life*, 9 (4), pp. 371–386.

Wheeler, M. (2001), 'Two threats to representation', *Synthese*, 129, pp. 211–231.

Wheeler, M. (2005a), 'Friends reunited? Evolutionary robotics and representational explanation', *Artificial Life*, 11 (1), pp. 215–232.

Wheeler, M. (2005b), *Reconstructing the Cognitive World: The Next Step*, (Cambridge, MA: MIT Press).

Wheeler, M. (forthcoming), 'How to do things with (and without) representations', forthcoming in *The Extended Mind*, ed. R. Menary (Aldershot: Ashgate)

Wheeler, M. and Clark, A. (1999), 'Genic representation: reconciling content and causal complexity', *British Journal for the Philosophy of Science*, 50 (1), pp. 103–135.

Wheeler, M. and Atkinson, A.P. (2001), 'Domains, brains and evolution', in *Naturalism, Evolution and Mind*, ed. D.M. Walsh (Cambridge: Cambridge University Press), pp. 239–66.

Wittgenstein, L. (1922), *Tractatus Logico-Philosophicus*, Translation: C.K. Ogden (London: Routledge).

CONTINUITY IN QUESTION

An afterword to *Is Language the Ultimate Artefact?*

Is Language the Ultimate Artefact? (henceforth ILUA) was originally published alongside a paper by Andy Clark called *Is Language Special? Some remarks on control, coding, and co-ordination* (Clark, 2004). One concern (among others) of the latter paper was to resist the argument of the former. In this short afterword, I shall attempt a counter-response to Clark's resistance. In so doing I hope to reveal, in a new and perhaps clearer way, what the most important issues really are in this (still unresolved) debate.

Let's begin by recalling the pivotal disagreement at the heart of the matter, as identified in the original exchange. Clark's position-defining claim is that language is 'an external resource that complements but does not profoundly alter the brain's own basic modes of representation and computation' (Clark, 1997, p. 198). The issue concerns the representational rather than the computational half of this continuity. The disputed point, reiterated by Clark in his response to me, is that '[the] brain represents [linguistic] structures, of course. But it does so in the same way it represents anything else. They do not re-organize neural routines in any way that is deeper or more profound than might occur, say, when we first learn to swim, or to play volleyball.' (Clark, 2004, p. 720) Now I agree that this claim holds in the case of on-line language use, that is, in the case of language-involving behaviour in which the relevant material symbols (such as printed text or ambient linguistic sounds) are present in the currently accessible environment and may thus form proper parts of a real-time distributed cognitive process.[19] However, I argue that it fails in the case of off-line language use such as linguistic inner rehearsal, in which the relevant material symbols are, by hypothesis, not present in the currently accessible environment. Here (again) is why.

Given a distributed approach to cognition (which is ground shared by Clark and me), how one understands the transition between on-line and off-line language use must be shaped by the general (i.e., non-language-specific) point that, in paradigmatic cases of distributed cognition, adaptive success ensues because, during the actual run-time of the behaviour, certain internal elements become directly causally locked onto the contributing external elements. When our reasoning is off-line, there are, by hypothesis, no such environmental factors onto which the mechanisms concerned could be locked. Nevertheless, the claim that fundamentally the same kind of computational processes are in play might survive, just so long as there exist certain inner surrogates for those missing environmental factors, surrogates which recapitulate certain structural properties of those factors, viz. the ones, whatever they may be, to

[19] The term 'material symbols' is due to Clark.

which the mechanisms concerned are designed so as to be mechanically keyed. So, in the linguistic case, what we need are inner surrogates that realize the critical structural properties of the very linguistic material symbols that support the corresponding on-line language-involving behaviour. Since the critical structural properties will be linguistic ones, the inner surrogates must themselves be linguistically structured (or so I suggested in ILUA). So Clark's claim that linguistic structures 'do not re-organize neural routines in any way that is deeper or more profound than might occur, say, when we first learn to swim, or to play volleyball' is violated. A sub-set of language-related cognition requires a transformation in the brain's own basic mode of representation, from one that is essentially non-linguistic in form to one that is essentially linguistic. Here's how Clark describes this alleged predicament ('my' and 'I' in the following quotation refer to Clark):

> [On the one hand, my position] means rejecting the idea that language processing requires some very special kind of internal processing and representation. On the other hand, I want to unpack offline cogitation, quite generally, in terms of internal recapitulations of the relevant-but-missing environmental structures. Since the environmental structures, in the linguistic case, are quite patently (perhaps tautologously) structured in a linguaform way, did not I just lose the farm, at least as far as the internal representations are concerned? Perhaps, Wheeler concedes, the *processing* can be unaffected ... But the *internal representations* really have been radically re-structured by the need for the offline use of linguistic resources. (Clark, 2004, p. 721)

Clark attempts to escape from this potential quandary by suggesting that my argument actually falls short of its intended mark.

> All [Wheeler's] argument shows is that the inner surrogates must amount to a representation, useable off-line, of the relevant environmental structures. But a representation of structure is not thereby ... a structured representation. Just as I can represent greenness without deploying a green inner vehicle, so too I can represent a sentence as involving three component ideas (John, loving, and Mary, to stick with the tired old example) without thereby deploying an inner vehicle that itself comprises three distinct symbols exhibiting that articulation. (Clark 2004, p. 722)

Now, Clark is surely right to point out that a representation of some X-with-a-certain-structure is not *thereby* an X-structured representation. So he is indeed correct that one can represent a structured sentence without *thereby* deploying an inner vehicle that itself comprises *all the very same elements and structure as that public sentence*. My original argument moved too quickly for its own good. But establishing that some inner surrogate need not recapitulate *all* the very same elements and structure as are realized by its representational target does not establish that that surrogate need not recapitulate *certain* structural properties of that target. And although it may well be obvious that representing greenness does not necessitate the presence of a green inner vehicle, it is rather less obvious that representing a *missing* structured syntactic object, in a way that secures competence in the relevant cognitive domain, does not necessitate some degree of significant structural recapitulation on the part of the inner element, and that's all my argument needs. So the unresolved question is *how much* structure is needed, and what the *character* of that structure is, in particular cases.

What Clark owes us, I believe, is a developed account of how linguistic inner rehearsal may take place *without* the kind of significant recapitulation of linguistic structure that, I suggest, is lurking in the explanatory wings. Fortunately, a sketch of how such an account might go is on offer. Clark calls it the *cognitive self-stimulation model* of off-line language use (Clark, unpublished). So let's see how it fares. As I understand it, the core of Clark's view is that, in off-line language-use, human beings do their thinking using inner *images* of words. The notion of an 'image' should be understood in a wide sense here, so as to include structures with an auditory or multi-modal character, as well as those of a purely visual kind. Thus, according to Clark, in on-line language use we access certain environmental inputs (e.g. the word on the page, the sentence in the air) that stimulate the brain, via sensation, so as to perturb it into different regions of its state space. This account of on-line language use is designed to cohere with the general distributed cognition approach to on-line intelligence. Subsequently, in off-line language use, we 'simply' self-create surrogates for the now-missing inputs, sometimes in the form of potentially observable structures such as audible vocalizations, but often in the form of inner images of the sort just mentioned. Given that these self-created surrogates are designed to preserve only the relevant sensory properties (the shapes that one sees, the sounds that one hears), they do not realize linguistic structure. Moreover, it is unmysterious how they might invoke essentially the same inner processes as are invoked by the environmental inputs in the on-line case. Thus continuity of representational structure and of computational process is preserved.

So why should there be cause to worry about this undeniably attractive story? The first thing to note is that Clark's flagship example of off-line mathematical reasoning (which, as I argue in ILUA, is analogous to the linguistic case) tends to skew one's receptivity to the self-stimulation model. Clark focuses on the example of using imagined Venn diagrams in our heads, and notes that 'there is no reason to suppose that ... [this requires] ... the installation of a different kind of computational device', different, that is, to the one active during cases of on-line reasoning involving Venn diagrams on the page (Clark, 1997, p. 199). A cognitive self-stimulation account would seem to have some cogency here. One simply self-creates images of the missing diagrams and deploys the same processing strategies. However, because of the fundamentally spatial, and therefore essentially visual, nature of the reasoning, the Venn diagram example rewards the idea of self-created pseudo-sensory inputs, but is potentially misleading as to the general prospects for the cognitive self-stimulation model, and thus for the kind of continuity that Clark advocates. To see this, consider another, and arguably more central, example of off-line mathematical reasoning, namely performing in one's head the kind of calculation that, in the on-line case, might standardly be tackled using pen and paper and the machinery of long multiplication, but which under pressure we can perform off-line. Do we really imagine the carryings of numbers that figure as on-the-page manipulations in the on-line case? That's the sort of thing that would seem to be required for cognitive self-stimulation to get any purchase. Phenomenological intuitions may vary, of course, but I'm willing to bet that, for most people, imagined carryings are just not part of our experience here. If this is right, then there is some evidence already to suggest that the door is far from closed on the sort of transformation in representational structure that I have argued is present in the transition from on-line cases of language-involving cognition to their off-line cousins.

So let's now open that door as wide as we can, by reflecting on Clark's own chosen example of an extant cognitive-scientific approach that demonstrates his key point, viz. that a representation of some X-with-a-certain-structure is not thereby an X-structured representation. That example is Elman's dynamical connectionist modelling of language (Elman, 1995). The relevant studies here feature what has come to be known as an Elman net, a simple recurrent connectionist network in which the widely used three-layer architecture of input, hidden, and output units is extended to include a group of context units. These units store the activation-values of the hidden units at any one time-step, and then feed that information back to the hidden units at the following time-step. The present state of such a network is thus a function of both the present input and the network's previous state, which, as Elman shows, allows this sort of system to encode sequential information, and thus to succeed at certain prediction-tasks. For example, given a corpus of simple sentences, constructed from a small set of nouns and verbs, and presented so that the only information explicitly available to the network was distributional information concerning statistical regularities of occurrences in the input strings, Elman was able to train a simple recurrent network to predict the cohort of potential word successors under various conditions of use. (A cohort is made up of all the words consistent with a given span of input.)

Subsequent statistical analysis of the network demonstrated that it had achieved its predictive capabilities by inducing several categories of words which were implicit in the distributional regularities in the input data. These induced categories had an implicitly hierarchical structure. Nouns were split into animates and inanimates, sub-categories which themselves were subdivided (into, for example, classes such as humans, nonhumans, breakables, and edibles). Verbs were grouped in the following categories: (a) requiring a direct object, (b) optionally taking a direct object, and (c) being intransitive. Conceptually similar words drive the network into regions of activation space that are close together, so conceptual similarity is captured via position in activation space. The most general linguistic categories, such as 'noun' and 'verb', correspond to large areas of this space, whilst more specific categories and (ultimately) individual words correspond to progressively smaller sub-regions of larger areas. Thus the space implicitly realizes the hierarchical structure described above.

According to Clark, this Elman net is a language-navigating system that represents linguistic structure while failing to realize linguistically structured representations. However, as far as I can see, this judgment can't be right. In my view the statistically visible states realized by this network *do* qualify as inner elements with linguistic structure. Of course, given the nature of the emergent groupings in question (see above), the states at issue do not perhaps obey the traditional syntax-semantics distinction, but that, in and of itself, doesn't stop those states from being linguistic in character. Its activation space is structured in terms of nouns, verbs, transitivity, intransitivity, and so on. How much more linguistic does it get?

At this point someone might be tempted to point out that, as with any connectionist network of this kind, there's a representational-computational level of description at which we don't see linguistically structured states, but rather weight matrices and patterns of activation values. However, that observation alone can't carry the day. As should be clear from my description of Elman's study, the statistically visible states here do genuine explanatory work. Under these circumstances I think we should unhesitatingly proceed to reify those states. And if that's correct, then what we have here is a system that realizes linguistic structure, and *not* a language-navigating system that represents linguistic structure while failing to realize linguistically structured representations.

One further objection that Clark might be tempted to make here is suggested by something else that he says in *Is Language Special?*. He notes there that my position depends on the assumption that it is theoretically possible to separate the structure of the representation from the nature of the associated processing, in such a way that it would be possible to speak of a fundamental transformation in the mode of representation but not in the associated mode of computation. I agree that the argument of ILUA depends on this assumption. Indeed, I'm up front about it (see ILUA footnote 18). But, according to Clark, this assumption is ultimately misguided, since 'for a representation to genuinely be structured in a certain way, just IS for the system to be able to operate upon it in certain ways' (Clark, 2004, p. 722, footnote 3). But now if representation and computation are intimately co-defined, one might refuse to reify the higher-order states of the Elman net on the grounds that since all the computational processing plausibly goes on at the level of the connection weights and unit activations, the higher-order states in question cannot be the objects of computational processes, and so cannot be representational in character, and so cannot figure in the fundamental representational-computational story. Of course, I'm inclined to reject the claim of intimate co-definition, but rather than argue for that here, I'd like to draw out a consequence of using that claim to resist the reification move. If the proposed alternative condition for reification (being the object of a computational process) were to be applied generally, and if we assume for the moment that connectionism provides a good model of the fundamental character of mind (as Clark does), then the only level at which one could speak of representations at all is at the level of weights and activation values. The present proposal would thereby mandate the elimination from our cognitive ontology of all sorts of higher-order psychological structures that are not reflected directly in the lower-level processing story. Writing blank cheques to eliminativism is not something that I think Clark would want to encourage. So this objection fails too.

To repeat by way of conclusion: The test-case Elman net is *not* a language-navigating system that represents linguistic structure while failing to realize linguistically structured representations. Rather, it is a system that navigates language by itself realizing linguistic structure. Thus it does not provide the kind of evidence that Clark needs in order to resist the argument of ILUA. In my view that argument is still well worth the pages on which it's written.

References

Clark, A. (1997), *Being There: Putting Brain, Body, and World Together Again* (Cambridge, MA, and London: MIT Press/Bradford Books).

Clark, A. (2004), 'Is language special? Some remarks on control, coding, and co-ordination', *Language Sciences*, 26:6, special issue on Distributed Cognition and Integrational Linguistics, ed. D. Spurrett, pp. 717–726.

Clark, A. (unpublished), 'The ins and outs of language'. Paper given at the University of Dundee, February 2006, in dialogue with Michael Wheeler.

Elman, J.L. (1995), 'Language as a dynamical system', in *Mind as Motion: Explorations in the Dynamics of Cognition*, eds. R. Port and T. van Gelder (Cambridge MA.: MIT Press/Bradford Books), pp. 195–225.

Section Three

PRACTICE

Rob Ellis

Grounding Visual Object Representation In Action

1. Representational Theories of Mind

A representational theory of mind forms a part of most models in cognitive science. Despite the ubiquitous presence of a concept of representation it remains a notoriously difficult one to tie-down. Palmer (1978) described the confused and confusing use of terms, most of which were applied inconsistently within the literature. His careful analysis of the variety of ways in which one system (the representing world) can stand for another (the represented world) focused upon the systematic relations which must exist between the two. To understand any particular use of the notion of representation the form of correspondence between the two systems must be established. In the so-called symbolic tradition in cognitive science the correspondence is established by convention: behaviour is the outcome of operations on a system of symbols which have a semantic interpretation in the sense of standing for objects or describing states of the world (Newell, 1980). Influential formulations of this view argue that the expressions that make up the symbol system have a compositional structure. Well-formed, molecular expressions are generated by the application of *rules* of combination to atomic *symbol* tokens. Operations applied to expressions are sensitive to their structure (Fodor, 1975; Fodor and Pylyshyn, 1988). This argument is perhaps most convincing in the case of language. Grammatical (well-formed) expressions are built from lexical components according to the rules of syntax, which determine how words may be combined together. In this sense expressions in natural language are compositional: they are complex structures containing atomic constituents. Compositional systems of this sort are generative in that an infinite set of expressions can be derived by repeated application of the rules of composition to the atomic parts. Language is said to be generative. So too are other mental faculties such as thought. For these reasons Fodor (1975) argued that mental representations in general were language-like. In short there was a 'language of thought'.

Ideas such as these are usually discussed in relationship to high level cognitive processes, but, also, lower level perceptual processes have been explained in similar ways. Marr's (1982) theory of vision, for example, asserts that seeing involves the derivation of useful *descriptions* of the world from images of it. The descriptions are formed by using representations, or formal systems, different types of which make different types of information explicit. It is not clear to what degree such visual descriptions are assumed to share the compositionality of the 'language of thought', but clearly they are intended to be symbolic structures which stand for aspects of the visual world.

However, *any* such representational theory of mind is faced by a problem which tends to be ignored by many psychologists, but worries most philosophers. That is how could a mind state or structure *represent* an object external to it (Fodor, 1980)? Whilst some current theories have, as Palmer (1978) demanded, specified what sort of correspondence there is between the representational state and what it represents, a further, deeper problem remains unresolved. Establishing the correspondence between a representational system and the world it represents, makes it possible for *an external agent* to interpret the representational state. However what is needed in the case of a mental state is some account of how it can stand for things in the world *for the agent whose mental state it is*. This has been called the 'symbol grounding problem'.

To solve this problem, what is needed are 'grounding relations' between the mental states and their referents. These relations are distinct from those that make the states symbolic (of the sort discussed above). If there is no way of connecting the symbols to the world, the system is trapped in a hermeneutic hall of mirrors (Searle, 1980; Harnad, 1990). That this is a fundamental issue is the major premise of this paper. We take for granted that it is not good enough to assume that brains simply *do* represent. The capacity to represent is one of the most basic assumptions in cognitive science and must itself be explained.

The problem is, of course, in specifying what sort of thing the grounding relations between mental symbols and their referents could possibly be. Here, Lockean solutions continue to receive critical attention (Fodor, 1980 and 1983; Harnad, 1990). In broad terms these assume that aspects of the world cause mental events which thereby serve as grounded representations in a compositional symbol system. The rules of combination allow the generation of complex expressions that inherit the grounding of the simple expressions or entities. In the case of visual object representation visual properties are tightly coupled or highly correlated with mental states because of the causal effects the visual properties have on the visual areas of the brain. The close coupling of visual properties and brain states makes it legitimate to say that the brain states stand for or represent those properties. Marr's (1982) theory of vision implicitly adopts this Lockean solution. The relative distance and orientation of surfaces in the world, for instance, have consistent effects in the visual areas of the viewer's brain. Those effects can be said to constitute a functional surface map of a visual scene: a 2-1/2D Sketch.

There is of course a notorious difficulty in making sense of how these brain states have the contents they have for the agent whose brain it is. It is almost certainly wrong to attribute a crude picture-in-the-head view to Locke. That is, he was aware of the fundamental flaw in the view that the end result of perceptual processes was a picture-like depiction in the head of, and seen by, the viewer. Mackie (1976) suggests the most coherent interpretation of Locke's notion is to treat representations as intentional objects: they are how things look to the viewer.[1] However, this view does not appear to correspond to many of the representational entities found in theories of vision. Continuing with the example of the 2-1/2D Sketch, this does not seem to be a description of how the things look to the viewer. It is not intended to be part of the conscious experience of the world. So, how can representations of *this* sort have content for the viewer?

The clarification of these matters depends on, we argue, on an elaboration of a causal theory of grounding which we develop in the next section. In broad terms we argue that visual representations can have content as a result of *the actions which they make available*. Their representational state is therefore independent of their being intentional or conscious states. They merely need to move the body in appropriate ways!

[1] *How* brain states give rise to intentional objects is the problem of consciousness, and beyond our scope!

2. Computation, Brain States, Visual Object Representation and Action

A powerful influence that has tended to blind most of us to the need for 'grounding relations' is our intuitions about computation. In general there is an implicit assumption that, as a complex information-processing machine, states of the brain can encode symbolic descriptions in the same way as other complex information processing machines, such as digital computers. In the case of vision, functional relations among brain states are supposed to encode descriptions of the visual world rather like the states of a digital computer can be said to encode and transform visual objects, when furnished with graphics software. The computational metaphor shows how a sufficiently rich functional repertoire can represent visual information in an entirely symbolic form. This is a view that, of course, sits very comfortably with the symbolic tradition sketched in the previous section. It is our contention that there is something seriously misleading about this metaphor. In fact, we argue, the internal states of a computer, running graphics software, can be construed as describing, say, a three dimensional object only because of the consequences of those states for some external device and an agent.

As we have agreed in the previous section functional states can be assigned an interpretation by convention. It is important to note that the states in and of themselves have no fixed interpretation. Putnam (1988) proves a theorem to the effect that any physical system can have every functional organisation. Informally,[2] since a physical system can be the subject of a large (if not unbounded) set of descriptions and since the functional organisation will vary as the descriptions vary, then any physical system can represent a large (if not unbounded) set of states of the represented world. By virtue of what, then, do we ascribe content to the functional states of a computer running graphics software? It is surely because the programmer has arranged for those states to control some external device in a (very) particular way. In fact it is only when the states of a digital computer are hooked-up to an external device that they can be reasonably said

---

[2] Putnam's theorem turns on the possibility of decomposing any physical system into a set of states that can be mapped onto machine states. Given that this mapping is arbitrary one can express any notional, finite automaton by having the sequence of physical states map to appropriate machine states. Interestingly Putnam's conclusion in the case of cognitive systems is that the ascription of content to internal, functional states reduces to a claim about the behavioural dispositions associated with those states.

to describe the *visual* properties of objects. Perhaps the states will map to a set of instructions for controlling the behaviour of a video display unit, which will, provided the hook-up is just right, yield images of visual objects. In these circumstances a user of the system may ascribe content to the code controlling the display devise, but notice the ascription depends on the user adopting the conventions of pictorial visual representation. The point is that the representational capacity of the graphics code does not reside in the *code*. Rather it is the code *together with the system in which it is embedded* that is ascribed meaning.

Ascribing meaning to the states of the system does not ground them of course. To continue with the example of a computer running graphics software, what more would be needed to say that its states were grounded visual representations? Fairly obviously in the case of on-line vision they would need to be causally related to visual properties of the world so that they were affected by events and objects in that world. More significantly however the states must be used by the system under their interpretation as visual representations in order to make sense of the claim that they have content *for the system*, and not merely an external observer. The key issue is: what use would count? Our conjecture is that a role in *guiding actions* would ground the internal states. For instance if the system were part of a robotic device which used visual information to avoid obstacles, the states representing *that* visual information has content for the system. States are grounded by virtue of their hook-up to the action systems.

The situation is similar in the biological case. Brain states hooked-up to some appropriate output device in just the right way may legitimise talk of internal visual representation. Consider again Marr's (1982) 2-1/2D Sketch which provides the viewer with information about the distance and orientation of visual surfaces in the world. Entertain the science fantasy that it was possible to rewire the visual areas, within which the 2-1/2D Sketch was implemented, so that a brain state that previously occurred in the presence of a close surface, of a given orientation, now did so when confronted with a distant one. What would one say about the representational state of the brain when the viewer was confronted by a distant surface? Since it is identical to a previous state that represented a far surface, perhaps one should say it continues to represent a far surface, but this is now a misrepresentation (Dretske, 1986). What would the effect be of acting upon that misrepresentation? If the viewer reached towards the surface, he or she might discover s/he could not make contact, thereby contradicting their representation of its distance based on visual information. What would be the consequence of this for the representational status of the brain-state coding surface distance on the basis of visual input?

We probably know the answer to this question because our fantasy is simply a version of the various distorting goggle experiments. When subjects wear, for extended periods, goggles that distort the visual world, adaptations occur. Kohler (1962), for example, describes the effects of wearing goggles fitted with prisms. Light rays entering the prism are bent, and the extent of this deviation, for a given prism, depends on the direction of the light relative to the front face of the prism. Light arriving at oblique angles is bent more than light arriving at right angles. The consequences for the viewer of these distortions is that straight lines look curved, right angles no longer look to be orthogonal, and perceived distances are altered. Kohler's subjects, on first wearing the goggles, described the visual world as rubber-like on account of the non-rigid transformations that resulted from their movement. If they moved their head horizontally objects changed in perceived width, evoking a concertina effect, and vertical head movements produced changes in the apparent slant of surfaces such that objects appeared to rock back and forth. After several weeks of wearing the goggles, adaptation occurs such that a normal visual world is seen. This adaptation is the more impressive when the variability of the distortions produced by the goggles is realised: given that the eyes could move relative to the prisms located a short distance in front of them, the prism effects change with eye movements. Removing the goggles after adaptation evokes the distortions once more, now reversed, and a further period is required for stability to return to the viewer's visual world.

The various distorting prism effects are well known, but almost entirely neglected by current theories of visual perception. Yet they seem to demonstrate something very important. What to us seems important about the adaptations to optical distortions is that they change the hook-up between the brain states that respond to aspects of the visual world, such as surfaces, and the systems that use this information, including the motor system.[3] It is the appropriate hook-up that makes a particular brain state representative of a visual

[3] O'Regan and Noë (2001) develop similar ideas arguing that visual awareness is a result of an observer's mastery of sensori-motor contingencies.

property. Moreover it appears that representational states grounded in action, in this manner, influence what the world looks like to the viewer. Action based representation affects representations *conceived of as intentional objects*.

3. Action potentiation and Embodied Cognition

If the mental representation of a visual object or property represents by virtue of its causal role in producing behavioural outputs, then a currently represented object should have observable effects on behaviour or the behavioural control systems. These effects are transparent in the case of tropisms. In other cases things are less clear. What might be expected given my attending to an object within my visual field? Which of the large number of relevant actions does the resultant visual representation cause? Surely none, since what I do depends on my current intentions and goals. To escape these difficulties we propose that visual representations have a causal role in the generation of behaviour in the sense of potentiating or facilitating relevant actions.

The action potentiation account of visual representation is obviously related to the idea of embodied cognition (Varela, Thompson, and Rosch, 1991; Newton, 1996; Clark, 1997). This emphasises the mutual influences of brain, body and the world and their joint action in the control of behaviour; and de-emphasises the distinction between the world and its mental representation. Indeed on some accounts the notion of mental representation is eliminated (including Varela et al., 1991; and Thelen and Smith, 1994). Others in the same tradition have proposed the idea of action-orientated representation in which internal states of the organism both code aspects of the world and enter into the control of relevant behaviours (Clark, 1995; 1997; see also Millikan, 1995). Our view of visual object representation is clearly entirely consistent with these latter ideas and this paper is an attempt to provide some empirical foundations for them.

3.1. Object affordance and Stimulus-Response Compatibility

If, as we claim, motor activity is partly constitutive of the representation of a visual object, it follows that merely representing an object should potentiate the actions associated with. This should happen irrespective of my intentions toward that object. Seeing a football should make it easier (other things being equal) for me to direct a kick, even when the kick is aimed at another object (but see section 4).

So: do seen objects produce action effects unrelated to the current activities or goals of the viewer? That they do may be one way of understanding very well established stimulus to response compatibility (SRC) effects. Broadly congruent mappings of response to stimuli, in a choice reaction time experiment, produce faster and more accurate responses than incongruent mappings (see Alluisi and Warm, 1990 and Kornblum, 1992 for reviews). For example when coloured stimuli are presented to the left or right visual field, and the colour cues the hand of response, responses are faster if the stimulus position corresponds to the hand of response (Simon, 1969). The traditional information processing account of these SRC effects is in terms of the similarity between the *mental representation* of sets of stimuli and sets of response options (Kornblum, 1992; Kornblum, Hasbroucq and Osman, 1990; Kornblum and Lee, 1995).

In contrast to the information processing account, Michaels (1988 and 1993) among others, has described an ecological account of SRC effects. Here the benefits of compatible mappings depend not on arbitrary pairings between mental codes for a stimulus and responses, but on the ecological relations between visual objects and action. Object affordance accounts for the compatibility advantage. A different, but related, idea is Hommel's (1997) notion of the action concept, which forms the basis of intentional action (see also Greenwald, 1970; Prinz, 1990). The action concept is an elaboration of the ideomotor notion of action effects. It is a representation of the sensory effects of a voluntary action, and becomes associated with the motor pattern producing the effects and so forms the basis of voluntary actions. An agent can produce an intended effect by choosing an appropriate action concept, which in turn selects the appropriate motor responses. Compatibility effects occur because stimulus codes may overlap with effect codes, leading to response competition in some cases.

3.2. Object-Action Compatibility

Most SRC experiments are entirely non-ecological, involving simple responses to highly abstract stimuli. To assess the idea that it is a relationship between objects and actions on them that underpins SRC effects, new questions must be posed, and appropriate experimental techniques devised. The studies that follow were an attempt to do this. They seek to establish that spatial location is not the only aspect of a visual object that may produce a Simon effect. In all the experiments participants viewed a real object or an image of a real object, and, simultaneously or shortly afterwards, made one of two responses determined by various criteria. The responses were designed to be components of a 'reach to' grasp. Three such components were investigated.

Hand of response. Tucker and Ellis (1998) describe participants viewing photographs of common, graspable objects. Each object was depicted in two vertical orientations: upright and inverted, and in two horizontal orientations. One of the horizontal orientations was designed to be optimal for a right-handed reach and grasp, the other with a left-handed action. For example a centrally placed teapot with a handle to the right of the viewer would be most compatible with a

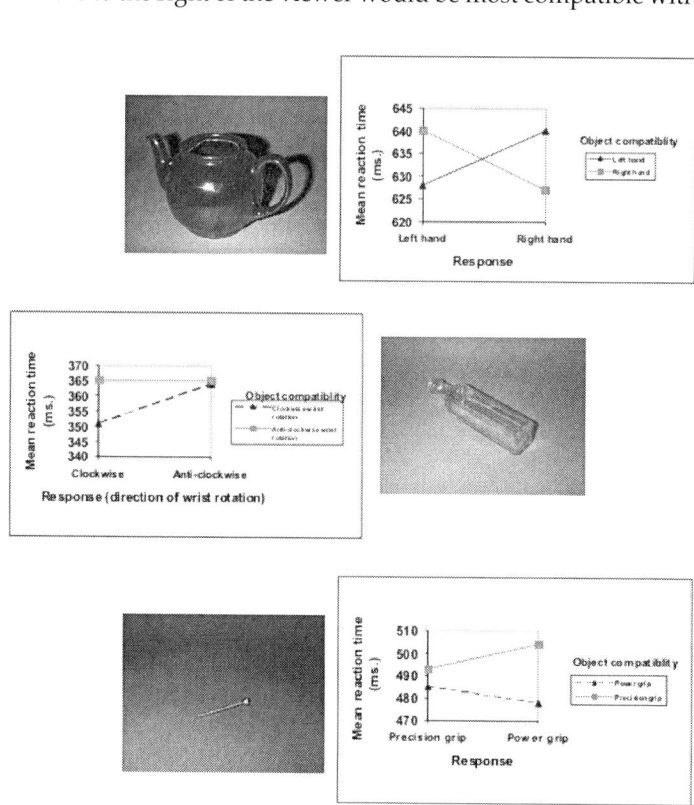

Figure 1. The Object-Action Compatibility effects, in response latency, when classifying objects which are orientated so as to have an optimal hand of grasp (as in the teapot example) or require a particular rotation of the wrist (as in the bottle example); or require a particular grip (as in the screw example).

right-handed reach and grasp. Participants had to decide whether the object was upright or inverted and signal their decision by a speeded right or left-handed key press. Performance was better when the hand of response was the same as the hand which would be optimal for reaching and grasping the object in its depicted orientation, compared to the incompatible case. The interaction of the object compatibility with the hand of response is is shown in figure 1.

Could this object-action compatibility effect be due to overlap between abstract stimulus and response codes? A second experiment suggests not. This was similar to the first, except participants now indicated the vertical orientation of the depicted objects by key-presses with the index and middle finger of their right hand. There was no object-action compatibility effect in these circumstances. Tucker and Ellis (1998) concluded that the effect observed in the first experiment was a real *object* to *action* compatibility effect of the sort predicted by the action potentiation account of visual representation. It was easier to respond to a teapot with its handle pointing to the observer's right-side because such an object's representation includes the associated action of reaching toward it with a specific hand. A second series of experiments tend to confirm this view in that they show an analogous effect of relations between object properties (their orientation with respect to the viewer) and an aspect of a response (the direction of wrist rotation) which appear not to share a common dimension. Their only plausible relationship is one based on action.

Direction of wrist rotation. Grasping an object requires a wrist rotation to align the hand with the opposition axis of the object to be grasped (Jeannerod, 1981; Jeanerod *et al.*, 1992). It has been shown that this element of an action is potentiated by the sight of a graspable object (Ellis and Tucker, 2000). Participants viewed two sorts of (real) object. One type consisted of tall cylindrical objects, such as bottles, which required a clockwise rotation to grasp, assuming the hand started from an orientation of having the thumb at 11 o'clock. The other sort of objects were small, a bottle top for instance, or had an elongated, horizontal, major axis at right angles to the line of sight, the bottle laid on its side for instance. For these objects, with the thumb at 11 o'clock, an anticlockwise wrist rotation would be needed to grasp the object.

Participants aligned their hand with their thumb at 11 o'clock (as measured by a mercury switch attached to the wrist). The object was then exposed and a short time later a high or low tone was sounded, whilst the object remained in view. Participants were told to remember the object for the purposes of a subsequent (dummy) recognition task, but their response was to the tone, which they classified as high or low with a clockwise or anti-clockwise wrist rotation. Despite this response being to an entirely different, auditory, stimulus it was affected by the seen object. As may be seen in figure 1 there was again an object by response interaction reflecting an advantage for responding to an object with a compatible action.

Hand shape. A third component of reaching and grasping for which we have observed object-action compatibility effects is the grip needed to handle an object (Tucker and Ellis, 2001). Participants decided whether a briefly presented real object was organic or manufactured. They responded with either a power grip, as in squeezing a lemon, or a precision grip, as in picking up a pin. The seen objects were ones which would be handled with either a precision or power grip: pins, lemons, grapes, hammers and such like. The significant interaction of object compatibility and response type is again illustrated in figure 1.

These data are consistent with the idea that seeing an object potentiates actions associated with it. We refer to such effects as micro-affordance. Related effects have been reported in participants making actual reach and grasp responses. Craighero, Fadiga, Rizzolatti and Umilta (1996 and 1998) demonstrated facilitation of reaching to and grasping an orientated bar, when a cue to respond was a picture of a bar having a similar orientation. This they termed visuomotor priming.

3.3. Micro-affordance and remembered objects

If action potentiation is the consequence of visual *representation*, and not simply the transient effect of (dorsal visual stream) visual to motor coordination, it would be expected in the case of imagined or remembered objects as well as seen. This is the case. Derbyshire, Ellis and Tucker (2006) observed the effects of the orientation of remembered objects. Participants viewed a sequence of four images of objects, one of which was orientated to be compatible with a left or right hand grasp. Each image was presented for one second, followed by a blank interval of 100 milliseconds, followed by a word that named an object. Participants responded with a left or right hand key press according to whether such an object had appeared in the sequence of images. The same object-action compatibility effect was observed as obtained in the case of seen objects. Importantly this effect did not depend on the position of the recalled object in the presentation sequence, and was not therefore the result of transient motor activation resulting from the presentation of the last image in the sequence. We conclude that micro-affordance is a product of the representation of an object, whether elicited by external or internal stimulation.

4. Object Based Attention and Object Based Ignoring

If seen objects potentiate associated actions regardless of intent, how is the problem of selection for action solved (Allport, 1987)? How do the actions on a goal object escape the competition from actions potentiated by non-goal objects? An obvious answer is that the actions of ignored objects are actively inhibited. Inhibition of the visual properties of an ignored object is well-established (Tipper, 1985). For instance ignoring a red letter so as to respond to a green letter will lead to a decrement in performance whenever the ignored letter appears as a target in the next trial. Does inhibition of this sort extend to the action properties of ignored objects?

Studies in which participants have to respond to one of two objects with precision or power grips, suggests that the actions associated with an ignored object are, indeed, inhibited (Ellis, Tucker, Symes and Vainio, 2007). The stimuli consisted of images of abstract three-dimensional objects. Each image contained two such objects drawn from a set of four: a small sphere, a small cube, a larger rectangular block and a larger cylinder. The small objects were sized so as to be compatible with a precision grip, the larger were compatible with a power grip. The target object was cued by its colour and participants had to signal whether it was 'curved' (sphere and cylinder) or 'straight' (rectangular block or cube) by making a power or precision grip.

The usual micro-affordance effect was observed for the target object: faster and more accurate responses were made when compatible with the action properties of the target than when incompatible. Performance was also strongly affected by the action properties of the distractor object, but effectively these were the mirror image of the target object effects. Responding to a target with a grip-type that was compatible with the action properties of the distractor object produced a decrement in performance relative to the incompatible cases. These two, different compatibility effects may be seen in figure 2, along with an example of the stimuli.

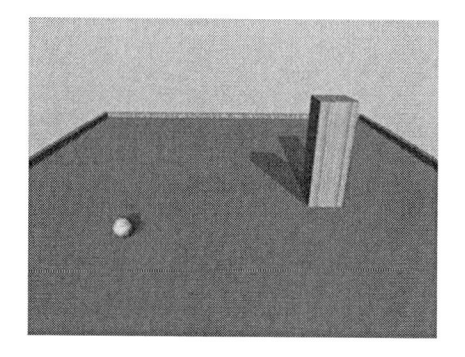

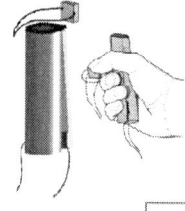

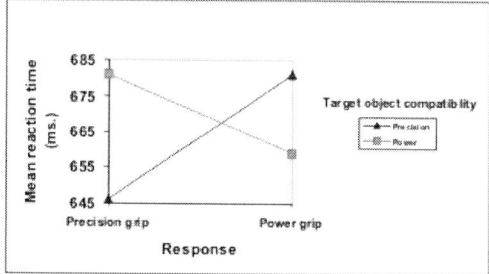

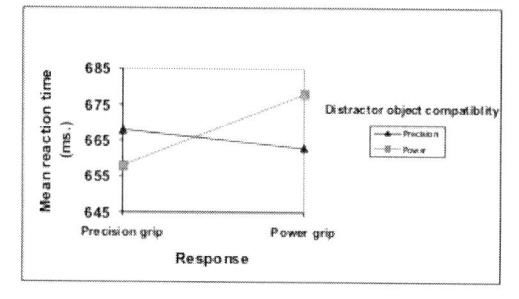

Figure 2. The Object-Action Compatibility effects, in response latency, for the target and distractor objects in two objects displays (as illustrated in the example), on precision and power grip responses (made on the response device also illustrated) classifying the shape of the target object (cued by its blue-grey colour).

This negative compatibility effect was not influenced by spatial configuration- it was observed regardless of whether the distractor was directly in front of the target (and therefore an obstacle) or behind the target (in experiment one) or when there was a wide separation between the target and distractor (experiments two and four). The distractor effect does not therefore appear to have arisen from physical, spatial clutter, but rather from 'representational clutter'.

Inhibition of the actions associated with a non-target was not observed when the location of the target was known in advance of its appearance (experiment 3 in Ellis, Tucker, Symes and Vainio, 2007).The most effective strategy in this situation would have been to allocate spatial attention, by default, to the known fixed location of the target. In these circumstances the distractor objects did affect responses, but this did not vary according to the actions associated with them. It was only their visual and spatial properties (such as size or their distance from the target object) which determined their interference effects, not whether the actions associated with them were compatible with the response being made. These data imply that micro-affordance (and the consequent need to inhibit actions of non-target objects) is an outcome of object-based attention. Only when an object is attended to and represented *as an object* do its associated actions become activated.

5. Effects of Action on Perception

Were representation, object selection and object affordance related in this way, then actions might be expected to have effects on perceptual processes. Not only should objects afford actions, but actions might afford objects. Evidence is accumulating that this is the case.

Wohlschlager's (2000) participants judged the direction of movement of ambiguous, apparent motion displays, whilst rotating their own hand. An anti-clockwise hand rotation induced the perception of an anti-clockwise rotation of the ambiguous display, a clockwise hand rotation induced a clockwise apparent motion of the object. Other studies show that action planning has a direct effect on visual attention, with stimulus compatible actions resulting in improved visual discrimination of that stimulus (Craighero, Fadiaga, Rizzolatti and Umilta, 1999; Pavese and Buxbaum, 2002; and Fagioli, Hommel and Schubotz, in press are examples). Symes, Tucker, Ellis and Vainio (under review) have demonstrated that the preparation of a grip leads to easier detection of objects compatible with that grip. Participants viewed two alternating scenes each containing an array of fruit and vegetables. Half of the items in each scene were small and would be typically grasped with a precision grip (a strawberry say). The others were larger and would be graspable with a power grip (an apple for example). The scenes differed in that just one of the items was replaced by another fruit or vegetable of roughly the same size. When a screen flicker disrupted the (150ms) interval between the two scenes the usual change blindness effect was observed. That is the change was surprisingly difficult to detect given its dramatic nature. When participants signalled detecting the change by pressing a key with their index finger the average response latency was 4809ms. When the finger response was replaced by either a power or precision grip an action to object compatibility effect was observed. When the change object was compatible with the response (a change in a strawberry signalled by a precision grip or a change in an apple signalled by a power grip for instance) reaction times were reduced compared to the incompatible cases (means of 4510ms and 4881ms respectively). It would appear that the preparation of a particular action has the consequence of directing (or at least biasing) visual attention to action compatible objects.

6. Conclusions

Represented visual objects, whether we are seeing them or recalling them in memory, propel us to act on them. If we are to ignore them we need to inhibit the tendencies to action, such is their potency. It also appears that our action intentions direct us to see aspects of the world that are congruent with those intentions. These observations provide evidence for a proposed solution to the symbol-grounding problem which builds on a Lockean account of perception. Causal mechanisms equip the brain with indicator states, that is states that are correlated with significant visual events or features. These indicator states are coupled, during the development of the species and the individual, with motor control systems as a result of behavioural adaptation to an ecological niche. This coupling of visual indicators and motor control forms a basis of visual representation in the brain. Such integration is the basis of Object-Action Compatibility effects and necessitates the inhibition of actions associated with non-selected objects.

Intuitions about vision are often heavily biased by a prevailing 'picture-metaphor' of seeing. To see is to construct descriptions (in the head of the viewer) of the visual properties of the world. As was suggested earlier, this description is most plausibly an intentional object: it is how things look to the viewer. What seems to have been forgotten in this approach is that sensory-motor integration can effect how things look, as adaptation to optical distortions demonstrates. We speculate that having vision and action in precise registrar is the foundation of veridical access to the visual world.

The model we have advanced here may also serve as a defence against the various forms of philosophical scepticism: that is, the observation that the external world is known to us only through our senses and is therefore in doubt. It seems to us that the precise registration of visual properties with micro-affordances required for successful action in the world squeezes out all but the most radical forms of scepticism. Actions confirm that what we see, in a narrow sense, is veridical. As for radical scepticism, we assume natural selection has squeezed that out.

References

Allport, D.A. (1987), 'Selection for action: some behavioral and neurophysiological considerations of attention and action', In H. Heuer and F. Sanders (Eds.) *Perspectives on Perception and Action* (Hillsdale, NJ: Erlbaum).

Alluisi, E.A. and Warm, J.S. (1990), 'Things that go together: a review of stimulus-response compatibility and related effects', In R.W. Proctor and T.G. Reeve (eds.) *Stimulus-Response Compatibility: An Integrated Perspective* (Amsterdam: North-Holland).

Clark, A. (1995), 'Moving minds: re-thinking representation in the heat of situated action', In *Philosophical Perspectives 9: AI Connectionism and Philosophical Psychology*, ed. J. Tomberlin.

Clark, A. (1997), *Being There: Putting Brain, Body, and World Together Again* (Cambridge, MA: MIT Press).

Craighero, L., Fadiga, L., Rizzolatti, G. and Umilta, C. (1996), 'Evidence for a visuomotor priming effect', *NeuroReport*, 8, pp. 347–349.

Craighero, L., Fadiga, L., Rizzolatti, G. and Umilta, C. (1998), 'Visuomotor priming', *Visual Cognition*, 5, pp. 109–126.

Derbyshire, N., Ellis, R. and Tucker, M. (2006), 'The potentiation of two components of the reach-to-grasp action during object categorisation in visual memory', *Acta Psychologica*, 122, pp. 74–98.

Dretske, F. (1986), 'Misrepresentation', In: *Belief: Form, Content and Function*, ed. R.J. Bogdan (Oxford University Press).

Ellis, R. and Tucker, M. (2000), 'Micro-affordance: the potentiation of actions by seen objects', *British Journal of Psychology*, 91(4), pp. 451–471.

Ellis, R., Tucker, M., Syms, E, and Vainio, L. (2007), 'Does selecting one visual object from several require inhibition of the actions associated with non-selected objects?', *Journal of Experimental Psychology*, 33(3), pp. 670–691.

Fagioli, S., Hommel, B. and Schubotz R.I. (in press), 'Intentional control of attention: action planning primes action-related stimulus dimensions', *Psychological Science.*

Fodor, J.A. (1975), *The Language of Thought* (Thomas Y. Crowell).

Fodor, J.A. (1980), 'Methodological solipsism considered as a research strategy in cognitive psychology', *The Behavioural and Brain Sciences*, 3, pp. 63–109.

Fodor, J.A. and Pylyshyn, Z.W. (1988), 'Connectionism and cognitive architecture: a critical appraisal', *Cognition*, 28, pp. 3–71.

Greenwald, A.G. (1970), 'Sensory feedback mechanisms in performance control: with special reference to the ideo-motor mechanism', *Psychological Review*, 77, pp. 73–99.

Harnad, S. (1990), 'The symbol grounding problem', *Physica D*, 42, pp. 335–346.

Hommel, B. (1994), 'Spontaneous decay of response code activation', *Psychological Research*, 56, pp. 261–268.

Hommel, B. (1997), 'Toward an action-concept model of stimulus-response compatibility', In *Theoretical Issues In Stimulus-Response Compatibility*, eds. B. Hommel and W. Prinz (Elsevier Science).

Jeannerod, M. (1981), 'Intersegmental coordination during reaching at natural visual objects', In *Attention and Performance IX*, eds. J. Long and A. Baddeley (Lawrence Erlbaum).

Jeannerod, M., Paulignan, Y., Mackenzie, C. and Marteniuk, R.M. (1992), 'Parallel visuomotor processing in human prehension', In *Control of Arm Movement in Space*, eds. R. Caminiti, P.B. Johnson and Y. Burnod (Springer-Verlag).

Kohler, I. (1962), 'Experiments with goggles', *Scientific American*, 206, pp. 62–72.

Kornblum, S. (1992), 'Dimensional overlap and dimensional relevance in stimulus-response and stimulus-stimulus compatibility', In G.E. Stelmach and J. Requin (eds.) *Tutorials In Motor Behaviour* (Amsterdam: North-Holland).

Kornblum, S., Hasbroucq, T. and Osman, A. (1990), 'Dimensional overlap: cognitive basis for stimulus-response compatibility – a model and taxonomy', *Psychological Review*, 97, pp. 253–270.

Kornblum, S. and Lee, J. (1995), 'Stimulus-response compatibility with relevant and irrelevant stimlulus dimensions that do and do not overlap with the response', *Journal of Experimental Psychology: Human Perception and Performance*, 21, pp. 855–875.

Lester, J., Converse, S., Kahler, S., Barlow, T., Stone, B. and Bhogal, R.(1997), 'The persona effect: Affective impact of animated pedagogical agents', in *Proceedings of CHI '97*, pp. 359–366.

Mackie, J.L. (1976), *Problems from Locke* (Oxford University Press).

Marr, D. (1982), *Vision* (San Francisco: Freeman).

Michaels, C.F. (1993), 'Destination compatibility, affordances, and coding rules: A reply to Proctor, Van Zandt, Lu and Weeks', *Journal of Experimental Psychology: Human Perception and Performance,* 19, pp. 1121–1127.

Michaels, C.F. (1988), 'S-R compatibility between response position and destination of apparent motion', *Journal of Experimental Psychology: Human Perception and Performance*, 14, pp. 231–240.

Millikan, R. (1995), 'Pushmi-Pullyu representations', In *Philosophical Perspectives 9: AI Connectionism and Philosophical Psychology*, ed. J. Tomberlin.

Newell, A. (1980), 'Physical symbol systems', *Cognitive Science*, 4, pp. 135–183.

Newton, N. (1996), *Foundations of Understanding* (Philadelphia: John Benjamins).

O'Regan, J.K. and Noe, A. (2001), 'A sensorimotor account of vision and visual consciousness', *Behavioural and Brain Sciences*, 24, pp. 939–1031.

Palmer, S.E. (1978), 'Fundamental aspects of cognitive representation', In *Cognition and Categorisation*, eds. E. Rosch and B.B. Lloyd (Hillsdale, NJ: Lawrence Earlbaum).

Pavese, A. and Buxbaum, L.J. (2002), 'Action matters: the role of action plans and object affordances in selection for action', *Visual Cognition*, 9, pp. 559–590.

Prince, W. (1990), 'A common coding approach to perception and action', In O. Neumann and W. Prinz (eds.) *Perspectives on Perception and Action* (Berlin: Springer-Verlag).

Putnam, H. (1988), *Representation and Reality* (Cambridge, MA: MIT Press).

Searle, J. (1980), 'Minds, brains and programs', *The Behavioural and Brain Sciences*, 3, pp. 417–457.

Simon, J.R. (1969), 'Reactions toward the source of stimulation', *Journal of Experimental Psychology*, 81, pp. 174–176.

Symes, E., Ellis, R., Tucker, M., & Vainio, L. (under review), 'Action-directed attention: Planning a grasp primes grasp-related stimulus features', *Journal of Experimental Psychology: Human Perception and Performance*.

Thelen, E. and Smith, L. (1994), *A Dynamical Systems Approach to the Development of Cognition and Action* (Cambridge, MA: MIT Press).

Tipper, S.P. (1985), 'The negative priming effect: inhibitory priming by ignored objects', *Quarterly Journal of Experimental Psychology*, 37A, pp. 571–590.

Tucker, M. and Ellis, R. (1998), 'On the relations between seen objects and components of potential actions', *Journal of Experimental Psychology: Human Perception and Performance*, 24(3), pp. 830–846.

Tucker, M. and Ellis, R. (2001), 'Micro-affordance of grasp type in a visual categorisation task', *Visual Cognition*, 8 (6), pp. 769–800.

Varela, F., Thompson, E. and Rosch, E. (1991), *The Embodied Mind: Cognitive Science and Human Experience* (Cambridge, MA: MIT Press_.

Wohlschlager, A. (2000), 'Visual motion priming by invisible actions', *Vision Research*, 40, pp. 925–930.

Jonathan Bishop

Ecological Cognition: A New Dynamic for Human-Computer Interaction

Introduction

Human computer interaction (HCI) is the study of the interaction between actors and their computer environments. It has long been argued that psychology has an important role to play in HCI, but that detailing its role has been difficult (Carroll, 1991). In the 20th century there were two dominant approaches to designing human-computer systems, one being the *cognitive* approach, (which was heavily based on the information processing model) and the other being the *behaviourist* approach, which was based on the stimulus-response theory that behaviour can be reinforced through rewards.

Kaptelinin (1996) points out that the cognitive approach to HCI may be limited and that it does not provide an appropriate conceptual basis for studies of computer use in their social, organisational, and cultural context, in relation to the goals, plans and values of an actor. The claim that all human behaviour can be explained as a result of information processing is just as implausible as the earlier assumption that the actions of an actor are the result of responses to stimuli. Mantovani (1996), in attempting to understand the relationship between goals and plans, indicates that the information-processing metaphor is limited and that the actions of actors cannot be fully captured by any preconceived cognitive schema.

The idea that actors interpret their environment through schemas is unsatisfactory, as actors will interact with artefacts intuitively, without reference to past experience or existing knowledge. The suggestion that these actors are interacting with artefacts as a result of reflexes is also unsatisfactory, as actors will use artefacts that have been invented as intuitively as those that have existed since the environment became a physical reality. The actor and the environment cannot be considered separately as one influences the other, which means that cognition must be ecological. The possibility of there being an ecological approach to cognition was put forward by Kyttä (2003), who asked whether it could exist. Kyttä drew upon the work of perceptual psychologists such as Gibson (1979) to suggest that it is possible for actors to interact with their environment based on what that environment offers (i.e. via 'affordances'.)

What Drives Actors To Act?

Understanding what drives actors to act is crucial in terms of developing human-computer systems that adapt to and influence them. There has been extensive research into discovering what drives people, which has led to a number of theories, including psychoanalytic theory (Freud, 1933), hierarchical needs theory (Maslow, 1943), belief-desire-intent theory (e.g. Rao & Georgeff, 1991), which see desires as goals, and other desire-based theories which see desires as instincts that have to be satisfied (e.g. Reiss, 2004). All of these theories suggest that actors are trying to satisfy some internal entity. This assumption ignores the role of the environment in shaping the behaviour of an actor and suggests that actors are selfish beings that only do things for shallow reasons.

Psychoanalytic theory as proposed by Freud (1933) argues that actors are driven by their 'id', which is challenged by their 'superego' and through the 'ego' they find a balance. The id creates instinctual desires in response to needs, including all the energy arising from the life instinct and the death instinct (Reef, 2001). The superego is like a conscience, which challenges the desires of the id and through the ego a balance is found resulting in an action. Freud (1933) argues that the actor is always trying to satisfy the id and the superego, a view that does not take into account the cognitive states of the actor that may be affected by the environment. The idea that everything an actor does is driven only by either a life or a death instinct seems implausible. These instincts could perhaps be considered to be one of the elements that drive an actor, in that actors will eat and procreate as well as sometimes cause harm to themselves, but they will also do things like socialising and making things creatively, which are neither existential or thanatotic.

More recent research suggests actors are driven by desires, but most still indicate that these desires are entities that have to be satisfied, as is the case with the theory of 12 desires proposed by Reiss (2004). In the literature relating to artificial intelligence and autonomous agents the words, 'desire' and 'goal', are often used interchangeably, as Rao & Georgeff (1991) indicate. In this context, if someone had a desire to quit smoking, that would be a goal to quit and they would not necessarily satisfy that goal if they did not have the intent. Bishop (2007) provided an alternative view that actors are driven to act by desires, and in this context a desire is a force that leads to a change of plan. These desires are created by intent, and an actor will act out their desires unless they decide not to after experiencing dissonance.

How Actors Decide and Plan Their Actions

Experiencing a desire to act results in a change in the cognitions of an actor. The cognitions that an actor uses to act out a desire are goals, plans, values, beliefs and interests. A goal can be a long-term aim, such as a goal to become a respected member of the community, or a short-term objective, such as a goal to learn about a specific topic. Plans are conceived as a result of experiencing desires and are stored in memory as a result of reflecting on a plan that has been acted out. Values are generalised things such as the values that 'you should always honour your parents' or 'you should always respect other people' and differ from the more specific and contextualised beliefs such as the belief 'I will not be being helpful by posting to this community'.

When an actor experiences a desire, such as a desire driven by social forces, they will develop a plan to be social, which will influence their other cognitions as they will have an interest in maintaining their plans, they may hold beliefs about that specific plan and they may have general values that apply to the situation they are in. If the actor's newly created plan to be social conflicts with an existing plan, or some other cognition, the actor will experience cognitive dissonance. According to Festinger (1957) cognitive dissonance is what an actor experiences when they cognitions are not consonant with each other. For example if an actor had a plan to be social, but a belief that this would be inappropriate, they would experience dissonance as a result of their plan not being consonant with their belief. Resolving this dissonance would achieve a state of consonance that would result in either temperance or intemperance. If this actor held a value that stated that they must never be social if it is inappropriate, they could achieve consonance by abandoning the plan to be social, which results in *temperance*. If the same actor had an interest in being social and a belief that it was more important to be social than not be social, they might resolve to disregard their belief, resulting in *intemperance*.

If an actor experiences a desire without experiencing *any* dissonance they experience *deference*, as they will act out the desire immediately. Vygotsky (1978) points out that infant actors will act out their desires immediately and will not wait for days to do so. The reason for this is that the infant actor is not experiencing dissonance when they desire to do something, and therefore immediately acts out the plan that resulted from the desire, thus experiencing deference.

The development and use of cognitions to shape action can clearly be seen in infant actors. An infant actor will experience an urge creating existential forces leading to a desire to (for example) excrete waste products. In the absence of dissonance, processes will occur that results in the excretion occurring. Through the intervention of a parental actor the infant can then develop their cognitions: this will eventually lead to the experience of dissonance (that will eventually result in temperance). For example the parent will impart the belief that it is wrong to excrete in certain contexts as well as the belief that in that context it will meet with their disapproval, and will assist the infant actor in developing plans to excrete into a container. After this training when the infant actor experiences the existential desire to excrete and develops a plan to do so, they will experience dissonance as a result of holding beliefs that they should refrain from acting out that desire in that context, as it will be against the wishes of their parents whom they have interest in, and will therefore modify their plan to act out their desire into a plan that creates consonance. Also observable in some infant actors is that the same beliefs will lead to intemperance as opposed to temperance depending on the desire. An infant may experience an affectance as a result of interacting with their parents that may lead to vengeance forces that create a desire. On experiencing a vengeance-driven desire some infant actors will modify their plan because they hold beliefs that excreting in a certain context will meet with the disapproval of their parents (as a result of parental training).

How Perception and Action Are Interlinked

It is accepted among most psychologists that perception and action are linked and that the environment has an impact on an actor's behaviour. Some have thought that an actor's actions are reflexes to stimuli (e.g. Watson, 1913) and these can be conditioned (e.g. Watson & Rayner, 1920; Pavlov, 1927) so that when an actor perceives a stimulus, such as an artefact, they respond with an action without reference to any cognitions. This concept will be referred to as stimulus-response theory. The idea that all animal behaviour could be explained by stimulus–response was a highly influential idea during the first half of the 20th century, but has been abandoned by many in recent years (Cahill, et al., 2001). However, there have been extensions to stimulus-response theory, most notably by Vygotsky (1978), who suggested that artefacts act as a mediator between the stimuli and the response. Even so, Vygotsky argued not that learning was a result of stimuli-response, but that through artefacts the response to the stimuli could be modified, a process that he called 'mediating'.

The role of affordances

The core principle of stimulus-response theory is that all behaviour is a reflex, or response, to a stimulus or stimuli. Whilst this *appears* to acknowledge the role of the environment in influencing behaviour, in actuality it fails to acknowledge that aspects of the environment can create an impetus that leads to action. Perceptual psychologists have introduced a new dimension to the understanding of perception and action, which is that artefacts suggest action through offering affordances, which are properties of an artefact that determine or indicate how that artefact can be used and are independent of the perceiver (Gibson, 1979). This suggests that when an actor responds to stimuli they are doing so not as the result of an internal reflex, but because of what the artefact offers. This is supported by neuroimaging studies, which suggest that when actors perceive affordances in artefacts they develop plans to interact with them (Winstein *et al.*, 1997; Grézes & Decety, 2002).

Vygotsky (1978) draws attention to the development of pointing in infant actors. He points out that the infant will grasp at something they want and then once a parental actor gives this to them they will (through the process of internalisation) learn to point when they want something. Stimulus-response theory would suggest that the grasping action is being reinforced through the so-called reward of receiving the artefact. What is actually happening here is that the infant actor perceives an affordance, that being that the artefact affords grasping and develops a plan to grasp it, and does not experience any dissonance so acts out the plan as a result of deference and although they do not reach the artefact they eventually get given it. As situated action theories suggest, the infant actor then reconstructs the plan based on their interpretation of what happened, which is what Vygotsky refers to as internalisation. The infant then develops the belief that pointing at something increases their chances of being given it, and may contextualise this belief to the situation they constructed, which then strengthens their new plan. When the infant actor next perceives that an artefact affords grasping they will develop a plan to grasp, experience dissonance, which leads then to adopt their reconstructed plan to point that resulted from the internalisation.

The concept of resonances

As demonstrated by Gibson (1979) affordances in artefacts can be directly perceived, so that a door handle can offer the affordance of grasping and opening. What Gibson did not deal with was the concept of the property of an artefact offers an affordance that evokes a plan. In the past these have been referred to as perceived affordances, a term which was introduced by Norman (2004) to describe what an artefact affords a user based on their experience, for example the blue underlined text in a hypertext system offers the perceived affordance of clicking. Pavlov (1927) describes an experiment with canine actors whereby the canines secrete saliva at the sound of a metronome. Pavlov argues based on traditional stimuli-response theory that the canine is demonstrating a reflex because the sound of the metronome has been paired with the stimuli of food, producing the response of salivation. Pavlov states that the canine actor was not aware that the food was edible until it had experienced it, suggesting that the desire to eat cannot come from the same impetus that leads to someone perceiving that a door can be opened, which is why the canine actor did not secrete saliva on sight of the food before it had experienced it, suggesting there is some learning necessary for the canine actor to salivate at the sight of the food. What happens with the canine actor is that they experience the food and develop a belief that it is edible. This belief will then be joindered with the interest in the food, so that the sight of the food leads the canine actor to believe that it is edible. The secreted saliva from the canine actor occurs as a result of them developing a plan to eat and acting on that plan. Often a human actor will experience something similar, such as hearing a phrase or seeing a scene, and will develop a plan to do something, such as saying something. What they see can be seen to resonate with them, and if this resonating experience results in a change in their cognitions the actor can be said to have experienced a resonance. A resonance can be seen to be a perceived affordance in that it is a social aspect of the environment that evokes a cognition.

The role of dissonance in influencing action

Even though plans result from actors experiencing desires, they will not act upon such plans if they resolve dissonance in such a way that results in temperance. Skinner (1938) describes experiments with rodents, whereby the rodent is presented with a lever that can be pressed. Skinner does not explain what makes the rodent press a lever, but the reason is that the lever offers the affordance of pressing and therefore leads the rat to experience a desire and develop a plan to press it — a plan which is acted out as a result of deference or intemperance. When the rat presses the lever and is presented with the food, this is not the result of a conditioned response as Skinner suggested, but the result of the rat developing a belief that pressing the lever delivers food, which is consonant with the plan to press a lever to deliver food.

The next time the rat perceives that the lever affords pressing it will develop a plan to press it, experience consonance as a result of holding a belief that food will be delivered (assuming it has a goal to eat) and therefore experience intemperance. If the rat is presented with food each time it presses the lever its belief will be strengthened. It is important to bear in mind here that it is not the so-called response that is being reinforced, but the belief that is being strengthened. If the same rat experiences a desire to eat it will develop a plan to eat. Using the belief that pressing the lever delivers food it will modify this plan (i.e. to press the lever) and will do so if it is in a state of consonance resulting in intemperance. If it gets this food it will strengthen its belief that pressing the lever delivers food and will act out its plan to eat. If, as was done in Skinner's experiments, the rat is no longer presented with food when the lever is pressed, this will challenge the rat's existing belief that pressing the lever leads to food, which will create dissonance the next time they desire to eat. It is *not* the case that the so-called conditioned response is becoming extinct. Instead what is happening is that the rat decides (through its 'belief structure') that it will not achieve its goal to eat by pressing the lever. The lever will still afford pressing, and the rat will still plan to press the lever, but it will experience dissonance that will lead it to abandon the plan, thus experiencing temperance.

The Ecological Cognition Framework and Its Application To Human-Computer Systems

Kaptelinin (1996) supporting the work of Engeström (1993), Kuutti (1996) and Nardi (1996) argues that the computer is just a tool that mediates between the actor and the physical environment, as opposed to the means for the actor to access the virtual environment.

To fully understand the role of the actor in human-computer systems the virtual environment must be treated on par with the physical environment. Virtual environments contain other actors, structures and artefacts, such as mediating artefacts (Bishop, 2005). Both virtual and physical environments can create impetuses in actors and actors will be driven to participate in both environments as a result of experiencing them.

The ecological cognition framework presented in Figure 2 suggests that there are five binary opposition forces that drive an actor and provoke changes in their cognitions. These are social-antisocial, creative-destructive, order-chaos, vengeance-forgiveness and existential-thanatotic. Examples of each of these forces can be seen in the functional systems that exist in virtual environments. Social-antisocial forces are very common in driving actors to take part in human-computer systems, which are often social spaces. Rhiengold (2000) describes 'the social Web' in which people like him participate as a result of being driven by their longings to participate and anti-social actions are easily discovered in virtual environments, as actors will often flame others. Actors in these virtual environments often experience creative forces and will create content as well as destructive forces, as some actors will 'blank' pages of content.

The existence of order forces is also apparent in human-computer systems, where actors will carry out actions such as organising book-

A New Dynamic for Human-Computer Interaction

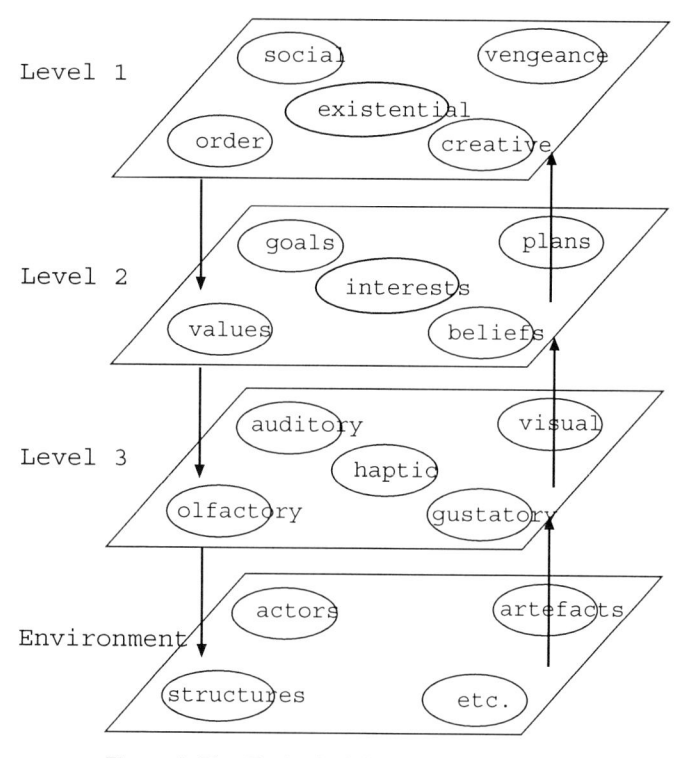

Figure 1. The Ecological Cognition Framework

marks, rearranging pages and some actors may take control of a situation, such as when members are flaming each other in a chat session, and others will attempt to create order when a bulletin board goes off-topic and will carry out actions to bring it back to the original topic, despite the fact that allowing bulletin board to go off-topic can increase sociability in the community (Bishop, 2002). Chaos forces can be seen in some functional systems that form part of virtual environments, as actors, who are often referred to as 'trolls' will create havoc through posting content, or carrying out actions that incite other actors.

Actions driven by vengeance forces are very apparent in human-computer systems, as actors in virtual environments are known to be very aggressive (Kiesler & Sproull, 1992; Wallace, 2001), carrying out actions such as flaming, and posting negative feedback on other community members. Indeed, Smith (2001) describes how some virtual community members that have been banned from the community will return with new identities to harass other individuals, disrupt the community and challenge the authority of leaders. The result of forgiveness forces can be seen in some functional systems, where actors will apologise to actors that they have had a disagreement with, often what has resulted from order forces.

Existential forces, such as eating, whilst not obvious in virtual environments have an impact on the actions of an action that is part of them. Thanatotic forces, like their existential opposites are not always apparent in the virtual environment, though some actors seek advice on committing thanatotic acts in some communities.

The second level of the framework presented in Figure 1 is an actor's cognitions, which are goals, plans, values, beliefs and interests. These cognitions will be influenced by five types of neuro-response driven by forces, namely *Conventions*, which create values, *Relations*, which create interests, *Epistemes*, which create beliefs, *Ambitions*, which create goals, and *Desires*, which create plans, and how an actor resolves them will determine which judgement they make, which will be either *Deference, Intemperance, Reticence, Temperance* or *Ignorance*.

Virtual Communities

Virtual communities are perhaps a good example of human-computer systems that can be considered to be a functional system that forms part of the virtual environment. Virtual communities consist of actors that share similar goals, values, beliefs and interests. Kim (2000) suggests that the actors that take part in these functional systems go through a membership lifecycle that determines how they contribute. These stages in the lifecycle include: lurkers, who are people who have never contributed to the community; novices, who are actors that have broken through a barrier to entry and are new to the community and only made a few contributions; regulars, who are actors that are regularly participating in community life; leaders, who are actors that have broken through another barrier and regularly participate through welcoming and nurturing novices and regulars; and finally elders, who are actors that are established leaders and have been in the community a long time. It has been suggested that as many as 9 in 10 of the actors that make up virtual communities are lurkers (Nonnecke & Preece, 2000) in that they have never contributed to the functional system they are part of. Preece et. al (2004) suggest that the reason that these actors do not participate is that they hold beliefs about the action of posting content, such as the belief 'I will not be helpful by posting'. Bishop (2007) suggests that lurkers will still have desires to post content, usually social or creative desires, but the beliefs that they hold will create dissonance that results in temperance.

The most obvious difference between a lurker and a regular is that regulars will often experience intemperance when it comes to acting out a plan to post content, whereas lurkers will experience dissonance that results in temperance. Nielsen (2006) argues that the existence of more lurkers than other members cannot be overcome. However, the author believes that leaders should challenge the beliefs that create dissonance in lurkers (e.g. by persuading them that comments they make will be welcome). This may well lead to more lurker participation.

Some members that take part in a virtual community can become so engaged that they will experience deference when they have a desire to participate. This is perhaps what Csikszentmihalyi (1977; 1990) refers to as a state of flow in that the actor will act with total involvement narrowing their attention focus and experiencing a loss of self-consciousness. Bishop (2007) suggests that if a virtual community has artefacts and actors that do not create dissonance with an actor's cognitions then the actor is more likely to become engaged in a state of flow and act out their desires, thus experiencing deference. However, whilst engaging an actor in a state of flow might mean that they are more likely to experience deference and act out their desires to be social, there is also the possibility that they will act out their vengeance desires as well. Indeed, some studies have indicated that in virtual environments where actors are likely to experience deference they are more likely to flame others (Orengo Castellá *et. al*, 2000). This suggests that any attempt to increase the flow experience of an actor should be done with caution.

Seductive Hypermedia

The term 'seductive hypermedia' is used to describe a human-computer system that orchestrates specific responses from the user in order to change their behaviour due to the system's ability to sustain appeal (Mbakwe & Cunliffe, 2003). Current understanding of seductive hypermedia is based on classical stimulus-response theory, suggesting that the user can become seduced if they are presented with stimuli and are then rewarded for responding to it. Mbakwe & Cunliffe (2003) argue that the first stage of seduction is inducement, which '*occurs instantaneously (or momentarily) prior to interaction, where its role is to evoke attraction, or to distract the user*'. What Mbakwe & Cunliffe refer to as an inducement is perhaps the impetus, such as an affordance. If an actor is using a hypermedia system and is then presented with a hyperlink, it may lead to a resonance, leading the actor to click on it. A strategically placed hyperlink could be considered an inducement if it is placed there to change the plans of the user. Such hyperlinks are referred to as persuasive mediating artefacts (Bishop, 2005). The next two stages of seduction Cunliffe & Mbakwe (2003) argue are negotiation and suggestion. In these stages they suggest that an actor is subject to an experience and then is convinced that they have achieved their goal. They also suggest that at this point the actor can cease using the interface if they feel their goals have not been met. Perhaps what Mbakwe & Cunliffe are trying to describe is the process of an actor achieving consonance, through developing beliefs about the system that are compatible with their cognitions. If an actor experiences a desire upon perceiving a mediating artefact and thus developing a plan to use it, they will use it if this leads them to achieve consonance. That is, they will use the artefact if the plan to use it is consonant with their existing plans, as well as their goals, values, beliefs and interests. If the actor uses the mediating artefact in the way suggested through its affordances they will have been persuaded, which is what Mbakwe & Cunliffe (2003) indicate is the final stage of seduction. Persuasion would have occurred as the actor will have developed specific beliefs about the system's ability to meet their goals, as opposed to their so-called responses being reinforced, which Mbakwe & Cunliffe (2003) indicate is necessary for the actor to be seduced by the system. This is clearly not the case. The actor will continue using the system and therefore be seduced by it so long as they achieve consonance when they experience impetuses offered by the system, and will not require so-called responses to be reinforced. The more plans created by the impetuses generated by the system, the more the actors will use the system providing that such plans are consonant with the actor's cognitions (in particular their goals), and which therefore result in deference or intemperance. If the system meets some of the goals of the user they may develop beliefs that it does, which will mean they are more likely to experience intemperance. Human-computer systems can be considered to be seductive if they create impetuses that lead to desires that result in plans that are consonant with an actor's cognitions and therefore result in the actors using the system for a longer period. A system could perhaps be considered highly seductive if it results in actors experiencing deference as opposed to intemperance.

Persuasive E-Learning Systems

Perhaps more challenging is developing human-computer systems that dispute an actor's beliefs whilst convincing them to continue to use the system, an application of persuasive technology particularly useful in the development of e-learning systems. E-learning systems are used to convey knowledge and information though a computer-based learning environment. An e-learning system can take many forms, from a simple hypertext application (such as an online encyclopaedia) to a complex multimedia system with interactive features, such as an educational video game (Bishop, 2005). Persuasive e-learning systems can be designed to be persuasive through changing the plans of an actor and through intervening to change the beliefs and values of actors and therefore influence their goals. Fogg (2003) argues that some persuasive systems can exploit the goals of an actor, such as the goals to be healthy and admired by others. E-learning systems could be persuasive by suggesting beliefs that are consistent with such goals so that the actor is more likely to adopt them without experiencing dissonance or by resolving dissonance in such a way that they accept the belief and change existing beliefs.

E-learning systems can be made persuasive through mediating artefacts which influence the plans of actors, as explored in earlier work by Bishop (2005). Through supporting the goals of the actor such e-learning systems can direct learners in specific directions so that they develop beliefs that are consonant with their goals. Fogg (2003) argues that systems can be persuasive if they intervene at the opportune moment. A potentially effective means of doing it is the Animated Pedagogical Agents (APAs), such as those developed by

Lester *et al.* (1997) and Bishop (2004). Lester *et al.* (1997) indicate that APAs can provide problem-solving advice to actors using a e-learning system, which will help the actor in developing beliefs, and can also play a powerful motivational role, which suggests that an APA can influence the actor so that they develop constructive desires and continue to use the system through developing plans. Indeed, Fogg (2003) suggests that computers can take on the role of social actors and persuade actors to do things, which would include assisting the actor in developing constructive desires that lead them to conceive plans to use the e-learning system and develop beliefs that are consonant with their goals. In order for such agents to be persuasive they must think and behave like human actors.

Discussion

In the 20th century there were two domination approaches to designing human-computer systems, that being the cognitive approach, which was heavily based on the information processing model and the behaviourist approach, which was based on the classical stimuli-response theory. In the second half of that century, understanding of what drives actors to act were heavily reliant on hierarchical-needs theory, while artificially intelligent agents were based on belief-desire-intent models. A core theme of these theories is that actors are internally orientated who respond to stimuli in the environment through internalised reflexes or schema and seek to satisfy internal entities such as needs. Such models are unsatisfactory when it comes to explaining the behaviour of actors. Actors will often perform actions as a result of perceiving affordances in the environment without reference to schemata or their so-called needs. Such affordances directly influence the plans of actors, which may lead them to act in a way different to how they initially intended to.

The plans of an actor are directly influenced by the forces that drive their desires. An actor in their lifetime will experience five binary-opposition forces, those being social-antisocial, creative-destructive, order-chaos, vengeance-forgiveness and existential-thanatotic. If an actor experiences an impetus and then intent, they will experience a desire directed by one of these forces which creates a plan and will act out that plan unless they experience dissonance that results in them modifying or abandoning the plan resulting in consonance. When an actor experiences a desire they will have to make a judgement as to whether to act on it. Deference occurs if the desire does not create any dissonance and is acted out or adopted almost without consideration, Intemperance occurs if the desire creates dissonance but the actor resolves to act it out or adopt it, Reticence occurs where dissonance occurs and by either acting on the desire or not the actor experiences regret, Temperance occurs if the actor experiences dissonance and decides not to accept the change in their cognitions, and Ignorance occurs if the actor declines to accept the change almost immediately without considering it.

Actors will interact within a functional system, such a workplace or virtual community by constructing an interpretation of the environment based on their goals, plans, values, beliefs and interests, which is referred to as a situation. Actors that form part of functional systems may share similar goals and beliefs, but the each will have constructed a different interpretation and therefore a different situation based on their cognitions and their individual competencies.

Human-Computer Interaction could benefit from a new approach based on the understanding that actors act as a result of experiencing an impetus, such as an affordance, developing the intent, experiencing forces, experiencing a neuro-response, such as a desire, and making a judgement by resolving dissonance. The design and management of virtual communities can be enhanced through realising that actors who do not contribute to these communities may have a desire to do so, but will have to resolve their dissonance to experience intemperance as opposed to temperance. Human-computer systems that attempt to seduce the user could be improved through developers understanding that actors will continue using a system if they believe their goals will be met and the affordances offered by the system are consonant with their existing goals, plans, values, beliefs and interests. E-learning systems could be made more persuasive through proposing beliefs that may be contradictory to the existing beliefs of an actor, but are consonant with their goals. Artificially intelligent agents could be made more lifelike, by experiencing desires and experiencing and resolving dissonance. Such agents could be useful in both e-learning system and systems that attempt to improve the health of actors. Computer-supported cognitive therapy systems could be improved by identifying and eliminating dissonance that an actor has experienced but not resolved.

Directions for future research

A challenge for researchers investigating functional systems, particularly human-computer systems that are part of the virtual environment is to develop research methods that allow them to research aspects of that system in a satisfactory manner. Traditional methods of gathering data from actors have acted on the assumption that actors provide accurate ('veridical') accounts of their internal mental states, but actually, actor's reflections on their behaviour or their motivations may not be accurate descriptions of what actually created the impetus for them to act. Neuroimaging has provided useful data on what an actor does when they perceive an affordance, but such methods may be limited in determining what desires an actor experienced that led to a particular action.

Some authors have suggested ethnographic approaches to researching virtual environments (e.g. Hine, 2000), and others have used techniques such as the Wizard of Oz technique to observe how actors behave when perceiving mediating artefacts (e.g. Bishop, 2005). New research methods must be identified to research the behaviour of actors, with perhaps one of the basic requirements of these methods being that they should research how actors act within *specific environments* as opposed to under laboratory conditions that are not necessarily reflective of how an actor would act in a less constrained setting.

Acknowledgements

The author would like to acknowledge all the anonymous reviewers that provided comments on earlier drafts of this chapter. Glamorgan Blended Learning is a Knowledge Transfer Initiative, supported by the University of Glamorgan though the GTi Business Network of which it is a member.

References

Bishop, J. (2002), *Development and Evaluation of a Virtual Community*, Unpublished dissertation, available online at: http://www.jonathanbishop.com/ publications/display.aspx?Item=11.

Bishop, J. (2003), 'The Internet for educating individuals with social impairments', *Journal of Computer Assisted Learning* , 19 (4), pp. 546–556

Bishop, J. (2004), 'The potential of persuasive technology in educating heterogeneous user groups', Unpublished thesis, available online at http://www.jonathanbishop.com/publications/display.aspx?Item=14

Bishop, J. (2005), 'The role of mediating artefacts in the design of persuasive e-learning systems', in: *Proceedings of the Internet Technology & Applications 2005 Conference*. Wrexham: North East Wales Institute of Higher Education.

Bishop, J. (2006), 'Social change in organic and virtual communities: An exploratory study of Bishop Desires'. *Paper presented to the Faith,*

Spirituality and Social Change Conference, University of Winchester, 8th April 2006.

Bishop, J. (2007), 'Increasing participation in online communities: A framework for human computer interaction', *Computers in Human Behavior*, 23, pp. 1881–1893

Cahill, L., McGaugh, J.L. & Weinberger, N.M. (2001), 'The neurobiology of learning and memory: some reminders to remember', *Trends in Neurosciences*, 24(10), pp. 578–581

Carroll, J.M. (1991), 'Introduction: The Kittle House Manifesto', in *Designing Interaction: Psychology at the Human-Computer Interface*, ed. J.M. Carroll (Cambridge: Cambridge University Press), pp. 1–16.

Csikszentmihalyi, M. (1977), *Beyond Boredom and Anxiety* (San Francisco: Jossey-Bass).

Csikszentmihalyi, M. (1990), *Flow: The Psychology of Optimal Experience* (New York: Harper & Row).

Engeström, Y. (1993), 'Developmental studies of work as a test bench of activity theory: The case of primary care medical practice', in *Understanding Practice: Perspectives on Activity and Context*, eds. J. Lave & S. Chaiklin (Cambridge: Cambridge University Press).

Festinger, L. (1957), *A Theory of Cognitive Dissonance* (Stanford, CA: Stanford University Press).

Fogg, B.J. (2003), *Persuasive Technology: Using Computers to Change What We Think and Do* (London: Morgan Kaufmann Publishers).

Freud, S. (1933), *New Introductory Lectures on Psycho-Analysis* (New York: W.W. Norton & Company, Inc).

Gibson, J.J. (1979), *The Ecological Approach to Visual Perception* (London: Lawrence Erlbaum Associates).

Grézes, J. & Decety, J. (2002), 'Does visual perception of an object afford action? Evidence from a neuroimaging study', *Neuropsychologia*, 40, pp. 212–222.

Grosso, M.D. (2001), 'Design and Implementation of Online Communities', Unpublished thesis, available online at: http://www.movesinstitute.org/darken/alumni/DelGrosso/delgrosso.pdf

Hine, C. (2000), *Virtual Ethnography* (London: Sage Publications Ltd).

Kaptelinin, V. (1996), 'Activity Theory: Implications for Human Computer Interaction', in *Context and Consciousness: Activity Theory and Human-Computer Interaction*, ed. B.A. Nardi, pp. 103–116

Kim, A.J. (2000), *Community Building on the Web: Secret Strategies for Successful Online Communities* (Berkeley: Peachpit Press).

Kim, H.C. (2005), *Bat Yam* (Philadelphia: The Hermit Kingdom Press).

Kiesler, S. & Sproull, L. (1992), 'Group decision making and communication technology', *Organizational Behavior and Human Decision Processes*, 52, pp. 96–123

Kuutti, K. (1996), 'Activity Theory as a Potential Framework for Human-Computer Interaction Research', in *Context and Consciousnesses: Activity theory and Human-Computer Interaction*, ed. B.A. Nardi (Cambridge, MA: The MIT Press), pp. 17–44.

Kyttä, M. (2003), 'Children in Outdoor Contexts: Affordances and Independent Mobility in the Assessment of Environmental Child Friendliness', Unpublished doctoral dissertation, Helsinki University of Technology, Finland.

Mantovani, G. (1996a), *New Communication Environments: From Everyday to Virtual* (London: Taylor & Frances Ltd).

Maslow, A.H. (1943), 'A Theory of Human Motivation', *Psychological Review*, 50, pp. 370–396.

Mbakwe, C. & Cunliffe, D. (2003), 'Conceptualising the Process of Hypermedia Seduction', in *Proceedings of the 1st International Meeting of Science and Technology Design: Senses and Sensibility – Linking Tradition to Innovation Through Design*, 25-26 September 2003, Lisbon, Portugal.

Nardi, B.A. (1996), 'Studying Context: A Comparison of Activity Theory, Situated Action Models and Distributed Cognition', in *Context and Consciousnesses: Activity theory and Human-Computer Interaction*, ed. B.A. Nardi, (Cambridge, MA: The MIT Press), pp. 69–102.

Nielsen, J. (2006), 'Participation Inequality: Encouraging More Users to Contribute'. Unpublished article, available online at:
http://www.useit.com/alertbox/participation inequality.html

Nonnecke, B. & Preece, J. (2000), 'Lurker demographics: Counting the silent', in *Proceedings of CHI 2000*, 1-6 April 2002 (The Hague: Amsterdam).

Norman, D.A. (c.2004), 'Affordances and Design', Unpublished article, available online at:
http://www.jnd.org/dn.mss/affordances-and-design.html

Orengo Castellá, V.; Zornoza Abad, A.M.; Prieto Alonso, F. & Peiró Silla, J.M. (2000), 'The influence of familiarity among group members, group atmosphere and assertiveness on uninhibited behavior through three different communication media', *Computers in Human Behavior*, 16, pp. 141–159

Pavlov, I.P. (1927), *Conditioned Reflexes* (London: Routledge and Kegan Paul).

Preece, J., Nonnecke, B. & Andrews, D. (2004), 'The top five reasons for lurking: improving community experiences for everyone', *Computers in Human Behavior*, 20, pp. 201–223.

Rao, A.S. & Georgeff, M.P. (1991), 'Modeling Rational Agents within a BDI-Architecture', in *Proceedings of the Second International Conference on Principles of Knowledge Representation and Reasoning*, KR91, ed. J. Allen, R. Fikes, & E. Sandewall, (San Mateo: Morgan Kaufmann, San Mateo, CA).

Reef, C. (2001), *Sigmund Freud: Pioneer of the Mind* (New York: Clarion Books).

Reiss, S. (2004), 'Multifaceted Nature of Intrinsic Motivation: The Theory of 16 Basic Desires', *Review of General Psychology*, 8 (3), pp. 179–193.

Rhiengold, H. (2000), *The Virtual Community: Homesteading on the Electronic Frontier* (London: The MIT Press).

Skinner, B.F. (1938), *The Behavior of Organisms: An Experimental Analysis* (New York: Appleton-Century-Crofts).

Smith, A.D. (2001), 'Problems of conflict management in virtual communities', in *Communities in Cyberspace*, ed. in: M.A. Smith & P. Kollock (London: Routledge).

Vygotsky, L.S. (1978), *Mind in Society: The Development of Higher Psychological Processes* (Cambridge, MA: Harvard University Press).
Wallace, P. (2001), *The Psychology of the Internet* (Cambridge: Cambridge University Press).
Watson, J.B. (1913), 'Psychology as the behaviorist views it', *Psychological Review*, 20, pp. 158–177.
Watson, J.B. & Rayner, R. (1920), 'Conditioned emotional reactions', *Journal of Experimental Psychology*, 3(1), pp. 1–14.
Winstein, C.J., Grafton, S.T. & Pohl, P.S. (1997), 'Motor task difficulty and brain activity: investigation of goal-directed reciprocal aiming using positron emission tomography', *Neurophysiology*, 77, pp. 1581–1594.

Erik Hollnagel

The Elusiveness of Cognition

1. Introduction

Although the interest for what goes on in the mind is as old as psychology itself, the study of cognition has several times gone astray. After a reasonably successful start, behaviorism effectively discouraged researchers from studying what went on in the mind and replaced it by studies of behaviour. The self-imposed ban on the use of mentalistic terms was eventually overcome by the analogy between the computer and the brain. But the new approach inadvertently created another obstacle, namely that cognition was treated as an epiphenomenon of information processing. As this view now slowly is waning, the question remains of which status 'cognition' should be given. This chapter proposes that cognition should be understood in terms of what it *does* rather than in terms of what it *is*, namely enabling some organisms—including some machines—to retain *control* of what they do

1.1 Cognition as a phenomenon or as an epiphenomenon

Is 'cognition' useful? An answer to this, admittedly, polemical question depends on how the constituent terms are interpreted and, more specifically, on what is meant by *cognition*. One possible definition is 'that which goes on between the ears' or, in more scientific terms, the *ability* of homo sapiens—and presumably other organisms as well—to become aware of or obtain knowledge of objects and events (including, of course, cognition itself) and thereby to *act* in a purposeful manner. Under this definition, cognition is not only useful but indeed necessary for our existence and survival as individuals and as a species. A second possible definition is 'the set of hypothetical *functions* or *processes* of the mind—or the brain—that are proposed as being necessary and sufficient to account for a certain range of human behaviours'. It is this second definition of cognition that constitutes the subject matter for disciplines such as cognitive psychology, cognitive science, cognitive neurosciences, cognitive ergonomics, and artificial intelligence—although the precise definition may differ among the disciplines.

Another way of answering the question is to look at cognition as either a phenomenon or en epiphenomenon, i.e., either in terms of how it appears or in terms of how it is explained. In the first case the phenomenon to be studied is actually behaviour—or performance—rather than cognition, since in the majority of cases we observe what people do rather than what goes on in their minds. The latter we can only find out about by means of introspection, and even here the verisimilitude of the verbal reports thus generated is open to debate (e.g., Morick, 1971; Nisbett, 1977; Prætorius & Duncan, 1988). In the second case, cognition is seen as a secondary phenomenon, most commonly as a result of (human) information processing. The focus of study therefore becomes the *information processing* that is assumed to constitute the material basis for cognition. The purpose of this chapter is to debate whether we can better understand cognition by studying it as a phenomenon or as an epiphenomenon (specifically as information processing).

In order to do that it is necessary first to understand how cognition came to be treated as an epiphenomenon. Although the study of cognition can reasonably be said to begin with the emergence of psychology as a scientific discipline, this development in itself rested on the dualistic principle of the separation of mind and body. Centuries of rationalism had further emphasised the importance of reasoning as a valid source of knowledge. Taken together this meant that scientific psychology set out to study, among other things, the process of knowing. To begin with cognition was studied as a phenomenon in its own right, i.e., a direct study of mental processes. The method was introspection under experimentally controlled conditions. The reason for taking this approach was based on Wilhelm Wundt's distinction between 'the exact, lawful nature of the hidden cause-effect relations to be discovered by psychologists and the chaotic surface circumstances that obscure such relations and thus confuse both the scientist and the behaving organism' (cf., Hammond, 1993, p. 206).

The purpose of controlled introspection and the meticulous reporting of inner experience was to unveil the structure of the conscious mind—to penetrate the obscuring 'surface circumstances.'

Despite its initial success the approach was dealt a devastating blow by the behaviorist manifesto (Watson, 1913), which presented psychology as an objective experimental branch of natural science to be studied without references to consciousness. The opening paragraph of this paper made the position abundantly clear:

> Psychology as the behaviorist views it is a purely objective experimental branch of natural science. Its theoretical goal is the prediction and control of behavior. Introspection forms no essential part of its methods, nor is the scientific value of its data dependent upon the readiness with which they lend themselves to interpretation in terms of consciousness. The behaviorist, in his efforts to get a unitary scheme of animal response, recognizes no dividing line between man and brute. The behavior of man, with all of its refinement and complexity, forms only a part of the behaviorist's total scheme of investigation (Watson, 1913, p. 158).

Since behaviorism left no role for introspection, there was consequently no need to limit psychological investigation to *homo sapiens*. The consequence of that, particularly in the United States, was that mainstream psychology turned to animal studies and tried to avoid all topics related to mental processes, mental events and states of mind.

2. The Circumnavigation

Although behaviorism held a firm grip on academic psychology for more than four decades, the interest in studying cognition never completely vanished. One example of that is Tolman's famous paper on 'Cognitive maps in rats and men', which argued that 'learning consists not in stimulus-response connections but in the building up in the nervous system of sets which function like cognitive maps' (Tolman, 1948, p. 197). The intellectual dominance of behaviourism was, however, so strong that mental phenomena in general and cognition in particular were deliberately neglected. Ritchie (1953) compared arguments about 'cognition' or 'behaviour' with arguments about a 'round' or a 'flat' earth and used this analogy to provide a scathing analysis of Kendler's (1952) proposal that it was useless to study learning as a mental process and that one instead should study only the observable behaviour.

> At the bottom of this seeming disagreement as to what is learned is the failure of many psychologists to utilize an adequate criterion of scientific explanation. All too often, propositions (usually involving phenomenological or physiological terms) which have

no deductive capacities are accepted as explanations because they instigate in some a sense of 'psychological understanding.' It is proposed that learning theorists avoid the problem of what is learned and come to grips with their undertaking in a positive forthright fashion. This can be accomplished by relating theoretical constructs to observables and unhesitatingly testing the explanatory capacities of their formulations (Kendler, 1952, p. 276).

Ritchie argued that studying learning while denying the existence of cognition was analogous to circumnavigating the globe without realising that it was round, and summarised the arguments against cognition as follows:

- Cognition/thinking is impossible because all that we can see are the results/products (i.e., behaviour).

- We can only know what cognition is when we have determined all the factors that produce it, but by that the answer is already given.

- Cognition may be possible, but rarely happens. The failure to find it is proof of that.

- Cognition is an inefficient way of explaining what happens.

- The problem is semantic, i.e., what do we really mean by 'thinking' and 'cognition'?

With the benefit of hindsight, the problem facing the study cognition of was the lack of a simple but powerful principle of explanation. Behaviourism was successful because it had such a principle, namely the stimulus-response association. The study of cognition withered until it found its own principle in the analogy between the (digital) computer and the human brain (e.g., von Neumann, 1958). The description of cognition as information processing overcame the problems that were the reason for the first circumnavigation of cognition and removed the stigmata of mentalism. Yet it also inadvertently became the cause of a second circumnavigation as described below.

3. The Second Circumnavigation

The possibilities offered by the computer analogy were recognised from the very start, i.e., from the time of the invention of the digital computer. One example of that is Boring's (1946) paper on 'Mind and mechanism', which was an almost programmatic statement of what was to come in information processing psychology, even though it was written at a time when electronic computers were still a marvel called 'electronic brains'. Boring described five steps in what he called 'the role of robotism in psychology' which pretty accurately describes the role of the computer analogy in psychology.

The first step was an analysis of the functional capacities of the human, e.g., as a listing of essential functions. The second step was to translate the functional capacities into properties of the organism, using the principles of operationism. The third, and in this context crucial, step was to reformulate these functions as properties of a hypothetical robot. In modern language this means reformulating them into operational descriptions for a computer system, e.g., in the form of flow charts or programs. The fourth step was to design and construct actual robots, which meant programming the functions in detail and verifying them by running a simulation. The fifth and final step was to explain it all by known psychophysiological principles. The simulation would serve to weed out any mentalistic terms and capacities (from the description, not from the domain). One would have to know how the simulation worked internally as well, otherwise little would have been gained. Boring also argued that the ultimate explanation should be given in terms of psychophysiology, so that 'an image is nothing other than a neural event, and object constancy is obviously just something that happens in the brain' (Boring, 1946, p. 182).

The consequence of this view was that the 'inner mechanisms' of an organism could be studied by simulation instead of by controlled introspection. Ironically, this maintained the behaviouristic emphasis on input-output (stimulus-response, S-R) relations, since the S-O-R (Stimulus, Organism, Response) paradigm is practically indistinguishable from the engineering concept of a black box (e.g., Arbib, 1964). That the S-O-R paradigm lived on in human information processing could be seen from the tenets of computational psychology. According to these, mental processes were considered as rigorously specifiable procedures and mental states were defined by their causal relations with sensory input, motor behaviour, and other mental states (e.g., Haugeland, 1985). This expressed the strong view that the human was an information processing system or a physical symbol system, which 'has the necessary and sufficient means for general intelligent action' (Newell, 1980; Newell & Simon, 1972). The phrase 'necessary and sufficient' meant that the strong view was considered adequate to explain general intelligent action and also implied that it was the only approach that had the necessary means to do so. Although the strong view has been criticized on several occasions, e.g., Searle (1980) or Weizenbaum (1976), it was rarely seriously questioned whether a human is at least an information processing system or whether, in the words of cognitive science, cognition is computational.

3.1 The complexity of behaviour

One controversial consequence of this view was that the apparent complexity of human behaviour was attributed to the environment rather than to cognition, as expressed by the so-called ant analogy (Simon, 1969). According to this, if a person describes an ant moving around its path, the description will come out as a sequence of irregular, angular segments. Although there may be an overall sense of direction, the movements on a smaller scale appear to be random. Simon made the point that the apparent complexity of the ant's behaviour over time for the most part was a reflection of the complexity of the environment, and that this also was the case for humans:

> A man, viewed as a behaving system, is quite simple. The apparent complexity of his behavior over time is largely a reflection of the complexity of the environment in which he finds himself (Simon, 1969, p. 25).

This argument made it legitimate to model human cognition independently of the context, which effectively was reduced to a set of inputs in the same way that actions were reduced to a set of outputs. So while the mistake of the first circumnavigation was to study behaviour without involving cognition, the failure of the second circumnavigation was to study information processing as if that was cognition, thereby relegating cognition to the status of an epiphenomenon.

4. Cognition in the Mind or Cognition in the World

Although the widespread acceptance of the analogy between the brain and the digital computer overcame the constraining influence of behaviorism, the computer analogy itself soon became as constraining as behaviorism had been. Since it was widely accepted that information processing was the material basis for cognition, the study of cognition became the study of 'cognition in the mind'. The study of the 'inner' functions under controlled conditions had been the preferred method from the very beginning of scientific psychology, and was initially also highly successful for information processing psychology and cognitive science (Newell & Simon, 1972). Yet after some years it was gradually realised that cognition — or information processing — could not be studied without considering also the socio-technical context in which it took place.

In cognitive science, the recognition of the need to go beyond what happened in the mind was awkwardly named situated cognition (e.g., Clancey, 1993). This maintained the focus on what happened in the brain — cognition as computation — but acknowledged that cognition emerged as a result of the interaction between the brain, the body and the world. The need to understand cognition as more than a mental process and to study it under more natural conditions led to a development that in the 1980s and 1990s culminated in the formulation of the principles for 'cognition in the wild' (Hutchins, 1995). Instead of studying subjects in laboratories under highly constrained conditions, situated cognition fortuitously echoed Brunswick's advice (1955) that data must be ecologically valid in the sense that they tell us something about how humans act in natural situations.

4.1 Cognition as control

Although the two viewpoints — 'cognition in the mind' and 'cognition in the wild' — differ considerably, both take for granted that it is meaningfully to study some underlying process called cognition. Yet cognition can also be seen as an aspect of what people do, rather than as something that goes on in their individual or collective minds. In this view of cognition, the main interest is to find the regularities of performance and how these can best be described and explained. In contrast to human information processing it is not assumed *a priori* that cognition, whether human or artificial, is the most important determinant. Indeed, the bulk of the evidence from studies of joint systems at work lends support to the view that the influence of working conditions and the situation as a whole are larger than the influence of cognition seen as the processes of thinking and reasoning. The unit of analysis must therefore be the performance characteristics of the *joint cognitive system* rather than the cognition that may — or may not — go on inside (Hollnagel & Woods, 1983; 2005).

Warnings against studying cognition as an 'inner' process are far from new and were issued even before information processing psychology became *de rigueur*. Neisser, for instance, reflecting on the then burgeoning discipline of experimental cognitive psychology, sternly warned that:

> '(w)e may have been lavishing too much effort on hypothetical models of the mind and not enough on analyzing the environment that the mind has been shaped to meet.'
> (Neisser, 1976, p. 8)

A few years later Broadbent concluded an extensive discussion of what he termed 'the minimization of models' with the following passage:

> ... one should (not) start with a model of man and then investigate those areas in which the model predicts particular results. I believe one should start from practical problems, which at any one time will point us towards some part of human life (Broadbent, 1980, p. 117).

If we accept that cognition is an aspect of what people do, the focus should be on problems that are *representative* of human performance. The argument is that the outcome of the regularity of the environment are a set of representative ways of functioning, and that these should be the subject of investigation rather than performances that are derived only from theoretical predictions or elicited under impoverished experimental conditions. Even earlier, Brunswik had made essentially the same point in his proposal for probabilistic functionalism:

> It is the contention of this paper that if there is anything that still ails psychology in general, and the psychology of cognition specifically, it is the neglect of investigation of environmental or ecological texture in favor of that of the texture of organismic structures and processes. Both historically and systematically psychology has forgotten that it is a science of organism-environment relationships, and has become a science of the organism (Brunswik, 1957).

The computer analogy made it irresistible to use a bottom-up approach, trying to base explanations based on model-defined elements rather than on what was necessary and sufficient to account for the observable complexity of behaviour. The bottom-up approach was reinforced by the ambition of psychology to model the total complexity of human behaviour (although reduced to manageable experimental conditions). Yet this approach was bound to fail because it could not transcend the limits of the analogy.

The organism-environment relationship is one of coping or maintaining *control* of a situation. Cognition can therefore be seen as that which makes coping possible, as a performance trait or feature, rather than as a process or function *in* the organism. It is a common lesson from studies in the field — or in the 'wild' — that behaviour in real world conditions clashes with the assumptions of 'cognition in the mind'. In order to understand what people do, it is necessary not only to focus on 'cognition in the world' but to extend the meaning of cognition far beyond the notions of human information processing. While behaviour may be shaped by the characteristics of the mind, it is determined by the environment. This environment, however, include other people whose behaviour is shaped by their minds and determined by their environments.

Cognition therefore cannot be isolated in the mind of a thoughtful individual, but involves people and artefacts distributed in space or time, and organised in larger groups, organisations, and institutions that together define the conditions for work – the constraints and demands as well as the resources. The scientific objectives of the study of cognition are still very much the prediction and control of behaviour. But in order to do that it is more important to understand what cognition *does*, than to understand what it *is*.

References

Arbib, M. A. (1964), *Brains, Machines and Mathematics* (New York: McGraw-Hill).

Boring, E. G. (1946), 'Mind and mechanism', *The American Journal of Psychology*, 59(2), pp. 173–192.

Broadbent, D. E. (1980), 'The minimization of models', In Chapman, A. J. & Jones, D. M. (Eds.), *Models of Man* (British Psychological Society).

Brunswik, E. (1955), 'Representative design and probabilistic theory in functional psychology', *Psychological Review*, 62(3), pp. 193–217.

Brunswik, E. (1957), 'Scope and aspects of the cognitive problem', In H. Gruber, K. R. Hammond, & R. Jessor (Eds.), *Contemporary Approaches to Cognition* (Cambridge, MA: Harvard University Press), pp. 5–31.

Clancey, W. J. (1993), 'A situated cognition perspective on learning on demand', Proceedings of *Fifteenth Annual Conference of the Cognitive Science Society* (Boulder, CO: Lawrence Erlbaum Associates), pp. 181–183.

Hammond, K. R. (1993), 'Naturalistic decision making from a Brunswikian viewpoint: Its past, present, future', In Klein, G. A., Oramasu, J., Calderwood, R. & Zsambok, C. (Eds), *Decision Making in Action: Models and Methods* (Norwood, NJ: Ablex).

Haugeland, J. (1985), *Artificial Intelligence: The Very Idea* (Cambridge, MA: MIT Press).

Hollnagel, E. & Woods, D. D. (1983), 'Cognitive systems engineering: New wine in new bottles', *International Journal of Man-Machine Studies*, 18, pp. 583–600.

Hollnagel, E. & Woods, D. D. (2005), *Joint Cognitive Systems: Foundations of Cognitive Systems Engineering* (BocaRaton, FL: Taylor & Francis).

Hutchins, E. (1995), *Cognition in the Wild* (Cambridge, MA: MIT Press).

Kendler, H. H. (1952), '"What is learned?" — A theoretical blind alley', *Psychological Review*, 59, pp. 269–277.

Morick, H. (1971), 'Cartesian privilege and the strictly mental', *Philosophy & Phenomenological Research*, 31(4), pp. 546–551.

Neisser. U. (1976), *Cognition and Reality: Principles and Implications of Cognitive Psychology* (W. H. Freeman and Company).

Newell, A. & Simon, H. A. (1972), *Human Problem Solving* (Englewood Cliffs, NJ: Prentice-Hall Inc.).

Newell, A. (1980), 'Physical symbol systems', *Cognitive Science*, 4, pp. 135–183.

Nisbett, R. E. & Wilson, T. D. (1977), 'Telling more than we can know: Verbal reports on mental processes', *Psychological Review*, 74, pp. 231–259.

Prætorius, N. & Duncan, K. D. (1988), 'Verbal reports: A problem in research design', In L. P. Goodstein, H. B. Andersen & S. E. Olsen (Eds.), *Tasks, Errors and Mental Models* (London: Taylor & Francis).

Ritchie, B. F. (1953), 'The circumnavigation of cognition', *Psychological Review*, 60, pp. 216–221.

Searle, J. R. (1980), 'Minds, brains, and programs', *The Behavioral and Brain Sciences*, 3, pp. 417–424.

Simon, H. A. (1969), *The Sciences of the Artificial* (Cambridge, MA: The MIT Press).

Tolman, E. C. (1948), 'Cognitive maps in rats and men', *The Psychological Review*, 55(4), pp. 189–208.

von Neumann, J. (1958), *The Computer and the Brain* (New Haven, CT: Yale University Press).

Watson, J. B. (1913), 'Psychology as the behaviorist views it', *Psychological Review*, 20, pp. 158–177.

Weizenbaum, J. (1976), *Computer Power and Human Reason. From Judgment to Calculation* (San Francisco: W. H. Freeman).

Brendan Wallace and Alastair Ross

Conclusion: The Future of an Illusion

What is the essence of a 'post-cognitivist' approach to human cognition? It is this: human cognition is not (as Socrates/Plato thought) necessarily the product of 'internal' rules, and the 'up to date' version of this theory (in which 'rules' are conceptualised as 'algorithms') is also not *necessarily* the case (Dreyfus, 1992),

Given that this view is problematic, its development by Descartes ('Cartesianism') is even more problematic. Moreover, the *neo*-Cartesianism of Cognitivism is even more problematic because so much of the Cartesian framework is (sometimes covertly) retained (i.e. the 'subject-object' distinction, 'dualism', the 'individual-environment' distinction etc.) and the actual mechanism of the 'switch' (i.e. the alleged switch from a Platonic/Cartesian framework to a materialist/naturalist framework) will not do the job which it is being called upon to do. This mechanism, of course, is the use of the word 'information' as a magic wand so that Cartesian 'mind stuff' (a *fundamentally* metaphysical concept) is described by seemingly rigorous and mathematical terms (specifically that 'cognition' is described as the 'processing' of 'bits' of information).

The analogous idea or theory (we have argued this is not in any sense a 'discovery') that the brain is a digital, algorithmic computer is also unworkable as a viable research program. Again, as Hubert Dreyfus pointed out this research program can be traced back to Plato and Socrates. This approach has been strongly criticised in recent years (correctly, we feel) and there is no particular need to go over the 'frame problem', the 'symbol grounding' problem, the 'Chinese room' problem and so forth, except to stress that in our opinion, these problems are unsolvable, *within the confines that the cognitivist/information processing research programme has set itself* (e.g. Searle, 1980; Harnad, 1990).

Beyond Cognitivism

So: when Tim van Gelder asked, 'What might cognition be, if not computation?' (van Gelder, 1995) he was asking a very important question. For many raised on the orthodox position, it has been taken for granted for so long that cognition is some form of computation (i.e. that cognition is rule bound, algorithmic) that to view it in any other way seems almost impossibly strange. Why should this be?

The mathematician and logician Keith Devlin answers this question rather nicely: 'The suggestion that much human activity is not based on rules has enormous implications for the logician's rule-based view of human thought ... having grown up in a culture whose intellectual traditions are heavily influenced by the Ancient Greeks ... most people find the very notion of rule-free expert performance hard to accept....' Devlin goes on to relate the (mainly unsuccessful!) attempts that he has made to persuade his students that cognition might not be rule or algorithm-bound. However he then makes an extremely important point: 'The (students) who most steadfastly stick to the rule-based view are *invariably the ones who have had a solid science education*....' (emphasis added). In order to explain this he argues: 'Western culture is dominated by an approach that goes back to Plato, and to his teacher, Socrates. Their love of mathematics and precise definitions led them to discount any ... skill ... that could not be explained (by) rational argument ... in the seventeenth century Galileo provided support for the rational approach by showing that it could be applied very successfully to the physical world.'

As we have shown in the introduction, this Galilean view of the physical world (as being law governed, these laws now being given metaphysical status) was developed by Newton, and then made the desideratum for ALL the sciences. And so, when the early pioneers of cognitive science (Chomsky, Turing, Newell and Simon, Minsky and others) began to attempt to create a new, 'cognitive' science, it seemed natural to turn to this Newtonian mode, which, it was hoped, would act as the framework for this new research programme (Devlin, 1997, pp. 180–184).

Rules and Metaphysics

The desire to put psychology on a firm foundation, the desire to make it a 'hard' rigorous science like physics or chemistry, explains the appeal of cognitivism. And this is why the question of 'what might cognition be, if not computation?' is so threatening. Psychologists are worried that without some overarching, rigorous 'physics-like' model, template or metaphor, psychology might simply collapse into a series of observations, empirical studies and interesting sounding theories with little or no predictive power. In other words it would have to give up its pretensions to ever being a 'real' *science*.

Now that we have reached the end of this book it is time to ask some speculative questions, and we are aware that some people might not like the answers. But it remains a fact that cognitivism's main appeal has been its promise of the discovery of *natural laws* of cognition whereby these laws would become a bedrock of psychology. However, much as some people might not like the idea, it should be pointed out that some contemporary philosophers are asking: do we really *need* the concept of timeless, context free, immutable 'laws of nature' at all? The philosophers Bas van Fraassen and Nancy Cartwright, amongst others, have argued that the concept of 'laws of nature' is not necessary for the progress of science, and may indeed be an anachronism, given their origin in neo-Platonic metaphysics (Van Fraassen, 2003: Cartwright, 1999).

We are not going to enter into such a charged philosophical debate. However we hope that simply by bringing these ideas to the attention of the psychological community might be of benefit, because if these were ideas were accepted, they might serve to clarify the task of a post-cognitivist psychology greatly. Freed from the assumption that science *must be* the discovery of universal 'laws', it would no longer necessarily be the case that the psychologists task is to 'discover' the universal laws of human behaviour. Still less would these 'laws' (rules, algorithms) *have to be* located inside the human brain.

Methodology

The purpose of this book has been to marshal evidence that cognitivism will no longer work as a research paradigm for 21st century psychology. But if we abandon cognitivism, with what do we replace it?

Firstly, it should not be presupposed that psychology actually *needs* a single major overarching theory or metaphor. Perhaps what is needed is more of a series of metaphors, images or models that are pragmatically useful in certain contexts. This conjures up an image of psychology as being more like a map, or a patchwork quilt, which we can journey over any number of times, in any number of directions, being guided not so much by overarching 'macro theories' as by various 'micro theories' that guide specific research projects. It would also help explain why, despite many false dawns, there has been no 'Newton' or 'Einstein' figure to unify psychology. Perhaps, due to its heterogeneous and contextually rich nature, no such unification is possible (cf. Cartwright, 1999).[1]

Situation Specificity.

The contextual aspects to cognition are worth emphasising. Cognitivist psychology tends to downplay the extent to which human behaviour is *situation specific*. To repeat Barker's aphorism (from the Introductory Chapter) 'when people are in Church, they behave Church. When people are in the post office they behave post office'. We would like to stress that we interpret this in a radical and fundamental sense. Specifically, we argue that there are no unvarying and discrete cognitive modules which might account for a range of behaviours.

In any case, the real question here is: what level of analysis will suit our investigation anyway? Cognitivism simply presupposed that what we should really be looking at was the 'inner' world of information in the brain, but this decision was predicated on commitment to reductionism.[2] Barker's idea of the behaviour setting (and Gibson's call for a systems approach to behaviour, that is, [to quote Maturana and Varela] an approach that looks at the 'structural coupling' between the organism and environment) would surely

[1] We quote this without necessarily accepting it, but we feel it is a point that should at least be considered. 'Particle physics is a child's game [...] compared to neuroscience [...] Anyone hoping to construct a unified theory of the mind must cope with an astronomical number of findings, many of them with contradictory implications. When it comes to the human brain, there may *be* no unifying insight that transforms chaos into order' (Horgan, 2000, p. 261). Note that this is NOT the same as the so called 'mysterian' position that posits the idea that there IS some unifying order that we can never access. Horgan is arguing that there may be no unifying order AT ALL (or to be more precise there may be no mathematical, logical order analogous to that provided by Newtonian or Einsteinian physics for physical phenomena).

[2] Not that there's anything wrong with reductionism *per se*, but there *is* something wrong with assuming any single research methodology (in this case, reductionism) without providing arguments or evidence as to why it is appropriate in a given context.

make more sense if the quest for hypothetical 'cognitive structures' is abandoned (Gibson, 1986: Maturana and Varela, 1987).

Situated Cognition

This change of emphasis is more or less synonymous with that has been termed the rise of 'situated cognition' (Clancey, 1997). Once one abandons the quest for *context free* 'laws' of human behaviour, whether 'programmed' into the brain or not, then the conceptual 'wall' that prevented us from seeing the *context specific* nature of human behaviour is broken down.

So Where Does This Leave Us?

Where this leaves us, is, of course, in uncharted territory. But following on from what we have been saying above, perhaps it also indicates that in moving from a monist to a pluralist paradigm in terms of theoretical psychology, we should make a similar move in terms of methodology and in terms of psychology's relationship with other sciences (and philosophy).

Pluralism

Given the relationship between epistemology and ontology (i.e. what you look for conditions what you find) it should also be obvious that a pluralist ontology therefore necessitates a pluralist epistemological approach.. In other words, if you ditch the idea of the 'one true' metaphor of the brain (in this case that it 'is' a digital computer) and instead look for pragmatic micro-models of how human beings work in specific environments, this necessitates the use of various techniques (and methodologies) to look at these behaviours. This is not to disparage the 'traditional' psychology experiment (that would just be to zoom from one extreme to the other) but instead to question the idea that *only* observations that have been validated via controlled experiments are to be accepted in 'the correct' view of psychology. Instead, we would argue, again, for a 'patchwork' view of how human beings work, which also, therefore, necessarily mean a 'patchwork' of methodologies. Discourse analysis, observational studies (both in *and* out of the lab), computer simulations and models, action research and so forth, can, and in our opinion *should* be used in the creation of a genuine psychology that genuinely illuminates human action and behaviour. To argue otherwise is, we would argue, to fall victim to 'physics envy', the idea that only methodologies that are based (however vaguely) on theoretical physics are valid.[3]

Implications for other Sciences

We also think that this proposed new approach in psychology will make it easier for psychology to 'talk to' the other social sciences, and that the growing trend for inter-disciplinary discussions between sociologists, anthropologists, linguists, economists and psychologists is to be welcomed: after all, these are simply more or less arbitrary names for specific approaches to the same problem: human behaviour. We would argue, strongly, that none of the sciences (let alone the social sciences) are autonomous, and that greater links between them should be welcomed. The demise of the cognitivist orthodoxy can only facilitate this.[4]

We hope, therefore, this book will act as a summary and a catalyst: a summary of the progress that has already been made, and a catalyst for the even more important work that is yet to come.

Bibliography

Cartwright, N. (1999), *The Dappled World* (Cambridge University Press). But see also the even more radical unpublished note: 'No God, No Laws': (http://personal.lse.ac.uk/cartwrig/Papers/NoGodNoLaws.pdf)
Clancey, W. (1997), *Situated Cognition* (Cambridge University Press).
Devlin, D. (1997), *Goodbye Descartes* (New York: John Wiley).
Dreyfus, H. (1992), *What Computers Still Can't Do* (Cambridge, MA: MIT Press).
Gibson, J.J. (1986), *The Ecological Approach to Visual Perception* (New York: Lawrence Erlbaum).
Harnad, S. (1990), 'The Symbol Grounding Problem', *Physica D*, 42, pp. 335–346.
Horgan, J. (2000), *The Undiscovered Mind* (London: Phoenix).
Maturana, H. and Varela, F. (1987), *The Tree of Knowledge: The Biological Roots of Human Understanding* (Boston, MA: Shambhala).
Searle, John (1980), 'Minds, Brains, and Programs', *Behavioral and Brain Sciences*, 3, pp. 417–424.
Van Fraassen, B. (2003), *Laws and Symmetry* (Oxford: OUP).
Van Gelder, T. J. (1995), 'What might cognition be, if not computation?', *Journal of Philosophy*, 91, pp. 345–381.

[3] The primacy in cognitivist psychology of the classic 'lab experiment' being a classic example of this.
[4] Because the truth is that very few anthropologists or sociologists ever accepted the cognitivist viewpoint: it was almost exclusively held by psychologists, (some) linguists, and (a few) philosophers.

Index

Activity theory 343-4
Affordances 76, 116, 178, 315-6, 319-20, 322, 324, 328, 331-3, 338, 340-2
Agency 63, 69, 71-2, 77, 79, 124, 126
Akhtar, 217
Aleksander, I. 117-8, 127-130
Anaximander 45
Anthropogenic 134-156
Aristotle 4-5, 45, 140, 143-4
Artificial Intelligence 7, 18, 20, 51, 92, 94, 130, 141, 147, 150, 152, 329, 340-1, 347
Artificial Life 25-6, 54, 57-8
Asch, Solomon 177
Ashby, W.R. 82, 103
Athens 2-4
Atkinson, A.P.(Tony) 175, 294
ATOM (agreement tense omission model) 198
Augustine, Saint 257, 262
Aurispa, Giovanni 5

Baars, B.J. 173
Barker, Roger 24, 359
Bechtel, W. 58, 132-3, 152
Beer, Randall 56, 65-7, 81, 133, 152
Behaviourism 1, 50, 148, 157, 166, 172-7, 348-9
Behaviourist(ic) 91, 93, 96, 104, 146, 149, 168, 173, 175-6, 327, 346, 348-9, 350
Bell Laboratories 8, 148
Binding 83, 117-8, 121-5, 128-9, 267
Biogenic 137-45, 150-9
Biology/biological(ly) 7, 14, 23, 34-5, 40, 50-8, 63-4, 66, 69, 71-6, 79, 81, 83-5, 128, 132-9, 141-5, 148, 150-9, 179, 233, 235, 251-3, 264, 271, 274, 313
Body-mind, see Mind-Body
Bohr, Neils 55-6

Boring, E.G. 349-50
Bowerman, M. 188-9
Bowling, M. 117-8, 128-30
Brahe, Tycho 96
Brentano, F.C. 149-50
Broadbent, D.E. 93. 124, 353
Brooks, Rodney 25, 56, 117-8, 128-9, 133, 147, 151, 174, 296
Browning, B. 118, 128, 130
Brunswik, E. 353
Buddhism 134
Burtt, E.A. 5, 171
Button, G. 11
Byzantine 4-5

Carruthers, Peter 116
Cartesian 5-6, 11, 13, 18-21, 24-6, 50, 134, 149, 153, 172, 356
Cartesianism 7, 11, 21, 356
Cartwright, Nancy 52, 358-9
Cartwright, T.A. 190
Categories 100, 119, 186-7, 190-1, 216-20, 238, 241, 244, 280, 303
Categorization 45, 170, 239-40, 266
Causal spread 77, 282-4, 287
Cavalli-Sforza, L.L. 236, 242, 245
Chalmers, D. 53, 282, 285
CHILDES database 193, 199, 218
Chomsky, Noam 18-20, 27, 91, 93, 96, 147-8, 152, 187, 209, 234, 251-2, 271, 357
Chomskyan 20, 27, 187, 251, 271-2, 293
CHREST 185-6, 193, 204, 210
Christianity 4, 6, 134, 143
Circumnavigation 348-51
Clancey, William 54, 95, 106, 352, 360
Clark, Andy 66, 75, 133, 269-82, 285-95, 298-305, 315
Closed-loop systems 77, 105
Cognition 1, 3-4, 6-12, 15-25, 33-5, 39, 46, 56, 78-80, 91-112, 118, 121, 132-160, 167-70, 172, 175, 179, 185,

187, 193, 204, 258-9, 264, 266, 269-71, 274, 281-3, 285-96, 299-302, 315, 327-342, 346-354, 356-60
  ecological 327-345
  embodied 25, 33, 35, 151, 159, 281, 315
  distributed 269, 281- 301
Cognitive
  architecture 117-8, 125-30, 253, 285, 296
  modelling 191
  science 12, 20, 33, 35, 38-9, 50, 66, 83, 132-8, 147-50, 152, 156, 159-60, 191, 281, 283, 291, 295-6, 309-10, 347, 351-2, 357
Cognitivism 1, 6, 11, 18-22, 24-7, 50-1, 82, 84, 92-3, 132-60, 166-7, 170, 173, 175, 177-9, 187, 192, 356-9
Competition 189, 233-56, 295, 316, 320
Complex dynamical systems 242
Compositionality 132, 233-56, 292, 310
Computer analogy 349-53
Conceptual
  metaphor 36, 38-46
  model (49-90) 51-3, 56, 58, 63, 66, 73, 78-9, 81-4
Constantinople 5
Constructivism 92, 103-6, 111, 189
Constructivist account 189-92, 216, 230
Cotterill, Rodney M.J. 117, 122-30
Csikszentmihalyi, M. 337
Cunliffe, D. 338

Damasio, Antonio 35, 78, 126
Darwin, Charles 93, 144, 233, 235, 254
Darwinian 234-5, 251, 272, 283, 295
De Boer, B. 234-7
De Waal, F.B.M. 134, 137, 152
Dennett, Daniel 57, 94, 106, 136, 150, 273, 293
Descartes, R. 5-6, 19-21, 118-20, 134, 141, 148-9, 153, 170-1, 174, 178, 356
Descombes, V. 11, 13
Devlin, Keith 357
Dewey, John 33-5, 38-40, 45-7, 166, 176-9
Di Paolo, Ezequiel 57, 66-9, 73, 75, 82, 296
Dilthey, Wilhelm 178
Discrimination network 185, 194, 203, 210-1, 215
Disembodied thought
  as illusion 33-48

Distributional
  account 190, 208-32
  analysis 185-207, 222
DNA 158, 235
Dreyfus, Hubert (& Stuart) 1, 2, 4, 7, 18, 22, 92, 94, 107, 147, 280, 356
Dualism 3-5, 11-2, 20, 134, 152-3, 170-9, 356
Dunmall, B, 117-8, 127-30

Eco, Umberto 260
Ecological Psychology 23-6
Edelman, Gerald 35, 46, 74, 78
Egyptian 3
E-learning/Computer-based learning 339-41
Elman, J.L. 72, 186, 188, 302-5
Embodied meaning 34-5, 37, 39-40, 43-4
Embodiment 25, 35, 38, 46, 51, 66-7, 71, 74, 78, 80, 83-4, 92, 95, 118, 129, 178
  see also Cognition, embodied
Emergent self 61-2, 74, 83
Engestrom, Y. 334
EPAM 185, 193, 210-1, 226
  EPAM-VOC 225-30
Epiphenomenon 346-7, 351
Episodic memory 258, 264-6
Europe(an) 5, 134, 149
Euthyphro, The 2
Evolution
  cultural 251
  of vowel systems 236-7
Evolutionary robotics 64-7, 83, 283-4

Fabre, Henri 136
Feldman, M.W. 236, 242, 245, 253
Festinger, L. 329
Flores, Fernando 97, 104, 133
fMRI 266
Fodor, Jerry 18, 100, 132, 140, 148-9, 169, 275-6, 291-3, 309-11
Fogg, B.J. 339-40
Fraser, J.T. 257
Freeman, W.J. 25, 74, 151, 192
Freud, Sigmund 328
Functionalism 50, 146, 148, 150, 152, 155, 353

Galileo 5-6, 19, 153, 171, 357
Gallese, V. 36, 132
Gaussian 108, 110
Georgeff, M.P. 328-9
Gettier, Edmund 101

Gibson, J.J. 24-5, 151, 178, 328, 331-2, 359-60
Givon, T. 258-60
Gobet, F. 185, 192-3, 210, 225, 227
God(s) 2, 6, 361
Godfrey-Smith, P. 52, 148, 162
Gold, E.M. 188-9
Gosselin, Frederic 106
Grady, J. 38
Greek 3, 138
Greeks, Ancient 148, 357
Green, Christopher 136
Greimas, A.-J. 260
Guignon, C.B. 280

Hahn, U. 192
Hall, Stuart 6, 171-2
Harnad, S. 137, 310-1, 356
Harre, Rom 173
Hartley, R. 8, 137
Harvey, Inman 64, 66, 283, 285-6, 296
HCI (human computer interaction) 327, 340
Hebb, Donald 173-5
Hebbian 68
Heidegger, Martin 92, 127, 279-80
Heideggerian 269, 280-1
Helmholtz, 149
Holland, O. 109
Hommel, B. 316, 322
Homo Sapiens 133,141, 251-2, 346, 348
Horizontal transmission 245-7, 314, 317
Hume, David 118-19, 121

Image schemas 36-42, 45-6
Imagination 116-131, 134
Implicit bottleneck 246, 250, 252
Information 7-14, 17, 20, 23, 53, 64, 74, 92-9, 101, 104-7, 111, 117, 121-9, 133, 147-9, 151, 155, 169-70, 186-91, 194, 196, 211-14, 219, 222-6, 230, 294, 303, 310, 312-4, 339, 356, 359
  processing 1, 8, 10-22, 24-6, 92-7, 106-7, 132, 316, 327-8, 340, 346-7, 349-52, 354-6
  producing 9, 106-7, 111
Input control 103-5
Integration 70, 117, 122, 127, 130, 158, 267, 269, 323-4
Intellectualism 177-8
Italy 5
Iterated learning 238, 242

James, William 34-5, 136, 144, 178, 261

Johnson-Laird, P. 172
Jonas, Hans 67, 71-2
Judeo-Christian 134

Kant, I. 117-130
Kantian 117, 121, 127
Kaptelinin, V. 327, 334
Karmiloff-Smith, A. 25
Kauffman, S. A. 58, 61
Keil, Frank 96, 102
Kendler, H.H. 348-9
Kepler, Johannes 96, 171
Kessen, William 169
Kim, A.J. 336
Kirby, Simon 237-8, 241-4, 247, 252, 272, 296
Knowledge 2, 33-6, 46-9, 52-6, 92-7, 100-7, 111-12, 117, 123, 125, 136, 147, 149, 159-60, 172-8, 185-8, 190-2, 197, 199, 203, 213, 217, 223, 225-6, 230, 238-41, 246, 252, 257, 264-5, 328, 339, 342, 346-7
Kohler, I. 68, 314
Koyre, Alexandre 171
Kuhn, Thomas 92
Kuutti, K. 334

Lakoff, George 5, 18, 25, 37, 40, 43-5, 95, 132
Lamarck, J.-B. 150
Langton, Chris 54
Language
  acquisition 18, 20, 116, 148, 185-207, 208-232, 272
  complexification of 253
  English 40, 143, 167, 186, 193, 197-200, 217, 223
  evolution 185, 233-8, 243-4, 250-1, 253-4, 272, 296
  external cognitive resource 271-4, 277-8, 280-1, 287, 290, 293-4, 299
  game 236, 238-40, 242, 245, 249
  narrow faculty 252
  origins 187, 234, 251, 263
  second-order thoughts 275-7
Lasa, A. 70, 78
Leder, Drew 43-4
LeDoux, Joseph 35
Leeper, Robert 168
Leslie, Alan 176
Lester, J. 340
Life, minimal models of 55-6, 58-60, 64, 73, 81, 83
Linguemes 234-6

Linguistic inner rehearsal 269, 275, 277-8, 290, 292, 294, 296, 299, 301
Llinas, Rodolfo 104
Locke, Lockean 311, 323
Logical Empiricism 33
Lurkers 336-7

Mackie, J.L. 311
MacWhinney, B. 188-90, 193, 199, 218
Mantovani, G. 327
Marr, D. 310-3
Masonic Texts 6
Maturana, Humberto 58, 67, 97, 104-5, 150-1, 156, 359-60
Mavelli, F. 58, 60, 63
Mbakwe, C. 338
McCulloch-Pitts, 146-7
McGovern, K. 173
Meaning
  bodily 34, 44
  drift 244
Meijsing, M. 117, 124
Meno, The 19
Mental life (49-90) 51-2, 54, 57, 69, 72-84
Merleau-Ponty, M. 92
Metaphor 17-18, 20, 23, 25, 36, 38-46, 83-4, 93, 146, 169, 172, 174, 258, 312, 323, 328, 358, 360
Miall, R.C. 123
Michaels, C.F. 316
Mind 2, 4-6, 11, 13, 21, 25-6, 33-48, 50-1, 54-7, 64, 67, 76, 78-84, 93, 96, 101, 104, 116, 118-21, 136-45, 148-50, 156, 159, 169-70, 172, 174-7, 251, 257-8, 260-5, 270, 274, 281, 286, 294, 304, 309-10, 334, 346-9, 351-6, 359
Mind-Body 11, 49, 126, 172
Minimalism/ist 19, 52, 53, 55-7, 64, 75, 79, 82
Mirror Neuron System 36
Model 7, 11, 20, 46, 49-90, 92, 97, 104, 106, 110, 124, 129-30, 133-4, 146-7, 153, 156, 170, 185-7, 190-200, 203-4, 208-11, 217-8, 222, 224-30, 233-9, 241-4, 251, 253-4, 259, 278, 287-8, 290, 292, 295-6, 301-2, 304, 309, 324, 327, 340, 351, 353, 358, 360
  see also Life, minimal models of
Monist 4, 11, 21, 360
Moreno, Alvaro 56, 59, 61, 63, 70, 78, 81, 85, 137
MOSAIC 186-7, 193-7, 200-4, 208-224, 230

MUN (minimalism, universality, naturalism) constraints 52-4, 63, 78
Muslim 4

Nardi, B.A. 334
Nativist theories 19, 187, 190, 192, 197, 209, 251
Natural selection 12, 71-2, 154, 235, 324
Naturalism 52-3, 152
Naturalist(ic) 11, 23, 34, 54-5, 64, 81, 186, 193,203, 210, 222, 356
Neisser, Ulric 92-3, 105, 133, 352-3
Neo-behaviorism: methodology 174
Neo-Platonic 4, 358
Nervous system 10, 34, 70, 78, 98, 104, 121, 150, 158-9, 348
Newton, 5-7, 17, 19, 315, 357, 359
Newtonian 11, 19, 357, 359
Nielsen, J. 337
Ninio, A. 216
Noë, A. 314
Norman, D.A. 122, 332
Nunez, Rafael 40, 44, 151, 192
NWR (nonword repetition) 223-30
Nyquist, Harry 8

O'Regan, Kevin 106, 314
On-line/off-line distinction 287-91, 293, 299
Online/Virtual communities 335-7, 341
Ontological project 154, 156
Optional infinitives 193, 197-202
Orphism 3
Oskaloosa 24
Overextensions 244
Ownership 116
Oyama, Susan 106

Palmer, S.E. 309-10
Pavlov, I.P. 331-2
Persuasion 338
PET scan 124, 266
Pinker, Steven 92, 188, 190-1, 204, 234, 251
Plato 2-5, 18-20, 45, 141, 143, 356-7
Platonic 4-6, 18-19, 21, 26, 356, 358
Platonism 5-6, 18, 44
Plotinus 4
Pöppel, Ernst 261-7
Popper, Karl 18, 93
Population size 242-8, 284
Population turnover 247
Positive feedback loop 58, 61, 246

Powers, W.T. 103-4
Pragmatism, American 34
Pre-Socratic thinking 45
Primary metaphor 38-42
Protolanguage 238, 251
Prototype 239
Putnam, Hilary 21, 104, 143, 148-9, 152, 312
PWM (phonological working memory) 225-7, 230
Pylyshyn, Z. 100, 172, 291-2, 309
Pythagoras 3-4, 15, 19-20

Quine, W. 152

Radical constructivism 92, 103-4, 106, 111
Rao, A.S. 328-9
Rayner, R. 331
Regier, T. 46
Representation(s) 12, 19, 53, 60, 84, 94-5, 97-8, 100, 107-8, 111, 121, 126, 128, 132, 147, 149, 151, 153, 167-72, 178, 189, 193, 198-9, 203, 238, 264, 271, 278, 285-6, 289-96, 299-305, 309-326
Representational(ism) 6, 50-1, 67, 75-6, 84, 92, 94, 107, 123, 149, 167,169-72, 178, 286, 289, 291, 293-4, 299, 301-2, 304, 309-15, 322
Rhiengold, H. 334
Ritchie, B.F. 348-9
Rose, Steven 23, 133
Roth, Gerhard 106
Ruiz-Mirazo, K. 58, 60-1, 63-4
Rumelhart, D.E. 203, 286, 288, 292
Rutherford, E. 55

Sampson, Geoffrey 20
Schank, Roger 3, 22-3
Schrödinger, E. 59
Schyns, Philippe 106
Searle, John 13-5, 49, 310, 351, 356
Seductive hypermedia 338
Self-consciousness 116-131, 337
Self-organising systems 233-4
Shannon, Claude 7-10, 13-4, 17-8, 147-8
Sharkey, N. 166
Shea, M. 5
Situated cognition 24-5, 281, 352, 360
Situatedness 51, 66, 75, 77, 84
Skinner, B.F. 91, 148, 187, 333-4
Sloman, A. 117-8, 126-30, 147
Socrates 2-4, 7, 17, 19, 22-3, 356-7

Socratic 22, 45
Spectator theory of knowledge 177-8
Spencer, Herbert 144
SRC effects 316
Stable state 242, 245, 254
Still, Arthur 26, 166-7
System-relative knowledge 111

Talking Heads experiment 238
Tallis, Raymond 10, 12
Temporality 257-268
Thales 45
Thelen, Esther 288, 315
Tibbetts, P. 11
Time
   fMRI studies of 266
   linguistic expression of 258
   psychological aspects of 260-1
Tolman, E.C. 149, 168, 348
Tomasello, M. 208, 216-8, 241, 251-2
Transmission bottleneck 233, 238, 242-6, 250, 252, 254, 272
Tucker, M. 317-22
Tulving, Endel 257-8, 264-5, 267
Turing, Alan 7, 15-8, 22, 146-7, 357
Turner, F. 263
Tye, M. 118-9

Universal Grammar 197, 234
Universal Law(s) 6, 358
Universalism 54, 79
Universality 52-3
Usage-based approach 240-1, 251

Van Duijn, M. 56, 137, 157-8
Van Fraassen, Bas 358
Van Gelder, Tim 25, 81, 92, 111, 133, 152, 357
Varela, F. 58, 61, 67, 74-5, 95, 101, 104-5, 117, 133, 156, 315, 359-60
Veloso, M. 118, 128, 130
Venn diagrams 288, 295, 302
Verb-island 193, 208-9, 216-8, 221-2
Vertical transmission 243-6
Vocabulary acquisition 191, 193, 208-10, 219, 222-3, 230
Von Foerster, Heinz 93, 95, 99, 105
Von Glasersfeld, Ernst 98, 104-5, 110
Von Neumann (computer) 146, 349
Vygotsky, L. 25, 330-2

Watson, John B. 91, 174-5, 331, 348
Weizenbaum, J. 351
Westermann, G. 192

Western
　culture 2, 357
　thought 1, 19
　tradition 4, 177-8
Wexler, K. 197-9, 202
Winograd, Terry 94, 97, 133
Wittgenstein, L. 25, 97, 279
Wohlschlager, A. 322
Wolpert, D.J. 123
Wray, A. 238
Wundt, Wilhelm 144, 174, 347